Communications
in Computer and Information Science
1093

Commenced Publication in 2007
Founding and Former Series Editors:
Phoebe Chen, Alfredo Cuzzocrea, Xiaoyong Du, Orhun Kara, Ting Liu,
Krishna M. Sivalingam, Dominik Ślęzak, Takashi Washio, and Xiaokang Yang

Editorial Board Members

More information about this series at http://www.springer.com/series/7899

Sergei O. Kuznetsov · Aleksandr I. Panov (Eds.)

Artificial Intelligence

17th Russian Conference, RCAI 2019
Ulyanovsk, Russia, October 21–25, 2019
Proceedings

 Springer

Editors
Sergei O. Kuznetsov (iD)
National Research University
Higher School of Economics
Moscow, Russia

Aleksandr I. Panov (iD)
Artificial Intelligence Research Institute
Federal Research Center "Computer Science
and Control" of the Russian Academy
of Sciences
Moscow, Russia

ISSN 1865-0929   ISSN 1865-0937 (electronic)
Communications in Computer and Information Science
ISBN 978-3-030-30762-2   ISBN 978-3-030-30763-9 (eBook)
https://doi.org/10.1007/978-3-030-30763-9

This Springer imprint is published by the registered company Springer Nature Switzerland AG
The registered company address is: Gewerbestrasse 11, 6330 Cham, Switzerland

Preface

You are presented with the proceedings of the 17th Russian Conference on Artificial Intelligence, RCAI 2019. RCAI 2019 was held in Ulyanovsk. The organizers of the conference were the Russian Association for Artificial Intelligence, Ulyanovsk State Technical University, the Federal Research Center "Computer Science and Control" of the Russian Academy of Science, and the Institute for Control Problems of Russian Academy of Sciences.

Being a long standing member of the European Association for Artificial Intelligence (EurAI, formerly – ECCAI), the Russian Association for Artificial Intelligence has a great deal of experience in running important international AI events since 1975, when the 4th International Joint Conference on Artificial Intelligence (IJCAI 1975) was held in Tbilisi, USSR (now Georgia).

The first Soviet (Russian, from 1992) Conference on AI was held in Pereslavl-Zalessky in 1988. Since then it was held every other year till 2018, when the conference became annual. The conference gathers the leading specialist from Russia, ex-Soviet Republics, and other countries, in the field of Artificial Intelligence. The participants were mainly the members of research institutes of the Russian Academy of Science and universities from all over Russia. Topics of the conference included data mining and knowledge discovery, text mining, reasoning, decision making, natural language processing, vision, intelligent robotics, multi-agent systems, machine learning, AI in applied systems, ontology engineering, etc. Each submitted paper was reviewed by three reviewers, experts in the field of Artificial Intelligence, to whom we would like to express our gratitude. The conference received 120 submissions in total, of which 30 were selected by the International Program Committee for publication in this volume. The editors of the volume would like to express their special thanks to Prof. Oleg P. Kuznetsov and Prof. Gennady S. Osipov, co-chairs of RCAI 2019, for their support in preparing these proceedings. We would also like to thank Prof. Nadezhda G. Yarushkina, the organizing chair of RCAI 2019, for the nice organization of the conference and hospitality in Ulyanovsk. We hope this volume will stimulate the further research in various domains of Artificial Intelligence.

August 2019

Sergei O. Kuznetsov
Gennady S. Osipov
Vadim L. Stefanuk

Organization

General Chair

Igor A. Sokolov   Federal Research Center "Computer Science
and Control" of the Russian Academy of Sciences,
Russia

General Co-chair

Gennady S. Osipov   Artificial Intelligence Research Institute, Federal
Research Center "Computer Science and Control"
of the Russian Academy of Sciences, Russia

Organizing Committee Chair

Nadezhda Yarushkina   Ulyanovsk State Technical University, Russia

International Program Committee Chair

Vadim Stefanuk   Institute for Information Transmission Problems
of the Russian Academy of Sciences, Russia

International Program Committee Co-chairs

Sergei O. Kuznetsov   National Research University Higher School
of Economics, Russia

Aleksandr I. Panov   Artificial Intelligence Research Institute, Federal
Research Center "Computer Science and Control"
of the Russian Academy of Sciences, Russia

International Program Committee

Alexey Averkin   Federal Research Center "Computer Science
and Control" of the Russian Academy of Sciences,
Russia

Jaume Baixeries   Universitat Politècnica de Catalunya, Spain

Ildar Batyrshin   Instituto Politecnico Nacional, Mexico

Nikolay Bazenkov   V. A. Trapeznikov Institute of Control Sciences
of the Russian Academy of Sciences, Russia

Gerhard Brewka   University of Leipzig, Germany

Aleksey Buzmakov   National Research University Higher School
of Economics, Russia

Pablo Cordero	Universidad de Málaga, Spain
Yves Demazeau	French National Center for Scientific Research, Grenoble Computer Science Laboratory, France
Vladimir Golenkov	Belarusian State University of Informatics and Radioelectronics, Belarus
Georg Gottlob	University of Oxford, UK
Valeriya Gribova	Institute of Automation and Control Processes of the Far Eastern Branch of RAS, Russia
Tom Hanika	University of Kassel, Germany
Dmitry Ignatov	National Research University Higher School of Economics, Russia
Dmitry Ilvovsky	National Research University Higher School of Economics, Russia
Giacomo Kahn	Computer Science Laboratory of Orleans, Université d'Orléans, France
Mehdi Kaytoue	Institut National des Sciences Appliquées de Lyon, France
Mikhail Khachumov	Artificial Intelligence Research Institute, Federal Research Center "Computer Science and Control" of the Russian Academy of Sciences, Russia
Vladimir Khoroshevsky	Federal Research Center "Computer Science and Control" of the Russian Academy of Sciences, Russia
Sergey Kovalev	Rostov State Railway University, Russia
Alla Kravets	Volgograd State Technical University, Russia
Oleg P. Kuznetsov	V. A. Trapeznikov Institute of Control Sciences of the Russian Academy of Sciences, Russia
Amedeo Napoli	French National Center for Scientific Research, University of Lorraine, France
Leonid Perlovsky	Harvard University, USA
Alexey Petrovsky	Federal Research Center "Computer Science and Control" of the Russian Academy of Sciences, Russia
Vladimir Redko	Scientific Research Institute of System Analysis of the Russian Academy of Sciences, Russia
Gregory Royzenson	Federal Research Center "Computer Science and Control" of the Russian Academy of Sciences Institute for Systems Analysis, Russia
Christian Sacarea	Babes-Bolyai University, Romania
Vasil Sgurev	Bulgarian Academy of Sciences, Bulgaria
Alexander Shvets	Universitat Pompeu Fabra, Spain
Ivan Smirnov	Artificial Intelligence Research Institute, Federal Research Center "Computer Science and Control" of the Russian Academy of Sciences, Russia

Contents

Intelligent Systems and Applications

Multi-Agent Systems, Intelligent Robots and Behavior Planning

Modeling the Structure of MIMO-Agents and Their Interactions

Liudmila Yu. Zhilyakova$^{(\boxtimes)}$ (iD)

V. A. Trapeznikov Institute of Control Sciences of Russian Academy
of Sciences, 65, Profsoyuznaya Street, Moscow 117997, Russia
zhilyakova.ludmila@gmail.com

Abstract. The paper describes a formal model of social network users who
have definite sets of interests in different subjects. The users are represented by
heterogeneous agents with multiple inputs of different types and multiple outputs of different types (MIMO-agents). Each *type* corresponds to one of the
interests of users. Agents have a cumulative activation function, depending on
current external influence from their neighbors and previous network states. If
the value of this function at a certain time step is above a specified threshold, the
agent becomes active according to one of the types. The choice of this type
depends both on his internal structure (personal preferences specified by a
vector) and on the proportion of active neighbors of every type. A network of
such agents is capable of generating various kinds of complex activity patterns.
We consider several examples of activity propagation and show the dependence
of stable activity patterns on the parameters of agents. Networks of MIMO-
agents with similar properties can be used not only to describe the interaction of
users of social networks, but also in modeling the transfer of heterogeneous
information in telecommunications networks.

Keywords: Networks of complex agents · Threshold models · MIMO-agents ·
Network activity

1 Introduction

In recent years, new data collection technologies have provided vast amounts of
information in various subject areas, such as genetics, neurophysiology, sociology,
cognitive sciences, and social networks. Such amount of raw data requires not only the
means of their processing, but first of all explanatory models capable of reproducing
and predicting the structural and functional features of the interaction of elements of
complex systems. Data analysis shows that intra-system interactions in different areas
can be described by large networks with similar statistical properties, so-called, complex or scale-free networks [1]. By origin, these networks can be divided into two large
classes. The first of them defines static connection structures, which represent all the
potential interactions; the second class consists of the dynamic subnetworks arising

This work was partially supported by the Russian Foundation for Basic Research, projects no. 17-
07-00541A, 18-29-22042мк, 19-07-00525A.

© Springer Nature Switzerland AG 2019
S. O. Kuznetsov and A. I. Panov (Eds.): RCAI 2019, CCIS 1093, pp. 3–16, 2019.
https://doi.org/10.1007/978-3-030-30763-9_1

from the spreading of a particular activity, i.e. functional networks [1–3]. Moreover, activity itself can be understood both as a homogeneous dynamic process that develops over time and consistently covers various nodes and groups of nodes [4–6], and as heterogeneous processes that differ in ways of influencing the same nodes, activation thresholds, propagation speed, etc. [7].

The general heterogeneous model described in [7] formed the basis for more specific models ([8] and, in part, [9, 10]). The paper [8] studies the propagation of two antagonistic activities in a network of agents with specified features. Each agent is characterized by a unique set of parameters, including two activation thresholds (one per each type of activity), two potentials characterizing the readiness to activation by a particular type, and signs indicating the attitude of the agent to each type of activity. In the articles [9, 10], a model of a heterogeneous neural network is constructed, in which neurons interact using several different neurotransmitters located in the common extracellular space. Neurons in this model have endogenous activity and are able to generate spikes in the absence of external influences. When activated, neurons emit their specific transmitter into the extracellular space; neurons have sets of receptors, each of which is capable of perceiving one transmitter. Transmitters, depending on the types of the receptors, can have inhibitory or excitatory effects on the neuron. Thus, the different chemical composition of the medium can generate different patterns of activity of neural ensembles.

In this paper, the formalisms from [7, 8] are modified to simulate heterogeneous interactions of users of a social network and study the dynamic processes of propagation of several interfering types of activity. Users are represented by agents that have many inputs of different types and many outputs of different types (moreover, the input and output sets do not always coincide). In this sense, we will call such agents MIMO-agents. In [11], the synchronization model of heterogeneous MIMO-agents is described. We will consider not the synchronization and search for consensus, but the distribution of several different types of activities in heterogeneous networks of MIMO-agents.

2   Model Description

2.1   The Main Entities of the Model

We define the heterogeneous network of interactions of social network users as a system $S = <N, C, R>$.

$N = \{1, ..., N\}$ is a set of *agents* with an internal structure.

$C = \{c_1, ..., c_m\}$ are *types* of informational interests of agents (generalized topics of posts and comments they create and read).

Matrix R is a *structural matrix* of the network. It corresponds to a weighted oriented graph of influence. If $r_{ij} > 0$, then agent i affects agent j with the power r_{ij}.

The system operates in discrete time t.

We assume that the agent can perceive all types of information, i.e. has *multiple inputs*, and that he can generate several types of information (posts and comments on different topics) – *multiple output*. That is, each user of the network is modeled by a MIMO-agent.

2.2   Network Structure

Each agent can be affected by many of his neighbors. If agent j affects agent i, we assume that there is an arc (j, i) in the influence graph. By *influence*, we mean the following. If agent j is active at time step t, then agent i when calculating its state at time step $t + 1$ takes into account the activity of agent j. Moreover, agent i calculates the power of influence taking into account two weight coefficients – *constant* and *variable*.

The *variable component* of the influence power is determined by the type of activity (i.e. produced information) of the agent j (it will be described in detail in Sect. 3.1).

The *constant* or *structural* component r_{ji} characterizes the degree of trust of agent i to agent j.

The weights r_{ji} define the structural matrix of the network R. In the study of real social networks, matrix R can be filled based on the frequency of comments and reposts, as well as the proximity of agents' interests (see Sect. 2.3). When constructing a simulation model of the interaction of agents in various subject areas (not necessarily social networks), a graph with a given set of statistical properties (small world, clustering, presence of hubs, regularity, etc.) can be taken for modeling connections between nodes. In Fig. 1 agent i with multiple inputs (structural influences) from other network agents is represented.

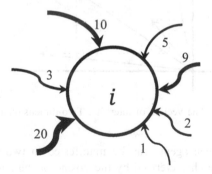

Fig. 1. Network node i and incoming arcs with weights r_{ji}

2.3   Types of Agent Interests

Depending on the research task, the semantics of the elements of the set C can be different. For an illustrative example, consider one of the possible interpretations – the study of the spread of several types of political activity in social networks. In this case, c_i can be "basic types" of beliefs, into which any politically charged activity (like publishing or commenting posts) can be decomposed.

In the study of network clustering and the identification of *echo chamber effects*, c_i will indicate the interests of users that lie in the basis of forming close communities. Relationships *within communities* are generated by the presence of the same common interest that prevails over all others. Then the connections *between communities* will be generated by "multimodal" agents who have several interests similar in strength of manifestation (frequency of posts and comments).

In general, C is a set of different types of activities, regardless of their semantics.

Each agent i is assigned a vector of length m consisting of weight coefficients $p_i = (p_{i1}, \ldots, p_{im})$ to characterize his interests. At least one coordinate of this vector is nonzero. Nonzero weights define the entire spectrum of the agent's output activities. The value p_{ik} characterizes the activation frequency of agent i by the type c_k.

If the network is based on empirical data, the weights correspond to the frequencies of posts and comments of every type. Weights should not be normalized: the characteristics of an agent who writes very rarely, and vice versa, who is always active, must be far enough from each other in the m-dimensional vector space, even though their interests are similar. Differences in interests are estimated as the angle between two vectors.

Thus, the interests of the agent are described by a vector in m-dimensional space. In Fig. 2 we present the two-dimensional case.

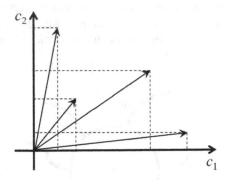

Fig. 2. The vectors of interests. Two-dimensional case

The difference between agents can be manifested in two ways. The differences between the interests are characterized by the cosine of the angle between the corresponding vectors:

$$d_c(i,j) = \cos \varphi = \frac{(p_i, p_j)}{|p_i||p_j|},$$

where (p_i, p_j) is a scalar product.

The distinctions in the activation frequencies of agents are characterized by the difference of the lengths of the vectors:

$$d_a(i,j) = ||p_i| - |p_j||.$$ (1)

Comment. It is necessary to use the difference of vector lengths in formula (1), not the distance between points (the length of the difference vector):

$$d_a(i,j) = |p_i - p_j|$$ (2)

The measure defined by formula (2) is not sufficient.
Consider the example (Fig. 3).

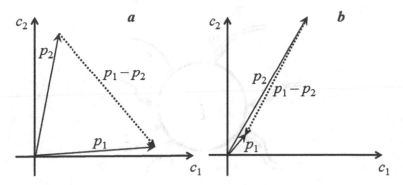

Fig. 3. Difference vectors of the same length between the vectors of interests of two agents

In Fig. 3a and b, the lengths of the vectors p_1–p_2 are the same in both cases. However, in Fig. 3b, two agents have similar interests, but at the same time significantly different activity rates, whereas in Fig. 3a, the interests of agents are very different, but the activation frequencies are similar. Formula (2) is not sensitive to this kind of difference. The formula (1), on the contrary, characterizes the absolute difference between the lengths of vectors. Measure d_a is the difference in the frequency of activation of a pair of agents, regardless of their beliefs.

In this case, the measures d_c and d_a contribute to the distance with different weight coefficients. The contribution of the measure d_c must exceed the contribution of d_a.

$$d(i,j) = \alpha_c \cdot d_c(p_i, p_j) + \alpha_a \cdot d_a(p_i, p_j), \text{ where } \alpha_c > \alpha_a.$$

We assume that the closer the agents are in this space (the smaller the value $d(i, j)$), the greater their degree of trust. In particular, the structural matrix R can be constructed depending on the values $d(i, j)$.

Another numerical characteristic, the *total activation frequency of the agent*, can be obtained from the vector p_i: $P(i) = |p_i|$.

3 Network Operation

3.1 Activity Propagation and Dynamic Weight Component of Influence

When several activities are spreading across the network, the neighbors of the agent (nodes affecting it) can be activated by different types. Then at each time step the agent can be influenced by many types. The effect on the agent at some time t is shown in Fig. 4. Unlike Fig. 1, a dynamic component is added here: the weights of the arcs remain the same as in Fig. 1, but different arcs conduct different types of activity to the agent.

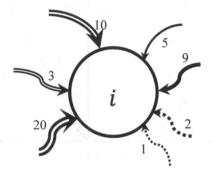

Fig. 4. Impact on the agent based on the network topology. Different types of lines represent different types of activity

Consider the reason why static weights given by matrix R may need to be adjusted.

Each agent i is characterized by a vector p_i. For clarity, it can be represented in graphical form (Fig. 5): the radius of the circle corresponds to the total activation frequency $P(i) = |p_i|$; the sizes of the sectors show the proportion of components of the vector p_i.

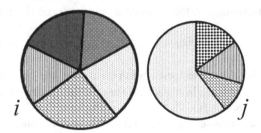

Fig. 5. Agent structure. The radius of the circle corresponds to the total activation frequency; the sectors denote the proportion of types of interest

The agent representation in Fig. 5 is dual to the representation in Fig. 2. They present the same information in different forms. Form of Fig. 5 is preferable when it comes to multidimensional space.

Let us denote the *dynamic*, or *functional*, component of the influence of agent j on agent i by $\beta_{ik}(j)$. Its value depends on c_k, i.e. on the type by which agent j is activated, and on the distribution of weights of agent i: $p_i = (p_{i1}, \ldots, p_{im})$.

We make the coefficients β_{ik} equal to the normalized coordinates of the vector p_i.

$$\beta_{ik} = \frac{p_{ik}}{\sum_{l=1}^{m} p_{il}}. \tag{3}$$

This means that the agent's trust in his environment as such is combined with the trust in the type of activity that is taking place at certain time step.

Then, if agent j is active at time $t - 1$ by type c_k, its effect on agent i at time t is calculated by the formula:

$$e_{jik}(t) = \beta_{ik}(j) \cdot r_{ji}. \tag{4}$$

The closer type of activity of agent j, $c_k(j)$, to the main interest of agent i, i.e., to the maximum component of the vector p_i, the higher the impact of this activity on agent i.

3.2 Transformer Slots

At each step t, the weights of the input arcs of a node undergo changes in accordance with formula (4). Changes in weights depend on the type of activity that comes along the corresponding arcs (see Fig. 4). In order for these changes to be taken into account at the structural level, we assign to each node a set of "transformer slots" of different types – one for each type of activity. Then the incoming arcs every time step are rearranged into the slots depending on conducting type of activity. The redistribution of the arcs across the slots occurs dynamically.

The impact of each type adds some coefficient to all static arc weights. It can be considered that the slot corresponding to some type amplifies or attenuates the incoming signal (Fig. 6).

Comment. According to formula (3), the signal is only attenuated. But if we add some factor greater than one to it, both amplification and attenuation would occur.

Then it is possible to derive formulas for calculating the impact on agent i for each type separately $e_{ik}(t)$ and the total impact $E_i(t)$ (Eqs. (5) and (6) respectively).

$$e_{ik}(t) = \beta_{ik} \sum_{j=1}^{N} r_{ji} y_{jk}(t-1), \tag{5}$$

$$E_i(t) = \sum_{k=1}^{m} e_{ik}(t) = \sum_{k=1}^{m} \beta_{ik} \sum_{j=1}^{N} r_{ji} y_{jk}(t-1), \tag{6}$$

where $y_{jk}(t) \in \{0, 1\}$ is the activity of agent j at time t by the type c_k (formula (9) below).

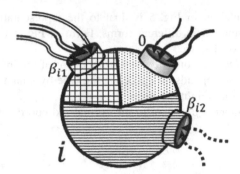

Fig. 6. Slots and their weight. All arcs leading from adjacent nodes that are not active on the current step are collected in the slot with weight 0

The sum in Eq. (5) determines the total weight of the arcs entering a slot of type c_k at time step t. Equation (6) combines the effects of all slots.

3.3   Agent Activity

At each time step, the agent undergoes the external influence described by formulas (5)–(6). In addition, the agent remembers the previous network states and takes them into account when determining the total impact.

The agent's activity at step t is specified by the vector $y_i(t)$ of length m, in which all components, except perhaps one, are equal to 0. If the agent i is active by type c_k, then $y_{ik}(t) = 1$.

Agent Memory. Each network agent has a memory of depth not more than Θ. To calculate the total excitation of the agent at the time t, a linear convolution of effects from all its neighbors, active in one or several steps in the interval $[t - \Theta, t]$, is performed.

By analogy with Eqs. (5)–(6), the agent readiness for activation can be calculated both for each type separately, and in a cumulative form.

$$a_{ik}(t) = \sum_{\theta=1}^{\Theta} \mu_\theta e_{ik}(t - \theta) = \sum_{\theta=1}^{\Theta} \mu_\theta \beta_{ik} \sum_{j=1}^{N} r_{ji} y_{jk}(t - \theta), \tag{7}$$

$$A_i(t) = \sum_{\theta=1}^{\Theta} \mu_\theta E_i(t - \theta) = \sum_{\theta=1}^{\Theta} \mu_\theta \sum_{k=1}^{m} \beta_{ik} \sum_{j=1}^{N} r_{ji} y_{jk}(t - \theta), \tag{8}$$

where μ_θ are non-negative discount factors that satisfy the relation:

$$1 = \mu_1 > \mu_2 \geq \cdots \geq \mu_\Theta.$$

Different agents can have different numbers of non-zero multipliers μ_θ.

Thanks to formulas (7)–(8), the model turns from synchronous into quasi-asynchronous. Even if some neighbors of agent i are not active at the present time step, he can be activated by experiencing their past effects (combined with some new ones).

The agent is active at t, if the value $A_i(t)$ (formula (8)) has exceeded the *threshold value*.

If the agent is activated at t, his memory resets. Memory accumulation occurs while the agent is not active.

Activation Threshold. The threshold value of agent Th_i characterizes his readiness for activation. If the agent responds to each message or comment, we will assume that his activation threshold equals to ε. This means that he supports any activity. If the agent itself starts an activity, his threshold is 0. The agent, which is practically unaffected by the environment, has a threshold close to unity. The remaining thresholds are distributed between the two extreme values [0, 1]. For the simulation model, you can set different threshold distributions – uniform, normal, etc.

Despite the fact that agents perceive the activity of many types, each agent has one threshold.

If the threshold Th_i is exceeded, the agent is activated according to one of the types defined by the components of the vector $a_i(t)$ (Eq. (7)).

Activation Type. Agent i is activated by the type c_k, if k satisfies the condition:

$$k = \arg\max_l a_{il}(t).$$

That is, the agent chooses the type from which he experiences the strongest impact. Then,

$$y_{ik}(t) = \begin{cases} 1, \text{if } A_i(t) \geq Th_i \,\&\, k = \arg\max_l a_{il}(t)); \\ 0, \text{otherwise.} \end{cases} \tag{9}$$

Network States. At each time step, each agent is in one of the $m + 1$ states (passive, or active by one of m types). Then the dynamics of the network as a whole can be considered as a change of some subset of N^{m+1} states $s_j(t)$ defined by the tuples $(\alpha_1, ..., \alpha_N)$, where $\alpha_i \in \{0, c_1,..., c_m\}$.

$$\alpha_i = \begin{cases} 0, \text{ if } y_{ij}(t) = 0, \, j = \overline{1, m}; \\ c_1, \text{ if } y_{i1}(t) = 1 \,\&\, \left(y_{ij}(t) = 0, \, j \neq 1\right); \\ \quad\quad ... \\ c_m, \text{ if } y_{im}(t) = 1 \,\&\, \left(y_{ij}(t) = 0, \, j \neq m\right). \end{cases}$$

We will call these states *external states* of the network.

Internal states are characterized by the values of the vectors $a_i(t)$, and, generally, the set of internal states has the power of the continuum.

Each external state is uniquely determined by the internal state. The arbitrary state $s_j(t) = (c_{j1},...,c_{jN})$. can be determined by the following system:

$$\begin{cases} j_1 = H(A_1(t) - Th_1) \cdot \arg\max_l a_{11}(t); \\ \quad\quad ... \\ j_N = H(A_1(t) - Th_N) \cdot \arg\max_l a_{Nl}(t). \end{cases}$$

Here $H(\cdot)$ is the Heaviside function.

4 Examples of Activity Propagation in the Network

Consider some examples demonstrating various effects in the activity propagation in the networks of MIMO-agents.

For illustration purposes, we construct a small network with a limited number of variable parameters. Figure 7 presents a network of three agents with two types of activity. We assume that all arcs of the graph have the same weights equal to r. Agents have the same total activation frequency, but the proportions of the types are pairwise different (numerical parameters will be set below).

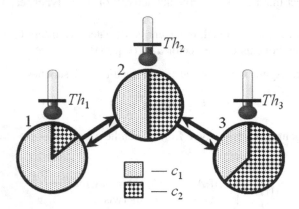

Fig. 7. A network of three agents with two types of activity. "Thermometers" denote the level of activity perceived by agents and their memory of previous network states; Th_i are activation thresholds.

A network of three elements with two types of activity can be in $3^3 = 27$ states s_j, defined by triples $(\alpha_1, \alpha_2, \alpha_3)$, where $\alpha_i \in \{0, c_1, c_2\}$.

$$\alpha_i(t) = \begin{cases} 0, \text{if } H(A_1(t) - Th_1) = 0; \\ c_1, \text{if } H(A_i(t) - Th_i) \cdot \arg\max_l a_{il}(t) = 1; \\ c_2, \text{if } H(A_i(t) - Th_i) \cdot \arg\max_l a_{il}(t) = 2. \end{cases} \qquad (10)$$

We number the states s_j in the lexicographical order from $s_0 = (0, 0, 0)$ to $s_{26} = (c_2, c_2, c_2)$.

Example 1. Let's set the parameters of agents for the network in Fig. 7. Let the total activation frequency for all agents be the same: $P(1) = P(2) = P(3) = 24$. Its distribution by types will be different – in accordance with the figure. In addition to the vectors p_i, we set thresholds Th_i:

1: $p_1 = (21, 3)$; $Th_1 = 0.5r$.
2: $p_2 = (12, 12)$; $Th_2 = 0.5r$.
3: $p_3 = (9, 15)$; $Th_3 = 0.5r$.

Here r are the same weights of arcs of the graph.

From the vectors p_i, the weights of slots β_{ij} are calculated:

$\beta_{11} = 0.875$, $\beta_{12} = 0.125$;
$\beta_{21} = 0.5$, $\beta_{22} = 0.5$;
$\beta_{31} = 0.375$, $\beta_{32} = 0.625$;

First, consider the agents without memory: $\Theta = 1$. In this case, Eqs. (7)–(8) turn into Eqs. (5)–(6), respectively, and the equalities hold: $a_i(t) = e_i(t)$; $A_i(t) = E_i(t)$.

For $t = 0$, set the initial state of the network $s_9 = (c_1, 0, 0)$ and calculate its dynamics.

$t = 1$

The first agent was active at $t = 0$; and there are no external influences on him. Then $\alpha_1(1) = 0$, according to formula (10).

The second agent is affected by the first agent by type c_1 with the force $e_{21}(1) = \beta_{21} \cdot r = 0.5r$. The excitation of the second agent reaches the threshold; he is excited by the type c_1: $\alpha_2(1) = c_1$.

No one is affecting a third agent; $\alpha_3(1) = 0$.

There is a transition: $(c_1, 0, 0) \rightarrow (0, c_1, 0)$ or $s_9 \rightarrow s_3$.

$t = 2$

The second agent affects both neighbors by type c_1. He himself is not affected, and therefore $\alpha_2(2) = 0$.

The impact on *the first agent* is calculated as $e_{11}(2) = \beta_{11} \cdot r = 0.875r$. The excitation is above the threshold; he is excited by type c_1: $\alpha_1(2) = c_1$.

The impact on *the third agent* is calculated similarly: $e_{31}(2) = \beta_{31} \cdot r = 0.375r$. This excitation is not enough to activate the agent, so $\alpha_3(2) = 0$.

We get the sequence: $(c_1, 0, 0) \rightarrow (0, c_1, 0) \rightarrow (c_1, 0, 0)$ or $s_9 \rightarrow s_3 \rightarrow s_9$.

Note that the network consisting of agents without memory, and, accordingly, without internal states, operates as a finite state machine. Then, since the state s_9 repeated, then the network enters the periodic behavior: $s_9 \rightarrow s_3 \rightarrow s_9 \rightarrow s_3 \rightarrow \ldots$

Agent 3 with the specified parameters and given initial state never becomes active.

Example 2. Consider a network with the same parameters.

Due to symmetry, it is easy to show that if at $t = 0$ the initial state of the network is $s_2 = (0, 0, c_2)$, then periodic behavior $(0, 0, c_2) \rightarrow (0, c_2, 0) \rightarrow (0, 0, c_2) \rightarrow (0, c_2, 0)\ldots$ or $s_2 \rightarrow s_6 \rightarrow s_2 \rightarrow s_6 \rightarrow \ldots$ will be generated.

To specify such a periodic behavior with a nonempty pre-period, it suffices to take the states $s_{18} = (c_2, 0, 0)$ or $s_1 = (0, 0, c_1)$ as the initial. Then the sequences of states will be respectively:

$$s_{18} \rightarrow (s_6 \rightarrow s_2) \text{ and } s_1 \rightarrow (s_3 \rightarrow s_9),$$

where the first members of the sequences correspond to pre-periods, i.e. states preceding repetitive cyclic activity (given in brackets).

Example 3. Consider a network with the same parameters as in Examples 1 and 2, but now *the third agent* has memory: $\Theta = 3$. Discount rates are: $\mu_{31} = 1$, $\mu_{32} = \mu_{33} = 0.9$.

Let, as in the first example, the initial state of the network is $s_9 = (c_1, 0, 0)$. Calculate its dynamics.

t = 1
The first agent was active at $t = 0$; and there are no external influences on him. Then $\alpha_1(1) = 0$.

The second agent is affected by the first agent by type c_1 with the force $e_{21}(1) = \beta_{21} \cdot r = 0.5r$. The excitation of the second agent reaches the threshold; he is excited by the type c_1: $\alpha_2(1) = c_1$.

No one is affecting a third agent; $\alpha_3(1) = 0$.

There is a transition: $(c_1, 0, 0) \rightarrow (0, c_1, 0)$ or $s_9 \rightarrow s_3$.

t = 2
The second agent affects both neighbors by type c_1. He is not affected, and therefore $\alpha_2(2) = 0$.

The impact on *the first agent* is calculated as $e_{11}(2) = \beta_{11} \cdot r = 0.875r$. The excitation is above the threshold; he is excited by type c_1: $\alpha_1(2) = c_1$.

The impact on *the third agent*: $e_{31}(2) = \beta_{31} \cdot r = 0.375r$. This excitation is not enough to activate the agent, so $\alpha_3(2) = 0$. Taking into account the memory, it is necessary to count for this agent not only the influence, but also the readiness for activation. At this time step we have $a_{31}(2) = e_{31}(2) = 0.375r$. This excitation is not sufficient for activation, so $\alpha_3(2) = 0$.

We get the sequence: $(c_1, 0, 0) \rightarrow (0, c_1, 0) \rightarrow (c_1, 0, 0)$ or $s_9 \rightarrow s_3 \rightarrow s_9$.

t = 3
This step externally coincides with step 1; the transition of external states is the same: $(c_1, 0, 0) \rightarrow (0, c_1, 0) \rightarrow (c_1, 0, 0) \rightarrow (0, c_1, 0)$ or $s_9 \rightarrow s_3 \rightarrow s_9 \rightarrow s_3$.

The exception is the internal state of the third agent:
$a_{31}(3) = 0 + 0.9 \cdot 0.375r = 0.3375r$.

t = 4
For agents 1 and 2 the state at $t = 4$ coincides with the state at $t = 1$: $\alpha_1(4) = c_1$; $\alpha_2(4) = 0$.

For *the third agent* holds: $a_{31}(3) = 0.375r + 0.9 \cdot 0.3375r = 0.7125r$, which exceeds the activation threshold and causes agent 3 to be activated by type c_1, although this type is not predominant for it. Therefore, the network enters the state $s_{10} = (c_1, 0, c_1)$.

The sequence of states is:

$$s_9 \rightarrow s_3 \rightarrow s_9 \rightarrow s_3 \rightarrow s_{10}.$$

t = 5
From state s_{10}, the network goes back to state s_3: agent 2 is activated, agents 1 and 3 become inactive, while the memory of agent 3 is reset to zero.

$$s_9 \rightarrow s_3 \rightarrow s_9 \rightarrow s_3 \rightarrow s_{10} \rightarrow s_3.$$

It is easy to see that further behavior of a network becomes periodic. The period here has the form: $(s_3 \rightarrow s_9 \rightarrow s_3 \rightarrow s_{10})$. Note that the external state s_3 is repeated twice, however, the internal states of the agents (here agent 3 only) are different.

This means that the behavior of such a network cannot be enclosed within the framework of a finite state machine. From Fig. 8 it is clear how externally indistinguishable states at steps 0 and 2, 1 and 3 differ in inner states.

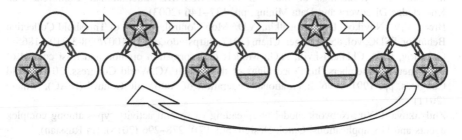

Fig. 8. The sequence of states of a network with memory

5 Conclusion

The paper proposes a heterogeneous network model of interactions between complex nodes capable of generating and perceiving several types of resources (this can be information on different subjects in social networks, packages of different nature in telecommunication networks, etc.) The nodes of such a network are complex MIMO-agents, each of which can perceive all types of recourses distributed over the network, as well as generate some of them.

As an application, a social network model is considered, in which each user has a certain set of interests. The "resource generation" concept corresponds to the user's publication activity. "Interests" are given by types of activity. It is assumed that users with similar interests trust each other more. An agent becomes active when his activation function has exceeded a certain threshold value. At any time, an agent can be active in no more than one type. The type by which an agent is activated depends both on his personal preferences and on the composition of the agent's environment activity at a given time step and in some retrospective (this is how the memory of agents about previous network states is implemented). Depending on the distribution of agent preferences and activation thresholds of agents, the activity patterns of various types can unfold over time in the network. The examples demonstrating the differences in the network activity depending on the changes in the parameters of its nodes are considered.

References

1. Newman, M.E.J.: The structure and function of complex networks. SIAM Rev. **45**(2), 167–256 (2003)
2. Baronchelli, A., Ferrer-i-Cancho, R., Pastor-Satorras, R., Chater, N., Christiansen, M.H.: Networks in cognitive science. Trends Cogn. Sci. **17**(7), 2013 (2013)
3. Bullmore, E., Sporns, O.: Complex brain networks: graph theoretical analysis of structural and functional systems. Nat. Rev. Neurosci. **10**, 186–198 (2009)
4. Kempe, D., Kleinberg, J., Tardos, E.: Maximizing the spread of influence through a social network. In: Proceedings of the 9-th ACM SIGKDD International Conference on Knowledge Discovery and Data Mining, pp. 137–146 (2003)
5. Breer, V.V., Novikov, D.A., Rogatkin, A.D.: Mob Control: Models of Threshold Collective Behavior. SSDC, vol. 85. Springer, Cham (2017). https://doi.org/10.1007/978-3-319-51865-7
6. Gubanov, D.A., Chkhartishvili, A.G.: Models of information opinion and trust control of social network members. In: Proceedings of the 18th IFAC World Congress, 2011 World Congress, pp. 1991–1996. International Federation of Automatic Control (IFAC), Milano (2011)
7. Zhilyakova, L.Yu.: Network model of spreading of several activity types among complex agents and ITS applications. Ontol. Design. **5**(3(17)), 278–296 (2015). (in Russian)
8. Zhilyakova, L., Gubanov, D.: Double-threshold model of the activity spreading in a social network. The case of two types of opposite activities. In: Proceedings of the 11th IEEE International Conference on Application of Information and Communication Technologies, AICT 2017, vol. 2, pp. 267–270 (2017)
9. Bazenkov, N., et al.: Discrete modeling of neuronal interactions in multi-transmitter networks. Sci. Tech. Inf. Process. **45**(5), 283–296 (2018)
10. Kuznetsov, O.P., Bazenkov, N.I., Boldyshev, B.A., Zhilyakova, L.Yu., Kulivets, S.G., Chistopolsky, I.A.: An asynchronous discrete model of chemical interactions in simple neuronal systems. Sci. Tech. Inf. Process. **45**(6), 375–389 (2018)
11. Zhu, L., Chen, X., Chen, Z., Hill, D.J.: Output synchronization of linear MIMO heterogeneous multi-agent systems via output communication. IFAC PapersOnLine **50**(1), 1748–1753 (2017)

Redistributing Animats Between Groups

Irina Karpova[✉][iD]

National Research University Higher School of Economics,
20 Myasnitskaya Ulitsa, Moscow, Russia
karpova_ip@mail.ru

Abstract. The paper refers to the research direction in which models of social behavior are the methodological basis for the functioning of robot (animat) groups. The purpose of this study is to implement a complex regulatory behavior of animat groups using previously created models and methods. The applicability of this approach is demonstrated by the task of redistributing animats between groups. To accomplish this, the paper proposes to implement a mechanism similar to the phenomenon of slavery that is characteristic of some species of ants. Slavery is a form of social parasitism and can be considered as a method for the redistribution of individuals between families (groups). The paper describes different types of slavery and the behavior of slave owners and slaves among species of ants. The main processes that make up this behavior are: exploring territory, organization of raids, seizure of slaves and their transfer to the slave-maker nests, and slaves adaptation in the new nest. It is proposed that this behavior is based on the "friend-alien" identification and is an evolutionary development of food and territorial behavior. The paper describes previously created methods, models, and mechanisms for implementing similar forms of animats' behavior: foraging, pack hunting, territory defense, and domination based on aggression. A method for identifying an animat and determining its internal state, which is necessary for organizing the interaction of animats, is proposed. Finally, the paper describes experiments confirming the applicability of the proposed method.

Keywords: Group robotics · Social behavior models · Ant slave-making · Foraging task · Aggressive behavior

1 Introduction

Consider the situation in group robotics, in which the robots are divided into groups. Each group is relatively stable and is designed, for example, to solve a separate problem. In this case, it may be necessary to redistribute robots between groups, if some task becomes more complicated and requires more "working hands" to solve it. It is necessary to develop a mechanism that would allow a fairly natural way, without the use of special techniques, to redistribute robots between groups.

Such stable formations are observed in nature—in particular, in social and eusocial animals—and are based on models of social behavior [1]. The most prominent representatives of eusocial animals are ants. Many researchers in the field of group robotics use them as a "role model" [2, 3].

© Springer Nature Switzerland AG 2019
S. O. Kuznetsov and A. I. Panov (Eds.): RCAI 2019, CCIS 1093, pp. 17–29, 2019.
https://doi.org/10.1007/978-3-030-30763-9_2

Let us consider what mechanisms for redistributing individuals between social groups exist in ants. Families of most species of ants are fairly stable. Family size usually changes due to reproduction and natural loss. As a result, there may be a separation of the family when an anthill is overpopulated or the two families are united into one after a mass death of individuals. It is also possible to capture alien ants and their brood during wars [4]; association of families of different species as a result of migration [5]. However, we are more interested in the phenomenon of slavery.

Slavery in ants is a form of social parasitism. Slave-making ants raid nests of other ant species, capture the developing offspring, and rear them to slave workers [6]. Subsequently, the captured individuals (the so-called slaves) are integrated into a foreign colony. The mobilization of alien individuals allows one to free oneself from the nesting activity inside and to increase the number of foragers. Accordingly, the increase in the number of workers is provided by the energy costs of another nest.

There are facultative and obligate slave-making ant species. Facultative slave-makers are able to forage, nurse their brood, and construct their nests like free-living ants, hence colonies without slaves are often found. For obligate slave-making species, the presence of slaves is a prerequisite for the survival of the species because such species are not able to perform certain vital functions (for example, caring for the brood). Raids and the integration of captured individuals in a new family can be viewed as a mechanism for the redistribution of individuals between groups.

The main idea of the proposed approach is to implement the redistribution of robots between groups without additional mechanisms and rules. We will try to limit ourselves to the models and mechanisms that were developed earlier in the application of social behavior models to solving group robotics problems. First, it is necessary to examine in detail the phenomenon of slavery and the behavior models on which slavery in ants is based.

The purpose of this study is to implement complex regulatory behavior of animats using previously created models, methods, and mechanisms. An animat is an artificial agent that acts autonomously in a real or virtual environment and simulates the behavior of a living organism. The problem to be solved is the following. How can animats belonging to one group recruit individuals from another group for the redistribution of forces?

2   The Behavior of Slaves and Slave-Makers

Ants of an obligate slave-making species periodically organize raids on the neighboring nests of the host species. In the process of raids, they seize brood or young workers and bring them to their own nest. Only those individuals who do not resist the invaders are subject to capture (resisting individuals are killed or expelled). Here it is necessary to mention the well-known phenomenon of the increasing aggressiveness of ants with age [7]. Consequently, young workers have lower aggressiveness than those who go on the raid.

It is well known that ants recognize each other by odor. All ants in the nest have a certain odor and perceive each other as "nestmates." Ants from other nests are "aliens," they have a different odor. In the new nest, captured young workers and individuals released from the brood quickly acquire the odor characteristic of this nest. Slave-making workers begin to perceive them as their own nestmates. In the beginning, the slaves are mainly engaged in the intra-nesting activity. As they grow older, they can participate in other work, including new raids. For example, according to Mori, Grasso, and Le Moli [8], among the workers of the Formica sanguinea nest there was no division of labor between slaves and slave-maker workers because the same ants were raiders during the campaign for slaves and foragers during the foraging.

Now consider the mechanism on which this behavior is based.

The evolutionary basis for raids is foraging [9]. Foraging is part of eating behavior. Scout ants mine protein foods. In search of food, the scout surveys his sector of the territory around the nest, memorizing the route. If the scout has discovered the food and cannot transfer it himself, he will return to his nest. He mobilizes other ants (passive foragers) near the nest.

Facultative slave-making species represent a parasitic group between free-living species and obligate species. According to the observations of Mori, Grasso, and Le Moli [8], scouts of obligatory slave-makers seek only slave colonies, while scouts of optional slave-makers (in particular, Formica sanguinea) seek both food and nests of potential slaves. This fact confirms the assumption that the purpose of scouting ants was to search for food. Only with the advent of slavery did the intelligence officers shift to the search for foreign nests as a source of resources.

The raid is organized like any other campaign: to go to war, to defend the territory, to eat, and so on. Before the raid, scouts survey a certain sector. They return to the nest if they discover the desired resource or reveal a situation that requires coordinated actions of many individuals [10]. Then they mobilize other ants using recruitment signals and lead them to the place where the problem arose or the resource was discovered. A resource, in general, can be not only food but also any other object (or subject) that the nest needs. In particular, representatives of another nest as free labor can be a resource.

In this way, initiating a raid is a simple search for a resource. Slaves for obligate slave-makers are a prerequisite for the survival of the species, so they can be considered as a resource. Raids occur periodically: when there is a shortage of manpower, hunger, cold, and other inconveniences. For our task, the reason for the organization of the raid in the first place is the group's need for additional labor. The causes for the emergence of this need in our case are insignificant.

Scouts lead mobilized passive foragers to an alien nest, which is a place of concentration of potential slaves. Scouts are dominant and give a recruitment signal, so passive foragers follow them. In addition, cohesion plays a significant role in coordinating group activities [11]. Near the attacked nest, fights take place between the raiders and local residents. There are two mechanisms here—aggression and imitative behavior [12]. On the one hand, when ants meet with aliens who are competitors, they have an aggressive reaction. The outcome of the confrontation depends primarily on the degree of aggressiveness of individuals and on the ratio of "nestmates" and "aliens." On the other hand, coordinated behavior of ants is usually achieved through a group hierarchy and mass imitation by the majority of individuals of activator ants.

During raids, individuals of the slave species are captured, destroyed, or they escape [10]. There are also no specific rules here, only the rules for the interaction of ants with representatives of other species (or other nests) [7]. When two representatives of different species (or nests) are encountered, the following situations are possible:

1. The ants ignore each other.
2. One ant behaves aggressively, the other does not (remains passive).
3. Both ants behave aggressively toward each other.

Aggressors cannot be passive, so the first option is not considered. In the second case, the aggressor can grab a passive individual, which folds up as a "suitcase" and allows itself to be carried. The third option leads to a fight, as a result of which one individual can be killed or damaged.

Captured young workers adapt to someone else's nest. The socialization of a slave is based on the following elements of behavior [6]:

– Nestmates do not kill the slave because he acquired the necessary odor and partially adopted the behavior patterns of the slave-makers. He has lower aggressiveness, therefore he does not cause an aggressive reaction in the slave-makers.
– The slave submits to the slave-makers because they are stronger and more numerous. Once in a strange nest, the slave cannot show the aggression that the inhabitants of the nest cause in him: there are too many of them, he will simply die. The threat turns into danger, and the need for self-preservation drives the slave to demonstrate submission (there is nowhere to run). On this basis, the general behavior of a slave is passive.
– The slave works because it fits his behavior program, individual needs, and the like.
– The slave can change the sphere of activity: as he grows, his aggressiveness increases with age, and there is a need to perform more active types of work than those inside the nest.

In the new nest, the slaves do the same work that they would have done in their nest. This can be explained by the fact that the slave is placed in an environment that is not very different from his own nest, and he does the same work that he would do in his nest. For him, after moving to a new nest, almost nothing changes, only the freedom to choose a profession (type of activity) is limited. On the other hand, even in slave-free nests, young workers are subordinate to senior and experienced workers. Seniors can, for example, take young workers outside to do a specific job. Or, they may drive young workers into the nest if there are too many workers outside and they interfere with each other. Therefore, the slave "can consider" that he continues to live and work as before, without realizing his "slave position."

Next, we consider how these mechanisms and behaviors were implemented in earlier studies in the field of group robotics.

3   Models and Mechanisms for the Implementation of Certain Types of Behavior

3.1   Previously Created Models and Methods

Animat Control System. Karpov [13] proposed an architecture of the need-emotional control system for the animat. In this system, emotions determine the overall assessment of the current situation and are the basis for controlling the behavior of the animat. This approach is based on the need-information theory of emotions P. Simonov [14].

In accordance with Simonov's theory, emotions are an assessment of the value of the current need and the possibility of satisfying it. The brain evaluates this possibility based on genetic predisposition and previously obtained individual life experience. This can be expressed as follows [13]:

$$E = f(N, p(I_{need}, I_{has})),   (1)$$

where E is the emotion (its force, quality, and sign); N is the force and quality of the current need; $p(I_{need}, I_{has})$ is the estimate of the possibility of satisfying the need using the inherent and gained life experience; I_{need} is the information about the method to satisfy the need; and I_{has} is information about the means, resources, and time the subject has presently at its disposal. The difference between the need and possibilities of their satisfaction determines the emotional estimate of the current situation. If we have some needs and the possibilities of satisfying them are sufficient, then we have a positive emotional estimate. Otherwise, the emotions are negative.

The condition for the initiation of any action is negative emotions associated with unrealized needs. In the robot control system, the state of each action block is characterized by its private emotion E_i. The condition for choosing an action C_a is determined by the emotional state of the agent (animat):

$$C_a = C_a(E),   E = \{E_i\}   (2)$$

The set of behavior rules is represented in MYCIN-like form, that is, in the form of productions with confidence coefficients

$$R_n :   Cond_1 \wedge \ldots \wedge Cond_i \rightarrow (a_n)   (3)$$

where $i = 1,\ldots, m$ and m is the number of actions performed by the robot. For example, the rule "eat" can be represented as

IF "There is need in food" (N_{food}) & "I'm hungry" (S_{hungry}) & "I see food" (S_{food}), THEN "Eat" (a_{eat}),

where N_{food}, S_{hungry} and S_{food} are the confidence coefficients and the coefficient a_{eat} in the rule is determined by $a_{eat} = \min(N_{food}, S_{hungry}, S_{food})$.

In this way, all the confidence coefficients a_i ($i = 1,\ldots, m$) for all rules can be determined at the current point in time, where a_i is the magnitude of the predicted necessity of the action I_{need}. However, the actual coefficient a_i^{actual} in the rule may be different from a_i because the robot can perform only one action at a time (this is our assumption). Thus, we can find the emotional estimate for all actions a_i:

$$E_i = N_i\left(a_i - a_i^{actual}\right) \tag{4}$$

The effect of emotions on the execution of an action is implemented as a positive feedback between the output signal (current action) and the behavior rules. A fragment of the emotional control system is shown in Fig. 1. The unit *Actions* contains a set of behavior procedures. Each such procedure is activated by signals received from the unit *Need* and the signals from the special element *Gate*. Gate is the element that receives the direct signal from the sensors and the feedback signal from the output elements (in Fig. 1 the internal sensor is indicated by yellow and external sensor is indicated by green color). Each output procedure has a specific emotional weight according to (4). This signal is the input for the gate element. Therefore, the positive emotions associated with the action a_i will increase the activity of this action. Each action corresponds to a fixed action patterns (FAPs) [1] which is implemented using one or more Mealy machines. Service neurons stabilize the output vector. At each time, the robot performs only one action. The signal from the output of each service neuron arrives at the input to the inhibition of all other service neurons, suppressing their activity.

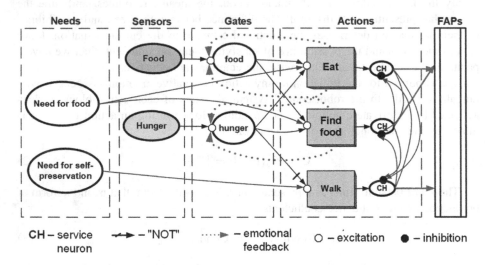

Fig. 1. Fragment of the emotional control system (Color figure online)

The need-emotional control system makes it possible not to introduce artificial rules for the functioning of the animat but to determine its activity in terms of needs and the possibilities for their satisfaction.

The Organization of Interaction. For the organization of joint action, animat must be able to recognize each other and distinguish between their own groups and others. Let each animat correspond to some number—its identifier (Id). This number is generated automatically at the beginning of work. The values of identifiers are divided into ranges —one per group; the belonging of the Id value to the range determines the belonging of the animat to the group (i.e., it imitates the smell tag of the nest). When meeting each other, animats generate a signal whose value is equal to the Id. By accepting this signal, they can understand who is in front of them: their own type or a different one. Moreover, the value of the Id can be interpreted as the rank of the animat, which depends on its internal state. Based on this rank, it is possible to determine the domination relationship between individuals.

The Mechanism of Foraging. Karpova [15, 16] proposed a method for solving the problem of searching resources (first of all, food) simulating the foraging mechanism of ants of the genus Formica rufa. Foraging consists of three stages:

1. The search for food in the feeding region.
2. The return home.
3. The repetition of the way to food and back.

Ants of the genus Formica rufa do not use pheromones, unlike many other ants species, when inspect the foraging area and returning home [12, 17]. They can be guided by a single light source (the Sun or the Moon), by the direction of light oscillations (the sky polarization in natural conditions) and by visible landmarks. In areas close to the nest, they use mostly visual reference points.

In [16], rules were developed for memorizing a route consisting of visual landmarks. The route contains landmarks in the sequence in which the animat saw them while moving in the process of searching for food. The route description included a list of visual landmarks and their position relative to the animat (left/right or forward in the direction of motion). In order for the animat to return home and repeat this route, rules have been created that interpret the route description. Difficult behavior "Pass a known route" was divided into relatively simple actions, such as "Bypass landmark X on the right/left," "Move to landmark X," and so on. The action is an elementary behavioral procedure; each behavioral procedure is implemented using Mealy machine.

Ants use various methods for mobilizing foragers. Ants of the genus Formica, for example, have two options [17]: (1) a scout transmits route information to foragers, and those independently go for food; (2) a scout leads foragers behind him. In Karpova's previous works the first option was considered, and now it is necessary to implement the second option. The process of mobilizing foragers (followers) must be initiated by some kind of a signal. The role of such a signal in ants is played by food exchanges (trophallaxis) and special poses that the scout takes.

Moskovsky, Burgov, and Ovsyannikova [18] describe the system of visual analyzer of an animat, which has the basic possibility of recognizing an animat's pose. But due to technical difficulties with the imitation and the recognition of the postures of a robotic device, we will initiate mobilization using signals. For example, Karpov and Karpova [19] describe the task of pack hunting. The leader of the pack generates some signal during the execution of a fixed behavioral procedure. In other words, the robot notifies its surroundings about its action or state. Other members of the group perceive the leader's signal as a call and follow him. This could be implemented on the basis of imitative behavior, as described by Karpov [20], but this is beyond the scope of this work. We assume that the signal starts an appropriate behavioral procedure, which is part of the eating behavior.

The Aggressive Behavior Model. Aggression is an integral part of many types of animal behavior: parental, territorial, group (hierarchical), and so on. Karpova and Karpov [21] considered a model of aggressive behavior that takes into account the experience of previous clashes (participation in conflicts) and simulates the phenomenon of increasing aggressiveness with the age of the animat and the effect of forgetting one's own experience. In addition, Karpova considered a model of territorial behavior based on aggression toward aliens [22]. These models are responsible for the realization of the domination relationship and the imitation of the struggle between individuals.

The model of aggressiveness proposed by Karpova and Karpov [21] includes two parameters and the internal sensor "aggressiveness," the value of which affects the animat behavior. The parameter A_0 sets the initial aggressiveness level, and the parameter A_C sets/measures/represents the current level. A_C determines the current tendency of the animat to enter into conflict. The A_C is increased by a certain amount δ in each time step, which imitates the increase in ant aggressiveness with age [7]. In addition, the value of A_C increases after the animat wins (W = 1) and decreases after its defeat (W = 0). The level A_C increases in case of victory at the moment of time t and is determined as monotonically increasing function with rage of values [0, 1), for example:

$$A_C(t) = 1 - e^{-\alpha t}, \tag{5}$$

where α is amplification factor of a synaptic connection.

In case of defeat the level decreases, and its value is defined as monotonically decreasing function with rage of values (0, 1], for example:

$$A_C(t) = e^{-\beta t}, \tag{6}$$

where β is attenuation factor of the synaptic connection.

In finite difference equations, the change in A_C can be expressed as follows:

$$\Delta A_C = \alpha(1 - A_C(t)), \text{ if } W = 1 \tag{7}$$

$$\Delta A_C = -\beta A_C(t), \text{ if } W = 0 \tag{8}$$

In fact, aggressiveness describes a measure of animat activity/passivity. This is a conditional indicator, which is convenient to use to describe the behavior of the animat. If desired, aggressiveness can be replaced by any other indicator, signal, or action. For us the main thing is to understand whether the animat is ready to obey. In ants, it depends primarily on the aggressiveness level. Therefore, we will not introduce any special parameters or signals but use precisely the aggressiveness level that has already been implemented in the animat's control system by Karpova and Karpov [21] ("Sensor A" in Fig. 2).

3.2   New Mechanisms and Methods

The control system has been supplemented by the "Recruitment signal" sensor and "Need for cohesion" [11] (see Fig. 2). This need coordinates the group behavior of the individuals during the raid. Also, a fixed action pattern "Follow the Leader" was implemented.

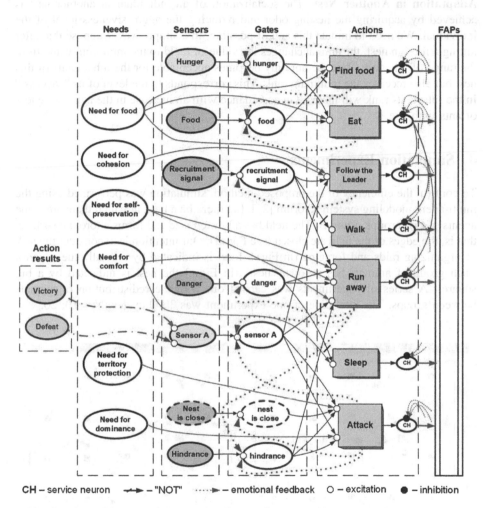

Fig. 2. The architecture of the emotional control system with an aggressive component

The Submission Mechanism. A mechanism of subordination is required to realize the phenomenon of slavery. Both food and a passive ant of another species are resources for active foragers. But a forager cannot change another individual and transfer it from an active to a passive state. The transition to a passive state must occur at the initiative of the one who obeys. Therefore, a weak ant takes the posture of submission when meeting an aggressor. For an animat, this means a change in the internal state, which leads to a decrease in its rank. Let the Id of the animat be interpreted as rank and depend on the level of aggressiveness. Then, we do not need additional alarms or artificial methods to simulate a duel, as shown by Karpova [22]. Changing the rank leads to the generation of the corresponding signal. This signal turns a weak animat into a resource attractive to foragers. And the forager transports this "resource" to its nest.

Adaptation in Another Nest. The socialization of an individual in another nest is achieved by acquiring the nesting odor and reducing the aggressiveness level of the individual. We need to imitate this and, if possible, in a simple way. Suppose that after hitting a foreign nest, the animat changes the value of its Id to the minimum value from the range of this nest. Thus, he not only becomes acceptable for the inhabitants of this nest but also receives the minimum rank. This corresponds to the level of its "success." In the future, its rank will increase in accordance with an increase in the aggressiveness of ants with age.

4   Simulation Experiments

To confirm the efficiency of the proposed method, simulation was performed using the multi-agent modeling system Kvorum [23]. Let there be a field in which there are some agents of two groups A and B. The field has a limited size and forms a toroidal surface, that is, the edges of the field are closed (see Fig. 3). Our intention is to consider the task of organizing raids and foraging (in Fig. 3 food is indicated by a small blue square). Each group of animats has its own "nest" (in Fig. 3 the nest is indicated by a big square). A series of experiments was carried out with the redistribution of animats between groups. The total time of one experiment was 3000 cycles, N = 10; 20.

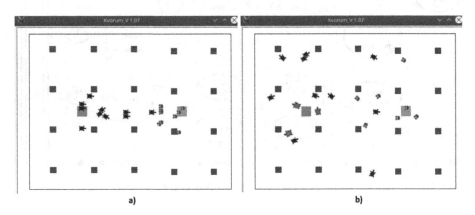

Fig. 3. Examples of experiments: (a) organization of the raid; (b) foraging after the animats redistribution (green animats moved to another group) (Color figure online)

To speed up the simulation, the experiments were carried out according to a simplified scheme:

1. The reconnaissance of the first group leads animats to the second nest.
2. Fights take place at the second nest.
3. The subordinate individuals of the second group are delivered to the first nest.
4. Both groups are engaged in foraging.

The stages of searching for food (resource) and returning to the nest have been described and implemented in [16]. For a raid, passive foragers are always recruited inside or near the nest [24], so this simplification does not contradict the observations of ants.

The animats had the following features. They could move back and forth, turn left and right. They have two internal sensors: the hunger sensor and the aggressive sensor. Also the animats were equipped with four IR sensors. Each sensor "hears" a signal from a certain side (in front, behind, to the left and to the right). The hearing area of the animat is limited. The animat generates a broadcast signal that can only be received by its close neighbors.

There is no sense in presenting any statistical data obtained in the course of the experiments and giving estimates. We can set different values of the model parameters and get any data: from the minimal susceptibility of animats to "enslavement" to the complete transition of all animats to one group. But these experiments faced another challenge. They were designed to confirm the applicability of the proposed approach and the efficiency of the developed models and algorithms. This goal was achieved.

5 Conclusion

The proposed approach allows us to solve the problem of redistributing animats between groups under the following conditions. The problem is solved in the conditions of local communication and without centralized control. Animats have a set of needs (dominance, self-preservation, food and so on), a set of procedures that implement some types of behavior (food, aggressive, contagious), and a set of rules that ensure the transition from one procedure to another. Each of them independently makes decisions about its actions, but together they form a society and act for the benefit of this society.

Of course, to solve the problem of redistributing animats between groups, a different, simpler method could be used. It is even possible that this other method would show better controllability and higher efficiency. But, first of all, the current work is designed to demonstrate that complex behavior can be implemented using previously created models, methods, and mechanisms in the framework of social behavior modeling. And secondly, the proposed method can be used to form heterogeneous robots groups in the future.

Acknowledgments. The project was supported by Russian Foundation for Basic Research, project № 16-29-04412 ofi-m.

The author would like to thank Valery E. Karpov and Eugeny V. Burgov for participating in the discussion of this work.

References

1. Tinbergen, N.: Social Behavior of Animals. Methuen, London (1953)
2. de Lope, J., Maravall, D., Quiñonez, Y.: Self-organizing techniques to improve the decentralized multi-task distribution in multi-robot systems. Neurocomputing **163**, 47–55 (2015)
3. Karpov, V.E.: Models of social behavior in group robotics. (Modeli social'nogo povedeniya v gruppovoj robototekhnike). Upravlenie bol'shimi sistemami **59**, 165–232 (2016)
4. Mabelis, A.A.: Wood ants wars. Neth. J. Zool. **29**(4), 451–626 (1979)
5. Zakharov, A.A.: Classification of ant nest complexes. Entomol. Rev. **95**(8), 959–971 (2015)
6. D'Ettorre, P., Heinze, J.: Sociobiology of slave-making ants. Acta Ethologica **3**(2), 67–82 (2001)
7. Zaharov, A.A.: Ants Community Organization (Organizaciya soobshchestv u murav'ev). Nauka, Moscow (1991)
8. Mori, A., Grasso, D.A., Le Moli, F.: Raiding and foraging behavior of the blood-red ant, Formica sanguinea Latr. (Hymenoptera, Formicidae). J. Insect Behav. **13**(3), 421–430 (2000)
9. Czechowski, W.: Recruitment signals and raids in slave-maker ants. Ann. Zool. **34**, 1–23 (1977)
10. Hasegawa, E., Yamaguchi, T.: Raiding behavior of the Japanese slave-making ant Polyergus samurai. Insectes Sociaux **41**(3), 279–289 (1994)
11. Leonhardt, S.D., Menzel, F., Nehring, V., Schmitt, T.: Ecology and evolution of communication in social insects. Cell **164**(6), 1277–1287 (2016)
12. Zaharov, A.A.: Ant, Family, Colony (Muravej, sem'ya, koloniya). Nauka, Moscow (1978)
13. Karpov, V.E.: Emotions and temperament of robots: behavioral aspects. J. Comput. Syst. Sci. Int. **53**(5), 743–760 (2014)
14. Simonov, P.V.: The need-information theory of emotions (Potrebnostno-informacionnaya teoriya emocij). Voprosy psihologii **6**, 44–56 (1982)
15. Karpova, I.P.: On the issue of the route for the robot in the foraging task (K voprosu o predstavlenii marshruta dlya robota v zadache furazhirovaniya). In: Proceedings of Fifteenth National Conference on Artificial Intelligence with International Participation (CAI-2016). vol. 1, pp. 169–178. Universum, Smolensk (2016)
16. Karpova, I.P.: On the issue of representing the route of a mobile robot based on visual landmarks (K voprosu o predstavlenii marshruta mobil'nogo robota na osnove vizual'nyh orientirov). Mekhatronika Avtomatizaciya Upravlenie **18**(2), 81–89 (2017)
17. Dlussky, G.M.: Ants of the genus Formica (Murav'i roda Formika). Nauka, Moscow (1967)
18. Moskovsky, A.D., Burgov, E.V., Ovsyannikova, E.E.: Animat's visual analyzer as the basis of the semantics of the robot's sensory system (Zritel'nyj analizator animata kak osnova semantiki sensornoj sistemy robota). Mekhatronika Avtomatizaciya Upravlenie **5**(19), 336–345 (2018)
19. Karpov, V., Karpova, I.: Leader election algorithms for static swarms. Biol. Inspired Cogn. Archit. **12**, 54–64 (2015)
20. Karpov, V.E.: Sensory model of the imitative behavior of robots (Sensornaya model' podrazhatel'nogo povedeniya robotov). In: Open Semantic Technologies for Intelligent Systems (OSTIS-2016) Proceedings of Conference, pp. 471–476. BGUIR, Minsk (2016)
21. Karpova, I., Karpov, V.: Some mechanisms for managing aggressive behavior in group robotics. In: 29th DAAAM International Symposium on Intelligent Manufacturing and Automation, pp. 566–573. Zadar, Croatia (2018)

22. Karpova, I.: About realization of aggressive behavior model in group robotics. In: Samsonovich, A.V., Klimov, V.V. (eds.) BICA 2017. AISC, vol. 636, pp. 78–84. Springer, Cham (2018). https://doi.org/10.1007/978-3-319-63940-6_11
23. Rovbo, M.A., Ovsyannikova, E.E.: Simulating robot groups with elements of a social structure using KVORUM. Procedia Comput. Sci. **119**, 147–156 (2017)
24. Topoff, H., LaMon, B., Goodloe, L., Goldstein, M.: Social and orientation behavior of Polyergus breviceps during slave-making raids. Behav. Ecol. Sociobiol. **15**(4), 273–279 (1984)

Hierarchical Reinforcement Learning with Clustering Abstract Machines

Skrynnik Alexey[1] and Aleksandr I. Panov[1,2(✉)]

[1] Artificial Intelligence Research Institute, Federal Research Center "Computer Science and Control" of the Russian Academy of Sciences, Moscow, Russia
{skrynnik,pan}@isa.ru
[2] Moscow Institute of Physics and Technology, Moscow, Russia

Abstract. Hierarchical reinforcement learning (HRL) is another step towards the convergence of learning and planning methods. The resulting reusable abstract plans facilitate both the applicability of transfer learning and increasing of resilience in difficult environments with delayed rewards. However, on the way of the practical application of HRL, especially in robotics, there are a number of difficulties, among which the key is a semi-manual task of the creation of the hierarchy of actions, which the agent uses as a pre-trained scheme. In this paper, we present a new approach for simultaneous constructing and applying the hierarchy of actions and sub-goals. In contrast to prior efforts in this direction, the method is based on a united loop of clustering of the environment's states observed by the agent and allocation of sub-targets by the modified bottleneck method for constructing of abstract machines hierarchy. The general machine is built using the so-called programmable schemes, which are quite universal for the organization of transfer learning for a wide class of tasks. A particular abstract machine is assigned for each set of clustered states. The goal of each machine is to reach one of the found bottleneck states and then get into another cluster. We evaluate our approach using a standard suite of experiments on a challenging planning problem domain and show that our approach facilitates learning without prior knowledge.

Keywords: Hierarchical reinforcement learning · Machine learning · Reinforcement learning

1 Introduction

Hierarchical reinforcement learning (HRL) is a promising approach for solving problems with a large state space and a lack of immediate reinforcement signal [3, 10, 21, 26]. Promising outlook of this approach was noted in early works on the automata theory [24]. The hierarchical approach allows decomposing the complex task into a set of sub-tasks using hierarchical structures. It is a natural procedure also performed by humans [20]. However, there is one aspect of human problem-solving that remains poorly understood, the ability to finding

© Springer Nature Switzerland AG 2019
S. O. Kuznetsov and A. I. Panov (Eds.): RCAI 2019, CCIS 1093, pp. 30–43, 2019.
https://doi.org/10.1007/978-3-030-30763-9_3

an appropriate hierarchical structure. Finding good decomposition is usually an art-form and it is a major challenge to be able to automatically identify the required decomposition. Despite the fact that a number of achievements have been made in this direction [7,17], discovering hierarchical structure is still an open problem in reinforcement learning.

Most of the efforts aimed at learning in hierarchies are concerned with the acceleration of Q-learning by identifying bottlenecks in the state space [15]. The most popular framework in these works is Options [19]. Within it, artificial agents are able to construct and extend hierarchies of reusable skills or meta-actions (options). A suitable set of skills can help improve the agent's learning efficiency in solving difficult problems. Another commonly used approach in HRL is the MAXQ framework [4], where the value function is decomposed over the task hierarchy. Automated discovery of options hierarchy [11] and task decomposition within the MAXQ approach [14] showed good results in a number of synthetic problems e.g. Rooms or Taxi environments. Most of the real problems in robotics are very different from these artificial examples. The tasks of manipulator control and robot movement in space are of great practical interest [6,23]. The existing attempts to adapt these approaches to continuous space [2] are of little use in these tasks. There are at least two reasons for this. The fist reason is the lack of mixed action and state abstraction [9]. The second is that pseudo-rewards should be specified to learn hierarchically optimal policies.

Particular attention in HRL is paid to the search for sub-targets using the so-called bottlenecks, i.e., special states of the environment that are key in terms of building successful trajectories with the maximum value of the total reward. The general ideas demonstrated in [12] and based on the calculation of the number of states visited, are subject to a large number of errors of the second kind, when the number of candidates for bottleneck gets a lot of "noise" states (for example, next to the local minimum remuneration). The idea of clustering (symbolization) of the environment states [1,8,11] may be useful when we try to distinguish similar classes both from the descriptive and functional points of view. For such classes, one can build separate sub-goals and thus organize a sequence of actions that lead from one cluster to another. Thus, we come to a simple idea stated in this work that the search for a hierarchical representation of the problem must be iterative, where the iteration steps are (a) the allocations of clusters, (b) the search for cluster bottleneck for each cluster and (c) the training of the corresponding cluster machine. Then the general machine formed by some principle serves as a base for a set of statistics at steps (a) and (b). A difficult place here is just the construction of a general abstract machine. In our work, we use the so-called programmable schemes approach [25]. It is a set of universal rules for combining subroutines (in our case, sub-plans) that are general enough to obtain a good generalizing ability of a single machine.

2   Background

2.1   Reinforcement Learning with HAMs

The HAM approach limits the possible actions of the agent by transitions between states of the machine [18]. An example of a simple abstract machine can be: "constantly move to the right or down." Transitions to certain states of the machine cause execution of actions in the environment and the remaining transitions are of a technical nature and define internal logic.

An abstract machine is a set of five elements $\langle M, \Sigma, \Lambda\mu, \delta \rangle$, where M is a finite set of machine states, Σ is an input alphabet corresponding to the space of states of the environment, Λ is the output alphabet of the abstract machine, $\delta(m, s_i)$ is the function of transition to the next state, with the current state $m \in M$ of the machine, and the state of the environment $s_i \in S$, $\mu(m) \in Lambda$ is the output function of the machine.

The machine's states are divided into several types: *Start*, this state starts the operation of any machine, *Action*, in this state, the action to be taken is performed when the machine goes to this state, *Choice*, if there are several transitions from this state, then the choice of the next one is stochastic, *Call*, a transition to this state suspends the execution of the current machine and calls the machine specified in this state,*Stop*, transition to this state stops execution of the current machine.

Since the choice of the next state for the transition is not deterministic only in the state of *Choice*, then Q value is updated for previous C and current C' *Choice* states. Iteration occurs with due account of the current state s of the environment:

$$Q(s, C) \leftarrow (1 - \alpha)Q(s, C) + \alpha(r_c + \gamma \max_{a'} Q(s', C'))$$

In addition to the standard approach, we use the idea of pseudo-rewards. In the machine, there can be vertices such that visits to them are internally rewarded, which applies only to a specific machine.

2.2   Bottlenecks

The states recommended for visiting are called bottlenecks $b_i \in \mathcal{B}$. Finding and using such states allows the agent to point in the right direction for exploring the environment. This approach is often used with the options framework. An option is a tuple of 3 components: $\langle I, \pi, \beta \rangle$, where I is a set of initial states., π is a policy, β is a termination condition. A set of options forms their hierarchy, where options can trigger elementary actions and other options. The found bottleneck states are used to determine the condition for completing an option β. This approach is well studied: [5,13,22].

3   Clustering HAMs

This article provides an algorithm for automatically building a hierarchy in which the source environment is divided into clusters and the search for bottlenecks, the scheme of the approach is presented in Fig. 1.

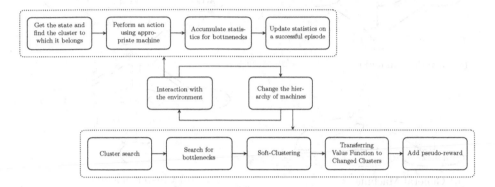

Fig. 1. Clustering HAMs scheme

The paper solves the following problems:

- Transfer learning is a task in which several environments have a similar structure. The knowledge gained by the agent on one of them can be applied to the other. The advantage of using the approach, in this case, is that the accumulated information can be used for a wide class of similar tasks. Consider a robot that can move around a room, it is much easier to train to move objects from one place to another than a robot that does not know how to move and learns from scratch.
- Restriction on the search space, in order to specify the direction of study by the agent of the original environment. In this case, the advantage is achieved due to the fact that there can be states in the environment visiting which is necessary to achieve the final goal. In such cases, it is beneficial to encourage the agent to achieve these conditions, thus directing the search. For example, a task in which an agent needs to get into a closed room with a key forces him to first find the key and only then move to the goal. The achievement by an agent of the state in which the key is located is necessary, and the agent's encouragement to achieve this state speeds up the learning process.

We use a method similar to that used in [5]. Bottlenecks are determined by frequency. In order for a condition to be chosen as a bottleneck, it is necessary that it is frequently visited in successful episodes $\widehat{Ep}$ (episodes in which the agent achieved his goal) $fr(s_i) = |s_i \in \widehat{Ep_k}|$. The application of this approach in cases where there is no information about the success of the episode is a direction of our future work.

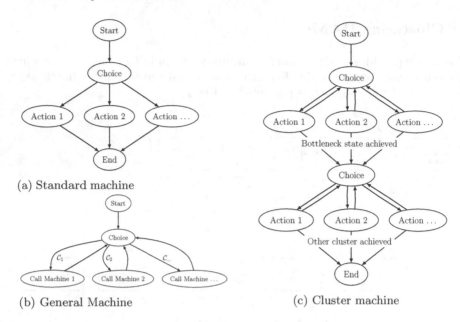

(a) Standard machine

(b) General Machine

(c) Cluster machine

Fig. 2. Predefined abstract machines

In our work, state clustering is used to determine the hierarchy structure. Clusters $\mathcal{C}$ are close environmental states. Consider the task in which the robot moves between several rooms. The rooms are numbered and then the cluster can be the number of the room in which the robot is currently located. If the robot solves the problem in a new environment, where states belonging to familiar clusters exist, then it will be able to apply the existing information (hierarchy structure), thereby increasing the speed and stability of learning. The comparison of the close states of the environment cannot be performed without any additional information about the $\mathcal{I}$ environment, so the method is not applicable to an environment where information about the environment is encoded only by a meaningless state identifier.

A significant advantage of our work is that the information about the environment is transmitted only at the moment of interaction with it, and is not determined in advance. In different environments, additional information may differ, as well as the information may not be provided at every step, for example, in some parts of the environment there may be a situation in which information cannot be obtained from sensors and devices (e.g. GPS is unstable). Examples of such information: coordinates of the agent; processed information from agent sensors; information from other sources that are not taken into account in the state of the environment. For clustering in the problem under consideration, a large number of algorithms can be used. The k-means method is used in this work, however later on we plan to use hierarchical clustering, since it allows us to build a hierarchical relationship between states, which in the future will allow you to create a multi-level hierarchy of machines.

We divide the algorithm into two stages: (i) using the current hierarchy to interact with the environment and accumulate statistics (ii) clustering, searching for bottlenecks and building a hierarchy. The process is cyclical, at each iteration the information obtained at the previous stage is used:

- At the stage of using the hierarchy and accumulating statistics, a hierarchy is applied with the structure defined at stage (ii).
- At the stage of building the hierarchy, the statistics accumulated at stage (i) is used.

At the first iteration of the algorithm, we do not have a built hierarchy, so we assume that all states belong to the same cluster, and it does not have any bottlenecks.

To search for clusters, we use additional information obtained from the environment, as well as information about the value function of each state, which we obtained using the previous hierarchy. The distance $d(p, \ldots, q, V)_{s1,s2}$ between the states $s1$, $s2$ for the Euclidean metric and the coefficient of significance of the value function c_V:

$$d(p, \ldots, q, V)_{s1,s2} = \sqrt{(p_{s1} - p_{s2})^2 + \cdots + (q_{s1} - q_{s2})^2 + (c_V(V_{s1} - V_{s2}))^2},$$

where $\langle p, \ldots, q \rangle$ is additional environment information, V is value function, c_V is value function of cluster c.

We add the value of the V value function as a parameter for clustering in order to take into account information about the proximity of states relative to the achievement of the goal. The usefulness of this function can be understood by an artificial example: Suppose there is a room from which there are doors to the other three, but you can only reach the target state through one of these rooms. Our task is to divide the state of these three rooms into 2 clusters. Naturally, the states inside the rooms are much closer to each other, relative to the states in the other rooms. In this case, taking into account the V value function will allow us to separate the room leading to the target state from the other two.

The following global parameters are used to search for clusters:

- Number of clusters C_{size}.
- Function significance coefficient V for clustering.

To search for bottlenecks, information about the frequency of states in successful trajectories is used. For each state, this indicator is equal to the ratio of successful trajectories in which it is encountered.

The following global parameters are used to search for bottlenecks:

- The coefficient of significance for a linear combination of the above parameters, according to the parameters and this coefficient, the states are sorted.
- The number of bottlenecks for each of the clusters. According to this indicator and sorted states, the required number of bottlenecks is selected for each cluster.

At this stage, the state of the environment is already divided in clusters. For each such cluster, a separate machine is built, which is applied only if the medium is in a state belonging to this cluster.

The machine that is used for each cluster is presented in Fig. 2c. The figure shows that the first goal of the machine is to achieve a bottleneck belonging to its arbitrary cluster and then exit from this cluster. Cluster machines are combined into one general Fig. 2b.

3.1 Algorithms

The pseudocode of the entire algorithm is presented as Algorithm 1. The input to the algorithm is the MDP, which is defined by the environment E. During initialization, the structure of the general machine $\mathcal{H}$ is given by the looped standard machine $\mathcal{H}_{standard}$, which is represented in Fig. 2a. $\mathcal{B}_{st}$ is initialized with an empty list.

Interaction with the environment takes place for a given number of $\mathcal{N}$ episodes. When each action is completed, the current cluster $\mathcal{C}_{cur}$ is determined, for which the corresponding machine $M_{\mathcal{C}_{cur}}$ is applied, using the general strategy $\mathcal{H}_{policy}$. During the interaction with the environment, $\mathcal{C}_{model\_info}$ of statistical information is updated, which is used for further clustering. After each episode, if the episode was successful, the information is updated to determine the bottlenecks $\mathcal{B}_{st}$. Then the hierarchy changes, using the accumulated statistics. In $\mathcal{H}^{\mathcal{C}}_{new}$ updated clusters are saved, new bottlenecks are preserved in $\mathcal{H}^{\mathcal{B}}_{new}$, the value function is transferred to $\mathcal{H}^{Q(s)}_{new}$. The pseudo-reward is added to the new $\mathcal{H}_{new}$ machine hierarchy. The pseudo-reward is determined only inside the machine for a particular cluster and is given to the agent for reaching the bottleneck and the subsequent transition to another cluster.

An important part of the algorithm is the clustering scheme since a large number of episodes can be carried out between finding clusters, the new partitioning of states can be very different from the previous one. For such a case, we propose a soft clustering algorithm that renumbers the class labels so that the new clustering is maximally similar to the previous one. The pseudocode of the algorithm is given as Algorithm 2. The main feature of the algorithm is that it is not tied to specific clustering methods. To use it, it is enough for the clustering method to have the functions *fit* and *predict*, which are responsible for learning and prediction, respectively.

4 Experiments

4.1 Dangerous Rooms Domain

The dangerous rooms domain is a modification of the well-known gridworld task. The agent is located in a maze consisting of several rooms, and his goal is to achieve a certain state. The agent appears in one of the random places in the first room and must reach a certain state in the last room. There is an abyss in the center of each room, the fall in which leads to the end of the episode with a

Algorithm 1. Clustering HAMs

Input: MDP E, τ frequency at which to update hierarchy

1: initialize hierarchy $\mathcal{H}$ with standard one $\mathcal{H}_{std}$
2: initialize $\mathcal{B}$ with empty dictionary
3: initialize $\mathcal{I}$ with empty set of tuples
4: **for** k = 0, ..., $\mathcal{N}$ − 1 **do**
5:     $G \leftarrow \emptyset$
6:     **while** terminate condition of env E_{done} is not True **do**
7:         find cluster $\mathcal{C}_{cur}$ which contains current state S
8:         make action in E using machine for cluster $\mathcal{C}_{cur}$
9:         collect S', R, $\mathcal{I}_{S'}$
10:        **if** $\mathcal{I}_{S'}$ not in $\mathcal{I}$ **then**
11:            add $\mathcal{I}_{S'}$ to set of additional states information $\mathcal{I}$
12:        **end if**
13:        update used machine policy with given reward R and next state S'
14:        **if** S' not in G **then**
15:            add state S' to set of visited in episode states G
16:        **end if**
17:     **end while**
18:     **if** completed episode was successful **then**
19:        $\mathcal{B}[S_i] \leftarrow \mathcal{B}[S_i] + 1$ for each state in G
20:     **end if**
21:     **if** k mod τ = 0 **then**
22:        make clusterization for $\mathcal{C}$ using accumulated information $\mathcal{I}$ via clustering
23:        find bottleneck states for clustered states $\mathcal{C}$ using $\mathcal{B}$
24:        create new hierarchy $\mathcal{H}_{new}$ with given $\mathcal{B}$ and $\mathcal{C}$
25:        transfer Q-function from $\mathcal{H}$ to $\mathcal{H}_{new}$
26:        add pseudo reward to $\mathcal{H}_{new}$ sub-machines
27:        set the new hierarchy as the main $\mathcal{H} \leftarrow \mathcal{H}_{new}$
28:     **end if**
29: **end for**
30: **return** $\mathcal{H}$

large negative reward. In each state of the environment, four actions are available to the agent: down, up, left, right. The environment is stochastic, so the action chosen by the agent occurs with a certain probability. With a probability of P_a, the agent will move in the selected direction (if possible) and with probability of $1 - P_a$, the agent will take a step in the direction different from that chosen. As additional information, the agent is informed of his coordinates in the maze. Figure 3 presents an example environment with four rooms and the size of each of them is 3 cells. Figure 3a shows the designation of colors.

4.2 Learning

The following general parameters were used for the experiments:

$P_a = 0.9$, probability of correct movement.
$R_t = +100$, reward for achieving the target state.

Algorithm 2. Soft Clustering Wrapper

Input: Set of observations $\mathcal{O}_{new}$, clustering algorithm $\mathcal{A}_{new}$

1: **if** saved $\mathcal{O}_{cur}$ doesn't exist **then**
2:     $\mathcal{O}_{cur} \leftarrow \mathcal{O}_{new}$
3:     $\mathcal{A}_{cur} \leftarrow \mathcal{A}_{new}$
4:     train $\mathcal{A}_{cur}$ with data from $\mathcal{O}_{cur}$
5:     initialize relabel dict $\mathcal{M}_{cur}$ with empty set $\emptyset$
6: **else**
7:     $\mathcal{O}_{cur} \leftarrow \mathcal{O}_{new}$
8:     make prediction $\mathcal{P}_{cur}$ with current algorithm $\mathcal{A}_{cur}$ for data $\mathcal{O}_{cur}$
9:     $\mathcal{A}_{cur} \leftarrow \mathcal{A}_{new}$
10:     make prediction $\mathcal{P}_{new}$ with new algorithm $\mathcal{A}_{cur}$ for data $\mathcal{O}_{cur}$
11:     make inverse mapping for $\mathcal{P}_{new}$ using $\mathcal{M}_{cur}$
12:     $\mathcal{M}_{cur} \leftarrow \emptyset$
13:     create $\mathcal{L}$ list of unique label pairs $\langle \mathcal{P}_{cur}^i, \mathcal{P}_{new}^i \rangle$
14:     sort $\mathcal{L}$ in decreasing order by the number of pairs where $\mathcal{P}_{cur}^i = \mathcal{P}_{new}^i$
15:     initialize empty set of used $\mathcal{U}_{cur}$ with $\emptyset$ for current labels
16:     initialize empty set of used $\mathcal{U}_{new}$ with $\emptyset$ for new labels
17:     **for** l_{cur}, l_{new} in $\mathcal{L}$ **do**
18:         **if** map$[l_{new}]$ is None and l_{cur} not in used $\mathcal{U}_{cur}$ **then**
19:             add l_{cur} to $\mathcal{U}_{cur}$
20:             add l_{new} to $\mathcal{U}_{new}$
21:             save mapping for l_{cur} with l_{new} to relabel dict $\mathcal{M}_{cur}$
22:         **end if**
23:     **end for**
24: **end if**
25: **return** $\mathcal{M}_{cur}$

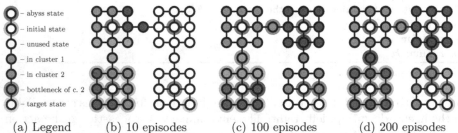

(a) Legend	(b) 10 episodes	(c) 100 episodes	(d) 200 episodes

Fig. 3. Clustering

$R_d = -20$, reward for falling into the abyss.
$R_a = -1$, reward for any other outcome.
$N_t = 30$, number of independent trials, which were carried out for each algorithm on N_{ep} episodes. The diagrams show the average result of these trials.
$\alpha = 0.1$, learning rate.
$\gamma = 0.9$, gamma.
$\epsilon = 0.1$, ϵ-greedy parameter, with fading factor 0.999, applied after each episode.

For the first experiment, we used the environment which consists of four rooms. The size of each of them is 5. The Fig. 4a shows the results of the following algorithms: Q-learning and CHAMs for 1, 2, and 4 clusters. Initially, the convergence curve goes down, due to the fact that at first, the algorithms choose a strategy "to go straight to failure", which gives a result close to −20. Then the policy is adjusted, the agent realizes that it is not rewarding to go into the abyss. However, he still cannot reach the target state, so he accumulates a large negative reward.

In the second experiment, we used an environment consisting of 6 rooms. The size of each room is 3. The results are presented in Fig. 4b. For clarity, s.d. compressed 5 times. It can be seen that it is initially small, and then increases, which confirms the above explanation of the fall of the convergence curve. Standard deviation hardly changes with the episodes, since the size of the room is small and the chance of accidentally falling into the abyss is high. Each of the experiments showed the advantages of the proposed method, the division into clusters and the allocation of bottlenecks improves convergence.

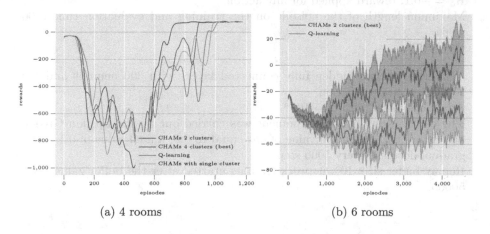

(a) 4 rooms   (b) 6 rooms

Fig. 4. Convergence diagrams

4.3   Transfer Learning

In the second experiment, we applied CHAM to the transfer learning task.

For this task, we used two environments of the dangerous rooms, which differed in the location of the target state in the last room. During the transfer of learning, only information about clusters and bottlenecks was reused.

With this experiment, we also wanted to show the universality of this approach, so we used a neural network as an approximator. For training, we used the DQN approach [16]. The state of the environment specified by the binary vector, as well as information about the current state of the abstract machine, is fed to the input of the network as an observation.

The state of an abstract machine is the index of the machine used and its current vertex, which are encoded by a binary vector. The output of the network is the probability distribution of actions taken by the agent.

To build the hierarchy, the same parameters of the DQN algorithm were used for the subsequent transfer of knowledge; these parameters will be presented below. Through the use of a neural network as approximator, it was possible to abandon the stage of the transfer of the value function. The hierarchy consisted of 6 clustering machines. The pseudo-reward for reaching the bottleneck and moving to another cluster was 5. The rebuilding of the hierarchy occurred at every 5000 step.

Dangerous rooms environment, with number of rooms 6, the size of each room is 5×5.

$P_a = 0.9$ and $P_a = 1.0$, the probability of the correct movement, for the stochastic and deterministic variants of the environment, respectively;

$R_t = +100$, reward for achieving a target state.

$R_d = -20$, reward for falling into the abyss.

$R_a = -0.1$, reward applied for any action.

Maximum length of the episode on the training and evaluation run, 1000 steps.

$\gamma = 0.95$.

Network with two hidden fully connected layers with 300 neurons and the ReLU activation function.

Adam optimizer with $\alpha = 10^{-3}$.

The exploration of the environment was carried out by the Epsilon Greedy algorithm, with an initial value of *eps* equal to 0.8, a final value of 0.1 and a gradual decrease every 5000 steps.

Replay buffer size: 10^5, network training started after the buffer gained size 50000.

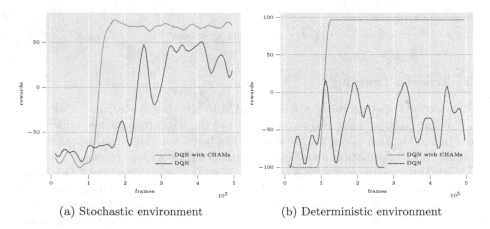

(a) Stochastic environment   (b) Deterministic environment

Fig. 5. Transfer learning task

The target network was updated every 500 step and the maximum number of steps $5 \cdot 10^5$.
The evaluation test was carried out at each 5000 step, the average total reward received for 10 of launches was used as a result.

Figure 5a shows the results for the stochastic environment. Figure 5b shows the results for the deterministic environment. The plots prove the effectiveness of the CHAM algorithm for the knowledge transfer task.

5 Conclusion

In this paper, we have proposed a new algorithm for automatic hierarchy construction in hierarchical reinforcement learning. As the basic framework of the SemiMDP solution, we used the method of abstract machines that are well adapted to robotics tasks. We used a well-known approach of bottlenecks, which have allowed us to define sub-goals as states of the environment mandatory to visit. We have proposed a modified metric to allocate sub-goals. In our algorithm, we used the idea of functional clustering, which assumes that each sub-goal must correspond to its class of states that will determine the reachability of this sub-goal. The main idea of our algorithm is the parallel allocation of such clusters and construction of a global abstract machine, which combines the hierarchy of sub-machines for the achievement of sub-goals for each cluster. In the iterative procedure of rebuilding clusters and changing the resulted machine, we have obtained an improvement in the convergence of the learning process. We have verified our approach in the environment of "dangerous rooms", which showed advantages of our algorithm compared to non-clustering methods.

Acknowledgements. This work was supported by the Russian Science Foundation, project no. 18-71-00143.

References

1. Abel, D., Arumugam, D., Lehnert, L., Littman, M.: State abstractions for lifelong reinforcement learning. In: Proceedings of the 35th International Conference on Machine Learning, vol. 80, pp. 10–19 (2018). http://proceedings.mlr.press/v80/abel18a.html
2. Daniel, C., van Hoof, H., Peters, J., Neumann, G.: Probabilistic inference for determining options in reinforcement learning. Mach. Learn. **104**(2–3), 337–357 (2016)
3. Dayan, P., Hinton, G.: Feudal reinforcement learning. In: Advances in Neural Information Processing Systems, pp. 271–278 (1993)
4. Dietterich, T.G.: Hierarchical reinforcement learning with the MAXQ value function decomposition. J. Artif. Intell. Res. **13**, 227–303 (2000)
5. Digney, B.L.: Learning hierarchical control structures for multiple tasks and changing environments. In: Proceedings of the Fifth International Conference on the Simulation of Adaptive Behavior on From Animals to Animats 5, pp. 321–330 (1998)

6. Gupta, S., Davidson, J., Levine, S., Sukthankar, R., Malik, J.: Cognitive Mapping and Planning for Visual Navigation. arXiv:1702.03920, February 2017
7. Hengst, B.: Hierarchical approaches. In: Wiering, M., van Otterlo, M. (eds.) Reinforcement Learning. Adaptation, Learning, and Optimization, vol. 12, pp. 293–323. Springer, Heidelberg (2012). https://doi.org/10.1007/978-3-642-27645-3_9
8. James, S., Rosman, B., Africa, S., Konidaris, G.: Learning to Plan with Portable Symbols, July 2018
9. Konidaris, G.: Constructing abstraction hierarchies using a skill-symbol loop. In: International Joint Conference on Artificial Intelligence, IJCAI, January 2016, pp. 1648–1654 (2016)
10. Kuzmin, V., Panov, A.I.: Hierarchical reinforcement learning with options and united neural network approximation. In: Abraham, A., Kovalev, S., Tarassov, V., Snasel, V., Sukhanov, A. (eds.) IITI 2018. AISC, vol. 874, pp. 453–462. Springer, Cham (2019). https://doi.org/10.1007/978-3-030-01818-4_45
11. Mannor, S., Menache, I., Hoze, A., Klein, U.: Dynamic abstraction in reinforcement learning via clustering. In: Twenty-first international conference on Machine learning - ICML 2004, p. 71. ACM Press (2004)
12. McGovern, A.: Autonomous discovery of abstractions through interaction with an environment. In: Koenig, S., Holte, R.C. (eds.) SARA 2002. LNCS (LNAI), vol. 2371, pp. 338–339. Springer, Heidelberg (2002). https://doi.org/10.1007/3-540-45622-8_34
13. Mcgovern, E.A.: Autonomous discovery of temporal abstractions from interaction with an environment. Power, May 2002. http://citeseerx.ist.psu.edu/viewdoc/download?doi=10.1.1.136.3079&rep=rep1&type=pdf
14. Mehta, N., Ray, S., Tadepalli, P., Dietterich, T.: Automatic discovery and transfer of MAXQ hierarchies. In: Proceedings of the 25th International Conference on Machine Learning - ICML 2008, pp. 648–655. ACM Press (2008)
15. Menache, I., Mannor, S., Shimkin, N.: Q-Cut—dynamic discovery of sub-goals in reinforcement learning. In: Elomaa, T., Mannila, H., Toivonen, H. (eds.) ECML 2002. LNCS (LNAI), vol. 2430, pp. 295–306. Springer, Heidelberg (2002). https://doi.org/10.1007/3-540-36755-1_25
16. Mnih, V., et al.: Playing atari with deep reinforcement learning. arXiv preprint. arXiv:1312.5602 (2013)
17. Panov, A.I., Skrynnik, A.: Automatic formation of the structure of abstract machines in hierarchical reinforcement learning with state clustering. In: ICML\IJCAI Workshop on Planning and Learning (PAL-18) (2018). http://arxiv.org/abs/1806.05292, https://sites.google.com/site/planlearn18/
18. Parr, R., Russell, S.: Reinforcement learning with hierarchies of machines. In: Neural Information Processing Systems (NIPS), pp. 1043–1049 (1998)
19. Precup, D., Sutton, R., Singh, S.: Multi-time models for temporally abstract planning. In: Advances in Neural Information Processing Systems 10, pp. 1050–1056 (1998)
20. Rasmussen, D., Voelker, A., Eliasmith, C.: A neural model of hierarchical reinforcement learning. PLOS ONE **12**(7), e0180234 (2017)
21. Shikunov, M., Panov, A.I.: Hierarchical reinforcement learning approach for the road intersection task. In: Samsonovich, A.V. (ed.) BICA 2019. AISC, vol. 948, pp. 495–506. Springer, Cham (2020). https://doi.org/10.1007/978-3-030-25719-4_64
22. Solway, A., et al.: Optimal behavioral hierarchy. PLoS Comput. Biol. **10**(8), e1003779 (2014). https://journals.plos.org/ploscompbiol/article?id=10.1371/journal.pcbi.1003779

23. Tamar, A., Wu, Y., Thomas, G., Levine, S., Abbeel, P.: Value iteration networks. arXiv, pp. 1–14, February 2016
24. Tsetlin, M.L.: Automaton Theory and Modeling of Biological Systems. Academic Press, New York (1973)
25. Verma, A., Murali, V., Singh, R., Kohli, P., Chaudhuri, S.: Programmatically interpretable reinforcement learning. In: Proceedings of the 35th International Conference on Machine Learning (2018). http://arxiv.org/abs/1804.02477
26. Wiering, M., Schmidhuber, J.: HQ-Learning. Adapt. Behav. **6**(2), 219–246 (1997)

Hierarchical Control Architecture for a Learning Robot Based on Heterogenic Behaviors

Maxim Rovbo$^{(\boxtimes)}$ (ID), Anton Moscowsky, and Petr Sorokoumov

National Research Center "Kurchatov Institute",
1, Akademika Kurchatova pl., Moscow 123182, Russia
rovboma@gmail.com

Abstract. The paper describes a hierarchical control architecture for robotic systems with learning that allows combining various goal-directed algorithms. A top-level control algorithm is proposed that switches control between base algorithms: Q-learning, random walk and a rule-based planning. The algorithm is implemented as a software module and is verified by the example of the task of finding a given door in a building of complex planning. The task is considered as a reinforcement learning problem in two distinct cases: with a goal fixed between the episodes and the goal changing from episode to episode. The simulation showed that the proposed method is more stable for different variants of the task than each of the basic ones separately, although it does not give the best result for each individual case.

Keywords: Robot · Control architecture · Behavior · Reinforcement learning

1 Introduction

Modern intelligent robots usually work in a changing, not completely defined environment to which they have to adapt. If we understand behavior as a response of a system to environmental signals (Gaaze-Rapoport and Pospelov 2004), then adaptation is the change of behavior to a more appropriate one for the current situation. The development of optimal or at least fairly well working in practice adaptation methods is still a problem that often has to be solved anew for each new task due to specific requirements. In this regard, it is of interest to create adaptation methods applicable to wide classes of mobile robotics problems.

Modern robots often have complex architecture, significant computational power (comparable to personal computers) and therefore they are capable to solve a number of complex tasks simultaneously. The individual behaviors they use are usually formalized in the form of algorithms, each of which is able to take control of the robot and achieve its goal with some success. The simultaneous operation of different behaviors is not feasible due to inconsistent instructions. At the same time, it is highly desirable to be able to combine different types of behavior in order to compensate for their weaknesses.

S. O. Kuznetsov and A. I. Panov (Eds.): RCAI 2019, CCIS 1093, pp. 44–55, 2019.
https://doi.org/10.1007/978-3-030-30763-9_4

Consider a specific task that can be put, for example, in front of an intelligent robot peddler or an automated wheelchair. Let the agent be inside the building that has numbered doors in the walls of the corridors. Usually but perhaps not always their numbering goes with an increase in the values to one of the sides along the wall. Some doors may have no number and the configuration of the corridors is arbitrary and not known in advance. The robot is required to get to the door with the specified number, relying only on local data (the immediate environment observed by the sensors).

It is obvious that such a task can be solved in many ways: by searching for a map compiled by SLAM methods, a SPA architecture (sense-plan-act) (Siciliano and Khatib 2008) with re-planning and even in some cases by following a predetermined route. In different situations, some approaches may work better than others. For example, the ordering of doors can be taken into account either explicitly (by setting appropriate constraints, for example, on a rule-based system) or implicitly (by processing numbers during machine learning of the system); finally, it is possible to ignore them altogether. It is not known in advance which approach in a particular type of environment will be more beneficial. The same uncertainty is observed with other aspects of behavior, such as introducing randomness into decisions made or using a map. Algorithms that rely heavily on a predetermined task model (fixed route) may not work properly after relatively small changes in the environment or detection failures (incorrectly recognized sign on one of the doors in the route). It can be seen that a combination of different behaviors has the potential to improve results.

Some methods for behaviors combining have already been proposed for limited applications. In reinforcement learning you can build a hierarchy of strategies, and some strategies can cause others (options) (Stolle and Precup 2007; Sutton and Barto 2018). Algorithms formed from component-behaviors are described for social mechanisms in robotics (Karpov et al. 2019b). Behaviors can also be combined with planning using knowledge bases and ontologies (Skarzynski et al. 2018; Vasiliu et al. 2014).

For more specialized systems in which behavior can be defined by state equations, it is sufficient to use a finite automaton to switch behaviors, as described in Marino et al. (2009) for loop traversal problems. When describing the state of a system not by one, as in a finite state machine, but by several discrete variables, we can associate behaviors with them and activate the most pronounced of them (Stoytchev and Arkin 2001). If we additionally select purely reactive from among possible actions, then one can arbitrarily include them in selectable behaviors, using, for example, fuzzy logical criteria (Aguirre and González 2000). The main problem of such approaches is narrow specialization: the automatic methods for customizing such solutions for universal control systems are unknown.

Combined systems are often built on a hierarchical basis. Multi-layer architectures have long been known that combine different levels of control and allow the control layer to choose the necessary algorithm to perform the task at the lower level. Behavior-based architectures (Siciliano and Khatib 2008) allow to manage the robot by setting a rigid structure connections between algorithms. However, both of these approaches require the developer to determine how the appropriate algorithm should be chosen.

If there are several ways to solve the problem, it makes sense to use algorithms that can themselves choose a more efficient solution depending on the environment. This is especially important for multi-agent systems in which not static but dynamic equilibrium can be optimal, such as, the distribution of roles in the foraging (Rovbo 2016), in which the role is basic behavior, as called in this paper, and the higher-level algorithm is random walk with some switching probabilities.

In this work, a hierarchical control system is proposed that has a learning algorithm at the top level. The basic actions of the system are the launches of underlying algorithms that are aimed at solving a user-defined task. Such a system is able to take advantage of the various algorithms and allows the developer to care less about the correspondence of the environment model of the selected algorithm to the environment itself. It solves the problem if at least one of the basic algorithms is suitable for solving it in this environment. This solution echoes the expansion of classical learning with reinforcement using options and hierarchical strategies described earlier (Sutton et al. 1999). Strategies can choose instead of actions other strategies (options) that have a certain chance of completion at each stage. Despite the proximity of this category of systems to the proposed solution, the basic algorithms in it are not considered as options and no restrictions on their properties are imposed.

An algorithm based on simpler components (finite machines) is described in Cetlin (1961) and Varshavsky et al. (1965), but this approach, despite the similarity of the central idea, is applicable only to systems based on finite automata, and the known properties of this group of algorithms are mainly effective for random environments in which the transitions between states are determined only by time but not by the actions of the robot. In this regard, it is impossible to directly transfer the results of these works to the robotic environments without further research. This is mainly due to the fact that in a typical mobile robotic system, the agent's actions directly affect the state of the environment and the associated rewards.

2   Control Architecture

In the proposed architecture only the continuous control module control robot. It receives instructions from the top level of the hierarchical control system, the meta-algorithm, and then controls their execution. The meta-algorithm itself never generates instructions, but only requests them from the basic set of behavioral algorithms (Fig. 1).

The idea of such scheme is similar to boosting in classification algorithms. A more efficient algorithm is created by combining a set of other algorithms that solve the same problem. Directly using such an approach is problematic due to the difference in the task of control (in particular, training with reinforcement) from the task of classification. Sometimes it is still possible; for example, an improvement strategy is described based on the work of another previously formed strategy with an increase in its interpretability (Brown and Petrik 2018). In contrast to this approach, in this work we propose to use the actions chosen by the underlying algorithms directly, without building a new strategy in the form of approximation of others.

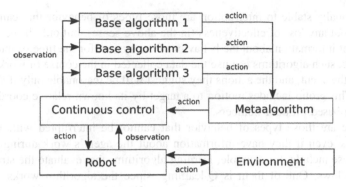

Fig. 1. Control system structure

3 Basic Algorithms and the Problem Under Consideration

The task can be solved by agents with different types of behavior. The following types of agents were selected as the base types: a randomly walking agent; a rule-based agent; and agent based on Q-learning. The first of them chooses the next action with a fixed probability from a fixed set. The rule-based agent plans actions taking into account the sequence of door numbers rescheduling when the previous plan failed. The last agent adjusts its actions during task execution, reestimating the actions based on experience and choosing the best of them from the point of view of the current assessment. Q-learning approach is used here because the combination of it with other algorithms has shown better performance than separate behavior components and algorithms in other works (McGlohon and Sen 2005), thus it was chosen as one of the basic algorithms.

In the process of reinforcement learning, the agent collects data on the effectiveness of his work over several episodes, and then changes the parameters defining the switching of behaviors to reflect this data. The model itself never gives instructions to the agent, but always delegates it to the component behaviors that belong to it.

Further, for simplicity, it is considered that the model should suggest actions for execution with a fixed period of time. In order for a particular behavior to perform a coherent set of actions and show its characteristic properties, switching is allowed not after each action, but after a fixed number of periods during which the same agent determines the behavior.

Each of the selected types of behavior allows to solve the problem either for the a priori estimated finite time, or (if there are elements of randomness) in a statistical sense. The applicability of this idea is fundamentally limited by the fact that some types of behavior cannot be interrupted, changed by another, and then re-used. In terms of interruption stability, it is possible to distinguish three groups: stable, conditionally stable, and unstable.

The stable to interruption behaviors can be interrupted without any loss of effectiveness. Such algorithms will continue to work from the new state no worse than if they were in it themselves. This group includes, for example, a random walk or movement towards a target, based on the absolute coordinates of the agent and the target.

Conditionally stable to interruption are those types of behavior that can be interrupted without any loss of effectiveness (in the above sense), but only if the algorithm has sufficient information about the behavior of the system for the time of interruption. For example, such algorithms can use the data collected in the course of work to assess the state of the agent, and the actions they suggest will be reasonable only if this data is complete. This group includes motion to a target by its known relative coordinates, or by planning based on door numbers.

Unstable are those types of behavior that cannot be interrupted without loss of effectiveness, even if they have information about the agent's work during the interruption. These include, for example, learning algorithms that evaluate the strategy that an agent follows. One of them is Q-learning, since the algorithm works under the assumption that the agent performs the actions selected by the algorithm.

On the basis of the classification proposed, it is clear that the algorithm for switching behaviors should not allow the transition to behavior unstable to interruption. In other words, this behavior can only be used at the beginning of the agent's work, and its launch after some other should not be allowed.

Let the model be constructed on the basis of a certain set of behaviors B, consisting of the elements b_i, $i = 1..N$. Then the work of the model is described by two components:

- an initialization vector S of size $N \times 1$, where each element s_i determines the probability of choosing the appropriate behavior b_i as the initial one;
- a transition matrix T of size $N \times N$, each element of which t_{ij} determines the probability of switching from the behavior of b_i to the behavior b_j.

Then the algorithm of the agent is as follows:

1. Initialize S and T. To do this, either uniform probability distributions or a priori assumptions about the desired transitions can be used. It should be noted that the probabilities of transition to non-resistant types of behavior from all types except himself should be zero here and hereafter;
2. Run some predetermined number of simulation episodes. In each episode:
   a. First, start the first behavior, defining it randomly according to probabilities from S;
   b. Periodically define a new behavior randomly according to the probabilities from the string T corresponding to the current behavior;
   c. Fix in each episode the reinforcements received and the sequence of transitions between the states performed;
3. Update S and T with the collected statistics, go back to point 2.

Updating the parameters for each behavior b_i is calculated by computing the average reward for the episodes started with this behavior, and the values obtained after normalization make up the new value of the vector S:

$$s_i = \frac{\sum_{x=1}^{k} r_x}{k},$$

where r_x is the reinforcement for episode x that began with behavior b_i, k is the number of such episodes.

For each transition from state i to state j, total reinforcement is calculated for all the episodes in which this transition was made. In this case, the reinforcement is pre-divided equally between all transitions of the episode. The new value of the matrix T is obtained from the values thus calculated by line normalization:

$$t_{ij} = \frac{\sum_{x=1}^{m} \frac{r_x k_x^{ij}}{k_x}}{m},$$

where k_x^{ij} is the number of transitions from the behavior of b_i to b_j in episode x, k_x is the total number of transitions in this episode, m is the number of episodes with this transition. Episodes without transitions are processed separately.

In the procedures described above, we considered that reinforcement was always non-negative. If necessary, a permanent offset should be added to it.

4   Experimental Base

A robotic wheelchair was used as a hardware platform (Karpov et al. 2019a). The wheelchair is a robotic platform that can move independently in space using an obstacle map and its own sensors. The user is able, through a number of interfaces, such as a joystick, keyboard, voice and brain-eye-computer, to give the wheelchair commands at a high level. A high-level command means giving the goal only, while the route to the goal and its operational movements are entirely performed by control system.

The basic elements of the system were implemented for the work in the hall of the robotics laboratory of the Research Center "Kurchatov Institute". The hall is a square room with a side of 17 m. To move the wheelchair through the hall (implementation of the basic actions described above), a pre-set map of obstacles is used, moving between the doors is performed using the Dynamic Window Approach algorithm (Fox et al. 1997), the position of the robot in each time point is determined using odometry. In the hall around the perimeter there are eight doors, the initial position of which is not marked on the map. For ease of recognition, each door is marked with a QR code sign, which contained the information of the "DoorXXX" format. The recognition system registers a QR code and determines the direction angle to it. Based on the knowledge of its location and the angle of the direction to the door, the system determines the coordinates of the door by the method of intersecting the rays and draws it on the map. The state of the system is visualized using standard ROS tools (Fig. 2).

The basic actions correspond to algorithms that travel along the map to the detected door using motion algorithms (in this case, the map itself is not used in the planning of the upper level). When performing actions in the motion, the robot can make special movements to detect doors in the immediate environment (these actions do not participate in the top-level control algorithms and, in fact, are part of the sensor system).

Fig. 2. Representation of the real robot in user interface

The system was implemented as a set of ROS nodes, its operability was tested both with the program model of the robot in the Gazebo environment (Fig. 3), and with the real robot (robotic wheelchair developed in the laboratory).

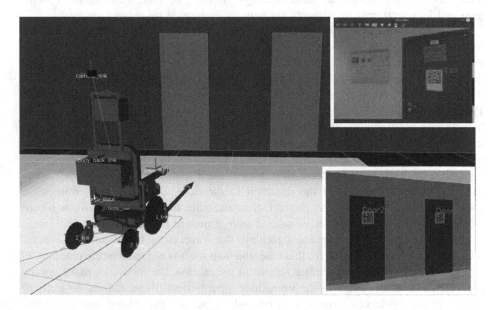

Fig. 3. Representation of the robot model in the system

5 Computational Experiments

Evaluation of the algorithm was performed on the task which is formulated as follows. The robot is located inside a building consisting of intersecting corridors and doors located in the walls of these corridors. The doors are numbered consecutively along one wall in one direction and some of the may not have a number. The numbers are displayed on the doors in the form of plates (QR codes were used for easier recognition). The building map is not known in advance for the control algorithm, and in general is randomly generated (in model experiments). The robot needs to reach the target door with the specified number.

To assess the performance of the control algorithm, one can consider this task as a continuous reinforcement learning task: the system must maximize the reward given for finding the target door, and the episode is the interval of time from receiving the task to find the target door to its achievement by the robot. After reaching the target door, two possible problem statements are considered: the robot remains at its current location, but it is given a new random target door (problem statement that is closer to real robotic problem), or the robot returns to its original position and receives the same door as a target (the classical problem statement for reinforcement learning). Note that within each episode a task can, in fact, be considered to be a task of finding the shortest route (but without a known map), and therefore, the use of a basic agent based on rules that build a plan based on the robot's understanding of the laws of the environment, also appears justified.

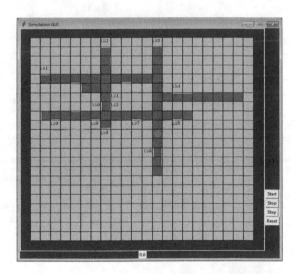

Fig. 4. Simulation environment

Thus, it is possible to formulate the problem under consideration as the task of maximizing the target criterion:

$$G(S) \doteq \sum_{t=0}^{t=\infty} r_t$$

Numerical evaluation of the effectiveness of the proposed approach was carried out on a program model using a specially developed environment that simulates the search for a given door in a two-dimensional cellular maze (Fig. 4). Part of the doors is numbered, and the numbering is always performed consistently within each wall, which allows the agent to put forward a hypothesis about the possible position of the desired door relative to the known ones. For example, if an agent needs to find door 103, and there is a wall with doors 109 and 110 in sight, it would be wise to try to move along this wall in the direction of descending room numbers.

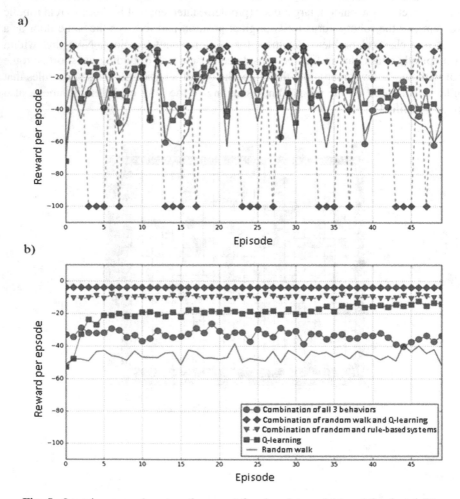

Fig. 5. Learning curve (agent performance) for changing goal (a) and fixed goal (b).

The following actions are available to agents:

1. Search for the nearest unvisited door;
2. The transition from the current door to its left neighbor on the same wall;
3. A similar transition to the right neighbor.

To facilitate the implementation of the simulation, it is believed that if there are no doors in the agent cage, actions 2 and 3 are performed equivalently to action 1.

The control system is implemented in such a way that it allows both working with the agent model and communication with a real robot using standard ROS interface tools.

Experiments were conducted for two cases: with a fixed target (Fig. 5b) and with a randomly changing target between episodes (Fig. 5a). The standard deviations of the intra-episodic values of the rewards changed little with each new episode, ranging from 5 to 8 for a changing goal and from 15 to 20 for a fixed goal (Table 1).

Table 1. Mean-squared error of rewards

	Epochs 1–10	Epochs 20–30	Epochs 40–50
Changing goal			
All 3 behaviors	7.3	6.8	6.8
Random walk + Q-learning	6.9	6.6	6.5
Random walk + rules	7.6	5.8	5.9
Q-learning	6.3	5.6	5.5
Random walk	7.5	7.2	7.2
Fixed goal			
All 3 behaviors	17.5	19.2	18.6
Random walk + Q-learning	17.7	15.1	16.2
Random walk + rules	16.0	13.1	13.0
Q-learning	17.4	15.0	15.1
Random walk	20.4	19.3	18.6

Graphs shows that for a changing goal (which is more realistic, since the robot needs to move to different doors during the work and fulfill different goals), simple application of existing learning algorithms is not always able to lead to improvement, however the same algorithm shows significant improvement for the case with a fixed goal. This illustrates the fact that different algorithms work within the framework of the usual operation of a robot under different conditions, in some of which model assumptions can be fulfilled, while others do not, and the graph shows that the proposed control structure allows for improved behavior, allowing the system to work relatively well in both cases.

6 Conclusion

The proposed approach to switching control algorithms was implemented both on software models and on a real robot and showed its capabilities. Evaluation of the effectiveness of this method on the software model of the chosen problem showed the difference in the operation of the basic algorithms depending on the assumptions about the immutability of the goal in the formulation of the problem. The proposed architecture allows one to slightly improve the result by switching to more efficient behavior in the process of work. The results show that the combination of the algorithms generally behaves in a more stable way for different instances of the problem than each of the algorithms separately, although it does not show the best performance in each individual case.

The analysis of the results allows to conclude that, despite the presence of a variety of effective learning algorithms, in practice it can be difficult to apply them directly because of the need to choose an appropriate algorithm. In such cases, the proposed method for constructing a robot control system can be used to improve the system performance on average for tasks that satisfy the assumptions of the basic algorithms used to varying degrees.

The performed computational experiments allow to conclude that the proposed architecture is applicable for the stated problem category. Further research may include other logic-based algorithms in the ensemble, especially planning algorithms, and more sophisticated top level optimization methods, such as gradient optimization algorithms.

Acknowledgements. This work was supported in part by the National Research Center "Kurchatov Institute" (Order No. 1601 of July 5, 2018) (Sect. 3) and the RFBR grant 17-29-07083 (Sects. 1, 2 and 4).

References

Aguirre, E., González, A.: Fuzzy behaviors for mobile robot navigation: design, coordination and fusion. Int. J. Approx. Reason. 25(3), 255–289 (2000). https://doi.org/10.1016/S0888-613X(00)00056-6

Brown, A., Petrik, M.: Interpretable reinforcement learning with ensemble methods, pp. 1–7 (2018)

Tsetlin, M.L.: O povedenii konechnyh avtomatov v sluchajnyh sredah. Avtom. i telemekhanika. **22**(10), 1345–1354 (1961). (in Russian)

Fox, D., Burgard, W., Thrun, S.: The dynamic window approach to collision avoidance. IEEE Robot. Autom. Mag. **4**(1), 23–33 (1997). https://doi.org/10.1109/100.580977

Gaaze-Rapoport, M.G., Pospelov, D.A.: Ot ameby do robota: modeli povedeniya, p. 296 (2004). (in Russian)

Karpov, V.E., et al.: Architecture of a wheelchair control system for disabled people: towards multifunctional robotic solution with neurobiological interfaces. Sovrem. Tehnol. v Med. **11**(1), 90–102 (2019a). https://doi.org/10.17691/stm2019.11.1.11

Karpov, V.E., Karpova, I.P., Kulinich, A.A.: Social'nye soobshchestva robotov, p. 352 (2019b). (in Russian)

Marino, A., et al.: Behavioral control for multi-robot perimeter patrol : a finite state automata approach. In: 2009 IEEE International Conference on Robotics and Automation, pp. 831–836 (2009). https://doi.org/10.1109/ROBOT.2009.5152710

McGlohon, M., Sen, S.: Learning to cooperate in multi-agent systems by combining Q-learning and evolutionary strategy. Int. J. Lateral Comput. 1(2), 58–64 (2005)

Rovbo, M.A.: Raspredelenie rolej v geterogennom murav'ino-podobnom kollektive. In: Pyatnadcataya nacional'naya konferenciya po iskusstvennomu intellektu s mezhdunarodnym uchastiem (KII-2016), pp. 363–371 (2016). (in Russian)

Skarzynski, K., Stepniak, M., Bartyna, W., Ambroszkiewicz, S.: SO-MRS: a multi-robot system architecture based on the SOA paradigm and ontology. In: Giuliani, M., Assaf, T., Giannaccini, M.E. (eds.) TAROS 2018. LNCS (LNAI), vol. 10965, pp. 330–342. Springer, Cham (2018). https://doi.org/10.1007/978-3-319-96728-8_28

Stolle, M., Precup, D.: Learning options in reinforcement learning. In: Koenig, S., Holte, R.C. (eds.) SARA 2002. LNCS (LNAI), vol. 2371, pp. 212–223. Springer, Heidelberg (2002). https://doi.org/10.1007/3-540-45622-8_16

Stoytchev, A., Arkin, R.C.: Combining deliberation, reactivity, and motivation in the context of a behavior-based robot architecture. In: Proceedings of IEEE International Symposium on Computational Intelligence in Robotics and Automation, CIRA, pp. 290–295, January 2001. https://doi.org/10.1109/CIRA.2001.1013214

Sutton, R.S., Precup, D., Singh, S.: Between MDPs and semi-MDPs: a framework for temporal abstraction in reinforcement learning. Artif. Intell. 112(1–2), 181–211 (1999). https://doi.org/10.1016/S0004-3702(99)00052-1

Sutton, R.S., Barto, A.G.: Reinforcement Learning: An Introduction (2018)

Varshavsky, V.I., Meleshina, M.V., Tsetlin, M.L.: Povedenie avtomatov v periodicheskih sluchajnyh sredah i zadacha sinhronizacii pri nalichii pomekh. Probl. peredachi Inf. 1(1), 65–71 (1965). (in Russian)

Vasiliu, L., et al.: RoboBrain: a software architecture mapping the human brain. In: 2014 IEEE-RAS International Conference on Humanoid Robots, pp. 160–165. IEEE (2014). https://doi.org/10.1109/HUMANOIDS.2014.7041353

Siciliano, B., Khatib, O.: Springer Handbook of Robotics. Springer, Berlin (2008). https://doi.org/10.1007/978-3-540-30301-5

Automated Reasoning and Data Mining

Stock Prices Forecasting with LSTM Networks

Tatyana Vasyaeva(iD), Tatyana Martynenko(iD), Sergii Khmilovyi(iD),
and Natalia Andrievskaya$^{(\boxtimes)}$(iD)

Donetsk National Technical University, 58 Artem str., Donetsk, Ukraine
vasyaeva@gmail.com, tatyana.v.martynenko@gmail.com,
hmelevoy_sergey@ukr.net, nataandr@yandex.ua

Abstract. An application of deep neural networks was studied in the area of
stock prices forecasting of pharmacies chain "36 and 6". The learning sample
formation in the time series area was shown and a neural network architecture
was proposed. The neural network for exchange trade forecasting using
Python's Keras Library was developed and trained. The basic parameters setting
of algorithm have been carried out.

Keywords: Machine learning · Deep learning · Recurrent neural networks ·
Long short-term memory · Time series · Stock prices

1 Introduction

Effective actions on the stock exchange are connected with a careful analysis of all events
happening in the market. Forecasting is the basis of exchange trade. In order to make the
forecasting as reliable as possible, and make the forecasts well grounded, traders use
exchange analysis. Widely used methods of analysis, to which most market participants
are accustomed [1], are not always effective. That's why over recent years, financial
analysts have become of great interest in such a direction as machine learning [2] and in
particular artificial neural networks [3]. In contrast to the classical methods of exchange
analysis [1], which involve the implementation of ready-made algorithms, machine
learning allows the system to learn how to recognize patterns and make forecasts.

In simplified version the exchange is understood as the place where the exchange takes
place. This can be an exchange of money for a product or a product is changed for money,
that is, there is a purchase and sale of something. At the same time, trading on exchanges
takes place not on physical goods, but on financial instruments. The mechanism of
exchange is designed so that it helps the buyer and the seller to find price which will be
suitable for both of them. Thus, the exchange acts as the arbitrage of all transactions.

In world practice exchanges are divided into stock, currency and commodity
(multi-commodity) w.r.t. type of product (asset) [1]. The methods of analysis of stock
exchanges are the focus of this research. In this context financial instruments are
represented by securities, such as shares, bonds, etc. In our work we will consider the
problem of predicting the future stock prices of the pharmacies chain "36 and 6" based
on the values of their stock prices in the past, as well as additional data of exchange
trade for the period under report. Future stock price prediction is probably the best
example of time series forecasting [4].

© Springer Nature Switzerland AG 2019
S. O. Kuznetsov and A. I. Panov (Eds.): RCAI 2019, CCIS 1093, pp. 59–69, 2019.
https://doi.org/10.1007/978-3-030-30763-9_5

To forecast the time series it is necessary to determine the following parameters:

- forecast interval, the time interval at which the forecast will be carried out: we will analyze the data for one day;
- forecast horizon, the number of intervals for which we want to make a forecast: forecast horizon in our work is one interval, i.e. one day;
- depth of immersion, the number of forecast intervals in the past that we will analyze to forecast next values. The determination of the depth of immersion [5] is a nontrivial task and we will not consider it in this paper.

We will predict the future stock prices of the pharmacies chain "36 and 6", based on its stock prices of the past 5 years.

2 Materials and Methods

2.1 Data Representation

The data that we are going to use for this article can be downloaded from servers "FINAM" and their web resource [6]. From the list of securities (instruments) provided by "FINAM" company we will take the data of quotations of the pharmacies chain "36 and 6". The received information provided by Moscow Exchange PJSC has the following format (Table 1): date, opening price, maximum price, minimum price, closing price, volume.

Table 1. Data representation.

DATE	OPEN	HIGH	LOW	CLOSE	VOL
20140326	13.410000	13.750000	13.400000	13.590000	255490
20140327	13.480000	13.690000	13.330000	13.420000	151960
20140328	13.540000	14.610000	13.440000	14.520000	433440
20140331	14.690000	14.910000	14.410000	14.760000	178030
...	...	...	...	...	...
20140401	14.750000	15.230000	14.650000	15.100000	151950
20140402	14.880000	14.950000	14.650000	14.790000	77570

Usually datasets for working with time series form a "sliding window" [4] with a width equal to the depth of immersion. After the data are prepared in this way they will have such form (see Fig. 1). As a rule of thumb, whenever you use a neural network, you should normalize or scale your data. We normalize the obtained data and divide it into parts.

For a long time it was common in machine learning to divide the data into training and test data set in relation to 70% by 30%. Although this approach still works, it is common to use the following datasets today [7]:

- Training set, a sample of the data that is used to train the algorithm;
- Development set or Validation set, the data sample used to select the parameters for the learning algorithm;
- Test set, a sample that is used to evaluate the performance of the algorithm, and it is not used to train the algorithm or the selection of algorithm parameters.

The size of the test set should be large enough to obtain high confidence in the quality of work. In today's era of big data, the proportion of data used for test and validation sets is decreasing. There is no need to use excessively large validation/test sets, they should simply be sufficient to assess the quality of the algorithms works.

№	OPEN	HIGH	LOW	CLOSE	VOL
1					
2					
3					
4					
...					
N					

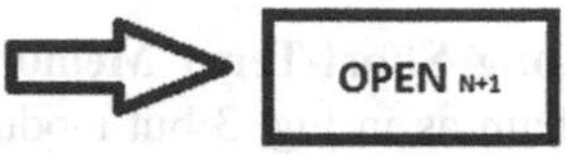

$\Longrightarrow$ OPEN $_{N+1}$

Fig. 1. Training data.

A common dataset after the transformations shown in Fig. 1, with depth of immersion = 100 has size of 5 × 100 × 1260. To build the model, we will use a set consisting of 851 simples (of 1260 total), and under the validation set we will allocate 1% of this data. The result is shown in Fig. 2.

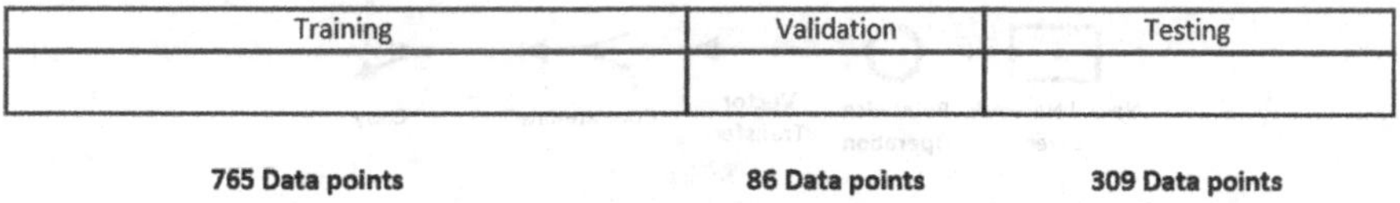

Training	Validation	Testing

765 Data points   86 Data points   309 Data points

Fig. 2. Training, validation and testing dataset.

2.2 Proposed LSTM Model

Nowadays deep neural networks become one of the most popular approaches to solving a wide variety of problems [8–11]. There is no unambiguous definition of what a deep neural network is. In this work, the term deep neural network will be understood as a neural network that contains more than one hidden layer.

To train neural networks, including deep ones, we use the error backpropagation algorithm [3] based on the gradient descent method. Deep neural networks with many hidden layers are difficult to train because of the vanishing gradient problem. The problem of vanishing gradient can be solved by the architecture of a recurrent neural network called a network of long short-term memory [12].

Recurrent Neural Networks (RNN). RNN [12] are the networks with loops in them, allowing information to persist. There is a chunk of neural network (see Fig. 3). The network takes the input value x_i and returns value h_i. A loop allows information to be passed from one step of the network to the next. A recurrent neural network can be thought of as multiple copies of the same network, each passing a message to a subsequent copy. If we unroll the loop, we will get the situation as in Fig. 3.

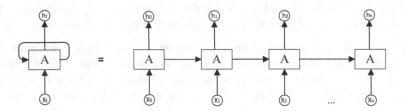

Fig. 3. A fragment of recurrent neural network and an unrolled recurrent neural network.

Long Short-Term Memory (LSTM). The structure LSTM [12] reminds of same chain as in Fig. 3 but modules look and interact in a different way, see Fig. 4.

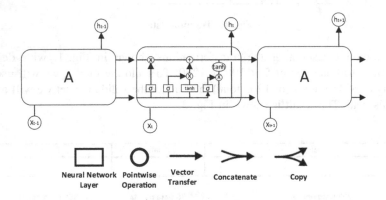

Fig. 4. Recurrent LSTM network.

The key component of LSTM is cell state. Cell state participates in several linear transformations. LSTM can erase information from cell state; this process is regulated by structures called gates. They are composed out of a sigmoid neural net layer and a pointwise multiplication operation, see Fig. 5. LSTM-network gates: "input gate layer", "output gate layer", and "forget gate layer".

"Forget gate layer". The "forget gate layer" in Fig. 6 controls erasing or saving the cell state information based on the new input value and the value received from the previous iteration. The sigmoid layer returns numbers from zero to one which indicate what part of information should be passed on the network. Zero in this case means " do not miss anything", one means "skip all".

"Input gate layer". "Input gate layer" (see Fig. 7) determines when data should be written to the cell. The sigmoid layer, as before, returns numbers from zero to one based on the new input value and the value from the previous iteration. Now the sigmoid layer indicates what part information will be recorded, and the tanh-layer generates values that can be added to the cell state.

As a result combination of new value and previous one will be recorded to the cell state (see Fig. 8). The neural network "decides itself" in learning process when the data should be saved and to what extent and when they should be replaced with new ones and to what extent.

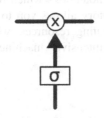

Fig. 5. Sigmoid layer.

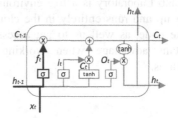

Fig. 6. "Forget gate layer".

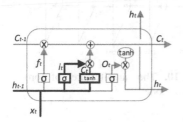

Fig. 7. "Input gate layer".

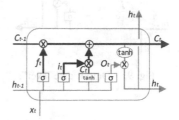

Fig. 8. State value update.

"Output gate layer". "Output gate layer" (see Fig. 9) determines what information we receive at the output. The output data will be based on the cell state and some gates will be applied to it. First, a sigmoid layer decides what information from the cell state we will output. The cell state values then pass through the tanh-layer to obtain values from the range −1 to 1 at the output and are multiplied with the output values of the sigmoid layer allowing only the required information to be displayed.

Neural Network Architecture. The following neural network architecture was developed experimentally (see Fig. 10). The network consists of an input layer, three LSTM layers and one dense output layer with activation function Relu. The input data sets are 5×100 in size (depth of immersion = 100). On the first LSTM layer there are 500 units and the other two have 100 units each. On the last layer there is 1 unit as we need only one output (forecast horizon = 1). After every LSTM layer the Dropout [13] is used, i.e. when training every training sample the network is rebuilt in such way that a certain set of units falls out (see Fig. 11). Developed neural network has the following view (see Fig. 12).

3 Experiment

In the environment of Colab Laboratory [14] a software implementation of a neural network was performed for future stock price prediction with LSTM using Python's Keras Library.

Colab Laboratory is a free environment for Jupyter notebooks which requires no setting up and runs entirely in the cloud. Colab Laboratory allows you to write and execute code, as well as to get access powerful computing resources, which is an important advantage when working with resource-intensive machine learning algorithms.

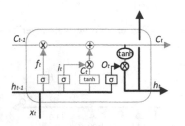

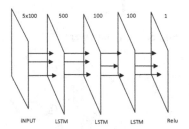

Fig. 9. "Output gate layer".

Fig. 10. The architecture of proposed model.

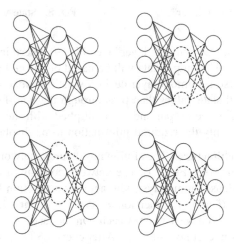

Fig. 11. Dropout.

Keras [15] is one of the most powerful and easy-to-use Python's libraries for the development and evaluation of deep learning models covering the effective libraries of numerical computations Theano and TensorFlow. The advantage of this is mainly the fact that it is possible to work with neural networks in a fairly simple way.

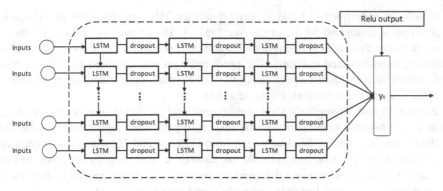

Fig. 12. Neural network architecture.

Let us conduct experiments on neural network training (Tables 2, 3 and 4). As an optimizer we will use a stochastic gradient descent optimizer (Table 2), which is traditional for neural networks training. Loss function (function of optimization estimation) is mean squared error. The metric (the function that is used to evaluate the model) is mean absolute error.

Analyzing the data in Table 2, we can draw the following conclusions. 150–250 epochs are enough for network training and then the network significantly relearns. It is recommended to use "RMSprop" optimizer for recurrent neural networks according to [12].

Table 2. Experiments on network training for optimizer = «SGD».

Epoch	Training set		Validation set		Test set	
	MSE	MAE	MSE	MAE	MSE	MAE
25	0.0048	0.0546	0.0055	0.0730	0.0144	0.1176
50	0.0027	0.0387	5.532e−04	0.0207	0.0012	0.0328
75	0.0025	0.0366	3.997e−04	0.0171	0.0008	0.0251
100	0.0024	0.0352	2.006e−04	0.0110	0.0002	0.0131
125	0.0023	0.0339	2.075e−04	0.0112	0.0003	0.0156
150	0.0024	0.0347	1.585e−04	0.0090	0.0002	0.0118
175	0.1967	0.4219	0.0538	0.2313	0.0148	0.1039
200	0.0021	0.0318	1.728e−04	0.0099	0.0002	0.0128
225	0.0019	0.0303	2.244e−04	0.0119	0.0004	0.0182
250	0.0019	0.0297	1.418e−04	0.0084	0.0001	0.0107
275	0.0019	0.0299	1.906e−04	0.0105	0.0002	0.0144
300	0.0019	0.0295	2.334e−04	0.0122	0.0004	0.0189
325	0.0020	0.0310	1.658e−04	0.0094	0.0003	0.0129
350	0.0018	0.0297	2.284e−04	0.0119	0.0005	0.0199
375	0.0018	0.0291	1.313e−04	0.0080	0.0002	0.0108
400	0.0017	0.0279	2.167e−04	0.0118	0.0005	0.0199

Results of experiments (Table 3) show that after 250 steps the network started to retrain. This is confirmed by the graph (see Fig. 13, 14, 15 and 16). Figure 13 shows the stock prices dynamics of opening trades and their predicted values on a full dataset (including validation and test sets). The predicted data was obtained by a neural network trained at 300 training epoch using the "RMSprop" optimizer. Figure 14 shows the results of the same network on the test data.

Figures 15 and 16 similarly show the original and predicted time series, obtained by the neural network with the previously discussed parameters, but trained on the 175 epochs of learning. As can be clearly seen from Figs. 14 and 16, a network trained on fewer steps shows much better results. At the same time, analyzing Table 3, we see that the training error on the training data with increasing of training epochs is decreased, but on the validation and test data generally vice versa is increased.

Table 3. Experiments on network training for optimizer = «RMSprop».

Epoch	Training set		Validation set		Test set	
	MSE	MAE	MSE	MAE	MSE	MAE
25	0.1967	0.4219	0.0538	0.2313	0.0148	0.1039
50	0.0021	0.0349	9.993e−04	0.0312	0.0148	0.1039
75	0.0015	0.0288	4.434e−04	0.0207	0.0005	0.0239
100	6.026e−04	0.0185	1.487e−04	0.0119	0.0003	0.0220
125	8.697e−04	0.0228	1.723e−05	0.0034	0.0003	0.0173
150	3.978e−04	0.0146	4.024e−05	0.0057	0.0005	0.0256
175	6.145e−04	0.0189	8.031e−05	0.0086	5.27e−05	0.0066
200	7.348e−04	0.0208	1.654e−04	0.0125	0.0002	0.0103
225	5.222e−04	0.0179	9.030e−05	0.0090	0.0008	0.0259
250	4.442e−04	0.0166	1.405e−05	0.0032	6.09e−05	0.0069
275	4.244e−04	0.0149	1.830e−04	0.0133	0.0003	0.0170
300	3.782e−04	0.0146	0.0013	0.0341	0.0083	0.0861
325	4.915e−04	0.0176	7.736e−05	0.0076	0.0026	0.0423
350	3.653e−04	0.0139	4.351e−04	0.0207	0.0007	0.0256
375	0.1967	0.4219	0.0538	0.2313	0.0148	0.1039
400	0.1967	0.4219	0.0538	0.2313	0.0148	0.1039

Table 4 shows the results using another common optimizer «adam». A good results are obtained for a neural network trained in 150 epochs, optimizer «adam». The best results are obtained for a neural network trained in 350 and 400 epochs (Figs. 17 and 18).

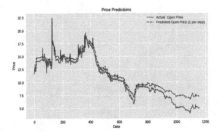

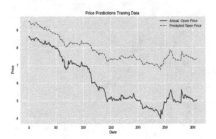

Fig. 13. Full dataset (Epoch = 300)

Fig. 14. Test dataset (Epoch = 300).

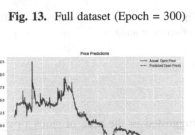

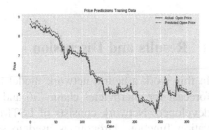

Fig. 15. Full dataset (Epoch = 175)

Fig. 16. Test dataset (Epoch = 175).

Table 4. Experiments on network training for optimizer = «adam».

Epoch	Training set		Validation set		Test set	
	MSE	MAE	MSE	MAE	MSE	MAE
25	0.0013	0.0265	1.936e−04	0.0112	0.0003	0.0146
50	0.0011	0.0242	5.513e−05	0.0050	6.729e−05	0.0060
75	0.0011	0.0246	4.723e−05	0.0045	9.985e−05	0.0085
100	7.984e−04	0.0215	3.716e−05	0.0041	3.699e−05	0.0041
125	4.735e−04	0.0159	1.196e−04	0.0099	0.0305	0.1746
150	5.438e−04	0.0174	2.580e−05	0.0036	3.443e−05	0.0043
175	4.084e−04	0.0153	2.176e−05	0.0032	4.759e−05	0.0058
200	3.547e−04	0.0141	2.767e−04	0.0162	0.0003	0.0177
225	3.273e−04	0.0134	1.448e−05	0.0028	5.055e−05	0.0061
250	2.565e−04	0.0117	5.378e−05	0.0065	4.586e−05	0.0061
275	0.0019	0.0306	2.211e−04	0.0118	0.0003	0.0165
300	2.810e−04	0.0126	2.514e−05	0.0041	2.935e−05	0.0048
325	2.309e−04	0.0110	9.775e−06	0.0024	2.619e−05	0.0041
350	1.855e−04	0.0096	8.276e−06	0.0022	3.346e−05	0.0049
375	2.038e−04	0.0102	1.619e−04	0.0124	0.0003	0.0166
400	1.756e−04	0.0098	8.633e−06	0.0022	1.664e−05	0.0033

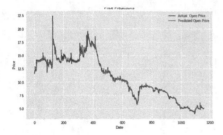

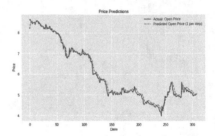

Fig. 17. Full dataset (Epochs = 150, optimizer = «adam»)

Fig. 18. Test dataset (Epochs = 150, optimizer = «adam»).

4   Results and Discussion

In this work a neural network model has been suggested in the area of stock prices forecast for pharmacies chain "36 and 6". The neural network architecture has been developed. Network consists of LSTM layers and a Dense layer with the Relu activation function. Dropout is used to solve the problem of retraining. Experimental studies have shown that the best results are achieved using the optimizer "adam". Error on a test set is MSE = 1.664e−05, MAE = 0.0033. This error makes it possible to forecast the price dynamics.

References

1. Iacomin, R.: Stock market prediction. In: 19th International Conference on System Theory, Control and Computing (ICSTCC), Cheile Gradistei, pp. 200–205 (2015). https://doi.org/10.1109/icstcc.2015.7321293
2. Shai, S.-S., Shai, B.-D.: Understanding Machine Learning: From Theory to Algorithms. Cambridge University Press, New York (2014). 416 pages
3. Schmidhuber, J.: Deep learning in neural networks: an overview. Neural Networks **1**, 85–117 (2015). https://doi.org/10.1016/j.neunet.2014.09.003
4. Brockwell, P.J., Davis, R.A.: Introduction to Time Series and Forecasting, 2nd edn. Springer, New York (2002). https://doi.org/10.1007/b97391
5. Sergii, K., Yurii, S., Tatyana, V., Natalia, A.: Feature selection for time-series prediction in case of undetermined estimation. In: Samsonovich, A.V., Klimov, V.V., Rybina, G.V. (eds.) Biologically Inspired Cognitive Architectures (BICA) for Young Scientists. AISC, vol. 449, pp. 85–97. Springer, Cham (2016). https://doi.org/10.1007/978-3-319-32554-5_12
6. Stock quotes. https://www.finam.ru/. Accessed 29 Mar 2019
7. Wang, H., Zheng, H.: Model validation, machine learning. In: Dubitzky, W., Wolkenhauer, O., Cho, K.H., Yokota, H. (eds.) Encyclopedia of Systems Biology. Springer, New York (2013). https://doi.org/10.1007/978-1-4419-9863-7_233
8. Vargas, R., Ruiz, L.: Deep learning: previous and present applications. J. Awareness **2** (Special 3), 11–20 (2018)
9. Chen, Y., Lin, Z., Zhao, X., Wang, G., Gu, Y.: Deep learning-based classification of hyperspectral data. IEEE J. Sel. Top. Appl. Earth Obs. Remote Sens. **7**, 2094–2107 (2014)

10. Bao, W., Yue, J., Rao, Y.: A deep learning framework for financial time series using stacked autoencoders and long-short term memory. PLoS ONE **12**(7), 1–24 (2017)
11. Chopra, S., Hadsell, R., LeCun, Y.: Learning a similarity metric discriminatively, with application to face verification. In: Proceedings of the IEEE Computer Society Conference on Computer Vision and Pattern Recognition (CVPR 2005), vol. 1, pp. 539–546. IEEE (2005)
12. Manaswi, N.K.: Regression to MLP in Keras. In: Deep Learning with Applications Using Python, pp. 68–89. Apress, Berkeley (2018)
13. Srivastava, N., Hinton, G., Krizhevsky, A., Sutskever, I., Salakhutdinov, R.: Dropout: a simple way to prevent neural networks from overfitting. J. Mach. Learn. Res. **15**(1), 1929–1958 (2014)
14. Google Colaboratory. https://colab.research.google.com/notebooks/welcome.ipynb. Accessed 11 Feb 2019
15. Keras: The Python Deep Learning library. https://keras.io/. Accessed 10 Mar 2019

Using a Hamming Neural Network to Predict Bond Strength of Welded Connections

Vitaliy Klimov, Alexey Klimov, and Sergey Mkrtychev[✉]

Togliatti State University, Togliatti, Russia
sm5006@yandex.ru

Abstract. The paper deals with using a Hamming neural network to predict the limiting destruction force under load of a welded connection in shear.

We propose an algorithm for encoding information on dynamic resistance into bipolar signals required for a Hamming neural network tuning and operation.

A computer program that implements a neural network based on the proposed algorithm has been developed. The results of the neural network training and testing are presented. The method proposed in the paper complies with the requirements of ISO 9000:2015 standard for continuous monitoring and documentation of each welded connection. The analysis showed that relative prediction error of the destruction force of a weld does not exceed 10%. Thus, the possibility of using a Hamming neural network to predict bond strength of welded connections based on dynamic resistance of the welding zone has been confirmed. The work was supported by the Russian Foundation of Basic Research (Grant Agreement 15-08-03125 A).

Keywords: Hamming neural network · Prediction · Resistance welding · Bond strength of welded connection

1 Introduction

In mass production of permanent connections, resistance welding holds leading positions due to high technical and economic rates in comparison with other welding methods [1].

Thus, in the global automotive industry, billions of welded spot connections are made annually. As a rule, to prevent possible negative consequences of poor product quality, the number of welds produced significantly exceeds the required value [2].

It should be noted that the quality of welded connections is influenced by such factors as current shunting, wear of welding electrodes, heating of the secondary circuit, presence of massive ferromagnetic inclusions in it, etc. To improve the quality of welding through adjusting the parameters of the welding process, automatic control systems are utilized [3].

Numerous research works show that the formation of a welded connection is fully characterized by the dynamic resistance Rd of the welding zone (the "electrode-to-electrode" section), which includes its own resistances of parts, as well as resistances of contacts "part-to-part" and "electrode-to-part" [4, 5].

S. O. Kuznetsov and A. I. Panov (Eds.): RCAI 2019, CCIS 1093, pp. 70–80, 2019.
https://doi.org/10.1007/978-3-030-30763-9_6

The change of this resistance is described with high accuracy by simple mathematical models that allow us to assess the quality of the surfaces of welded parts and the accuracy of their assembly and, therefore, predict the quality of welding [6, 7].

To study the electric processes in a resistance welding machine, its equivalent electric schema is used (see Fig. 1).

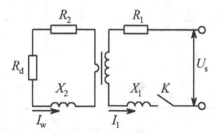

Fig. 1. An equivalent electric schema of a resistance welding machine.

The welding current I_w flows through the elements of the secondary circuit and the secondary coil of the welding transformer represented by active R_2 and inductive X_2 resistances.

The primary current I_1 flows through the primary winding of the welding transformer represented by active R_1 and inductive X_1 resistances. The switch K simulates the operation of the thyristor contactor when the mains voltage goes through 0 [8]. Electrically welded specimens are the time-varying resistance R_d of the weld zone. At the same time, a small R_d value and electrical disturbances make it difficult to conduct measurements and analyze their results without computer technologies.

To solve this problem, intelligent computational methods were applied, including neural networks, which increase the prediction accuracy of welds quality by automatically adjusting R_d quantification algorithms that are implemented with specialized software [9, 10].

However, they are not universal and require time-consuming reconfiguration to weld a new type of parts [11, 12].

Thus, it is necessary to develop a universal method for the prediction of bond strength of welded connections ensuring reliability of the obtained results.

2 Methodological Approach

To increase the versatility and reliability of the prediction of welded connections bond strength, we suggest applying the method of qualitative assessment of the welding zone dynamic resistance based on a recurrent neural network [13, 14].

For that, we chose a Hamming neural network, the main advantage of which is simplicity of establishment and lower computational costs with relatively high accuracy of solving prediction tasks [15].

The proposed Hamming net is a two-layer neural network with feedback (see Fig. 2) [16, 17].

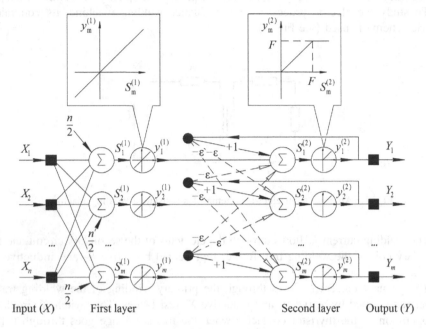

Fig. 2. A structure of the Hamming neural network.

The bipolar signals $X_1, X_2,..., X_n$ are fed to the input of the neural network corresponding to the graph of the measured dynamic resistance $R_d(t)$.

The first layer of the neural network contains information on pattern graphs $R_d(t)$ in the amount of m corresponding to different welding results depending on the adopted quality criterion (bond strength, diameter of the cast core, effective heat release rate, etc.).

The second layer of the neural network is used to search for a pattern as close as possible to the set of input signals $X_1, X_2,..., X_n$. At the output of the neural network there is one of the signals $Y_1, Y_2,..., Y_m$, corresponding to the number of the selected pattern. Further, we assume that the characteristics of the diagnosed connection correspond to the characteristics of the selected pattern [18].

To obtain bipolar signals $X_1, X_2,..., X_n$, the values of which are -1 or $+1$, the $R_d(t)$ graph is transformed into a matrix of dimension $[n \times 1]$, for which the $R_d(t)$ graph is rationed by linear conversion to the range $[0, 1]$. A rectangular grid $a \times b = n$ with the same cells is imposed on the result of the transformation. If the rationed graph crosses the corresponding cell, a value of this cell is assumed to be $+1$ and otherwise equals -1 (see Fig. 3).

The cell values of the bipolar matrix obtained this way are transmitted to the corresponding inputs of the neural network.

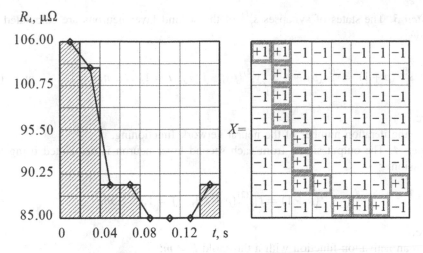

Fig. 3. Converting the graph $R_d(t)$ into a bipolar matrix.

3 Neural Network Building Algorithm

The Hamming neural network building algorithm for the prediction of welds bond strength is based on coding information on dynamic resistance into bipolar signals and consists of the following steps.

Step 1. Information on the pattern graph $R_d(t)$ in the amount of m is stored in the first layer of the neural network in the form of a matrix of weight coefficients of dimension $[m \times n]$. Each j-th column stores information on $X_1, X_2,..., X_n$ signals corresponding to the j-th pattern:

$$\omega(.j) = \begin{pmatrix} X_1 \\ X_2 \\ \vdots \\ X_n \end{pmatrix} \cdot 0,5, \quad j = 1, \ldots, m \tag{1}$$

In the prediction process, a bipolar matrix X is fed to the neural network input. Then the state of the axons (outputs) of the first layer neurons is calculated using the formula:

$$y_j^{(1)} = \sum_{i=1}^{n} \omega_{i,j} X_i + \frac{n}{2}, \quad j = 1, \ldots, m$$

Step 2. Using the obtained values of $y_j^{(1)}$, the values of $y_j^{(2)}$ axons (outputs) of the second layer are initialized:

$$y_j^{(2)} = y_j^{(1)}, \quad j = 1, \ldots, m.$$

Step 3. The states of synapses $s_j^{(1)}$ of the second layer neurons are calculated as follows:

$$s_j^{(2)}(p+1) = y_j^{(2)}(p) - \varepsilon \sum_{i=1}^{m} y_i^{(2)}(p), \quad i \neq j, \ i = 1, \ \ldots, \ n, j = 1, \ \ldots, \ m, \quad (2)$$

where:

p - the iteration number of the neural network functioning.

Step 4. The output signal from each second layer neuron is calculated using the expression:

$$y_j^{(2)}(p+1) = f[s_j^{(2)}(p+1)], \quad j = 1, \ \ldots, \ m, \quad (3)$$

where:

f – an activation function with a threshold $F = m$:

$$f(x) = \begin{cases} 0, & x < 0; \\ x, & 0 \leq x < F; \\ F, & x \geq F. \end{cases}$$

With further functioning of the neural network, the output signals from the second layer of neurons are checked out for the presence of changes during the last iteration. If there are changes, the signals are fed through feedback to the inputs of the second layer of neurons. From this point on, the next iteration of the neural network functioning begins, and, using Eqs. (2) and (3), new output signals are calculated. If the output signals of the second layer of neurons for the last iteration have not changed, they are transmitted to the output Y of the neural network:

$$Y_j = y_j^{(2)}, \quad j = 1, \ \ldots, \ m.$$

The number of the neuron at the output Y of the neural network, the signal of which is greater than 0, corresponds to the number of the pattern closest to the input signal X.

4   Computer Simulation of the Neural Network

The proposed algorithm was implemented with specialized software that allows us to automate the process of obtaining $R_d(t)$ graphs and their conversion into bipolar matrices (see Fig. 4).

Furthermore, this program provides training and functioning of the neural network and contains means of the work results visualization.

The connection of the computer with the resistance welding machine is carried out with a galvanic isolation unit, an adapting interface, and a controller.

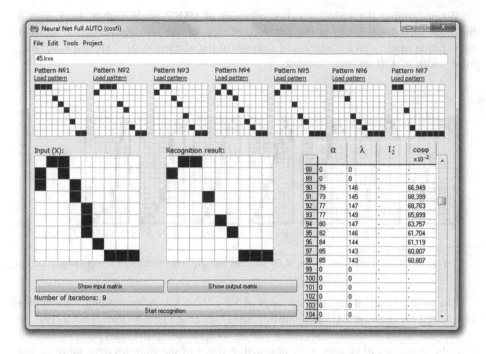

Fig. 4. A screen form of the transformation of graphs $R_d(t)$ into bipolar matrices.

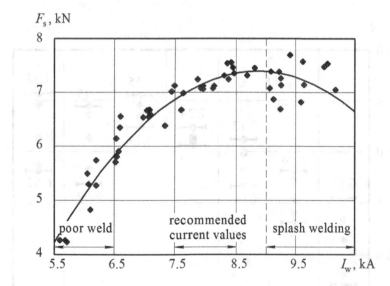

Fig. 5. A graph of destruction force change during the training of the neural network.

When training the neural network, samples of 08KP grade carbon steel with a thickness of 0.8 + 0.8 mm at the 5th voltage step of the transformer in the current stabilization mode with a compressive strength of the electrodes of 3 kN and a welding pulse width of 180 ms were welded.

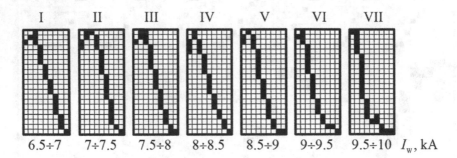

Fig. 6. Bipolar matrices of the $R_d(t)$ patterns for different welding current ranges.

The welding current varied in the range of 5.5 ÷ 10.5 kA. After welding, the samples were tested for shear on a H50KT tensile testing machine (Tinius Olsen TMC) [19].

Subject to the measurements results of 50 samples using the least squares method [20], the dynamics of change in F_s destruction force of the samples depending on the welding conditions was defined (shown in Fig. 5).

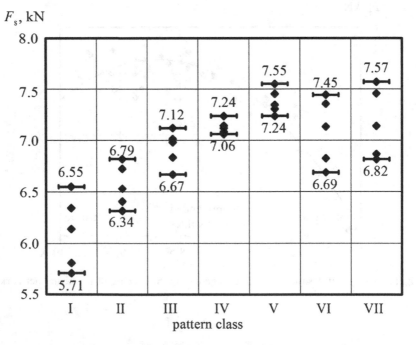

Fig. 7. A range of destruction force for each pattern during the training of the neural network.

Seven welding current I_w ranges from 6.5 kA to 10 kA with 0.5 kA step were allocated, for which the $R_d(t)$ patterns as the arithmetic mean of all experimental graphs obtained for the corresponding welding current values were built.

Then, for each $R_d(t)$ pattern bipolar matrices were obtained (see Fig. 6) and inserted into the neural network using expression (1).

Each pattern has its own range of destruction force (shown in Fig. 7).

Testing of the neural network in the welding process was carried out at the welding current of 6.5, 8 and 9.5 kA for the diameter of the electrode 5, 6 and 7 mm.

The neural network compared the bipolar matrices of the test welds with previously obtained pattern matrices (see Fig. 8).

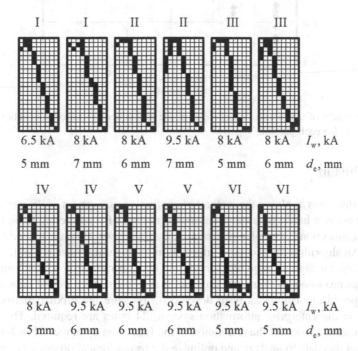

Fig. 8. The bipolar matrices of the test welds for different values of the welding current (I_w) and electrode diameters (d_e) with indication of the closest pattern.

The strength characteristics of the studied welded connection were taken subject to the characteristics of the pattern closest to it. The destruction force of experimental samples in most cases was in the range of the destruction force of the corresponding pattern (see Fig. 9).

The relative prediction error did not exceed 10%.

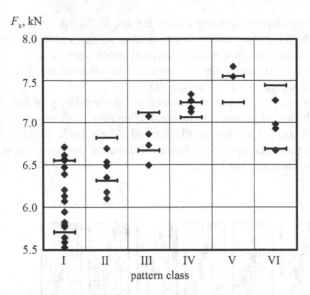

Fig. 9. The results of the bound strength tests of the experimental welded connections and the range of values for each pattern.

5 Conclusion

The article discusses applying the method of qualitative assessment of the welding zone dynamic resistance based on a recurrent neural network for predicting bound strength of welded connections. To solve this problem, a two-layer Hamming neural network was used. An algorithm for encoding information on dynamic resistance of the welding zone into bipolar signals required for tuning and operating of a Hamming neural network was proposed. A computer program that implements a neural network based on the proposed algorithm has been developed. To store the bipolar matrix of each weld point in the enterprise information system, 24 bytes are required. The accumulated information allows for the restoration of the formation dynamics of each point and for the use of this data to analyze and optimize the technological processes of resistance welding. The results of the neural network training and testing are presented. The analysis showed that the relative prediction error of the welds destruction force does not exceed 10%.

Thus, the possibility of using a Hamming neural network to predict bond strength of welded connections based on the dynamic resistance of the welding zone has been confirmed. The proposed method complies with the requirements of ISO 9000:2015 standard [21] for continuous monitoring and documentation of each welded connection and can be recommended for solving problems of predicting and diagnosing the quality of resistance welding.

Acknowledgment. The work was supported by the Russian Foundation of Basic Research (Grant Agreement 15-08-03125 A).

References

1. Ambroziak, A., Korzeniowski, M.: Using resistance spot welding for joining aluminium elements in automotive industry. Arch. Civil Mech. Eng. **10**(1), 5–13 (2010). https://doi.org/10.1016/S1644-9665(12)60126-5
2. Ivy, J.S., Pollock, S.M.: Classification of spot welds using power factor time profiles. Int. J. Prod. Res. **39**(3), 549–566 (2001). https://doi.org/10.1080/00207540150504340
3. Control of Welding Processes: Report of the Committee on Welding Control. National Academy Press, Springfield (1987)
4. Bhattacharya, S.: Significance of dynamic-resistance curves in the theory and practice of spot welding. Weld. Metal Fab. **9**, 296–301 (1974)
5. Livshits, A.: Universal quality assurance method for resistance spot welding based on dynamic resistance. Weld. J. **76**(9), 383–390 (1997)
6. Sampaio, D., Moscato, L., Link, N.: Quantitative estimation of a resistance spot weld quality using a simple model. In: ABCM Symposium Series in Mechatronics, vol. 3, pp. 831–838 (2008)
7. Raoelison, R., Fuentes, A., Pouvreau, C., Rogeon, P., Carre, P., Dechalotte, F.: Modeling and numerical simulation of the resistance spot welding of zinc coated steel sheets using rounded tip electrode: analysis of required conditions. Appl. Math. Model. **38**(9–10), 2505–2521 (2014). https://doi.org/10.1016/j.apm.2013.10.060
8. Klimov, V.S., Komirenko, A.V.: Control and diagnostics of the resistance welding process on single-phase AC machines using a thyristor contactor. Test. Diagn. **13**, 50–56 (2013). (in Russian)
9. Martín, Ó., López, M., Martín, F.: Artificial neural networks for quality control by ultrasonic testing in resistance spot welding. J. Mater. Process. Technol. **183**(2), 226–233 (2007). https://doi.org/10.1016/j.jmatprotec.2006.10.011
10. Yongyan, L., Weimin, Z., Haitao, X., Jian, D.: Defect recognition of resistance spot welding based on artificial neural network. In: Wu, Y. (ed.) Software Engineering and Knowledge Engineering: Theory and Practice, vol. 2, pp. 423–430 (2012). https://doi.org/10.1007/978-3-642-25349-2_56
11. Cho, Y., Rhee, S.: Quality estimation of resistance spot welding by using pattern recognition with neural networks. IEEE Trans. Instrum. Measur. **53**(2), 330–334 (2004). https://doi.org/10.1109/TIM.2003.822713
12. El-Banna, M., Filev, D., Chinnam, R.: Online qualitative nugget classification by using a linear vector quantization neural network for resistance spot welding. Int. J. Adv. Manuf. Technol. **36**, 237–248 (2008). https://doi.org/10.1007/s00170-006-0835-5
13. Ivezic, N., Alien, J., Zacharia, T.: Neural network-based resistance spot welding control and quality prediction. In: 2nd International Conference on Intelligent Processing and Manufacturing (1999). https://doi.org/10.1109/ipmm.1999.791516
14. Shah, D., Patel, D.: Prediction of weld strength of resistance spot welding using artificial neural network. J. Eng. Res. Appl. **3**(5), 1486–1491 (2013)
15. Lippman, R., Gold, B., Malpass, M.: A comparison of Hamming and Hopfield neural nets for pattern classification. MIT Lincoln Lab. Tech. Rep. TR-769 (1987)
16. Ikeda, N., Watta, P., Artiklar, M., Hassoun, M.: A two-level Hamming network for high performance associative memory. Neural Networks **14**(9), 1189–1200 (2001). https://doi.org/10.1016/S0893-6080(01)00089-2

17. Koutroumbas, K., Kalouptsidis, N.: Generalized Hamming networks and applications. Neural Networks **18**(7), 896–913 (2005). https://doi.org/10.1016/j.neunet.2005.02.003
18. Klimov, V.S., Klimov, A.S., Kudinov, A.K.: Diagnostics of resistance spot welding using Hemming neural network. Part 2. Modeling of neural network. Vestnik mashinostroyeniya **11**, 32–35 (2016). (in Russian)
19. Tinius, O.: Testing Machine Company. https://www.tiniusolsen.com. Accessed 28 Apr 2019
20. Abdi, H.: The Methods of Least Squares. Encyclopedia of Measurement and Statistics. Sage, Thousand Oaks (2007)
21. ISO 9000:2015. Quality management systems - Fundamentals and vocabulary, https://www.iso.org/standard/45481.html. Accessed 28 Apr 2019

Thematic Mapping and Evaluation of Temporary Sequence of Multi-zone Satellite Images

Vitaliy Dementiev, Andrey Frenkel[✉], Dmitriy Kondratiev,
and Anastasia Streltsova

Ulyanovsk State Technical University, Ulyanovsk, Russian Federation
dve@ulntc.ru, j.skvoll@gmail.com,
kondratev.dmitriy@gmail.com, nastya94strel@mail.ru

Abstract. The goal of this paper is to present and compare algorithms for thematic mapping of multispectral satellite images. The paper proposes a non-linear multi-dimensional filter to combine the results of processing of several multi-temporal multispectral images. Options for implementation of procedures are discussed.

Keywords: Earth remote sensing · Satellite monitoring · Image sequence processing · Least squares method · Segmentation

1 Introduction

Recently there has been a significant increase in the number of diverse satellites of Earth remote sensing (ERS). Satellite images are widely used for monitoring of the atmosphere, the oceans, polar areas, agricultural lands, urban areas, deserts, and forests.

A main difficulty to the widespread use of high-resolution data is the lack of suitable tools for automated analysis and interpretation of such data. One of the fundamental stages in the processing of remote sensing images is segmentation, which is carried out with the aim of dividing the image into segments containing the same type according to their visual characteristics of the pixels. Each pixel is assigned a certain label (the number of the segment to which it is assigned) with the subsequent formation of the card segments. This treatment allows to distinguish images of homogeneous areas (forest, field, urban areas, etc.) on the satellite, subsequent analysis of which is substantially more simple in comparison with the baseline studies of heterogeneous satellite images.

There are two general approaches to solving the problem of image segmentation, which are based on alternative methodological concepts (Gonzalez 2006; Bakut 1987; Vasiliev et al. 2014; Potapov 2008). The first approach is based on the "discontinuity" of the properties of image points when moving from one area to another (Gonzalez 2006; Bakut 1987; Fursov 2014). This reduces the segmentation task to the task of demarcating regions. The second approach is to isolate image points that are homogeneous in their local properties and combine them into a region (Vasiliev et al. 2014; Potapov et al. 2008; Tarabalka 2009).

© Springer Nature Switzerland AG 2019
S. O. Kuznetsov and A. I. Panov (Eds.): RCAI 2019, CCIS 1093, pp. 81–92, 2019.
https://doi.org/10.1007/978-3-030-30763-9_7

Using standard segmentation algorithms for thematic mapping of satellite images in most cases leads to significant errors for two reasons. Firstly, these algorithms are mostly not able to take into account the multispectral nature the remote sensing, i.e., the fact that each satellite image contains the results of the registration of the earth's surface in different spectral ranges. Secondly, the existing approaches do not allow to use for segmentation the observed territory data obtained at previous time points. The purpose of this work is to overcome these shortcomings by modifying the factorization segmentation algorithm and neural network segmentation and classification of multidimensional data, as well as combining information from images taken at different time points.

2 Factorization Segmentation Algorithm

Consider the task of automatically classifying a multizone satellite image recorded at a time point t. This means that the image should be divided into disjoint regions, and each region have identification data. We assume that the identification is given a list of M objects corresponding to a particular area. Let us imagine that at the t time moment we have n processed multi-zone images of the territory obtained at the time points t_1, t_2, ..., t_n. At the same time, the technical characteristics of the images coincide and spatial displacements and geometric distortions are absent. Otherwise, you can apply well-known (Vasiliev et al. 2014) image combining methods, for example, pseudo-gradient procedures that allow subpixel alignment accuracy to be provided (Vasiliev et al. 2013). To reduce the likelihood of failures, it is possible to use preliminary estimates of distortions based on the analysis of RFM models (Gonzalez 2006) of recording devices.

To perform automatic classification, let us use the texture segmentation algorithm based on the image factorization procedure (Dementiev 2017). At the first stage of his work, several auxiliary images are formed using a Laplace filter. Then, we calculate local spectral histograms for the each $N = N_1 \times N_2$ image pixels (where N_1 and N_2 is the spatial resolution of the original image and the images obtained after the filter operation). If we form a vector of some properties M for each pixel, then this array can be represented as V, where dimension of the matrix is $M \times N$. Suppose that each property can be represented as a linear combination of characteristic features. Based on this assumption, an image model can be written as

$$Y = ZV + \xi, \tag{1}$$

where Z is of dimension $M \times L$ and its columns represent the characteristic features; V is a matrix of dimension $L \times N$ containing the weight vector of characteristic features in the columns; ξ is model error. Matrix Z is calculated from manually selected windows in each homogeneous region using the least squares method:

$$V = (Z^T Z)^{-1} Z^T Y \tag{2}$$

Segmentation is carried out according to the results of the analysis of matrix V. Each pixel is assigned to the segment in which the corresponding characteristic feature has the greatest weight.

Figure 1 shows the original and segmented images as a result of the algorithm for $M = 2$.

Fig. 1. The original and segmented images

A certain disadvantage of this algorithm is the need to know the number of objects in the image. However, in the case of processing a large array of satellite images of one territory, this drawback is not fundamental, since the number of objects can be determined already during the processing of the first image.

3   Neural Network Segmentation Algorithm

Algorithms based on the usage of neural networks would be another approach to image segmentation. Many neural network architectures are aimed at solving problems of clustering heterogeneous data, including image segmentation. Convolutional neural networks with fully connected layers (FCN) are the most convenient, allowing the output to form a matrix of probabilities that each pixel in the input image belongs to each segment. An analysis of the available literature has shown that, at present, the FCET network UNET is most often used to solve the problem of image segmentation. Out of ten winners of the international DSTL competition, five used this particular network option.

A key feature of UNET networks is the orientation to the processing of a single image (two-dimensional or multi-zone). Meanwhile, modern satellite systems are a source of regular updates of Earth remote sensing data. At the same time, the period between surveys ranges from several days to several weeks, while multi-temporal multi-zone images themselves, due to the specificity of modern measuring and recording equipment, can be considered combined with accuracy of 1 pixel. In connection with the above, it is necessary to modify the architecture of the neural network in order to use the data not only of the current multi-zone image, but also of some material preceding in time. This is especially important because the structure of objects in the satellite image changes quite slowly. Therefore, the use of historical data can potentially significantly reduce processing error.

To achieve this goal, we expand the input layer of the UNET network (consisting of the spectral layers of a multi-zone image by default) with three auxiliary two-dimensional half-tone images obtained from the source using NDVI, EVI, SAVI transformations and two two-dimensional arrays representing the segmentation results of the area at the previous time moment and one year ago. The use of two such reference markings at once makes it possible to reduce the classification error in the event of rapid terrain changes due to a change in the season and in the absence of a marking array at a previous time point, e.g., due to cloudiness. Figure 2 shows the architecture of the network used.

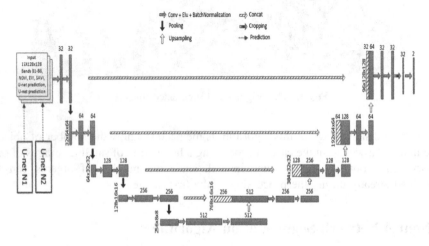

Fig. 2. The architecture of the neural network used

To train such a network, time sequences of multi-zone satellite images of the Ulyanovsk region obtained in the period from 2013 to 2017 were used from Landsat 8 spacecraft. At the same time, the spatial alignment of these images was performed and three groups of sequences consisting of at least 30 multi-zone images were formed. The spatial size of these images was 8000 by 8000 pixels with a resolution of 30 m per pixel and eight spectral ranges used (B1–B8) and three auxiliary layers of indices (NDVI, EVI, SAVI). Each of the images used for training was accompanied not only by markup of terrain objects at the time of registration of the image itself, but also by similar markings formed for images that were obtained two weeks and one year before the main image was recorded. Each marking contained objects of five types: forests, fields, settlements, rivers, and other objects.

The network training itself was carried out over 50 epochs. In the process of learning, each era was trained in 500 games. In turn, each batch was formed from 128 random fragments selected from a random location of the original image, 128 × 128 in size.

Figure 3 shows the results of automatic classification of multi-zone images obtained in different periods in 2017. Thus, in Figs. 3a, b, the allocated forest in the Melekessky region of the Ulyanovsk region is shown, Figs. 3c and d show city of Ulyanovsk with its suburbs.

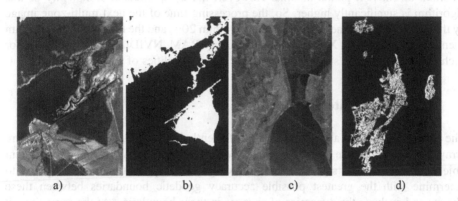

a)   b)   c)   d)

Fig. 3. Results of automatic classification of satellite multi-zone images

A visual analysis of the presented fragments shows that the accuracy of the proposed procedure is comparable to that of the results of processing by a qualified operator.

4   Comparative Analysis of the Results

Note that the achieved results are largely related to the use of markup layers obtained at previous points in time when training the network and its application. For illustration, the following table shows the classification accuracy results (percentage of correctly classified pixels) of forests, water bodies and settlements for the same satellite image fragment when using the ISODATA algorithm (Vasiliev 2016), the combined factorization algorithm (Dementiev 2017), the proposed procedure for cases of processing a single spectral channel, eight spectral channels, and joint processing of the current multi-zone image and data obtained in the previous treatments (Table 1).

Table 1. Comparison of the quality of segmentation algorithms

Type of object selected	ISODATA Algorithm	Factorization algorithm	Treatment single spectral channel (B1)	Co-processing eight spectral channels (B1–B8), NDVI, EVI, SAVI layers and archival segmentation results
"Forest"	64,2	87,8	78,3	93,2
"River"	71,4	96,3	83,2	96,5
"Locality"	61,8	91,1	79,1	94,7

The analysis of the presented results gives grounds to conclude that the segmentation efficiency is significant (up to 12%) due to the joint processing of the multizonal image and the results of its processing over the previous time. Similar results are shown by a factorization algorithm aimed at processing several multi-zone images that were recorded at different points in time. However, the computational complexity of this algorithm is significantly higher. So, the processing time of the next multi-zone image by the presented neural network procedure is 4 min 20 s, and the factorization algorithm spends 26 h 11 min (4x Xeon E5-4600, 26 GB of RAM, NVIDIA Tesla K80 GPU) for such processing, which significantly reduces the possibilities of its practical use.

5 Synthesis of Filtering Results

The solutions proposed above allow with sufficiently high accuracy to divide the entire array of pixels that make up the image into separate classes that correspond to different objects. However, in a significant number of practical applications, it is required to determine with the greatest possible accuracy geodetic boundaries between these objects and evaluate the dynamics of changes in these boundaries. At the same time, it is intuitively clear that the presence of temporal sequences of multispectral images can potentially significantly improve the accuracy of determining these estimates.

To solve these problems, we assume that the segmentation of the multi-zone image at the $t - 1$. time point results in selecting an object that is described on the image by a set of elementary geometric shapes, the size of which is determined by the spatial resolution of the original image. Most often such figures are the squares corresponding to the pixels of the original image. Since it is possible to assign the geodesic coordinates of its angles to each of these squares, it becomes possible to assign the set of observed geodesic coordinates of the points $\{P_i^{t-1} = (z_{xi}^{t-1}, z_{yi}^{t-1})\}_{i=1}^{N_{t-1}}$ that make up its boundary to the selected object.

Similarly, it is possible to select the same object at a point in time in a subsequent multi-zone image. At the same time, due to the errors that occur when registering an image, combining it with the previous one, segmentation, calculating geodetic coordinates $\{P_i^t = (z_{xi}^t, z_{yi}^t)\}_{i=1}^{N_t}$, the set of geodetic coordinates will not unambiguously correspond to $\{P_i^{t-1} = (z_{xi}^{t-1}, z_{yi}^{t-1})\}_{i=1}^{N_{t-1}}$ even if the actual boundaries of the object did not change between the moments $t - 1$ and t. At the same time, it is clear that if this gap is large enough, then one cannot speak of the immutability of the actual boundaries of the object. For example, the boundaries of a water body are very mobile in spring during the flood period, or the boundaries of the forest are very significantly shifted over a sufficiently long period of time due to natural overgrowing and logging. In this case, the point with real coordinates at time $t - 1$ determined by the vector $(x_i^{t-1}, y_i^{t-1})^T$, can move at time t to point $(x_i^t, y_i^t)^T$. In this case, the following relations take place:

$$z_{xi}^{t-1} = x_i^{t-1} + n_{xi}^{t-1}, \; z_{yi}^t = y_i^t + n_{yi}^t, \; x_i^t = x_i^{t-1} + v_{xi}^t, \; y_i^t = y_i^{t-1} + v_{yi}^t, \quad (3)$$

where v_{xi}^t and v_{yi}^t is the displacement of a point with an index i along x and y axes, respectively. The question arises as to the correspondence between the points $\{x_i^t, y_i^t\}$ and observations $\{z_{xi}^t, z_{yi}^t\}$, located on the identified boundary of the object. One of the options for finding points corresponding to observations $\{z_{xi}^t, z_{yi}^t\}$ can be the following algorithm. Let there be sets of points $\{P_i^{t-1} = (z_{xi}^{t-1}, z_{yi}^{t-1})\}_{i=1}^{N_{t-1}}$ and $\{P_i^t = (z_{xi}^t, z_{yi}^t)\}_{i=1}^{N_t}$, describing the selected boundaries of the same object at times $t-1$ and t, respectively. For definiteness, we will assume that these points sequentially form a closed set of segments that are the boundaries of the specified object. Then consider a single point P_i^{t-1}. Together with the points P_{i-1}^{t-1} and P_{i+1}^{t-1} it forms two segments that make up the boundary of the object. We define a line L_i^{t-1} that coincides with the bisector of the angle $(P_{i-1}^{t-1}, P_i^{t-1}, P_i^{t-1})$, and find the nearest point of its intersection with any of the segments defined by pairs of points $\{P_i^t, P_{i+1}^t\}, i = 1, .., N_t$. Denote this point by $\tilde{P}_i^t$ and let us assume that it is this point with coordinates $\{z_{xi}^t, z_{yi}^t\}$ that corresponds to the point with coordinates $\{z_{xi}^{t-1}, z_{yi}^{t-1}\}$ at t the moment of time (Fig. 4). Continuing in this way the process of searching for correspondence between the points of the border at different points in time, it is possible to construct the following arrays of observations: $\{z_{xi}^{t-1}, z_{yi}^{t-1}\}$, $i = 1, .., N_1, t = 1, .., T$.

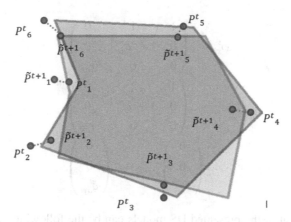

Fig. 4. The process of finding a match between observations at different points in time

Note that in the approach presented, the number of points constituting the boundary of the object does not change with time and corresponds to the number of points to this boundary at the first time point. Our experiments show that this simplification is not fundamental and does not lead to a noticeable degradation of the processing algorithms. We assume that the set of arrays of observations: $\{z_{xi}^t, z_{yi}^t\}$, $i = 1, .., N_1, t = 1, .., T$ corresponds to the changing boundaries of some object. We also assume that changes in this boundary may occur unevenly. For example, a ravine or cliff area can increase by several tens of centimeters over the years, and at a certain point acquire a dynamic that is hundreds of times greater than the indicated values. Similarly, the area of a lake can be almost unchanged throughout the year, but it can increase several times in the spring with the snow melting. Under these conditions, we change the model (3) with respect to the unknown coordinates $\{x_i^t, y_i^t\}$, $i = 1, .., N_1$, $t = 1, .., T$, as follows

$$
\begin{aligned}
x_i^t &= 2x_i^{t-1} - x_i^{t-2} + a_{xi}^t \left(x_i^{t-1} - x_i^{t-2} \right), \\
y_i^t &= 2y_i^{t-1} - y_i^{t-2} + a_{yi}^t \left(y_i^{t-1} - y_i^{t-2} \right), \\
a_{xi}^t &= r_{ax} a_{xi}^{t-1} + \xi_{axi}^t, \; a_{yi}^t = r_{ay} a_{yi}^{t-1} + \xi_{ayi}^t,
\end{aligned}
\tag{4}
$$

where r_{ax}, r_{ay} - scalar parameters that determine the rate of change of acceleration a_{xi}^t and; a_{yi}^t; ξ_{axi}^t, ξ_{ayi}^t are independent normal random variables with zero expectation and variance σ_ξ^2. Model (5) is called double stochastic (DS) and allows describing essentially non-stationary processes (Vasiliev et al. 2018). Denote by $v_{xi}^t = x_i^t - x_i^{t-1}$, $v_{yi}^t = y_i^t - y_i^{t-1}$, and by $\overline{X}_i^t = (\; x_i^t \quad v_{xi}^t \quad a_{xi}^t\;)$, $Y_i^t = (\; y_i^t \quad v_{yi}^t \quad a_{yi}^t\;)$. Then model (4) can be rewritten in the form:

$$
\overline{X}_i^t = \wp_{xi}^t \overline{X}_i^{t-1} + \overline{\xi}_{xi}^t, \; \overline{Y}_i^t = \wp_{yi}^t \overline{X}_i^{t-1} + \overline{\xi}_{yi}^t
\tag{5}
$$

where

$$
\wp_{xi}^t = \begin{pmatrix} 1 & 1 & 0 \\ 0 & 1 + a_{xi}^{t-1} & 0 \\ 0 & 0 & r_{ax} \end{pmatrix},
$$

$$
\wp_{yi}^t = \begin{pmatrix} 1 & 1 & 0 \\ 0 & 1 + a_{yi}^{t-1} & 0 \\ 0 & 0 & r_{ay} \end{pmatrix},
$$

$$
\overline{\xi}_{xi}^t = \begin{pmatrix} 0 \\ 0 \\ \xi_{axi}^t \end{pmatrix}, \; \overline{\xi}_{xi}^t = \begin{pmatrix} 0 \\ 0 \\ \xi_{ayi}^t \end{pmatrix}.
$$

Another variant of the presented DS models can be the following nonlinear vector stochastic expressions describing an independent change of coordinates:

$$
\overline{X}_i^t = \varphi_{xi}^t \left(\overline{X}_i^{t-1} \right) + \overline{\xi}_{xi}^t, \; \overline{Y}_i^t = \varphi_{yi}^t \left(\overline{Y}_i^{t-1} \right) + \overline{\xi}_{yi}^t
\tag{6}
$$

Then

$$
\varphi_{xi}^{t\prime} \left(\overline{X}_i^{t-1} \right) = \begin{pmatrix} 1 & 1 & 0 \\ 0 & a_{xi}^{t-1} & v_{xi}^{t-1} \\ 0 & 0 & r_{ax} \end{pmatrix}
$$

and

$$\varphi_{yi}^{t}\left(\overline{Y}_{i}^{t-1}\right) = \begin{pmatrix} 1 & 1 & 0 \\ 0 & a_{yi}^{t-1} & v_{yi}^{t-1} \\ 0 & 0 & r_{ay} \end{pmatrix}.$$

In this case, the model of observations can be rewritten in the form:

$$z_{xi}^{t} = C_{x}\overline{X}_{i}^{t} + n_{xi}^{t}, \; z_{yi}^{t} = C_{y}\overline{Y}_{i}^{t} + n_{yi}^{t}, \; i = 1, .., N_{o}, \; t = 1, .., T,$$

where $C_{x} = C_{y} = (1 \quad 0 \quad 0)$.

The notation allows us to apply twice stochastic nonlinear filtering for filtering observations and building predictions of the behavior of a region relative R_{0} to an object T_{o}. At the same time, we introduce $\overline{X}_{3i}^{t} = \varphi_{xi}^{t}(\overline{X}_{i}^{t-1})$ and $\overline{Y}_{3i}^{t} = \varphi_{yi}^{t}(\overline{X}_{i}^{t-1})$, extrapolated predictions of the coordinates of point T_{Ei} at time t from previous observations z_{xi}^{t-1} and z_{yi}^{t-1}. The covariance error matrices of such extrapolation will be:

$$P_{3xi}^{t} = M\left\{\left(\hat{\overline{X}}_{3i}^{t} - \overline{X}_{3i}^{t}\right)\left(\hat{\overline{X}}_{3i}^{t} - \overline{X}_{3i}^{t}\right)^{T}\right\} = \varphi_{xi}^{t}{}'(\overline{X}_{i}^{t-1})P_{x}^{t-1}\varphi_{xi}^{t}{}'(\overline{X}_{i}^{t-1})^{T} + V_{x_{\xi}i}^{t} \quad (7)$$

$$P_{3yi}^{t} = M\left\{\left(\hat{\overline{Y}}_{3i}^{t} - \overline{Y}_{3i}^{t}\right)\left(\hat{\overline{Y}}_{3Ei}^{t} - \overline{Y}_{3i}^{t}\right)^{T}\right\} = \varphi_{yi}^{t}{}'(\overline{Y}_{i}^{t-1})P_{yi}^{t-1}\varphi_{yi}^{t}{}'(\overline{Y}_{i}^{t-1})^{T} + V_{y_{\xi}i}^{t}, \quad (8)$$

where P_{xi}^{t-1}, P_{yi}^{t-1} are the covariance matrices of filtering errors at the time moment $(t-1)$, $V_{x_{\xi}i}^{t} = M\{\overline{\xi}_{xi}^{t}\overline{\xi}_{xi}^{tT}\}$, $V_{y_{\xi}i}^{t} = M\{\overline{\xi}_{yi}^{t}\overline{\xi}_{yi}^{tT}\}$ are the diagonal covariance matrices of random additions $\overline{\xi}_{xi}^{t}$.

Then you can write the following relations for double-stochastic nonlinear coordinate filters:

$$\hat{X}_{i}^{t} = \hat{\overline{X}}_{3i}^{t} + B_{xi}^{t}(z_{xi}^{t} - \hat{x}_{3i}^{t}) \quad (9)$$

$$\hat{Y}_{i}^{t} = \hat{\overline{Y}}_{3i}^{t} + B_{yi}^{t}(z_{yi}^{t} - \hat{y}_{3i}^{t}) \quad (10)$$

where $\hat{x}_{3i}^{t}, \hat{y}_{3i}^{t}$, is the first elements of the vectors and

$$\hat{\overline{X}}_{3i}^{t} \text{ и } \hat{\overline{Y}}_{3i}^{t}; \; B_{xi}^{t} = P_{3xi}^{t}C_{x}^{T}D_{xi}^{t}{}^{-1} \quad (11)$$

$$fB_{yi}^{t} = P_{3yi}^{t}C_{y}^{T}D_{yi}^{t}{}^{-1}f \quad (12)$$

$$sD_{xi}^t = C P_{\Im xi}{}^t C^T + \sigma_n^2 f \tag{13}$$

$$fD_{yi}^t = C P_{\Im yi}{}^t C^T + \sigma_n^2 f \tag{14}$$

The variance of the filtering error at each step is determined by the matrices

An important feature of a double stochastic filter is the possibility of retracing, i.e., refining the estimates for subsequent observations. In this case, the following relations hold:

$$\hat{X}_{Wi}^{t-1} = \hat{X}_i^{t-1} + A_{xi}{}^t \left(\hat{X}_{Wi}^t - \hat{x}_{\Im i}^t \right) \tag{15}$$

$$\hat{Y}_{Wi}^{t-1} = \hat{Y}_i^{t-1} + A_{yi}{}^t \left(\hat{Y}_{Wi}^t - \hat{y}_{\Im i}^t \right) \tag{16}$$

where

$$A_{xi}{}^t = P_{xi}{}^t \varphi_{xi}{}^{t-1\prime} \left(\bar{\hat{x}}_i{}^t \right)^T P_{\Im xi}{}^{t-1} \tag{17}$$

$$A_{yi}{}^t = P_{yi}{}^t \varphi_{yi}{}^{t-1\prime} \left(\bar{\hat{y}}_i{}^t \right)^T P_{\Im yi}{}^{t-1} \tag{18}$$

$$\bar{\hat{x}}_{Wi}{}^{Nt} = \bar{\hat{x}}_i{}^{Nt}, \; \bar{\hat{y}}_{Wi}{}^{Nt} = \bar{\hat{y}}_i{}^{Nt} \tag{19}$$

Thus, to realize the reverse stroke of the coordinate-wise double stochastic filter, it suffices to store the values of filtering errors P_{xi}^t and P_{yi}^t, as well as extrapolation errors, $P_{\Im xi}{}^t$ and $P_{\Im yi}{}^t$, for all points and moments of time.

6 Analysis of the Filtering Results

To analyze the effectiveness of the presented algorithms, a series of fragments of satellite images of a forest area in the Cherdaklinsky district of the Ulyanovsk region for the period 2001–2017 was processed. The volume of the series was 42 multi-zone images. Figures 5a, b and c present fragments of such images for years 2001, 2009, and 2017, respectively. The spatial resolution of each image was 12 m. Each of the multi-zone images was segmented based on the neural network algorithm described in Sect. 3. As a result of the segmentation, each of the selected areas was assigned to several classes. Figure 5d presents the result of such a classification in the form of automatic selection of the forest area. A visual analysis of the quality of the results of such segmentation shows very high efficiency. The actual processing accuracy is comparable to the accuracy of the operator.

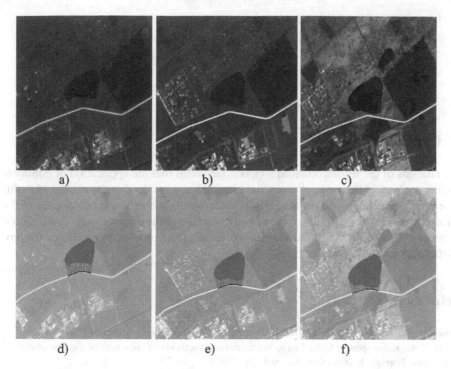

Fig. 5. Selection of the forest on multi-zone images registered at different points in time

For the first of the images in the sequence, according to the results of the analysis of the coordinates of the geodetic binding, a set of points $\{P_i^1 = (z_{xi}^1, z_{yi}^1)\}_{i=1}^{N_1}$ was determined that define the borders of the forest area. For each of the subsequent images on the basis of the approach presented in Sect. 4, the corresponding arrays of points were obtained $\{P_i^t = (z_{xi}^t, z_{yi}^t)\}_{i=1}^{N_1}$, $t = 2, .., 42$. For these arrays, direct coordinate-wise nonlinear double stochastic filtering was performed, which allowed to determine arrays of estimates, $\{(\hat{x}_i^t, \hat{y}_i^t)\}_{i=1}^{N_1}, t = 2, .., 42$, and inverse coordinate-wise double stochastic filtering, which resulted in estimates. In this case, an empirically selected value of the noise variance was used, $\sigma_m^2 = \frac{\Delta^2}{2}$, where Δ is the spatial resolution of the image. The estimates found were compared with accurate measurements obtained during geodetic surveys in the area in 2009 and 2017. As a result, the following average errors were obtained (Tables 2 and 3).

Table 2. Coordinate error x

	Mean error $AVG(z_{xi}^t - x_i^t)$	Mean error $AVG(\hat{x}_i^t - x_i^t)$	Mean error $AVG(\hat{x}_{wi}^t - x_i^t)$
2009	10.6	3.9	3.0
2017	10.2	3.1	3.1

Table 3. Coordinate error y

	Mean error $AVG(z^t_{yi} - y^t_i)$	Mean error $AVG(\hat{y}^t_i - y^t_i)$	Mean error $AVG(\hat{y}^t_{wi} - y^t_i)$
2009	10.8	4.1	3.1
2017	10.7	3.0	3.0

7 Conclusion

The analysis of the results obtained supports the claim that the application of nonlinear double stochastic filtering to observations obtained as a result of segmentation of multizone images has improved the accuracy of determining the geodetic coordinates of the object boundaries by up to 25% of the spatial resolution of the original image, i.e. 3–3, 5% of direct observations. This allows us to recommend the proposed procedures for processing real satellite data.

References

Gonzalez, R., Woods, R.: Digital Image Processing. Technosphere, Moscow (2006)

Bakut, P.A., Kolmogorov, G.S.: Image segmentation: methods of selection of the boundaries of regions. Foreign Radioelectronics, vol. 10 (1987)

Vasiliev, K.K., Krasheninnikov, V.R.: Statistical Image Analysis. UlSTU, Ulyanovsk (2014)

Potapov, A.A., Gulyaev, Y.V., Nikitov, S.A., Pakhomov, A.A., German, V.A.: The Latest Image Processing Techniques. FIZMATLIT, Moscow (2008)

Vasiliev, K.K.: Optimum processing of signals in discrete time, Radio engineering (2016)

Vasiliev, K.K., Krasheninnikov, V.R., Tashlinsky, A.G.: Statistical analysis of sequences of multidimensional images. Science-intensive technologies, vol. 14, no. 5 (2013)

Fursov, S.A., Bibikov, O.A., Baida, V.A.: Thematic classification of hyperspectral images by conjugacy index. Comput. Opt. **38**(1), 154–158 (2014)

Zimichev, E.A., Kazansky, N.L., Serafimovich, P.G.: Spatial classification of hyperspectral images using the k-means++ clustering method. Comput. Opt. **38**(2), 281–286 (2014)

Tarabalka, Y., Benediktsson, J.A., Chanussot, J.: IEEE Trans. Geosci. Remote Sens. **47**(8), 2973–2987 (2009)

Satellite Imagery Feature Detection. https://www.kaggle.com/c/dstl-satellite-imagery-feature-detection. Accessed 25 Apr 2019

Dementiev, V.E., Vasiliev, K.K., Andriyanov, N.A.: Estimating image parameters. Pattern Recogn. Image Anal. (Adv. Math. Theor. and Appl.) **26**(1), 240–247 (2016)

Dementiev, V.E., Kondratiev, D.S.: Method of thematic mapping of sequences of satellite images. Inf.-measuring Control Syst. **15**(12), 49–53 (2017)

Andriyanov, N.A., Dementiev, V.E.: Segment field of satellite images, CEUR Workshop Proceedings, vol. 1814 (2018)

Vasiliev, K., Dementiev, V., Andriyanov, N.: Representation and sequences of satellite images and sequences. Proc. Comput. Sci. **126**, 49–58 (2018)

Hierarchical Representation of Information Objects in a Digital Library Environment

Nikolay Kalenov⬤, Irina Sobolevskaya⬤,
and Alexandr Sotnikov$^{(\boxtimes)}$⬤

Joint Supercomputer Center of the Russian Academy of Sciences — Branch
of Federal State Institution "Scientific Research Institute for System Analysis
of the Russian Academy of Sciences" (JSCC RAS — Branch of SRISA),
Leninsky av., 32 a, 119334 Moscow, Russia
asotnikov@jscc.ru

Abstract. This paper studies the problem of building a modern information society as a task of forming a virtual knowledge space. This task can be implemented on the IT platform of a digital library, which ensures the formation and provision of information resources in various areas to general public users. It shows how electronic copies of objects of a library, archive and museum storage represented in the form of texts, graphic images, and audio/video objects, including 3D-models, can be integrated using digital library facilities. The concept of a hierarchical level of electronic objects is introduced. The definitions of objects of various levels are given and the principles of work with objects of each level are formulated. The hierarchical representation of electronic objects in a digital library environment is proposed. A distinction between thematic, theme-specific, and interdisciplinary collections is shown. The information environment for forming subtheme collections is represented as a set of databases created by information fund holders. This environment is distributed and unified in terms of the software and hardware used, as well as in terms of a set of requirements for digital images being formed. The paper formulates the basic principles of forming collections of various levels in a digital library environment and reflects the developed digital solutions that ensure their implementation. For each hierarchical level, it gives examples of objects and collections provided on the portal of the Scientific Heritage of Russia Digital Library (SHR DL) and formed in compliance with the proposed principles and digital solutions. In particular, the paper describes in detail the thematic collection of publications in mathematics being a database formed through LibMeta DBMS; interdisciplinary collection "Garden of Life" created in collaboration with one of the Russian museums, and some other collections.

Keywords: Scientific Heritage of Russia Digital Library ·
Theme-specific collections · Thematic collections ·
Interdisciplinary collections · Virtual exhibitions · Digital 3D-models ·
Museum objects

S. O. Kuznetsov and A. I. Panov (Eds.): RCAI 2019, CCIS 1093, pp. 93–104, 2019.
https://doi.org/10.1007/978-3-030-30763-9_8

1 Introduction

The formed digital knowledge space is one of the most important elements of the modern information society. Access to objects of the knowledge space is provided via the Internet, which offers many opportunities for combining various information sources, extracting knowledge and forming a virtual information space on their basis. An effective means of integrating information resources is a complex of technological, technical, and organizational solutions united by the concept of a digital library that ensures the formation and provision of information resources in various areas to general public users.

There exist several integrators that combine different types of information resources. An example is the European electronic library Europeana [1], which aims at combining digital images of European cultural heritage sites and making their content available to users. At the same time, Europeana provides access to full texts of electronic printed publications. The other example of the pooling of resources is the European library [2], which is a portal that provides a free search for resources available to the leading national and scientific libraries in Europe. From 2011 to 2017, the European library managed the Europeana Libraries project, which was created to include more than 5 million objects from 19 scientific libraries in Europe. In 2017, the European library project was closed, and all the processes associated with the unification of European digital objects of cultural significance is provided by Europeana.

Unlike the European media, most cultural and scientific centers of the United States have long been creating their digital collections and cooperate only for the organization of thematic projects. Since 1990, the Library of Congress has launched an American Memory project called the National Electronic Library. However, this project did not involve pooling the resources of most US public libraries. There were many thematic library projects in the country without centralized management. In 2013, the electronic resources of libraries, universities, museums, and archives were combined and made available through a single portal [3], the electronic public library of America (DPLA), which should provide online access to the cultural heritage of the whole country. DPLA, unlike Europeana, does not contain digital copies of documents but provides metadata about their resources transferred by participating libraries. The DPLA database contains records redirecting the user to the provider library site that contains the corresponding digital document. The digital public library of USA portal serves as a single point of access to millions of objects, providing search across all DPLA-enabled digital libraries [4].

Several large aggregators of information resources described above provide access not only to digital copies of printed publications, but also allow viewing thematic collections or virtual exhibitions provided by participants [5]. However, none of the above resources allows to dynamically form user collections of the presented information objects united by some features [6].

In particular, the task of integrating electronic objects of library storage, archival storage and museum storage presented in the form of text files, graphic images, and multimedia into a unified resource is solved with the help of electronic libraries [7].

We have considered in sufficient detail the approaches to the digital library design and principles of their formation using the example of the Scientific Heritage of Russia Digital Library (SHR DL) in [8–10].

SHR DL provides integration of electronic copies of scientific objects stored in institutions of memory (libraries, archives, museums), presented in the form of text files, graphic images, and multimedia. Objects that are reflected in the SHR DL are accompanied by extensive information about their creators, scientists who have made a significant contribution to the development of Russian science.

SHR DL is based on a combination of the principles of decentralization (preparation of metadata and digitization of materials by resource owners) and centralization (editing, storing information and providing it to users upon their requests).

The main functionalities of SHR DL include:

- formation and storage of content provided by institutions of memory;
- search for metadata objects of electronic funds of institutions of memory;
- search, metadata about scientists and publications;
- thematic search;
- viewing of collections available in the SHR DL;
- forming and editing custom collections;
- searching by collection;
- work with media objects, allowing you to view media objects;
- viewing full texts of digital copies of publications;
- import of metadata from external systems.

User access to the SHR DL is through any browser. The basis of the SHR DL software is the "LibMeta" platform. The core of this platform performs the following functions [11]:

- management of the static content of the SHR DL;
- storage of objects of the SHR DL represented by RDF-triples in relational Database Management System (DBMS);
- batch download;
- indexing;
- full-text search;
- system security;
- news management.

The participants of the project for the creation of the SHR DL (scientific libraries, museums, archives of the Russian Academy of Sciences and several scientific institutes) form and edit the metadata of their resources on-line in the technological database. The ontology of the SHR DL envisages that each object to be included in the SHR DL is characterized by a set of properties fixed for each type of objects (persons, publications, museum objects, etc.). As the formation (editing) of the object metadata is completed, they are loaded in batch mode into the central database with the automatic establishment of links with other objects.

It should be noted that SHR DL is developing as an integral part of the Russian digital knowledge space towards the integrator of scientific information resources of memory institutions.

The formation and maintenance of information funds of digital libraries and the provision of access to them require a specific technological environment that supports relevant procedures. The study of the fund creation process and the nature of material requests has demonstrated that users often need to select information objects from the entire set of interconnected digital library resources united by one feature or some combination of them. This, in turn, provokes a need to develop and analyze the hierarchical representation of digital objects in a digital library environment. To build the above hierarchy, let us introduce the following concepts:

"objects" – images of items of information funds;

"type of an object" – an object property that reflects its membership in one of the resource groups determined in a digital library space (publications, archive materials, museum objects, etc.);

"theme of an object" – an object property that reflects its content identity with the group determined by a certain semantic concept (e.g. a section of science, historical period, attitude to this person, etc.);

"collection" – a set of objects of one or several types and (or) themes.

The proposed hierarchical representation of objects in a DL environment containing 4 levels is given in Fig. 1.

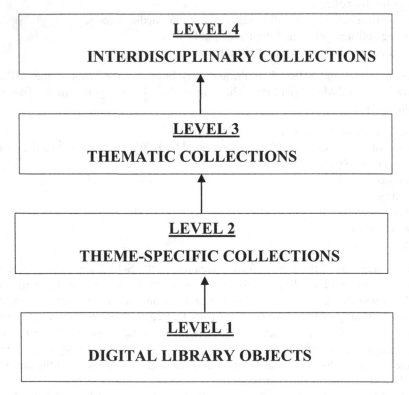

Fig. 1. Hierarchical levels of information objects.

Combining digital objects of various hierarchical levels according to some features allows developing and implementing numerous analysis and processing procedures for them, as well as representations according to the needs of the user. At the same time, it significantly enhances the ability to reflect the results of the search in digital library funds: from exhibiting a separate object to providing collections created by it and the arrangement of virtual exhibitions.

2   Elements of Hierarchical Levels of Information Objects

The elements of **Level 1** are digital library **objects**. The elements of the first level can be presented by digital copies of printed publications, archive materials, museum objects, audio/photo/video items.

Consider collections of objects of the first level relating to the same type and theme as elements of **Level 2**. For example, a collection of e-books in a given scientific area or a collection of museum objects of the same type (collection of minerals, sculptures, etc.). Objects formed in this way are called **theme-specific collections**.

Consider collections of objects of various types relating to a particular topic as elements of **Level 3**. For example, a collection dedicated to a certain scientific area, event or person, which includes at least two types of objects on a given topic: a collection of books, archive materials, museum objects. Such collections are called **thematic**. For example, the thematic collection on the botany of the 1920s–1930s may include a collection of books on this topic, biographies of biologists, as well as multimedia materials of the period, etc. [12, 13].

Objects of **Level 4,** which are formed by combining objects of the previous level, are called **interdisciplinary collections**. Thematic collections (Level 3) may exist by themselves, but may also be a part of interdisciplinary collections. If a collection includes materials relating to various fields of science (knowledge) and intersected by one or several parameters, then such a collection comprises several thematic collections. For example, an interdisciplinary collection dedicated to space exploration may include materials on astronomy, space physics, history of cosmonautics, as well as those related to the problems of space exploration, etc.

Collections of natural history museums are of particular interest for applied and fundamental research. They are used for informative and educational purposes [14]. One of the ways of representing interdisciplinary collections in a distributed digital library environment is to form a virtual exhibition. A virtual exhibition is a multimedia information resource in the Internet environment, demonstrating to the user heterogeneous pieces of information (digital copies of printed materials, archive documents, museum items, etc.), combined according to given characteristics. The chief distinction of a virtual exhibition is the provision of information in an interactive form. Along with materials of various types being represented, multimedia objects, digital 3D-models of museum objects, in particular, are necessary to form digital natural history collections. Virtual exhibitions, in contrast to museum exhibitions, are not limited by the duration of an exhibition [15, 16].

It is important to note that the arrival of virtual exhibitions in a digital library environment may be one of the directions in the integration of heterogeneous resources and representation of the digital museum content.

2.1   Examples of Information Objects of Various Hierarchical Levels in a Digital Library Environment

Consider examples of objects of various levels represented in the Scientific Heritage of Russia Digital Library.

Objects of Level 1 are presented by "scientists", "publications", "museum objects", etc., available in the portal for SHR DL (http://e-heritage.ru) and selected by the user. [9]. A search in this portal can be carried out by several parameters with a fragment of the field value entered for a search indicated. Figure 2 shows the result of the search of D. Bernoulli's letters to L. Euler published in Latin (Excerpta ex litteris a Daniele Bernoulli ad Leonhardum Euler). The displayed bibliographic description is an active link, following which you can get a complete text of this publication (Fig. 3), is an object of Level 1 in this case.

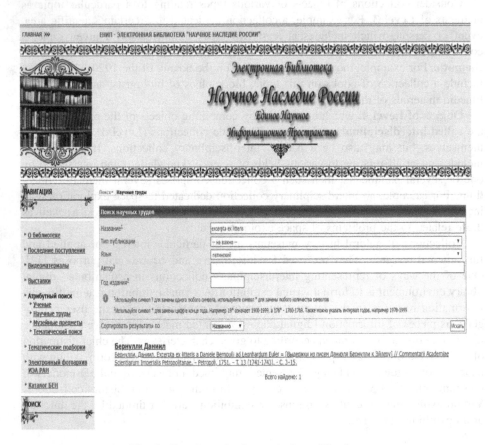

Fig. 2. Search result of a particular publication.

Fig. 3. Fragment of the e-book "Excerpts from Daniel Bernoulli's Letters to Euler".

Theme-specific collections are most popular among the users of the Scientific Heritage of Russia Digital Library. They allow, for example, to see the overall picture of the development of a specific scientific area or to form an updated bibliographic collection of scientific works. Some theme-specific collections formed in the information space of the Scientific Heritage of Russia Digital Library are given below.

One of the examples of a theme-specific collection is publications in mathematics available in the digital library. This collection contains bibliographic data and complete texts of 969 publications in mathematics.

The majority of the collection publications are in Russian (70,07%). In addition to publications in Russian, the collection includes books in Latin (21,67%) and French (5,06%). Publications in English, German and other languages make up about 3,2%.

The percentage distribution of available publications into periods is given in Table 1.

A dramatic reduction in the number of available works since the second half of the 20th century is primarily due to the copyright law, following which SHR DL members prepare materials to be included in the Library.

Another example of a theme-specific collection is "Scientific publications of XIX century in the Scientific Heritage of Russia Digital Library". The main distinction of this collection from the previous one is that (a) in this case, the selection of publications

Table 1. Time distribution of publications

Period	%
1700–1799	20
1800–1899	14
1900–1949	54
1950–1999	10
2000–2018	6

is limited to a specific historical period – XIX century, (b) this collection includes works in various scientific areas. This collection includes 4848 scientific publications published in 1800–1899 in Russian, English, German, French, Latin and other languages.

An example of a **thematic** digital collection formed by SHR DL is "Minerals in P.V. Yeremeyev's publications". This thematic collection offers the user to get acquainted with digital images of minerals, which are studied in P.V. Yeremeyev's works, as well as his published works, in which these minerals are described (Fig. 4).

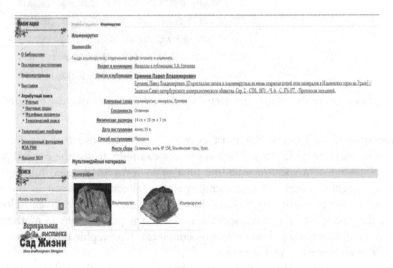

Fig. 4. Thematic collection "Minerals in P.V. Yeremeyev's publications".

The virtual exhibition "Garden of Life", dedicated to the 160th anniversary of the birth of I.V. Michurin (Fig. 5), and the exhibition "Portraits from Skeletons", dedicated to M.M. Gerasimov's scientific work (Fig. 6), are examples of **interdisciplinary** collections created in the form of virtual exhibitions.

The first virtual exhibition includes archive materials dedicated to I.V. Michurin and his scientific school (including text documents, digitized newsreel, and photos) and two theme-specific collections on this topic – digitized publications from library funds and 3D-model fruit of I.V. Michurin, stored in K.A. Timiryazev State Biological

Fig. 5. The main page of the virtual exhibition "Garden of Life".

Fig. 6. The main page of the virtual exhibition "Portraits from Skeletons".

Museum. The exhibition is freely available at http://vim.benran.ru/ and referred to in the portal of SHR DL.

The exhibition "Portraits from Skeletons" dwells on M.M. Gerasimov's scientific heritage, his school, and anthropology development. This exhibition has the same structure as the above one and includes, among other things, digital 3D-models of M. M. Gerasimov's anthropological reconstructions and his students, interactive component allowing the visitor to get acquainted with M.M. Gerasimov's work in a playful form (Fig. 7).

Fig. 7. The page of joint virtual exhibition "Portraits from Skeletons" describing M.M. Gerasimov's work.

Both exhibitions created on the platform of the Scientific Heritage of Russia Digital Library in association with K.A. Timiryazev State Biological Museum and Russian State Documentary Film and Photo Archive.

3   Conclusion

In the course of studying the problems of organizing various collections, the following basic principles of their formation have been formulated:

- The IT platform of the digital library should support the ability to form and providing collections of various levels.
- The information environment for forming collections is a set of distributed databases created by information fund holders. This principle presupposes the existence of a single space of information support ensuring the creation, dynamic updating, and accumulation of information resources by organizations participating in the formation of DL funds.

- The technological environment for the formation of digital objects is distributed and unified in terms of the software and hardware used and a set of requirements for digital images being formed. The conceptual basis for the organization of such environments is a distributed formation and storage of large data arrays. At the same time, a centralized metadatabase equipped with common search and navigation services is also created in the distributed information environment. Along with it, metadata are also stored on the servers of participants of the formation of DL funds, which enables their use in local systems of information search and provision [15].
- Provision of complete and sufficient digital object (metadata set) description means for their inclusion in a collection and their representation in information funds of the digital library.
- Independent collection formation by information fund holders combined with their availability.

The developed hierarchical approach to the formation of collections within the digital library makes it possible to more effectively and dynamically meet the information needs of users of different categories.

According to these principles, the dispatch system for stages of integration of interdisciplinary collections has been developed. It allows immersing various digital objects (images of museum objects, printed publications, archive materials, multimedia objects) into the distributed SHR DL environment online. The subsystem of data packet exchange allows exchanging data in the RDF/XML format according to the ontology metadata model. In its turn, the architecture of formation of the information support system for interdisciplinary collections and the application profile of the extended data storage support allow forming such collections in the distributed SHR DL environment.

Thematic collections presented in the SHR DL environment have been created in compliance with the available technology of forming and representing thematic collections in a distributed information environment of the digital library [6, 17, 18].

The research is carried out by JSCC RAS — branch of SRISA within supported by Russian Foundation for Basic Research (projects 17-07-00400 and 18-07-00893).

The computational capacity of JSCC RAS, MVS-100 K cluster, in particular, was used to build 3D-models.

References

1. LNCS Homepage. https://www.europeana.eu/portal/ru. Accessed 13 Nov 2018
2. LNCS Homepage. http://www.theeuropeanlibrary.org/tel4/. Accessed 13 Nov 2018
3. LNCS Homepage. https://dp.la/exhibitions. Accessed 13 Nov 2018
4. Marttila, S., Botero, A.: Infrastructuring for cultural commons. Comput. Support. Coop. Work (CSCW) 26(1–2), 97–133 (2017)
5. Díaz-Corona, D., Lacasta, J., Nogueras-Iso, J.: Barriers for the access to knowledge models in linked data cultural heritage collections. In: ACM International Conference Proceeding Series Vol. Part F137707. 5th Spanish Conference on Information Retrieval, CERI, Zaragoza (2018)

6. Shahzad, F., Alwosaibi, F.M.: Development of an e-Library Web application. In: Proceedings of the 11th International Multi-Conference on Society, Cybernetics and Informatics, IMSCI Orlando, pp. 153–158 (2017)
7. Anagnostopoulos, I., Zeadally, S., Exposito, E.: Handling big data: directions and future directions. J. Supercomputing 72(4), 1494–1516 (2016)
8. Kalenov, N., Sobolevskaya, I., Sotnikov, A.: Hierarchical levels of representation of information objects in a digital library environment. Inf. Innov. 13(2), 25–31 (2018)
9. Kalenov, N., Savin, G., Serebryakov, V., Sotnikov, A.: Principles of building and formation of the Scientific Heritage of Russia Digital Library. Softw. Prod. Syst. 4(100), 30–40 (2012)
10. Kalenov, N., Sobolevskaya, I., Sotnikov, A.: Digital museum collections and representation of objects of natural history museum storage in the Scientific Heritage of Russia Digital Library. Sci. Tech. Inf. Serv. 1(10), 33–38 (2016)
11. Antopolsky, A., Atayeva, O., Serebryakov, V.: Environment of integration of data of scientific libraries, archives, and museums "LibMeta". Inf. Resour. Russia 5(129), 8–12 (2012)
12. Kalenov, N., Sobolevskaya, I., Sotnikov, A.: On the interaction of the Scientific Heritage of Russia Digital Library with natural history museums. Inf. Resour. Russia № 148, 2–6 (2015)
13. Ivanov, V.M., Strelkov, S.V., Kholina, A.A., Avtyushenko, A.L.: Virtual reconstructions in multimedia exhibitions of objects of cultural heritage. Virtual archaeology. Collection/Hermitage, pp. 41–49 (2015). http://www.virtualarchaeology.ru/pdf/281_va_book2015.pdf. Accessed 13 Nov 2018
14. Barutkina, L.P.: Multimedia in a modern museum exhibition. Bulletin of St. Petersburg State University of Culture and Arts. SPbSUCA, pp. 106–108 (2011)
15. Vassileva, S., Kovatcheva, E.: The innovative model for interactivity in Bulgarian museums. In: 10th Annual International Conference of Education, Research and Innovation (ICERI), pp. 5407–5412. CERI Proceedings (2017)
16. Maggio, A., Kuffer, J., Lazzari, M.: Advances and trends in bibliographic research: examples of new technological applications for the cataloging of the georeferenced library heritage. J. Librarianship Inf. Sci. 49(3), 299–312 (2017)
17. Frandsen, T.F., Tibyampansha, D., Ibrahim, G.R., von Isenburg, M.: Library training to promote electronic resource usage: a case study in information literacy assessment. Inf. Learn. Sci. 118(11–12), 618–628 (2017)
18. Mi, X.Y., Pollock, B.M.: Metadata schema to facilitate linked data for 3D digital models of cultural heritage collections: a university of South Florida libraries case study. Cataloging Classif. Q. 56(2–3), 273–286 (2018)

Extended Stepping Theories of Active Logic: Declarative Semantics

Michael Vinkov[1] and Igor Fominykh[2](✉)

[1] Bauman Moscow State Technical University, Moscow, Russia
vinkovmm@mail.ru
[2] Moscow Power Engineering Institute, Moscow, Russia
igborfomin@mail.ru

Abstract. Active Logic is a conceptual system with reasoning formalism that allows for correlation of their results with specific points in time and that has tolerance to inconsistencies. Currently, tolerance to inconsistencies (paraconsistency) in Active Logic systems is theoretically justified in the works of the authors of this paper and is attributed to the so-called formalisms of stepping theories, which integrate the principles of Active Logic and Logic Programming. More specifically, the argumentation semantics of so-called formalisms of stepping theories with two kinds of negation has been proved to be paraconsistent. This formalism has more expressive power than the other formalisms of stepping theories and to a greater extent satisfies the principles of Logic Programming. This case study proposes the declarative semantics for formalisms of stepping theories and represents its equivalency with respect to the argumentation semantics of this type of formalism. This, in turn, means that the proposed declarative semantics is also paraconsistent, and logical inconsistencies existing in these theories do not result in their destruction.

Keywords: Active Logic · Reasoning situated in time · Stepping theories · Declarative semantics · Paraconsistency

1 Introduction

It is known that Active Logic [1, 2] is a conceptual system that combines a number of formalisms (reasoning in time) that are not viewed as a static sequence of beliefs, but as a process that flows through time. The principles established in Active Logic systems are relevant to solving the tasks of operating complex objects under tight timing constraints. Such task solving is attributive for situations when the excess of the admissible amount of time allocated for their solution is fraught with catastrophic consequences. Furthermore, information coming in the process of solving such problems often proves to be contradictory and requires special processing techniques. Reasoning that fit the Active Logic concept has two important properties:

(1) Their results can be linked with the moments of time which a cognitive agent is able to perceive (temporal sensitivity);
(2) This reasoning is tolerant to inconsistencies that occur during reasoning (reasoning systems characterized by such feature are called paraconsistent).

© Springer Nature Switzerland AG 2019
S. O. Kuznetsov and A. I. Panov (Eds.): RCAI 2019, CCIS 1093, pp. 105–114, 2019.
https://doi.org/10.1007/978-3-030-30763-9_9

Although, assuming a temporal sensitivity in active logic systems was not associated with serious theoretical problems, until recently the attempts to create declarative paraconsistent semantics for such logic systems failed, as shown in the work of [2]. This state of things remains until in the case study of [3] paraconsistent argumentation semantics was introduced into one of stepping theory formalism variants that combines the principles of Active Logic and Logic Programming. Later, this result was scaled up with respect to another, more general variant of a stepping theory formalism of Active Logic, a stepping theory formalism with two kinds of negation (hereinafter, the formalism of extended stepping theories), [4] for which the paraconsistency of its argumentation semantics was shown [5].

As it is known, paraconsistent logic is a section of modern non-classical logic, in which the logical principle that allows to derive an arbitrary sentence from the logical contradiction, does not hold. In classical logic a theory called controversial when both a sentence and its negation can be proved. If an arbitrary proposal can be proved in this theory, the theory is called trivial. In conventional systems, the logics of the concept of triviality and inconsistency do not differ, i.e. there is a contradiction in theory leads to its triviality. Paraconsistent logic treats inconsistency differently than classical logic. The possibility to derive any proposition from contradictions is ruled out in it, thereby ceases to be a contradiction of the theory of the threat of destruction. However, this does not resolve the fundamental need to get rid of contradictions in the course of further development of the theory. This brings about another definition of paraconsistent logic, somewhat less general than the previous one: a logic is called paraconsistent if it can be the basis of contradictory, but not trivial theories.

The strict definition of paraconsistent logic is associated with the characteristic of relation of logical consequence. It can be called explosive if it satisfies the condition that for any formulas A and B, A and Non-A will be an arbitrary to formula B (symbolically: $\{A, \neg A\} \vdash B$).

This paper proposes a declarative semantics for a stepping theory formalism. Similarly to logical program formalisms, this type of semantics is implemented using sets of literals distinct from more complex structures like Kripke-style semantics. The study results show that the proposed declarative semantics to a certain extent is equivalent to the existing argumentative semantics of extended stepping theories, in view of this, the declarative semantics, like the latter, has the paraconsistency property of a logical system.

2 Extended Stepping Theories of Active Logic

A stepping theory formalism of Active Logic was first introduced in [6]. Let us take a pair $T = (R, Ck)$ as a *stepping theory*, where R is a finite set of the rules, Ck is a so-called clock of a stepping theory.

The rules look as follows:

$$N : a_1 \wedge a_2 \ldots \wedge a_m \Rightarrow b, \tag{1}$$

where N is a character string that indicates the name of the rule, b is a propositional literal, and $a_1 \ldots a_m$ are propositional literals or first-order logic literals of the form later (j) or $\neg$ later(j), where j is a natural number. The rules reflect the following principle: if the formula $a_1 \wedge a_2 \ldots \wedge a_m$ is feasible, then it is admissible to assume that the formula b is feasible. In this case, $-b$ means a literal that is a supplement to a complementary pair for the literal b. In the situations where it is convenient, the rule antecedents are viewed as sets of literals. Hence, the system of stepping theories can be considered as a variant of the Active Logic system, which is completely rule-based and satisfying the principle of Logic Programming, according to which the formula models are sets of literals rather than more complex structures like Kripke-style semantics.

The clock of a stepping theory represents a finite subsequence of the sequence of natural numbers. Members of this subsequence identify duration of successively performed deductive cycles determining a reasoning process in all systems of Active Logic (see, for example, the case study [7]. Here, to ensure the generality of derived results, for simplicity's sake we assume that $Ck = Ck^1 = (1, 2, 3, 4, \ldots)$. We'll use the symbol Ck^* to denote the set of all member of this sequence.

Further, for any stepping theory $T = (R, Ck)$ notation R [q] denotes the set of all rules whose consequent is q. The set of literals forming the antecedent of the rule r will be denoted by A (r). A consequent of the rule r is denoted by C (r). Let Lit_T be the set of all literals occurring in the rules of stepping theory T. *The belief set* of stepping theory $T = (R, >)$ is a set of the form $\{now (t)\} \cup L_T^t$, where *t* is a natural number representing a point in time on the clock or 0, $L_T^t \subset Lit_T$. Let us consider operator ϑ_T that transforms the belief sets into other belief sets in such a way that if B is a belief set such that now (t) $\in$ B, then now (t + 1) $\in \vartheta_T(B)$. The sufficient conditions under which the objective literals will belong to belief set $\vartheta_T(B)$ will be different for different stepping theories, (see, for example, the case study [8]. Below we will review these conditions as they apply to a system of extended stepping theories in the context of their argumentation semantics (see examples below).

Now let B be the belief set of theory T, such that literal now (t) $\in$ B. We take B *as a quasi-fixed point* of operator ϑ_T iff for any B_1, such that now $(t_1) \in B_1$, where $t_1 \geq t$, the sequence includes $B_1 \backslash \{now (t_1)\} = \vartheta_T (B_1) \backslash \{now (t_1 + 1)\} = B \backslash \{now (t)\}$. *The history* in stepping theory T is a finite sequence of belief sets $\boldsymbol{B}$. Therein $\boldsymbol{B}(i)$ is the i-th member in the history, $\boldsymbol{B}(0) = \{now (0)\}$, for any t $\boldsymbol{B}$ (t + 1) = $\vartheta_T(\boldsymbol{B}(t))$. The last element in the history is a belief set denoted by B_{fin}, *(final)*. It is the smallest quasi-fixed point of operator ϑ_T in the sense defined above. *An inference step* in stepping theory $T = (R, Ck)$ is any pair of the form $(\boldsymbol{B}(i), \boldsymbol{B}(i + 1))$, where *the inference step number* is the number equal to (i + 1). The consequent (t-*consequent*) of the stepping theory T is a literal belonging to belief set B_{fin} (a literal belonging to the belief set $\boldsymbol{B}(t)$, t $\in Ck^*$).

A formalism of an extended stepping theory of Active Logic was introduced in the work of (6). Compared to other stepping theories, the subjective negation operator not^t has been added to the alphabet of the rule language. The rules look as follows:

$$N : a_1 \wedge a_2 \ldots \wedge a_m \wedge not^t c_1 \wedge not^t c_2 \ldots \wedge not^t c_n \Rightarrow b, \qquad (2)$$

where N is a character string that indicates the name of the rule, b is a propositional literal, and, $a_1, a_2, \ldots, a_m$, are propositional literals or first-order logic literals of the form later (j) or ¬ later(j), where j is a natural number and c_1, c_2, ..., c_n are propositional literals. Propositional literals can be objective or subjective, it will be discussed below.

The rules of the extended stepping theory reflect the principle of negative introspection in the following interpretation: if the formula $a_1 \wedge a_2 \dots \wedge a_m$ is feasible and at this inference step it is not known, whether the formula $c_1 \wedge c_2 \dots \wedge c_n$ is feasible, then it is admissible to assume that the formula b is feasible. In this case, as it was said above, – b denotes a literal that is a supplement to the complementary pair for the (always objective) literal b. It is noteworthy that the rules of extended stepping theories in outward appearance are similar to R. Reiter's default theories with default logic options. The issue of correlation between the rules of extended stepping theories of Active Logic and extended logic programs under answer set semantics (which are known as specific variants of Reiter's default theories) is presented in the case study of [9].

One of the two kinds of negations in the extended stepping theories of the type under review will be called *subjective* negation and denoted as the not^t operator. While in logic programming the expression not q means that the attempt to infer the literal q using the given logical program failed, the expression not^{t}q in the antecedent of a rule of a stepping theory means that a reasoning agent has not managed to infer the literal q by the current point of time (=at the given inference step). Another kind of negation, used in this type of stepping theories, is denoted by the unary logical connection ¬, we shall henceforth call it a *strong negation* as this type of negation is called in Logic Programming.

Hereinafter, any propositional literal of type a_i, which is not preceded by the subjective negation operator not^t will be referred to as an objective literal. Any literal of type not^t c_j will be referred to as a subjective literal. In this regard it should be noted that any further reasoning will remain valid even when the first-order logic literals without functional symbols, i.e. with the finite Herbrand universe, are used instead of the propositional literals.

3   Argumentation Semantics for Extended Stepping Theories

The argumentation theory [10] proved to be quite fertile in presenting of nonmonotonic reasoning [11]. Argumentation semantics for formalisms of active logic stepping theories was suggested in some previous works [6, 7]. A variant of such kind of argumentation semantics with the consideration of specifics of extended stepping theories introduced by [5] will be given below.

Definition 1. We assume that T = (R, Ck) is an extended stepping theory. Let an argument for T be referred to as follows:

(1)   any literal 1 (of first order logic) of type later (t) or ¬later (t), where t > 0, and where there exists rule r ∈ R such that l ∈ A (r);

(2)   sequence of the rules Arg = $[r_1, r_2, ..., r_n]$, where $r_1, r_2, ..., r_n \in R$, so that for any $1 \geq i \geq n$, if $p \in A(r_i)$, where p is the objective propositional literal, then there might be such $j < i$ that $r_j \in R[p]$;
(3)   any subjective literal of type $not^t q$ is such that there exists rule $r \in R$ and $m \in A(r)$.

For this extended stepping theory $T = (R, Ck)$, *a set of all its arguments* is denoted by $Args_T$. If an argument is the first order logic literal of type later(t) ($\neg$later (t)), then we will call such argument as *limiting* (the function of other arguments after and before in time).

An argument of type Arg = $[r_1, ..., r_n]$ is called *supporting argument*. Propositional literal b is called *the conclusion* of supporting argument Arg = $[r_1, r_2, ..., r_n]$ iff $r_n \in R$ [b].

The argument of type $not^t q$ is called a *subjective argument*.

Any subsequence of $[r_1, r_2, ..., r_n]$ sequence, meeting the Definition 1 is called *a supporting subargument* of argument Arg = $[r_1, r_2, ..., r_n]$. A limiting or subjective argument is a *subargument* of the argument Arg = $[r_1, r_2, ..., r_n]$ if the corresponding first-order logic literal or a subjective literal is included in the antecedent of any of the rules $r_1, r_2, ..., r_n$.

Any supporting subargument of the argument Arg = $[r_1, r_2, ..., r_n]$ is called its maximum subargument, if a literal being a conclusive inference of this subargument is included in the antecedent of the rule r_n. A limiting or subjective argument is a maximum subargument of argument Arg = $[r_1, r_2, ..., r_n]$, if a corresponding literal is included in the antecedent of the rule r_n.

Example 1. Let R_1 set of the stepping theory $T1 = (R_1, Ck^1)$ consist of the following elements:

$$\{N1: \Rightarrow p,$$
$$N2: p \Rightarrow q,$$
$$N3: q \Rightarrow r,$$
$$N4: later (4) \land not^t r \Rightarrow \neg task\_is\_solved,$$
$$N5: \neg later (4) \land r \Rightarrow task\_is\_solved,$$
$$N6: task\_is\_solved \Rightarrow task\_is\_solved\}.$$

The supporting arguments of T_1 theory are Arg_1 = [N1, N2, N3, N5, N6] and all of its supporting subarguments, as well as Arg_2 = [N4]. The supporting subargument Arg_3 = [N1, N2, N3, N5] is the maximum supporting subargument of argument Arg_1. $Arg_4 = \neg$ later (4) and Arg_5 = later (4) are limiting arguments of T_1 theory (and corresponding subarguments of arguments Arg_1 and Arg_2). $Arg_6 = not^t r$ is a subjective subargument of argument Arg_2.

Going over to the definition of an argument status and a conflict between arguments of extended stepped theories, we should take into consideration that unlike other systems of argumentation, where the relationships of various arguments are studied "in statics", here, speaking informally, we have to discuss the development of these relationships over time, i.e. in inference steps of the stepped theory. On a certain step of inference, a specific argument may not have been yet constructed, i.e. is not in time to become active, and after putting into action an argument may be in action until the time

(=step of inference) of its withdrawal from action. The latter means that a specific argument (on a specific given step) is denied (=disposed of) due to the consequences of a conflict with other arguments. Thereby, the notion of "putting an argument into action" plays a key role in determining the status of arguments and a conflict between them. For the purpose of simplicity hereafter we will refer to the inference step numbered i as to simply step i.

Definition 2. Putting arguments of extended stepping theories in action is performed according to the following rules:

1. Any limiting argument of type later (t) R_1 of extended stepping theory $T_1 = <R_1$, $Ck^1>$ is put into action on step i, so that i = t. Any limiting argument of type $\neg$ later (t) is activated on step 1 (at time point 0).
2. If a supporting argument does not have any subarguments, then it will be activated on step 1.
3. Any supporting argument is activated on step i, if all of its subarguments are in action, have been put into action on the previous steps and there is its maximum subargument activated on step (i − 1).
4. Any subjective argument is put into action on step 1.

Definition 3. Withdrawal of limiting arguments from action is performed by the following rule:

Any limiting argument of type $\neg$ later(t) is withdrawn from action on step i, where i is such, that (i − 1) = t.

All other arguments, including limiting arguments of the type later(t) after they are put into action on subsequent steps of inference, have the status *active*.

The notion of arguments attacking each other, which is present in practically all argumentation systems, has its specific feature in Active Logic.

Definition 4 (attacking arguments)

1. Arg_1 supporting argument *attacks* the other supporting arguments with conclusion q or subjective argument $Arg_2 = not^t$ q on step i, iff the following conditions are simultaneously fulfilled:
   (1) the conclusion of Arg_1 is literal − q;
   (2) Arg_1 (like all of its subarguments) is active on step i;
   (3) none of the Arg_1 subarguments is attacked on step i by any other supporting or subjective arguments.
2. Subjective argument $Arg_1 = not^t$ q *attacks* subjective argument $Arg_2 = not^t$ −q on step i, iff it is not attacked on step i by any supporting argument with the conclusion q.

Any set of beliefs in the stepping theory, in addition to a meta-literal of type now (i), consists of objective literals. The definition given below establishes necessary and sufficient condition of attributing of an objective literal to a belief set in the extended stepping theory under argumentative semantics.

Definition 5. Let B (i) be a belief set of a certain extended stepping theory. The objective literal $q \in B$ (i) iff there is the supporting argument Arg_1 of a specific extended stepping theory, which conclusion is literal q, such that all its subarguments are valid on step i and it is put into action no later than on step i, whereby Arg_1 or any of its subjective subarguments are not attacked on step i by any other supporting or subjective arguments.

4   Declarative Semantics for Extended Stepping Theories of Active Logic

In what follows below, we present the semantics for extended stepping theories of Active Logic formulated in terms of literal sets in the conventional style of definition of Logic Program semantics.

Consider the extended stepping theory $T = <R, Ck^1>$, where Ck^1 is used to avoid cumbersome expressions, but without loss of generality.

Definition 6. We call literals of the form later (j), $\neg$ later (j) as limiting literals. We assume that they are *passive on step i* iff, respectively, $i > j$ and $j \geq i$.

Definition 7. A subjective literal of the form not^t q is *active on step i,* iff the following two cases occur simultaneously.

1. No rule $r \in R$ in action exists on step i (see definition below) such that C (r) = q;
2. No subjective literal not^t-q in the antecedents of the rules R exists, or there exists the rule $r' \in R$ in action on step i such that C (r') = $-$ q.

Definition 8. The rule $r \in R$ is *active on step 1* iff there are no objective literals in its antecedent, and all the subjective and restrictive literals in the antecedent are, respectively, active and passive literals.

Definition 9. The rule $r \in R$, C (r) = q *is in action on step i,* iff it is active on this step and no active rule $r' \in R$ exists on step I, such that C (r') = $-$ q.

Definition 10. The rule $r \in R$ is *active on step i* iff all subjective and limiting literals in its antecedent are, respectively, active and passive, and for any objective literal $p \in A$ (r) there is the rule $r' \in R$ that acts on step i and starting to act no later than step (i $-$ 1), such that C (r') = p.

Definition 11. Let us assume that the theory $T = <R, Ck^1>$ is an extended stepping theory, B (i) is its set of beliefs on step i, q is an objective literal. $q \in B$ (i) iff there is the rule $r \in R$ in action on step i and such that C(r) = q.

Example 2. Assume that the set R2 of the extended theory T2 = (R2, Ck^1) consists of the following rules:

$$\{N1: \Rightarrow a,$$
$$N2: a \Rightarrow b,$$
$$N3: b \Rightarrow c,$$
$$N4: later (2) \Rightarrow \neg b,$$
$$N5: c \Rightarrow b\}.$$

Consider step 3. The set of beliefs on step 3 will be $B(3) = \{now\ (3), a\}$. In this case, the rule N1 will be valid, and the rules N2 and N4 will be active on this step. Rules N3 and N5 will not be active by definition.

Example 3. Let the set R3 of the extended theory T3 = (R3, Ck^1) consist of the following rules:

$$\{N1: not^t a \Rightarrow b,$$
$$N2: not^t b \Rightarrow a\}.$$

A final set of beliefs of this extended theory looks as follows: $B(1) = B_{fin} = \{now\ (1)\}$. On its only step 1, this theory has no active rules.

Example 4. Let the set R4 of the extended theory T4 = (R4, Ck^1) consist of the following rule:

$$\{N1: not^t a \Rightarrow b\}.$$

The final set of beliefs of this extended theory is as follows: $B(1) = B_{fin} = \{now\ (1), b\}$. On its single step 1, this theory has active rule N1.

Theorem 1. Assume that T = <R, Ck^1> is an extended stepping theory, r ∈ R is one of its rules, C (r) = q. The rule r is active on step i (under the declarative semantics introduced in this section) iff there is a supporting argument for this stepping theory Arg_1, so that its conclusion is literal q, all its subarguments are active on step i, it has come into effect no later than on step (i), and neither Arg_1 nor any of its subarguments were attacked on step i by any other arguments of theory T.

The proof of the theorem is carried out in both directions using induction by inference step number.

This theorem establishes the equivalence of argumentation and declarative semantics in the sense that the history of any extended stepping theory will be the same, regardless of whether it fits the declarative or argumentation semantics.

5 Paraconsistentency of Declarative Semantics for Extended Stepping Theories of Active Logic

Paraconsistency issues were covered in detail in the case study of [5], here we only indicate that a rigorous definition of paraconsistent logical semantics is associated with a specific relationship of logical implication. It can be called excessive (explosive), if it satisfies the condition that for any of formulas A and B, a non-arbitrary formula B (symbolically: $\{A, \neg A\} \vdash B$) follows from A and not-A. Classical logic, intuitionistic logic, multivalued logic, and most other standard logics have excessive semantics. Logical semantics is called paraconsistent iff a corresponding relationship of logical implication is not excessive.

The following theorem is true.

Theorem 2. Declarative semantics of extended stepping theories is paraconsistent.

The proof immediately follows from Theorem 1 on equivalence of declarative and argumentative semantics based on the previously proved theorems [5] on the paraconsistency of the latter.

6 Conclusion

In this article we have proposed a declarative semantics for stepping theories of Active Logic and we have shown the equivalence of this semantics to the previously introduced argumentation semantics for the type of theories under review. The work proves that declarative semantics is paraconsistent. The stepping theories of this type can contain inconsistencies, but this does not result in their destruction.

Acknowledgment. This work was supported by Russian Foundation for Basic Research (projects 19-07-00439, 19-07-00-123, 17-07-00696, 18-07-00213, 18-51-00007, 18-29-03088, 17-07-01374).

References

1. Elgot-Drapkin, J.J., Perlis, D.: Reasoning situated in time I: basic concepts. J. Exp. Theor. Artif. Intell. **2**(1), 75–98 (1990)
2. Hovold, J.: On a semantics for active logic, MA thesis, Department of Computer Science, Lund University (2011)
3. Fominykh, I., Vinkov, M.: Paraconsistency of argumentation semantics for stepping theories of active logic. In: Abraham, A., Kovalev, S., Tarassov, V., Snášel, V. (eds.) Proceedings of the First International Scientific Conference "Intelligent Information Technologies for Industry" (IITI'16). AISC, vol. 450, pp. 171–180. Springer, Cham (2016). https://doi.org/10.1007/978-3-319-33609-1_15
4. Vinkov, M.M., Fominykh, I.B.: Stepping theories of active logic with two kinds of negation. Adv. Electr. Electron. Eng. **15**(1), 84–92 (2017). il.Web of Science

5. Vinkov, M., Fominykh, I.: Extended stepping theories of active logic: paraconsistent semantics. In: Kuznetsov, S.O., Osipov, G.S., Stefanuk, V.L. (eds.) RCAI 2018. CCIS, vol. 934, pp. 70–78. Springer, Cham (2018). https://doi.org/10.1007/978-3-030-00617-4_7
6. Vinkov, M.M.: Argumentation semantics for step theories of active logic. In: Proceedings of the Xth National Conference on Artificial Intelligence with International Participation, KAI-2006, vol. 1, pp. 64–72. Fizmatlit Publ., M. (2006). (in Russian)
7. Vinkov, M.M., Fominykh, I.B.: Modeling the behavior of an intelligent agent with an unexpected increase in the duration of its deductive cycle under hard time constraints. In: Proceedings of the XIVth National Conference on Artificial Intelligence with International Participation, KAI-2014, vol. 1, pp. 14–22. RIC «School», Kazan (2014). (in Russian)
8. Vinkov, M.M., Fominykh, I.B.: Argumentation semantics for step theories of active logic with time granulation. In: Artificial Intelligence and Decision Making, № 3, pp. 95–101. URSS, M. (2015). (in Russian)
9. Fominykh, I., Vinkov, M.: Step theories of active logic and extended logical programs. In: Abraham, A., Kovalev, S., Tarassov, V., Snasel, V., Vasileva, M., Sukhanov, A. (eds.) IITI 2017. AISC, vol. 679, pp. 192–201. Springer, Cham (2018). https://doi.org/10.1007/978-3-319-68321-8_20
10. Dung, P.M.: Negation as hypothesis: an abduction foundation for logic programming. In: Proceedings of the 8th International on Logic Programming. MIT Press, Paris (1991)
11. Vagin, V.N., Zagoryanskaya, A.A.: Argumentation in plausible reasoning. In: Proceedings of the IXth National Conference on Artificial Intelligence with International Participation, KAI-2000, pp. 28–34, vol. 1. Fizmatlit Publ., Moscow (2000). (in Russian)

Logical Classification of Partially Ordered Data

Elena V. Djukova[1(⊠)], Gleb O. Masliakov[2(⊠)],
and Petr A. Prokofyev[3(⊠)]

[1] Federal Research Center "Computer Science and Control,"
Russian Academy of Sciences, Moscow 119333, Russia
edjukova@mail.ru
[2] Moscow State University, Moscow 119899, Russia
gleb-mas@mail.ru
[3] Mechanical Engineering Research Institute, Russian Academy of Sciences,
Moscow 101000, Russia
p_prok@mail.ru

Abstract. Issues concerning intelligent data analysis occurring in machine learning are investigated. A scheme for synthesizing correct supervised classification procedures is proposed. These procedures are focused on specifying partial order relations on sets of feature values; they are based on a generalization of the classical concepts of logical classification. It is shown that learning a correct logical classifier requires solution of an intractable discrete problem to be solved. This is the dualization problem over products of partially ordered sets. The matrix formulation of this problem is given. The effectiveness of the proposed approach for solution of the supervised classification problem is illustrated on model and real-life data.

Keywords: Logical data analysis · Supervised classification ·
Monotone dualization · Dualization over products of partially ordered sets ·
Irreducible covering of a Boolean matrix ·
Ordered irredundant covering of integer matrix

1 Introduction

In classification problems, the training data is a set of examples of objects under examination where each object is represented by a numerical vector obtained by measuring or observing its parameters. The properties of objects to be measured or observed are called features. In a simple case, the examples are divided into two classes — the class of positive and the class of negative examples. In the general case, the number of classes may be greater than two. Given a description of an unknown object in terms of features, it is required to find out (recognize) the class it belongs to.

The main advantage of the logical approach to the classification (recognition) problem is the possibility to obtain a results without additional probabilistic

This study was partially supported by the Russian Foundation for Basic Research, project no. 19-01-00430-a.

S. O. Kuznetsov and A. I. Panov (Eds.): RCAI 2019, CCIS 1093, pp. 115–126, 2019.
https://doi.org/10.1007/978-3-030-30763-9_10

assumptions and using a small number of training objects (using a small number of precedents). The analysis of training data is reduced to finding certain dependences or elementary classifiers (which are subsets of feasible values of some features) that differentiate objects belonging to different classes. An object is classified judging by the presence or absence of such elementary classifiers in the object's description. Special attention is given to synthesizing correct algorithms, i.e., algorithms that unmistakably classify the training objects.

Models of correct logical classifiers based on finding "correct" elementary classifiers are most effective in the case of integer data with a small number of possible values, especially binary data. Examples are classification by the vote of tests or by the vote of representative sets or by the vote of class coverings. The first models of such classifiers were proposed in Baskakova et al. (1981) and Dmitriev et al. (1966), and their description using the concept of elementary classifier was first proposed in Djukova and Peskov (2002).

There are complicated problems where no sufficient number of informative correct elementary classifiers can be found. For example, such a situation occurs when the features can take a large number of possible values. Features that can take real values are often treated as integer valued features with a large number of possible values. A way to solve such problems is to use logical correctors. Here we mean correct recognition algorithms based on constructing correct sets of elementary classifiers from incorrect elementary classifiers (Djukova et al. 2017a) and (Djukova et al. 1996).

In Djukova et al. (2017a), a generic scheme for synthesizing correct logical classification procedures was proposed; within this scheme, classical models and logical correctors were described.

If the feature space is large, computationally complex (intractable) problems have to be solved. The central place among these problems belongs to the monotone dualization problem, i.e., the problem of constructing a reduced disjunctive normal form of a monotone Boolean function specified by a conjunctive normal form. The intractability of the monotone dualization problem has two aspects: exponential growth of the number of solutions as the problem size increases and the complexity of finding (enumerating) these solutions. The most efficient algorithms are algorithms with a polynomial delay. However, polynomial algorithms are known only for some special cases of monotone dualization (e.g., see Johnson et al. (1988), Eiter et al. (2008)).

Application problems cannot always be described within the classical statement of logical classification in which feature values are compared for equality. In many classification problems, each feature can take values from a partially ordered set. Previously, the questions of logical analysis of partially ordered data in classification were considered in the context of Formal Concept Analysis (see e.g., Ganter and Kuznetsov (2001), Kaytoue et al. (2015)) and in the context of classification using expert knowledge based on the algorithms of evaluation of monotone Boolean functions (see for example Korobkov (1965), Kozhevnikov and Larichev (1999), Sokolov (1982)).

In this paper, we propose a scheme for synthesizing correct logical classification algorithms under the condition that partial order relations are specified on the sets of values of integer-valued features. The basic concepts used in the logical analysis of integer data in the supervised classification problem are generalized, and conditions of the correctness of the basic logical classification procedures are obtained. It is found that the analysis of training samples with partial orders requires dualization over the product of finite partial orders; a simple special case of this problem is monotone dualization. We give a matrix formulation of the general dualization problem and show that this problem is reduced to enumerating special coverings of an integer matrix, which are called in this paper ordered irredundant coverings. The concept of the ordered irredundant covering of an integer matrix is a generalization of the well-known concept of irreducible covering of a Boolean matrix used in the matrix formulation of the monotone dualization problem. Using real-life data, we establish the dependence of the quality of logical classification on the choice of partial orders on the sets of feature values.

2 Logical Classification of Integer Data in the Classical Statement

Consider the supervised classification problem. Let M be a set of objects under examination; this set is divided into l classes $K_1, \ldots, K_l$. Let the objects in M be described by the features $x_1, \ldots, x_n$. Let us define the basic concepts used in designing the classical logical classification procedures. Assume that the set of values of each feature consists of integer numbers and this set is finite.

Let $H = \{x_{j_1}, \ldots, x_{j_r}\}$ be a set of r different features, and $\sigma = (\sigma_1, \ldots, \sigma_r)$, where σ_i is a possible value of the feature x_{j_i}, $i = 1, 2, \ldots, r$. The pair (σ, H) is called an elementary classifier (el.cl.) of rank r. The proximity of the object $S = (a_1, \ldots, a_n)$ in M to the el.cl. (σ, H) is determined by the quantity $B(\sigma, S, H)$, which is equal to 1 if $a_{j_t} = \sigma_t$ for $t = 1, 2, \ldots, r$ and is equal to 0, otherwise. If $B(\sigma, S, H) = 1$, then the object S is said to generate (contain) the el.cl. (σ, H). The el.cl. (σ, H) is correct for the class K ($K \in \{K_1, \ldots, K_l\}$) if no pair of training objects S' and S'' exists such that $S' \in K$, $S'' \notin K$, and $B(\sigma, S', H) = B(\sigma, S'', H) = 1$.

The classification algorithm A in the phase of learning constructs a set of correct el.cl. $C^A(K)$ for each class K. The classification of object S is based on computing the quantity $B(\sigma, S, H)$ for each el.cl. (σ, H); i.e., each element of the set $C^A(K)$ takes part in the voting procedure. As a result, an estimate of the membership of the object S in the class K is found. Let us consider the basic models.

In the general case, the elementary classifier (σ, H) can possess one of the following two properties with respect to the class K: (1) some training objects in K contain (σ, H); (2) none of the training objects in K contains (σ, H).

Every correct el.cl. of the first type is called a representative el.cl. for the class K. A representative el.cl. (σ, H) for the class K is said to be an irredundant representative el.cl. of the class K if any el.cl. (σ', H') such that $\sigma' = (\sigma_1, \ldots, \sigma_{t-1}, \sigma_{t+1}, \ldots, \sigma_r)$ and $H' = H \backslash \{x_{j_t}\}$ for $t \in \{1, 2, \ldots, r\}$ is not a representative el.cl. for K.

A set of features H is called a test if each precedent of each class K ($K \in \{K_1, \ldots, K_l\}$) contains a representative el.cl. for K of the form (σ, H). A test is called irredundant if its every proper subset is not a test.

The elementary classifier of the second type is called a covering of the class K. A covering (σ, H) of K is said to be an irredundant covering of K if any el.cl. (σ', H')

such that $\sigma' = (\sigma_1, \ldots, \sigma_{t-1}, \sigma_{t+1}, \ldots, \sigma_r)$ and $H' = H \backslash \{x_{j_t}\}$ for $t \in \{1, 2, \ldots, r\}$ is not a covering of K.

In simple modifications of classification algorithms based on construction of a set of representative el.cl., the estimate for the class K is computed by summing the values $P_{(\sigma, H)} B(\sigma, S, H)$, where $(\sigma, H) \in C^A(K)$ and $P_{(\sigma, H)}$ is the number of training objects in K containing (σ, H). In the classification algorithms based on construction of a set of class coverings, the estimate for the class K is computed by summing the values of $1 - B(\sigma, S, H)$ over $(\sigma, H) \in C^A(K)$.

Elementary classifiers of small rank are most informative. For this reason, in applications the rank of el.cl. is limited or only irredundant correct el.cl. are considered (and even not all of them). However, in problems where the features have a large number of possible values, almost all correct elementary classifiers have a large rank, and consequently all such classifiers have low informativity. Problems in which features have too large number of possible values are too complicated for the logical classifiers considered above; in this situation, as has been mentioned in the Introduction, the use of logical correctors is more effective.

3   Data Analysis Over Product of Partially Ordered Sets

In this section, we give the basic definitions of logical data analysis with partial order relations and formulate two key problems of this analysis: the problem of finding the maximal independent elements of the product of partial orders and the problem of finding the minimal independent elements of the product of partial orders.

Let $P = P_1 \times \ldots \times P_n$, where $P_1, \ldots, P_n$ are finite partially ordered sets. An element $y = (y_1, \ldots, y_n) \in P$ follows an element $x = (x_1, \ldots, x_n) \in P$ (x precedes y) if y_i follows x_i (x_i precedes y_i) for $i = 1, 2, \ldots, n$. We use the notation $x \preccurlyeq y$ to denote that $y \in P$ follows $x \in P$ (x precedes). The notation $x \prec y$ means that $x \preccurlyeq y$ and $y \neq x$. The elements $x, y \in P$ are called comparable if $x \preccurlyeq y$ or $y \preccurlyeq x$. Otherwise, x and y are said to be incomparable. The greatest element in P is the element x for which $y \preccurlyeq x$ for every $y \in P$.

Let $R \subseteq P$. We introduce the following notation: $R^+ = R \cup \{x \in P | \exists a \in R, a \prec x\}$ is the set of elements following the elements of R; $R^- = R \cup \{x \in P | \exists a \in R, x \prec a\}$ is the set of elements preceding the elements of R. The element x in $P \backslash R^+$ ($P \backslash R^-$) is called the maximal (minimal) element of P independent of R if, for any other element y in $P \backslash R^+$ ($P \backslash R^-$), the relation $x \prec y$ ($y \prec x$) does not hold.

Denote by $I(R^+)$ the set consisting of the maximal independent of R elements of the set P, and denote by $I(R^-)$ the set consisting of the minimal independent of R elements of P. For the given set R, we want to construct the sets $I(R^+)$ and $I(R^-)$. The sets $I(R^+)$ and $I(R^-)$ are dual of each other: if $Q = I(R^-)$ or $Q = I(R^+)$, then, respectively, $I(Q^+) = I(R^+)$ and $I(Q^-) = I(R^-)$. In what follows, each of these problems is called the dualization problem over the product of partial orders.

One of the most popular and well-studied case is the one in which the sets $P_1, \ldots, P_n$ are chains, i.e., any two elements in these sets are comparable. An antichain is a set in which any two elements are incomparable. The sets $I(R^+)$ and $I(R^-)$ are antichains.

The simplest case of dualization over the product of chains is monotone dualization. The problem is formulated as follows.

Let a conjunctive normal form realizing the monotone Boolean function $F(x_1, \ldots, x_n)$ be given. We want to construct a reduced disjunctive normal form of F. It is easy to verify that monotone dualization is equivalent to the problem of constructing the set $I(R^-)$ under the condition that P is the n-dimensional Boolean cube, $P_i = \{0, 1\}$ for $i = 1, 2, \ldots, n$, the order $0 \prec 1$ is defined in each P_i, and R is the set of zeros of the function F containing the set of upper zeros of F. The elements of $I(R^-)$ are lower units of the function.

The task of monotone dualization can be formulated in terms of hypergraphs (Murakami and Uno 2014) and in terms of matrices using the concept of irreducible covering of a Boolean matrix (Djukova and Prokofyev 2015).

Theoretical estimates of the effectiveness of dualization algorithms are based on evaluating the complexity of a single step, i.e. the complexity of finding a new solution. In the most efficient algorithm, the step complexity is polynomial in the input size. Algorithm of this kind is called a polynomial-delay algorithm. However, polynomial algorithms have been constructed only for some particular cases of monotone dualization, for example, for the case of 2-CNF (Johnson et al. 1988). Currently, there are two main areas of research.

The first direction aims to construct so-called incremental algorithms, when the algorithm is allowed to review the solutions obtained in previous steps. The complexity of the algorithm step is estimated for the worst case (for the most complex variant of the problem). In Fredman and Khachiyan (1996) an algorithm of monotone dualization that has step with quasi-polynomial complexity determined by the size of both its input and its output was proposed.

In Boros et al. (2002) for the case where each P_i, $i = 1, 2, \ldots, n$, is a chain and $|P_i| \geq 2$, a quasi-polynomial incremental algorithm based on the algorithm proposed in Fredman and Khachiyan (1996) was constructed. A similar result was obtained for some other special finite partial orders (semi-lattices of bounded width, lattices defined by a set of real closed intervals, forests (Elbassioni 2009)). For lattices given by sets of irreducibles the impossibility of constructing a polynomial incremental algorithm (if $P = NP$ does not hold) was proved in Babin and Kuznetsov (2017), and for the case of distributive lattices a subexponential incremental algorithm (output subexponential algorithm) is proposed. It should be noted that the incremental approach is mainly of theoretical interest because in the worst case the number of dualization solutions (the output size) increases exponentially with the increase of the input size.

The second direction is based on the construction of asymptotically optimal dualization algorithms (Djukova 1977; Djukova and Prokofyev 2015). In this case, the algorithm is allowed to execute additional steps with polynomial delay under condition that their number is almost always sufficiently small compared to the number of all solutions of the problem. This has resulted in the construction of algorithms for monotone dualization that are efficient in the typical case (efficient for almost all variants of the problem). These algorithms have a theoretical basis and are leaders w.r.t. the computational time.

In Djukova et al. (2017b) and Djukova et al. (2018), an asymptotically optimal algorithm RUNC-M+ for the dualization over the product of chains was constructed. The proof of the asymptotic optimality of RUNC-M+ is based on proving the asymptotic equality of two quantities—the typical number of steps of this algorithm and the typical number of solutions to the problem (the cardinality of $I(R^+)$). To this end, a matrix formulation of the problem of constructing $I(R^+)$ for the case of product of chains was given, and the technique of obtaining asymptotic estimates that were earlier used for proving the optimality of monotone dualization algorithms was elaborated. Below, we give a matrix formulation of the problem of constructing the maximal independent elements for the product of finite partial orders P based on a more general concept of ordered irredundant covering of a matrix the rows of which are sets from $R \subseteq P$ than the concept used in Djukova et al. (2018) for the case of chains.

Let us introduce the following notation. Let $Q_1(x, P)$ $(x \in P)$ be the set of all elements in P that immediately follow x ($Q_1(x, P) = \{y \in P : x \prec y, \forall a \in P : x \prec a \Rightarrow a \not\prec y\}$); $Q_2(x, y, P)$ $(x \in P, y \in Q_1(x, P))$ is the set of all elements a $\in$ P that do not precede x and precede y ($Q_2(x, y, P) = \{a \in P : a \not\preceq x, a \preceq y\}$).

We also define the ordered irredundant covering of the matrix L_R the rows of which are sets from $R \subseteq P$.

Let H be the set of columns of the matrix L_R with indexes $j_1, \ldots, j_r$ and $\sigma = (\sigma_1, \ldots, \sigma_r)$ where $\sigma_i \in P_{j_i}$ for $i = 1, 2, \ldots, r$. Then H is said to be an ordered irredundant σ-covering if the following two conditions are satisfied: (1) for every $i \in \{1, 2, \ldots, r\}$ and every $y \in Q_1(\sigma_i, P_{j_i})$, the submatrix L_R^H of L_R formed by columns of H contains each row of the form $(\beta_1, \ldots, \beta_{i-1}, \beta_i, \beta_{i+1}, \ldots, \beta_r)$ where $\beta_i \in Q_2(\sigma_i, y, P_{j_i})$ and $\beta_t \preceq \sigma_t$ for $t \neq i$, $t \in \{1, 2, \ldots, r\}$; (2) the submatrix L_R^H does not contain rows preceding σ.

Note that if P_i $(i \in \{1, 2, \ldots, n\})$ is a finite chain and $x \in P_i$ is not the greatest element in P_i, then the set $Q_1(x, P_i)$ consists of a single element, which is denoted by $x + 1$ below; therefore $Q_2(x, x + 1, P_i) = \{x + 1\}$. For this reason, in the case of the product of finite chains, condition (1) in the definition of the ordered irredundant σ-covering turns into the following condition: for every $i \in \{1, 2, \ldots, r\}$, the submatrix L_R^H of the matrix L_R formed by columns from H contains the row $(\beta_1, \ldots, \beta_{i-1}, \sigma_i + 1, \beta_{i+1}, \ldots, \beta_r)$ where $\beta_t \preceq \sigma_t$ for $t \neq i, t \in \{1, 2, \ldots, r\}$.

Consider the element $x = (x_1, \ldots, x_n) \in P$ in which the component $x_{j_i} = \sigma_i$ $(i \in \{1, 2, \ldots, r\})$ is not the greatest element in P_{j_i} and each of the other components x_j $(j \in \{1, 2, \ldots, n\} \setminus \{j_1, \ldots, j_r\})$ is the greatest element in P_j. Define $\sigma = (\sigma_1, \ldots, \sigma_r)$. We have the following result.

Theorem 1. *Element x is a maximal element independent of R if and only if the set of columns of the matrix L_R with the indexes $j_1, \ldots, j_r$ is an ordered irredundant σ-covering of L_R.*

Proof. The sufficiency is obvious. Let us prove the necessity.

Let x be maximal independent of R. Then condition (2) from the definition of an ordered irredundant covering follows from x independence. Let us show the validity of condition (1) from the same definition.

The component x_{j_i} of x is not the greatest element in P_{j_i} for every $i \in \{1, 2, \ldots, r\}$. Therefore $Q_1(\sigma_i, P_{j_i}) \neq \emptyset$ for every $i \in \{1, 2, \ldots, r\}$. Let $i \in \{1, 2, \ldots, r\}$ and $\sigma' \in Q_1(\sigma_i, P_{j_i})$. Consider the element $x' = (x'_1, \ldots, x'_n)$ which is obtained from x by replacing of equal to σ_i component x_{j_i} with the component x'_{j_i} equal to σ'_i. Since x is maximal independent of R, we have $x' \in R^+$. It follows, that element $x'' = (x''_1, \ldots, x''_n)$, $x'' \preccurlyeq x'$, exists in R. Let $x''_{j_t} = \beta_t$, $t \in \{1, 2, \ldots, r\}$. Then $\beta_t \preccurlyeq \sigma_t$, $\sigma'_t = \sigma_t$ for $t \neq i$ and $\beta_i \preccurlyeq \sigma'_i$, $\sigma'_i \in Q_1(\sigma_i, P_{j_i})$. Since relation $\beta_i \preccurlyeq \sigma_i$ contradicts the independence of x, we have $\beta_i \not\preccurlyeq \sigma_i$. It follows, that $\beta_i \in Q_2(\sigma_i, x_{j_i}, P_{j_i})$. Since σ_i and $\sigma'_i \in Q_1(\sigma_i, P_{j_i})$ could be arbitrary, we obtain condition (1) from the definition of an ordered irredundant covering. The necessity is proved.

By Theorem 1, the logical classification of data that are the product of finite partial orders is effectively reduced to finding ordered irredundant coverings of an integer matrix.

Remark 1. The concept of ordered irredundant σ-covering of the matrix L_R defined in this section is a generalization of the irreducible covering of a Boolean matrix. Indeed, if every $P_i = \{0, 1\}$ and the order $0 \prec 1$ is defined on P_i, then the ordered irredundant $(0, \ldots, 0)$-covering of L_R is an irreducible covering.

4 Logical Classification Over Product of Partially Ordered Sets

In this section, we propose a more general statement of the logical classification problem aimed at solving problems in which each feature takes values in a finite partially ordered set of numbers.

Let $M = N_1 \times \ldots \times N_n$ where N_i ($i \in \{1, 2, \ldots, n\}$) is a finite set of values of the feature x_i with a partial order defined on it. We assume that each set N_i, $i \in \{1, 2, \ldots, n\}$, has the greatest element k_i. If there is no such an element in N_i, then we complete N_i with such an element.

The proximity of the object $S = (a_1, \ldots, a_n)$ in M to the el.cl. (σ, H), where $H = \{x_{j_1}, \ldots, x_{j_r}\}$, $\sigma = (\sigma_1, \ldots, \sigma_r)$, and $\sigma_i \in N_{j_i}$ for $i = 1, 2, \ldots, r$, is the quantity $\hat{B}(\sigma, S, H)$ that is equal to 1 if $a_{j_i} \preccurlyeq \sigma_i$ for $i = 1, 2, \ldots, r$ and equal to 0, otherwise. The object S is said to generate the el.cl. (σ, H) if $\hat{B}(\sigma, S, H) = 1$.

The definitions of the correct el.cl. of class K, the representative el.cl. of class K, the covering of class K, and test are completely extended for the general case under considerations if $B(\sigma, S, H)$ is replaced by $\hat{B}(\sigma, S, H)$.

Let (σ, H) be an el.cl. in which $H = \{x_{j_1}, \ldots, x_{j_r}\}$, $\sigma = (\sigma_1, \ldots, \sigma_r)$, $\sigma_i \in N_{j_i}$ for $i = 1, 2, \ldots, r$. We assign to the el.cl. (σ, H) the set $S_{(\sigma, H)} = (\gamma_1, \ldots, \gamma_n)$ from $M = N_1 \times \ldots \times N_n$ in which $\gamma_t = \sigma_i$ for $t = j_i$ ($i = 1, 2, \ldots, r$) and $\gamma_t = k_t$ for $t \notin \{j_1, \ldots, j_r\}$.

A covering (σ, H) of the class K is said to be irredundant if every el.cl. (σ', H') such that $S_{(\sigma,H)} \prec S_{(\sigma',H')}$ is not a covering of class K. A representative el.cl. (σ, H) for the class K is said to be irredundant if every el.cl. (σ', H') such that $S_{(\sigma,H)} \prec S_{(\sigma',H')}$ is not representative for the class K.

By $R(K)$ we denote the set of training objects in the class.

Proposition 1. *The covering (σ, H) of the class K is an irredundant covering of K if and only if $S_{(\sigma,H)} \in I\big(R(K)^+\big)$.*

Let $\bar{K} = M \backslash K$. We will consider $\bar{K}$ as a separate class; i.e., we assume that there are only two classes K and $\bar{K}$. The following result is obvious.

Proposition 2. *The el.cl. (σ, H) is an irredundant representative el.cl. for the class K if and only if $S_{(\sigma,H)} \in I\big(R(\bar{K})^+\big)$ and $S_{(\sigma,H)} \in R(K)^+$.*

Propositions 1 and 2 imply that, in the case of partially ordered data, the construction of logical classifiers based on construction of a set of irredundant coverings of a class or a set of irredundant representative el.cl. for a class requires the construction of maximal independent elements of the product of partial orders.

Note that the existence of representative el.cl. for the class K is not guaranteed in the general case, and for a classification algorithm (based on construction of a set of representative el.cl.) to be correct, it is necessary that the descriptions of objects belonging to different classes are incomparable.

We show that, in the case of disjoint classes, there exists a transformation of the feature description of the set M as a result of which a nonempty set of irredundant representative el.cl. is formed for each class K and every object in K generates at least one el.cl. in this set.

Denote by $\tilde{P}$ the set coinciding the set P with the reversed order relation; i.e., $x \preceq y$ in P if and only if $y \preceq x$ in $\tilde{P}$.

Let $\tilde{M} = \tilde{N}_1 \times \ldots \times \tilde{N}_n$. Define the mapping $\varphi : M \to M \times \tilde{M}$ as follows. The mapping φ takes the object $S = (a_1, \ldots, a_n)$ in M to the object $\varphi(S) = (a_1, \ldots, a_n, a_{n+1}, \ldots, a_{2n})$ in $M \times \tilde{M}$ where $a_{i+n} = a_i$ for $i \in \{1, 2, \ldots, n\}$. In other words, the feature description of S is duplicated with the reversed order relation.

Let $\varphi(A)$ $(A \subset M)$ be the image of A under the mapping φ. We have the following theorem.

Theorem 2. *If the classes of the set M are disjoint, then every precedent of the class $\varphi(K)$ generates an irredundant representative el.cl. of the class $\varphi(K)$.*

Proof. Let $S \in R(K)$. We show that the element $\varphi(S)$ doesn't belong to $\varphi(R(\bar{K}))^+$ $(\varphi(S)$ is independent of $\varphi(R(\bar{K}))$ in $\varphi(M))$. Suppose $\varphi(S) \preceq \varphi(\bar{S}), \bar{S} \in \varphi(R(\bar{K}))$. By the definition of mapping φ, it follows that $S \preceq \bar{S}$ and $\bar{S} \preceq S$. Since $\preceq$ is antisymmetric, we have $S = \bar{S}$. This contradicts $R(\bar{K}) \cap R(K) = \emptyset$. By the finiteness of $M \times \tilde{M}$, it follows that maximal independent of $\varphi(R(\bar{K}))$ element $\varphi(S') \in M \times \tilde{M}$, $\varphi(S) \preceq \varphi(S')$, exists. This proves the theorem.

Remark 2. If each set $N_i (i \in \{1, 2, \ldots, n\})$ is an antichain with the added greatest element, then $R(K)^+ = R(K)$, $\hat{B}(\sigma, S, H) = B(\sigma, S, H)$, and therefore, we have in this case the classical statement considered in Sect. 1.

Figures 1 and 2 show illustrative examples that demonstrate the advantage of the more general statement of the logical classification problem. We consider two classification problems each of which has two classes and the system of features $\{x_1, x_2\}$. The training objects of the classes K_1 and K_2 are shown by crosses and circles, respectively. The set of possible values of each feature is the set of integers.

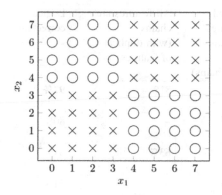

Fig. 1. Model example 1   **Fig. 2.** Model example 2

Consider the first example in Fig. 1. It is easy to verify that, for every value of feature x_1, the number of objects in each class for which x_1 takes this value, is four. The same is true for feature x_2. It is also easy to verify that in the classical case each el.cl. of rank 2 is correct either for the class K_1 or for K_2 and that it is generated by only one object in the training set. Therefore, every correct el.cl. of any of the two classes has low informativeness. Such an el.cl. is not generated by any of the objects not included in the training set. The situation in the second example (see Fig. 2) is similar. On the one hand, there are only two correct el.cl. of rank 1—these are the el.cl. $((0), \{x_1\})$ and $((0), \{x_2\})$; each of them is generated by only few objects of the class K_2. On the other hand, if we define the natural order $(\cdots \preccurlyeq 0 \preccurlyeq 1 \preccurlyeq \cdots)$ on the set of possible values of the features x_1 and x_2, then the decision rules for both examples become quite simple. Let $S = (a_1, a_2)$ be an object to be classified. Then, the decision rule for the first example is as follows: if $(a_1, a_2) \preccurlyeq (3, 3)$ or $(a_1, a_2) \succcurlyeq (4, 4)$, then $S \in K_1$; otherwise, $S \in K_2$. The decision rule for the second example is as follows: if $(a_1, a_2) \preccurlyeq (x, 7 - x)$ for at least one $x \in \{0, 1, \ldots, 7\}$, then $S \in K_2$; otherwise, $S \in K_1$.

5 Experiments with Real-Life Data

The quality of classifiers was experimentally compared for five data sets taken from www.kaggle.com and archive.ics.uci.edu. For testing, we used the triple cross validation procedure, and the quality was assessed by the fraction of correct classifications.

The results are presented in Table 1. The first column shows the name of the data set and its parameters (the number of objects m, the number of features n, the number of classes l, and the maximum number of values of feature k). Each of the following four columns corresponds to one variant of ordering the feature values in the algorithms in which the voters are irredundant representative el.cl. In addition, the classical logical corrector model developed in Djukova et al. (2017a) was used. This model uses a preliminary selection of informative el.cl. and boosting in learning.

Table 1. Experiment results

Data set name (m, n, l, k)	All features are antichains	All features are chains	Mixed features (chains and antichains)	All features are chains (with duplication of features)	Logical corrector
Car (1728, 4, 4, 4)	73%	70%	84%	81%	**97%**
Heart (302, 13, 2, 151)	76%	74%	**81%**	–	80%
Ph (427, 3, 15, 256)	43%	10%	51%	**63%**	31%
Dermatology (336, 34, 4, 75)	**95%**	82%	**95%**	–	51%
Turkey (129, 14, 6, 6)	35%	30%	35%	39%	**42%**

These results confirm that the classical approach (where each feature is an antichain) does not take into account the dependences in the values of attributes; for this reason, this approach tends to overfit. The linear order (chain) is very sensitive to the choice of linear order ($k!$ variants of chains for a feature with k admissible values are possible). The decision of which feature is a chain and which is an antichain is ambiguous. The practice showed that features with a large number of admissible values that have a natural linear ordering (e.g., age) are good candidates for the role of chains. The presence of several chains among antichains (the version of mixed features) in the majority of problems improved the quality and reduced the computation time. For the data sets Car, Ph, and Turkey, a heuristic with duplicating features in reversed order was also considered (see Theorem 2). It was shown that when all features are chains, duplication yields better results than in the version without duplication. For the data sets Heart, Ph, and Dermatology, which have a large number of feature values, the new algorithms demonstrated higher quality compared with logical corrector.

6 Conclusions

For the supervised classification problem (machine learning), the logical analysis of data represented by the product of partially ordered finite sets (product of partial orders) is studied for the first time. Based on a generalization of the basic concepts, the conventional approach to constructing logical classification procedures is improved. Results of testing the new classification algorithms on model and real-life data are presented. This study has an important scientific methodological significance and considerably extends the field of practical application of the methods of logical data analysis.

References

Baskakova, L.V., Zhuravlev, Yu.I.: A model of recognition algorithms with representative samples and systems of supporting sets. U.S.S.R. Comput. Math. Math. Phys. **21**(5), 189–199 (1981)

Dmitriev, A.N., Zhuravlev, Y., Krendelev, F.P.: On mathematical principles of objects or phenomena classification. Discrete Anal. (Diskretnyi analiz) **7**, 28–40 (1966). (in Russian). In-t matem. SO Akad. Nauk SSSR, Novosibirsk

Djukova, E.V.: On an asymptotically optimal algorithm for constricting irredundant tests. Dokl. Akad. Nauk SSSR **233**(4), 527–530 (1977)

Djukova, E.V., Zhuravlev, Y., Prokofyev, P.A.: Logical correctors in the problem of classification by precedents. Comput. Math. Math. Phys. **5**(11), 1866–1886 (2017a)

Djukova, E.V., Zhuravlev, Y., Rudakov, K.V.: On the logical algebraic synthesis of correct recognition procedures based on elementary algorithms. Comput. Math. Math. Phys. **36**(8), 1161–1167 (1996)

Djukova, E.V., Maslyakov, G.O., Prokofjev, P.A.: About product over partially ordered sets. J. Mach. Learn. Data Anal. **3**(4), 239–249 (2017b)

Djukova, E.V., Maslyakov, G.O., Prokofjev, P.A.: Dualization problem over the product of chains: asymptotic estimates for the number of solutions. Doklady Math. **98**(3), 564–567 (2018)

Djukova, E.V., Peskov, N.V.: Search for informative fragments in descriptions of objects in discrete recognition procedures. Comput. Math. Math. Phys. **42**(5), 711–723 (2002)

Djukova, E.V., Prokofyev, P.A.: Asymptotically optimal dualization algorithms. Comput. Math. Math. Phys. **55**(5), 891–905 (2015)

Babin, M.A., Kuznetsov, S.O.: Dualization in lattices given by ordered sets of irreducibles. Theor. Comput. Sci. **658**, 316–326 (2017)

Boros, E., Elbassioni, K., Gurvich, V., Khachiyan, L., Makino, K.: Dual-bounded generating problems: all minimal integer solutions for a monotone system of linear inequalities. SIAM J. Comput. **31**(5), 1624–1643 (2002)

Eiter, T., Makino, K., Gottlob, G.: Computational aspects of monotone dualization: a brief survey. Discrete Appl. Math. **156**(11), 2035–2049 (2008)

Elbassioni, K.M.: Algorithms for dualization over products of partially ordered sets. SIAM J. Discrete Math. **23**(1), 487–510 (2009)

Fredman, L., Khachiyan, L.: On the complexity of dualization of monotone disjunctive normal forms. J. Algorithms **21**, 618–628 (1996)

Johnson, D.S., Yannakakis, M., Papadimitriou, C.H.: On general all maximal independent sets. Inf. Process. Lett. **27**(3), 119–123 (1988)

Ganter, B., Kuznetsov, S.O.: Pattern structures and their projections. In: Delugach, H.S., Stumme, G. (eds.) ICCS-ConceptStruct 2001. LNCS (LNAI), vol. 2120, pp. 129–142. Springer, Heidelberg (2001). https://doi.org/10.1007/3-540-44583-8_10

Kaytoue, M., Codocedo, V., Buzmakov, A., Baixeries, J., Kuznetsov, S.O., Napoli, A.: Pattern structures and concept lattices for data mining and knowledge processing. In: Bifet, A., et al. (eds.) ECML PKDD 2015. LNCS (LNAI), vol. 9286, pp. 227–231. Springer, Cham (2015). https://doi.org/10.1007/978-3-319-23461-8_19

Korobkov, V.K.: O monotonnyh funkciyah algebry logiki. V sb. "Problemy kibernetiki", **13**, 5–28 (1965). Nauka

Kozhevnikov, D.L., Larichev, O.I.: Comparison of algorithms for decoding monotone functions by the statistical simulation method. Comput. Math. Math. Phys. **39**(8), 1356–1362 (1999)

Murakami, K., Uno, T.: Efficient algorithms for dualizing large-scale hypergraphs. Discrete Appl. Math. **170**, 83–94 (2014)

Sokolov, N.A.: On the optimal evaluation of monotonic Boolean functions. Comput. Math. Math. Phys. **22**(2), 449–461 (1982)

Natural Language Processing and Understanding of Texts

Ontology-Driven Processing
of Unstructured Text

Olga Nevzorova[1,2](✉) [iD] and Vladimir Nevzorov[3] [iD]

[1] Tatarstan Academy of Sciences, Bauman Street, 20, Kazan 420111, Russia
`onevzoro@gmail.com`
[2] Kazan Federal University, Kremlevskaja Street, 18, Kazan 420008, Russia
[3] Kazan National Research Technical University n.a. A.N. Tupolev,
K. Marks Street, 10, Kazan 420111, Russia
`nevzorovvn@gmail.com`

Abstract. A lot of projects on ontologies focus on describing some aspect of reality: objects, relations, states of affairs, events, and processes in the world. Another approach is using ontologies for problem-solving. In this paper we discuss an approach for designing NLP tasks based on a multilevel system of ontological models. We developed a system of ontological models which is used for ontology-driven computational processing of unstructured texts. The components of the system are the ontology of task designing, the ontology of applied models, and the domain ontology. We discuss the general schema of designing solutions of applied tasks and some applications.

Keywords: Ontology of task designing · Ontology of applied models · Domain ontology · Natural Language Processing

1 Introduction

At the present time there exist various widely used frameworks for Natural Language Processing (Core NLP Suite, Natural Language Toolkit, Apache OpenNLP, GATE and Apache UIMA, etc.). To give a brief overview, Stanford CoreNLP [1] provides tools for natural language analysis; it can give word lemmas and their parts of speech, normalize dates, times, and numeric quantities, mark up the structure of sentences in terms of phrases and word dependencies, indicate which noun phrases refer to the same entities, indicate sentiment, extract particular or open-class relations between entity mentions, etc. Natural Language Toolkit [2] (NLTK) is a leading platform for building Python programs to work with language data. It provides easy-to-use interfaces to over 50 corpora and lexical resources such as WordNet, along with a suite of text processing libraries for classification, tokenization, stemming, tagging, parsing, and semantic reasoning, and wrappers for industrial-strength NLP libraries. Apache OpenNLP [3] library is a machine learning toolkit for processing natural language texts. GATE framework [4] comprises a core library and a set of reusable Language Engineering modules. The framework implements the architecture and provides facilities for processing and visualizing resources, including representation, import and export of data.

© Springer Nature Switzerland AG 2019
S. O. Kuznetsov and A. I. Panov (Eds.): RCAI 2019, CCIS 1093, pp. 129–142, 2019.
https://doi.org/10.1007/978-3-030-30763-9_11

Unstructured Information Management applications (UIMA) [5] are software systems that analyze large volumes of unstructured information in order to discover knowledge that is relevant to an end user. For example, UIMA application might ingest plain text and identify entities, such as persons, places, organizations; or relations, such as works-for or located-at. UIMA enables applications to be decomposed into components. Each component implements interfaces defined by the framework and provides self-describing metadata via XML descriptor files. The framework manages these components and the data flow between them. UIMA additionally provides capabilities to wrap components as network services.

For the Russian language, general classes of computational linguistic tools have been developed, including those based on semantic technologies. Let us mention some of the systems. OntosMiner system [6] uses semantic ontologies to analyze natural language text. The outcome is a set of searchable and conceptually structured data which can be categorized, browsed, and visually presented in semantic networks. Tamita parser [7] is a linguistic tool for extracting structured data (facts) from texts. The extraction of facts is based on context-free grammars and dictionaries of keywords.

Compreno technology [8] is a universal linguistic platform for applications that solve a variety of applied tasks for NLP. In Compreno project, the ultimate goal is to achieve the syntactic and semantic disambiguation. Semantic and syntactic representations are viewed as two facets of the same structure. Another (interrelated) feature of Compreno parsing technology is that syntactic and semantic disambiguation run parallel to each other from the very start (in contrast to the architecture that is more usual for the NLP systems when the semantic analysis follows the syntactic one).

However, a lot of NLP systems are commercial and do not provide an enough explicit clarification of the details of the main processes. To give a better insight into the issue, this article discusses a framework named "OntoIntegrator" system which is developed for ontology-driven computational processing for NLP [9].

This system is based on the linguistic ontology approach which integrates conceptual and technological solutions for NLP based on a system of ontological models. On the one hand, the system of ontological models structures semantic space, and on the other hand, it controls problem-solving methods. The tools developed in the OntoIntegrator system are focused on text processing in Russian and include a number of specialized databases built on the basis of the Russian national corpus [10].

We use ontologies as a means of linking the domain analysis and an applied system. Our basic approach is to consider ontology as a framework for specifying models in a particular problem domain, i.e., a meta-model that provides a vocabulary for formulating application models in this problem domain. On this basis, concepts in the ontology can be explicitly linked to software component capability descriptions, enabling the ontology to serve both as a mechanism for indexing and retrieving relevant software components and as a specification of overall configuration requirements.

More generally, the association of component capabilities with concept definitions in the ontology promotes a direct configuration of executable systems from specification of an abstract domain model.

To adjust our approach to NLP tasks we have developed a new conceptual model of a multilevel system of ontological models. This system allows one to build and use problem-solving methods for NLP tasks based on specialized ontologies. We have designed a system of ontological models which includes three ontologies: the ontology of task designing, the ontology of applied models and the domain ontology.

2 Related Work

In recent years, software reusability has become a key to reducing the time and cost of construction and maintenance of applied software. Ontologies may be used to help achieve that goal. We shall give a brief analysis of the approaches that are focused on developing systems with ontologies for problem solving.

Happel and Seedorf [11] suggested concrete approaches for using ontologies in all software engineering phases: analysis and design (requirements specification and component reuse), implementation (software modeling, domain object model, coding support and documentation), deployment and runtime (semantic middleware and Web services), and maintenance (project support, updating and testing).

In [12] the major elements of a first-level ontology of a generic instance of problem solver are discussed. They are as follows:

1. A problem-solving goal;
2. Domain data describing the problem-instance;
3. Problem-solving state;
4. Problem-solving knowledge (PSK);
5. Domain factual knowledge (DFK).

Design systems have goals of synthesizing object configurations that will behave as intended. In our approach, the problem-solving goal corresponds to the target task.

A problem instance is described in terms of domain factual ontology. In design, it is a set of constraints and specifications. Second-level ontology for problem instance data parallels that of the goal. Data for design goals are specifications, constraints, and functions; for prediction goals, they are initial conditions, and actions, and so on. The problem-solver creates and changes a number of internal objects during the process of problem solving. A problem state is a set of values of state variables representing these internal objects. Problem state includes information about current goals and subgoals. It would also include all knowledge inferred during problem solving: e.g., elements of candidate solutions, their plausibility values, rejected solutions and reasons for them.

The basic unit of problem solving knowledge (PSK) is a mapping of the following form:

- conditions on the problem state (including goals);
- conditions on domain knowledge;
- conditions on data describing the problem instance;
- changes to problem state (including goal components).

The ontology for domain knowledge is determined by the needs of the goal and the problem-solving knowledge. A problem solving method is an organized package of PSK units, indexed by the problem solving goal to which it is applicable.

We would like to mention some ontology projects for problem solving tasks. First, the OZONE ontology [13] provides a generic perspective for building scheduling systems.

The central component of OZONE is its scheduling ontology which defines a reusable and extensible base of concepts for describing and representing scheduling problems, domains and constraints.

The CommonKADS [14] ontology also provides modeling behaviour for scheduling tasks.

The paper [15] describes an ontology-based software architecture for the support of knowledge reuse in the aviation domain. The central part of the system architecture relies on three ontologies: Documentation Ontology, Model Ontology, Design Ontology. These ontologies have been developed independently of one another and they make different ontological commitments in order to meet the representational and computational requirements of the software components that rely on them.

An important trend is the use of ontologies for crisis management. The paper [16] presents the important results, including the identified domains involved in crisis management, the applied ontologies, a detailed analysis on the design and usability of the ontologies.

In this paper we discuss a framework for problem solving NLP tasks. Our approach may be categorized as ontology-driven development of software. While developing we use ontologies to describe the problem to be solved and the problem domain.

Our technology focuses on developing a multilevel system of ontological models used for designing and implementing NLP tasks. It includes all basic units of problem solving knowledge and is implemented in OntoIntegrator system developed by the authors of this paper.

The rest of the paper is organized as follows. Section 3 presents basic structure of OntoIntegrator system that is used for designing and implementing NLP tasks. Section 4 describes the general schema of designing solutions of applied tasks. Section 5 presents basic components of the developed ontological models. The task of building mathematical text annotations in the mathematical texts based on the proposed approach is considered in Sect. 6. Then we discuss the conclusions and outline the prospects of future work.

3   Basic Structure of OntoIntegrator System

The OntoIntegrator system is used for designing and implementing NLP tasks but its current version only supports processing Russian texts. We will discuss basic ideas of the proposed approach and give some examples of using our technologies for solving various applied linguistic tasks.

The OntoIntegrator system consists of the following functional subsystems (see Fig. 1):

- Integrator System;
- OntoEditor+ System;
- Text Analyzer System;
- Linguistic Resource Manager;
- Ontology System Manager.

The OntoEditor+ System provides basic functions which are necessary in processing ontologies (adding, changing, and deleting records; automatically checking the

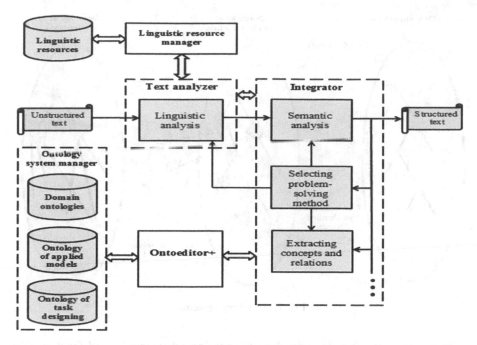

Fig. 1. OntoIntegrator high-level architecture.

record; merging ontologies; importing ontology; getting ontology statistics; searching chains of relations). The system supports different graphic modes of ontology visualization.

The Text Analyzer system includes basic linguistic tools developed by authors, which are used in a morphological and syntactic analysis, ontological annotating, ambiguity resolution, segmenting and text mining in various applications. Linguistic Resource Manager supports basic linguistic resources including annotated grammatical vocabularies and various specialized databases. The Integrator System provides an integration basis for solving applied linguistic problems and manages the construction of applied solutions.

While solving an applied linguistic problem the system of ontological models is used. Ontology System Manager supports the ontology system that includes three types of ontologies: the domain ontology, the ontology of applied models, and the ontology of task designing (see Fig. 2).

Each of the ontologies is formally described by a set of concepts and a set of relations. For the ontology of task designing we defined a set of concepts-tasks and specific relations between the concepts-tasks. For the ontology of applied models we defined a set of concepts-models and also specific relations between them. The domain ontology includes a set of concepts from the domain and relations between them.

The corresponding components of the ontological system are linked as shown in Fig. 2.

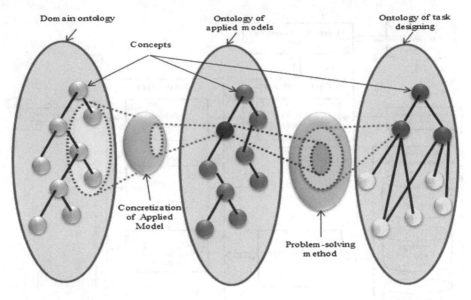

Fig. 2. Ontology system.

In the next section we describe how the ontological system is used for designing solutions of applied tasks.

4   General Schema of Designing Solutions of Applied Tasks

In Fig. 3 we present the general schema of designing solutions of applied tasks. Building a new solution of an applied task is implemented in 3 stages. On the first stage we create a new concept-task using the ontology of task designing and decomposing the concept-task into a graph-based solution to define the structure of the solution of the new task.

As a result we form the graph-based solution using the concepts of the ontology of task designing. Decomposing the new concept-task is implemented interactively by a special program tool named "Task Constructor" module. The graph model of the abstract solution is shown in Fig. 4. For building an abstract solution we use different classes of concepts of the ontology of task designing, and determine the computational schema.

Second, we create a new concept model (or apply the existing one) using the ontology of applied models and decompose the concept model into a graph model. The concept model is also built in an interactive mode. An example of the "Term" concept-model is presented in Fig. 9. Then it is necessary to embed the developed concept model into the developed concept task. Thus we construct a method of problem solving.

Third, the components of the ontology of applied models are mapped into the components of the domain ontology; thus we customize the concept model for the

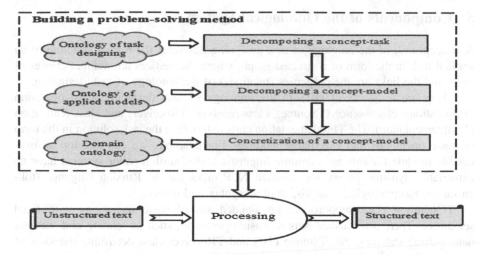

Fig. 3. General schema of designing solutions of applied tasks.

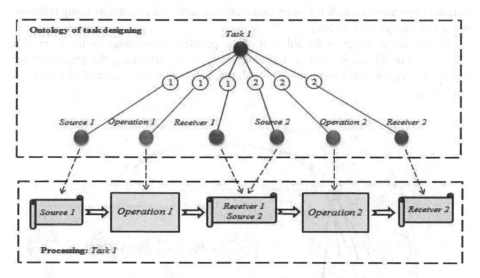

Fig. 4. A graph model of an abstract solution.

domain. At this stage we determine the specification of the developed relations or properties (as the models) and/or the specification of computational models.

At the final step we apply the developed method to the unstructured input text and extract the objects which satisfy the model requirements.

5 Components of the Ontological System

A concept task of the ontology of task designing describes the formal structure of an applied task in the form of a directed graph, where the vertices are definite classes of tasks and the links are the properties (relations) of the ontology of task designing.

There are 4 classes of tasks in the ontology of task designing: class-operation (TOperation), class-source (TSource), class-receiver (TReceiver) and class-realization (TImplementation). The TImplementation class determines the task solution in the form of basic operations and executable modules. For example, we can develop an executable module for solving a definite linguistic task. OntoIntegrator systems have an extendable dynamic library for standard NLP tasks for the Russian language (tokenization, morphological analysis, shallow syntax and others).

TOperation class supports an open-ended set of basic operations with fixed semantics. There are standard sets of basic operations, such as loading and viewing data, getting statistics, etc. TSource class and TReceiver class determine the tools of data transformation.

Creating an object of class TImplementation is based on a special mechanism for assigning operations, which forms an executable sequence of operations using relations of the task designing ontology.

The logical structure of the solution of the problem is presented in the form of a graph (see Fig. 5) and is generated automatically after performing the procedure for assigning a sequence of operations. This solution is saved in the system library and can be reused.

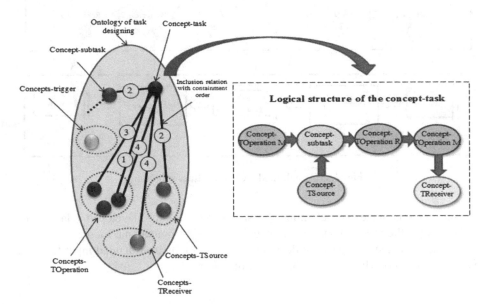

Fig. 5. Logical structure of a concept-task.

In Fig. 5 we present a general scheme of assigning operations used in the process of building a new concept-task. We have developed a special method of assigning a sequence number to each element of the created graph-based solution.

There are 4 classes of applied models in the ontology of applied models: property (a unary predicate), relation (an n-ary predicate), reference (a reference type), and m-implementation (a library module).

A proper hierarchy can be constructed for each class of this ontology (e.g., a hierarchy of properties, a hierarchy of relations, a hierarchy of m-implementations). Development and usage of hierarchies depend on the type of the problem being solved. Actually, the ontology of applied models represents a system of hierarchies of concepts (properties, relations) and hierarchies of computational models (classes of implementations). Some elements from hierarchies of concepts can be related to the classes (methods) of hierarchies of computational models.

A concept model is generated in two steps. First, one needs to define the model type using a special method of model specification, then a model is constructed to solve the concrete task. The implementation model (a library model) might be constructed using the method of aggregation of objects.

In Fig. 6 we demonstrate a simple example of building a solution of a standard simple task of statistical analysis of grammatical homonyms in a Russian text. For this task, it is not required to involve the ontology of applied models and applied ontology. The solution is built on a set of standard basic operators.

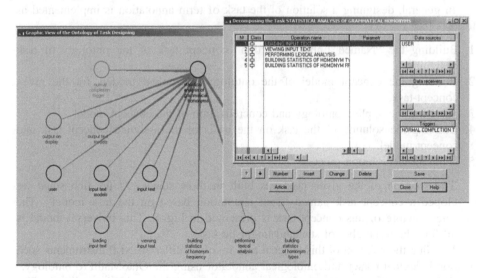

Fig. 6. Building the solution of the task of statistical analysis of grammatical homonyms in a Russian text.

First, we created a new concept task by the name of "Grammatical homonyms in Russian text" and performed the decomposing this concept task. We defined a set of subtasks needed to solve this problem and represented the solution in the form of a directed graph.

This concept task includes the following sequence of subtasks:

- K1: TOperation // Loading input text
- K2: TOperation // Viewing input text
- K3: TOperation // Performing lexical analysis
- K4: TOperation // Building statistics of homonym types
- K5: TOperation // Building statistics of homonym frequency

Building the solution of this problem can be fulfilled in graphical and text modes. The graph of the task determines the sequence of operations (with input and output data and special flags (conditions) for implementation). The same sequence of operations can be given in the tabular mode.

To evaluate the strength of our approach we have tested it on different NLP tasks. We have implemented standard linguistic tasks (tokenization, morphological analysis), shallow parsing (extracting groups of words such as NP (noun phrases), VP (verb phrases), PP (preposition phrases)) for the Russian language. We have obtained new results of extracting multiword NP in mathematical texts [17].

6 Terminology Annotation Case

As an example, consider a solution of a well-known problem of generating mathematical text annotations. For this case we also used OntoMathPro ontology [17].

In general, designing a solution of the task of term annotation is implemented as follows (see Fig. 7).

1. Building the "Named Entity extraction" concept task of the ontology of task designing.
2. Building the concept model of the ontology of applied models for the given concept-task.
3. Selecting the applied ontology and concretization of the concept model.
4. Building the solution of the task on the basis of the assigned concept task and concept model.
5. Running the solution process.

The solution of the given task was built in three stages. At the first stage we developed a concept task named "Text annotation based on the task model". The graphic structure of this concept task is presented in Fig. 8. This universal model is useful for a large number of standard linguistic tasks.

Building the solution of this concept task involves different NLP instruments such as morphological parser and ontological annotator using the OntoMathPro ontology.

This stage results in a set of text strings that satisfy specified conditions. The algorithm finds elements of this set which are recognized as the task model. These elements are marked with appropriate text tags.

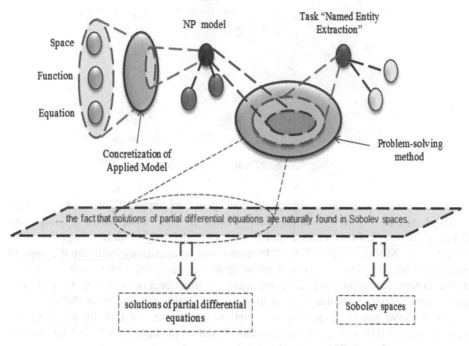

Fig. 7. The "Named Entity extraction" task.

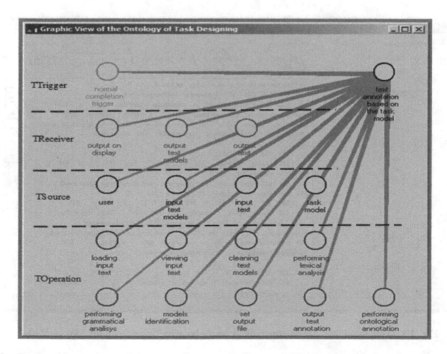

Fig. 8. Graphic structure of the general concept-task named "Text annotation based on the task model".

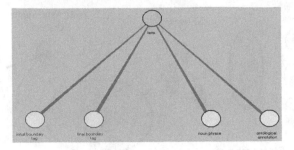

Fig. 9. The "Term" concept-model.

At the second stage we designed the concept-model named "Term" which is represented in Fig. 9. This concept-model includes an NLP component, a component defining the applicability criteria and components defining boundary tags for noun phrases. The NLP component is used for extracting noun phrases including the applied ontology concepts. The component defining the applicability criteria allows one to define criteria for recognizing all components of this concept-model in the text. The component defining boundary tags is used for annotating noun phrases (NPs).

At the third stage we developed a method of solving the task by selecting the general concept task named "Text annotation based on the task model" and the concept model named "Term". This method is implemented for text processing.

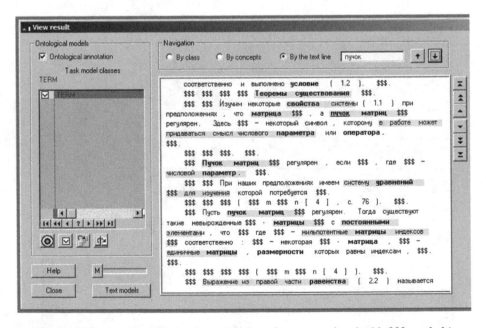

Fig. 10. Annotated text file (mathematical formulas were replaced with $$$ symbols).

The result of text processing is an annotated xml file. The developed method was implemented for a Russian mathematical text collection which consists of papers in XML format. The terminological noun phrases were annotated with tags TERM1 (NP), TERM2 (NP with formula), TERM3 (PP) and TERM4 (PP with formula). The result of term annotation is shown in Fig. 10 (here the result is represented in the OntoIntegrator system). Colored text strings are the extracted terminological NPs.

7 Conclusion

The proposed approach for building solutions of applied tasks can be presented as a knowledge discovery tool in various domains. The given ontological framework provides main facilities that are needed to solve NLP tasks. The system can help the user in designing NLP tasks and in selecting effective methods from its own dynamic library. The demo version of OntoIntegrator system is available upon request.

In future we are planning to use our approach as a major building block for designing new applications of NLP methods in various domains, especially for semantic representation of mathematical knowledge in mathematical texts.

Acknowledgments. This work was funded by the subsidy allocated to Kazan Federal University for the state assignment in the sphere of scientific activities, grant agreement no. 1.2368.2017.

References

1. Manning, C.D., Surdeanu, M., Bauer, J., Finkel, J., Bethard, S.J., McClosky, D.: The stanford CoreNLP natural language processing toolkit. In: Proceedings of the 52nd Annual Meeting of the Association for Computational Linguistics: System Demonstrations, pp. 55–60 (2014)
2. Natural Language Toolkit. http://www.nltk.org/. Accessed 04 Oct 2019
3. Apache OpenNLP. http://opennlp.apache.org/. Accessed 04 Oct 2019
4. Cunningham, H., Tablan, V., Roberts, A., Bontcheva, K.: Getting more out of biomedical documents with GATE's full lifecycle open source text analytics. PLoS Comput. Biol. 9(2), e1002854 (2013)
5. Ferrucci, D., et al.: Unstructured information management architecture (UIMA) version 1.0. OASIS Standard, March 2009
6. Khoroshevsky, V.F.: Ontology driven multilingual information extraction and intelligent analytics. In: Proceedings of NATO Advanced Research Workshop on Web Intelligence and Security, Ein-Bokek, Israel, 18–20 November 2009
7. Tamita parser. https://tech.yandex.ru/tomita/doc/tutorial/concept/about-docpage/. Accessed 04 Oct 2019
8. Anisimovich, K.V., Druzhkin, K.J., Minlos, F.R., Petrova, M.A., Selegey, V.P., Zuev, K.A.: Syntactic and semantic parser based on ABBYY Compreno linguistic technologies. In: Computational Linguistics and Intellectual Technologies Papers from the Annual International Conference "Dialogue", Issue 11, Volume 2 of 2. Papers from special sessions, pp. 91–103 (2012)

9. Nevzorova, O., Nevzorov, V.: Terminological annotation of the document in a retrieval context on the basis of technologies of system "OntoIntegrator". Int. J. Inf. Technol. Knowl. **5**(2), 110–118 (2011)

10. Russian National Corpus. http://ruscorpora.ru. Accessed 04 Oct 2019

11. Happel, H., Seedorf, S.: Applications of ontologies in software engineering. In: Proceedings of the 2nd International Workshop on Semantic Web Enabled Software Engineering, (ESE 2006), pp. 1–14 (2006)

12. Chandrasekaran, B., Josephson, J.R., Richard Benjamins, V.: Ontology of tasks and methods. AAAI Technical report SS-97-06. http://web.cse.ohio-state.edu/~chandrasekaran. 1/Ontology-of-Tasks-Methods.PDF. Accessed 04 Oct 2019

13. Smith, S.F., Becker, M.A.: An ontology for constructing scheduling, systems. In: Proceedings of AAAI-1997, Spring Symposium on Ontological Engineering (1997)

14. Breuker, J., Van de Velde, W.: CommonKADS Library for Expert Modelling. IOS Press, Amsterdam (1994)

15. Lehmann, J., Shamiyeh, M., Ziemer, S.: Towards integration and coverage assessment of ontologies for knowledge reuse in the aviation sector. In: Joint Proceedings of SEMANTiCS 2017 Workshops Co-located with the 13th International Conference on Semantic Systems (SEMANTiCS 2017) Amsterdam, Netherlands (2017). CEUR Workshop Proceedings (CEUR-WS.org), vol. 2063. http://ceur-ws.org/Vol-2063/lidari-paper3.pdf. Accessed 04 Oct 2019

16. Liu, S., Brewster, C., Shaw, D.: Ontologies for crisis management: a review of state of the art in ontology design and usability. In: Comes, T., Fiedrich, F., Fortier, S., Geldermann, J., Müller, T. (eds.) Proceedings of the 10th International ISCRAM Conference – Baden-Baden, Germany, May 2013, pp. 349–358 (2013)

17. Nevzorova, O., et al.: Bringing math to LOD: a semantic publishing platform prototype for scientific collections in mathematics. In: Alani, H., et al. (eds.) ISWC 2013. LNCS, vol. 8218, pp. 379–394. Springer, Heidelberg (2013). https://doi.org/10.1007/978-3-642-41335-3_24

Towards Automated Identification of Technological Trajectories

Sergey S. Volkov[1(✉)], Dmitry A. Devyatkin[2(✉)],
Ilia V. Sochenkov[2,5], Ilya A. Tikhomirov[3], and Natalia V. Toganova[4]

[1] Peoples' Friendship University of Russia, Moscow, Russia
volksergl@gmail.com
[2] Federal Research Center "Computer Science and Control" of Russian
Academy of Sciences, Moscow, Russia
devyatkin@isa.ru
[3] Ministry of Science and Higher Education of the Russian Federation,
Moscow, Russia
[4] Institute of World Economy and International Relations of Russian Academy
of Sciences, Moscow, Russia
[5] Lomonosov Moscow State University, Moscow, Russia

Abstract. The paper presents a text mining approach to identifying technological trajectories. The main problem addressed is the selection of documents
related to a particular technology. These documents are needed to identify a
trajectory of the technology. Two different methods were compared (based on
word2vec and lexical-morphological and syntactic search). The aim of developed approach is to retrieve more information about a given technology and
about technologies that could affect its development. We present the results of
experiments on a dataset containing over 4.4 million of documents as a part of
USPTO patent database. Self-driving car technology was chosen as an example.
The result of the research shows that the developed methods are useful for
automated information retrieval as the first stage of the analysis and identification of technological trajectories.

Keywords: Text mining · Technological trajectories ·
Similar document retrieval

1 Introduction

One of the modern fundamental research questions is the identification of technologies
development trajectories. "Technological trajectory" as well as "technological paradigm" are basic concepts associated with the research of science and technology
development. Each "technological paradigm" defines its own concept of "progress"
based on its specific technological and economic trade-offs; and has its own set of
procedures, its own definition of the "relevant" problems and of the specific knowledge

This work was supported by the RFBR grant № 17-29-07016 ofi_m.

S. O. Kuznetsov and A. I. Panov (Eds.): RCAI 2019, CCIS 1093, pp. 143–153, 2019.
https://doi.org/10.1007/978-3-030-30763-9_12

related to their solution. The development path within a technological paradigm is a technological trajectory [1].

The prediction of the development of technological trajectories can accelerate innovation progress. However, the development of technologies is the everyday process. It is impossible to keep track of all changes or to clearly classify a change as essential and another one as insignificant. We gain too much information, partly also because of interdisciplinary approach in the development of products and services. A possible way to address this problem is to analyze various scientific and technical information. But it requires a special methodology of automation and information retrieval tools.

In this paper we address the problem of technological trajectories identification. The proposed approach helps experts to get an answer to the question, what is the level of development of a given technology. With the help of our method one can analyze the retrieval results to predict the direction of technology development.

Text mining can be one of the methods for solving this problem. Analysis of representative scientific and technical information will reveal the technology development for a given period.

The process of technological trajectory identification can be divided into steps:

(1) Selecting the information sources, crawling and indexing documents.
(2) Document retrieval from the index database and selecting the subset of documents which are related to the technology which is the point of interest.
(3) Detailed expert analysis of metadata on the previously selected documents. Experts study publication and patent activity, main patent right holders and R&D centers, then this information is used to identify how the technology has been developing.

The second step needs further consideration. To get representative results we need to select a complete set containing a huge number of documents. It is a time consuming procedure, which is hard to be done manually. Thus, the automation of this stage is highly demanded. Therefore, tools for topically similar document retrieval are helpful on this stage of technological trajectory identification. We manually select some "seed" documents relevant to the chosen technology (i.e. self-driving car, particular aspects of robotics, distillation machines, etc.) using keywords and expert knowledge. After that, we use the proposed exploratory search tools to get the complete set of relevant documents. In our research, we compare two methods to retrieve relevant documents: word2vec and lexical-morphological and syntactic search. USPTO patent database is the dataset for our experiments. In practice, the additional databases (i.e. scientific papers, PhD. theses, scientific and technical reports) must be taken into the consideration.

The main goal is to find more information about a given technology and about technologies that could affect its development. The experimental result shows that the proposed methods are useful for automated information retrieval as the first stage of the analysis and identification of technological trajectories. Since both methods have drawbacks, the best accuracy and recall can be achieved by using them together.

This way, we expect to receive more complete information about the state of technology development. This information allowed us to study the development of the crucial components of unmanned vehicle technology. We also detected the starting point of active diffusion of this technology itself.

2 State of the Art

There are many cases when breakthroughs are carried out by a new combination of existing technologies, the innovation diffusion framework. Among the works devoted to new methods of trajectories detection, we can single out, for example, [2], in which a hybrid method for comparing scientific and technical documents was proposed, taking into account their thematic similarity and the presence of joint citations. Information on the development of technology can also be obtained from the analysis of the patent databases. In [3], a method was proposed for isolating patents related to a single technology using the clustering of full texts and analyzing the dynamics of clusters obtained. This method uses the metric clustering algorithm and a semantic measure of the proximity of patents. Paper [4] proposes a hybrid method for identifying patents devoted to a certain group of technologies, which simultaneously considers key vocabulary and international patent classification codes. Experimental approbation of the proposed method was carried out on the collaborations between countries.

We can note paper [6] in the field of patent search methods. It shows that semantic search has better accuracy than binary (by NDCG - Normalized Discounted Cumulative Gain measure). In [7], a patent search method was proposed, which includes statistical and semantic analysis of patent documents and the calculation of semantic similarity based on the extracted "subject-action-object" triplets. Statistical analysis is performed using the LDA method (Latent Dirichlet Allocation) [11]. The authors implemented this method and developed the software to solve the problem of patent expertise, which is intended to reduce the time that an expert spends looking for similar patents.

Another important task for the analysis of technological trajectories is the information extraction from the texts of scientific and technical documents. Paper [8] presents open source software for recognizing named entities and identifying the relationships between named entities in patent documents. A promising method for extracting named entities and relations between them from scientific and technical texts using supervised machine learning and graph probability models is presented in [12]. The results of the full linguistic analysis of texts were used as input data for analysis. The efficiency of the method was empirically confirmed by experts.

Based on these works, it can be concluded that the problem of technological trajectories detection can be solved using text mining. Therefore, one can understand the current state of technology development using information retrieval methods, analyzing scientific publications, patents, journals, popular science literature.

3 Methods for Identification of Technological Trajectories

This study is focused on the problem of searching for documents from the index database and filling the custom collection of documents. One of the methods of searching for information in large text arrays is semantic search. A disadvantage of this method is the need to use the query language. The user must formulate the correct requests to obtain the necessary information. Only then he can add the results to the collection for further analysis. The process can take a lot of time. It makes sense to consider options for automatic filling of collections.

In this work two methods of automatic collection filling were compared. Both methods are based on similar document search. USPTO patent database was chosen as an information source. Over 4.4 million documents have been indexed. We used the natural language processing and information retrieval methods implemented in Exactus Expert [9] and Exactus Patent [10], as well as methods for automatically generating keywords of documents [10], to solve the problem of documents indexing and text analysis. We manually selected 10 "seed" documents and tried to expand the collection.

The presented methods use extracted keywords of documents at a certain stage. In this case keywords are most informative lexical descriptors in the text of the document [16]. Lexical descriptors are

- individual lexemes as sets of paradigmatic forms (word forms) of one word, i.e., different forms of the same word do not differ;
- phrases in canonical forms (the main word is reduced to the dictionary form, and the form of dependent words is subject to the control of the main word), irrespective of various forms.

The information significance of the lexical descriptor is determined by the formula tf-idf (tf for term frequency, idf for inverse document frequency):

$$tf(t, d) = \frac{n_t}{\sum_k n_k} \tag{1}$$

n_t is the number of occurrences of a t-word in a document. Denominator is the total number of words in the document.

$$idf(t, D) = \log \frac{|D|}{|\{d_i \in D | t \in d_i\}|} \tag{2}$$

$|D|$ is the number of documents in the collection.
$|\{d_i \in D | t \in d_i\}|$ is the number of documents from collection D that contain t-word.

$$\text{tf-idf}(t, d, D) = tf(t, d) \times idf(t, D) \tag{3}$$

The first method is based on word2vec [13]. Word2vec is a two-layer neural network that processes texts. Its input is a text corpus and its output is a set of vectors: feature vectors for words in that corpus. We trained word2vec model on full texts of patents from United States Patent and Trademark Office (USPTO) [15]. Database contains more than 4.4 million documents from 1976 to 2019 years. For each document, keywords were extracted and sorted by tf-idf. After that sorted keywords were handed into the model. Summing all the keyword vectors, one vector corresponding to the one document is generated. These operations were performed for the top keywords ranked w.r.t. tf-idf. The top size was 5, 10, 15. Next, search for the closest vectors to "seed" was performed. Cosine similarity was used as a measure of similarity. Threshold of similarity was chosen for each case. The process of collection extension is divided into several steps. The first step is to search for documents similar to the "seed". At each next step, we search for the documents similar to already retrieved ones.

The second method is also based on similar document retrieval (lexical-morphological and syntactic search). The method described here [5] was modified. For all documents in the collection, keywords have been extracted. These keywords formed a new search descriptor. A descriptor is considered as a pattern and the algorithm starts searching for documents that are like it. All documents filtered by the similarity threshold are added to the collection. Hamming similarity measure was used as a measure of similarity. In this method the process of collection extension is also divided into several steps. At each step, document is re-generated from the keywords of all documents in the extensible collection and similar documents retrieval is repeated.

4   Results

The dataset [17] was collected by experts using information retrieval tools [9, 10]. The document was considered valid if it is contained in the dataset.

The tables show results on the "seed" collection which was collected by human experts. For 5, 10 and 15 keywords we have considered several cases by iterating a threshold parameter from 0.1 to 0.2 with a step of 0.005.

In Table 1 one can see the accuracy rate for each case. The columns of the table stay for combinations of parameters (number of keywords – kw, minimal proximity threshold of documents – thr), and the rows stay for steps.

Table 1.   Results of the method based on word2vec model

Step\keywords number, threshold	5kw, thr = 0.13	10kw, thr = 0.15	15kw, thr = 0.135
1	75%	78.3%	70.6%
2	81.8%	81.6%	75%
3	**95.8%**	87.5%	78.6%
4	66.5%	65.4%	93.8%
5	43.2%	54%	81.8%
6(extra)			75.7%

After a certain step the accuracy starts to decrease. It means that more and more documents are no longer satisfying the condition (document must be in dataset). To verify this behavior for case with 15 keywords, 1 extra step was performed. The combination of the number of keywords and the threshold value (15kw, thr = 0.135) shows the best accuracy. Figure 1 shows the change of accuracy.

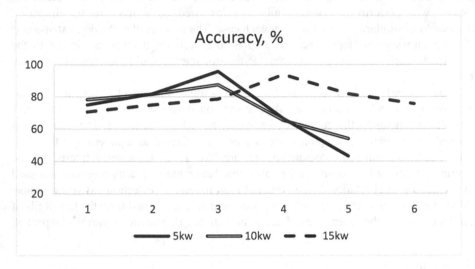

Fig. 1. Accuracy of the method based on word2vec model

The second method shows a different result. The more new keywords are considered, the less weight they have. It means that at a certain point in the next step no new documents will be found. In order to artificially increase the number of steps, the maximum number of documents added at each step were limited to 50 documents.

The cells of Table 2 contain accuracy rate for each case with number of found documents on each step. The columns of the table stay for combinations of parameters (number of keywords – kw, minimal proximity threshold of documents – thr), and the rows stay for steps.

Table 2. Accuracy of the method based on lexical-morphological, syntactic and semantic search.

Step\keywords number, threshold	5kw, thr = 0.13	10kw, thr = 0.15	15kw, thr = 0.135
1	82% (50 docs)	96% (50 docs)	94% (50 docs)
2	76% (50 docs)	82% (17 docs)	82% (50 docs)
3	**100%** (3 docs)	70% (10 docs)	64% (50 docs)
4	(0 docs)	(0 docs)	40% (5 docs)

The feature of this method is that the resulting lists of documents with different parameters are quite different from each other. This phenomenon is explained by the fact that the collection is expanding in the direction of the largest subset of topically similar documents. So, in the first case (5 keywords) the method collected a lot of documents about "roadway trajectories for self-driving vehicles" and similar to it. In the second case (10 keywords) the method could find patents about "visual object detection" and similar to it. In the third case (15 keywords) there are a lot of documents about navigation systems. Figure 2 shows the change in accuracy.

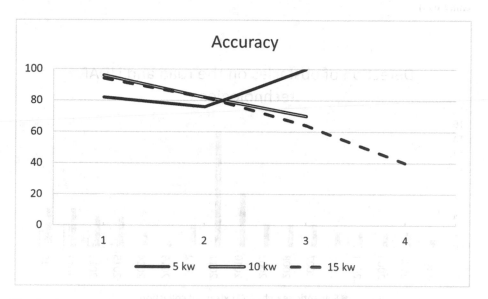

Fig. 2. Accuracy of the method based on lexical-morphological, syntactic and semantic search

Another important thing is the number of retrieved documents that describe the technologies that are components of the given technology. The more such documents were found, the more information we can get, which covers related sub-technologies. The second method solved this problem with a higher quality. Namely, the case using 15 keywords. In the process of searching for similar documents, the following topical directions were found (Table 3).

Since both methods have drawbacks, the best results can be achieved by using them together.

Then each direction was analyzed in detail. Since the new founded directions relate to unmanned vehicles, we found out when they began to be commercially used as a component of the technology. The semantic search method [18] was also used for solving this task. The found documents were grouped by issue date. As a result, we got the yearly patent activity for each of direction. Figures 3 and 4 show when each direction began to mention unmanned vehicles.

Table 3. Selected directions in the extended collection.

Direction	Documents count
Self-driving/unmanned and autonomous vehicle	86
Navigation systems/route planning	19
Detection of obstacles on the road and LIDAR technologies	10
Traffic analyze/Traffic control systems/Vehicle collision avoidance system	7
Other (mobile communication devices, lighting devices, in-vehicle virtual reality etc.)	33

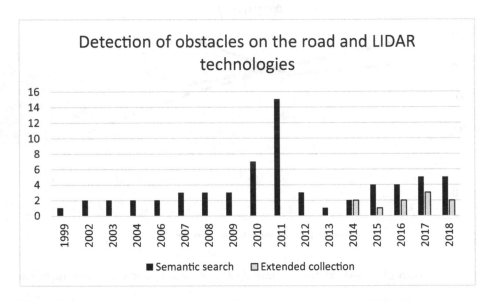

Fig. 3. Patent activity related to the obstacles detection on the road and LIDAR technologies

In Fig. 3, one can see that starting in 2014, there is an activity of patenting technologies that detect obstacles on the road in the context of unmanned vehicles. The same situation we see for navigation systems and route planning technologies (Fig. 4).

The largest group of documents is about unmanned vehicles themselves. The results of semantic search for query directly about self-driving cars also was compared with documents from group of extended collection (Fig. 5). This diagram shows that the method was able to find a significant proportion of documents.

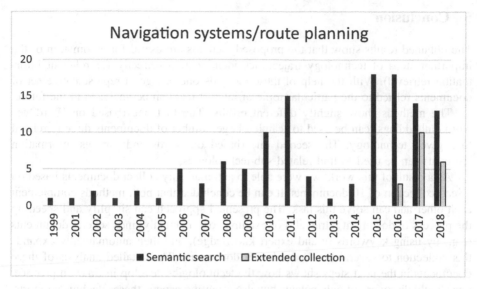

Fig. 4. Patent activity related to the navigation systems/route planning

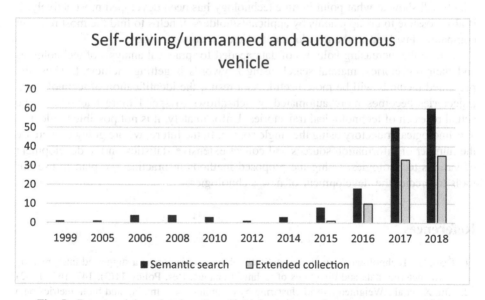

Fig. 5. Patent activity related to the self-driving/unmanned and autonomous vehicle

5   Conclusion

The obtained results show that the proposed methods are useful for automation of the important steps of technology trajectories identification (directly for relevant information retrieval). With the help of these methods one can get a representative set of documents related to the particular topic of interest that can be analyzed in the future.

The methods show slightly different results. The first one (based on Word2vec word embeddings) can be used to search a large number of documents directly related to a given technology. The second one (based on words and phrases information retrieval) can be used to find related sub-technologies.

As a result of this work, we were able to automatically collect documents based on a seed collection of 10 documents. It can be concluded that both methods complement each other and can solve this task. The presented approach can simplify and speed up the process of document retrieval. For example, one manually finds several documents (e.g., by using keywords or/and expert knowledge), and then automatically expands this collection to several hundred relevant documents. The detailed analysis of these documents in the next steps shows how the technologies develop in time. In practice, one should discover not only patents but also scientific papers, theses, technical reports, and other sources. On the example of patents, one can analyze patent activity by years, which will show at what point in time technology has been developed most actively. It is also possible to group patents by applicants/holders. It helps to find the most relevant companies involved in the development of the given technology.

Due to the increasing volumes of data needed for practical analysis of technologies and their trajectories, manual search using keywords is getting inefficient. Thus, the presented methods will be more useful. As a result, the identification of technological trajectories becomes more automated, which allows to spend more attention to the actual research of technological trajectories. Unfortunately, it is not possible to identify a technological trajectory using the single source. In the future, we are going to increase the number of information sources and collect extensive statistics on the development of various technologies. Using the proposed methods in practice, we plan to use our tools to predict the development of new technologies.

References

1. Dosi, G.: Technological paradigms and technological trajectories: a suggested interpretation of the determinants and directions of technical change. Res. Policy **11**(3), 147–162 (1982)
2. Liu, X., et al.: Weighted hybrid clustering by combining text mining and bibliometrics on a large-scale journal database. J. Am. Soc. Inf. Sci. Technol. **61**(6), 1105–1119 (2010)
3. Niemann, H., Moehrle, M.G., Frischkorn, J.: The use of a new patent text-mining and visualization method for identifying patenting patterns over time: concept, method and test application. Technol. Forecast. Soc. Change **115**, 210–220 (2017)
4. Ozcan, S., Islam, N.: Patent information retrieval: approaching a method and analysing nanotechnology patent collaborations. Scientometrics **111**(2), 941–970 (2017)

5. Sochenkov, I.V.: Metod sravneniya textov dlya resheniya poiskovo-analiticheskikh zadatch (Text comparison method for solving search and analytical tasks). Intellectualniy poisk informacii (Intelligent information retrieval), vol. 2, pp. 32–43 (2013)

6. Möller, A., Moehrle, M.G.: Complementing keyword search with semantic search—introducing an iterative semiautomatic method for near patent search based on semantic similarities. Scientometrics **102**(1), 77–96 (2015)

7. Korobkin, D.M., et al.: Prior art candidate search on base of statistical and semantic patent analysis. In: Multi Conference on Computer Science and Information Systems 2017, pp. 231–238 (2017)

8. Alves, T., Rodrigues, R., Costa, H., Rocha, M.: Development of text mining tools for information retrieval from patents. In: Fdez-Riverola, F., Mohamad, M., Rocha, M., De Paz, J., Pinto, T. (eds.) PACBB 2017. AISC, vol. 616, pp. 66–73. Springer, Cham (2017). https://doi.org/10.1007/978-3-319-60816-7_9

9. Osipov, G., Smirnov, I., Tikhomirov, I., Sochenkov, I., Shelmanov, A.: Exactus expert—search and analytical engine for research and development support. In: Hadjiski, M., Kasabov, N., Filev, D., Jotsov, V. (eds.) Novel Applications of Intelligent Systems. SCI, vol. 586, pp. 269–285. Springer, Cham (2016). https://doi.org/10.1007/978-3-319-14194-7_14

10. Osipov, G.S., et al.: Exactus patent–sistema patentnogo poiska i analiza (Exactus Patent–patent search and analysis system)

11. Blei, D.M., Ng, A.Y., Jordan, M.I.: Latent dirichlet allocation. J. Mach. Learn. Res. **3**, 993–1022 (2003)

12. Okamoto, M., Shan, Z., Orihara, R.: Applying information extraction for patent structure analysis. In: Proceedings of the 40th International ACM SIGIR Conference on Research and Development in Information Retrieval, pp. 989–992. ACM (2017)

13. Mikolov, T., et al.: Distributed representations of words and phrases and their compositionality. In: Advances in Neural Information Processing Systems, pp. 3111–3119 (2013)

14. Smirnov, I.V., et al.: Semantic-syntactic analysis of natural languages. Part II. Method for semantic-syntactic analysis of texts. In: Iskusstvenny intellekt i prinyatie resheniy–Artificial Intelligence and Decision Making, vol. 1, pp. 11–24 (2014)

15. Search for patents–USPTO. https://www.uspto.gov/patents-application-process/search-patents

16. Suvorov, R.E., Sochenkov, I.V.: Opredelenie svyazannosti nauchno-technicheskikh dokumentov na osnove kharakteristiki tematicheskoy znachimosti (Determination of the connectedness of scientific and technical documents based on the characteristics of thematic significance). Iskusstvenniy intellect I prinyatie resheniy (Artificial intelligence and making decisions)

17. Dataset trajectories-uspto. http://nlp.isa.ru/trajectories-uspto. Accessed 04 July 2019

18. Sochenkov, I.V., Suvorov, R.E.: Servisy polnotekstovogo poiska v informacionno-analiticheskoy sisteme (chast 1) (Full-text search services in the information and analytical system). In: Informatsionnie tekhnologii i vichislitelnie sistemy (information technologies and computing systems), no. 2, p. 69 (2013)

Development of the Lexicon
of Argumentation Indicators

Irina Kononenko[✉] and Elena Sidorova

A.P. Ershov Institute of Informatics Systems SB RAS,
Novosibirsk 630090, Russia
irina_k@cn.ru, lsidorova@iis.nsk.su

Abstract. The paper presents the results of a preliminary analysis of the argumentation indicators observed in the corpus of popular science texts in Russian. Main pragmatic aspects of the argumentation signaled by discursive indicators are outlined. The classification of indicators takes into account pragmatic meaning and the type of language means used. Special attention is paid to insufficiently studied indicator constructions and classes of their core content words. We consider constructions with verbs and nouns of mental state, speech, inference, and mental impact. The process of creating a lexicon of argumentation indicators is described. Indicators are presented in the form of lexical units and lexical-grammatical patterns, which are automatically generated from annotated text fragments and can be manually corrected by the expert. The pattern description language allows to represent grammatical and semantic constraints, nested constructs, alternatives, and discontinuity. The lexicon of indicators will be used for automatic annotation of argument indicators in unannotated text, as well as for experiments in argument mining.

Keywords: Argumentation indicator · Lexical-grammatical pattern · Argumentative annotation · Popular science discourse · Text corpus

1 Introduction

In the last decade, an interdisciplinary field of research has been actively developing at the intersection of philosophy, psycholinguistics and computational linguistics. Its purpose is to create models of argumentation for various types and genres of discourse and automatically identify and extract argument components and structure including premises and conclusions, and the relations between them based on typical argumentation schemes. The main prerequisite for the development of this area is the creation of annotated corpora, in which textual fragments are matched with components of argumentative structures and relations between them.

So far, there exist only a few resources with annotated argumentation structures over monologue texts, mainly for the English language. The best known is AIFdb[1], the

---

[1] AraucariaDB, http://corpora.aifdb.org/araucaria, last accessed 2019/04/30.

S. O. Kuznetsov and A. I. Panov (Eds.): RCAI 2019, CCIS 1093, pp. 154–168, 2019.
https://doi.org/10.1007/978-3-030-30763-9_13

former Araucaria corpus [1], which contains news articles, records of parliamentary and political online debates. Resources are created in German: University of Darmstadt Corpus[2] includes subcorpora of student essays [2], news texts and scientific articles; the Potsdam corpus[3] contains a small set of microtexts on a given topic, later translated into English [3]. There exist projects for some other languages (Italian, Greek, Chinese). As for the Russian language, such resources, as far as we know, do not yet exist. In most cases, corpus annotation includes text segmentation with highlighting of argumentation units, markup of roles (premise, conclusion) and relations (support, attack), without matching the argumentation schemes on which the reasoning is based. An exception is Araucaria, where argumentative structure annotation is related to particular argumentation scheme based on the theory of Walton [4].

The proposed work was performed as part of an on-going research project aimed at creation of an argumentation annotated corpus for the Russian language. A popular science discourse that is not presented in well-known argumentatively annotated corpora is being studied. Popular science discourse is defined as a way of transmitting scientific knowledge or innovation projects by the author-scientist (or a journalist as an intermediary) for their understanding by a mass audience. The corpus of popular science online articles on linguistic topics has been selected with the help of catalogs of Russian search engines Yandex and Rambler. Corpus includes about 70 texts with an average volume of 1057 words (minimum – 167 words, maximum – 4094 words), with no restrictions on the subject, structure, and the type of presentation. Some articles are transcripts of oral presentation, interviews, etc.

The texts are annotated manually based on the argumentation model developed by the project participants. An important linguistic aspect of the process of arguments annotation is registration of argumentative indicators, which constitute keystones in the discourse, facilitating the identification and reconstruction of argumentative moves that are made in argumentative discussions and texts (see [5]). Argumentative indicators are language means (words, constructions) that serve as discourse clues in identifying the structure of argumentation: they help determine the presence of arguments in a given segment of text, reconstruct the connections between statements, relate the argument to a specific reasoning pattern (inference form expressing the relations of premises and conclusions).

The purpose of this study is to create a lexicon of argumentative indicators used in popular science discourse. The work outlines the preliminary results of the analysis of argumentative indicators selected in the corpus of popular science articles. The questions of their classification, structural features and methods of formal representation are discussed.

---

[2] TU Darmstadt Homepage of Argumentation Mining, www.informatik.tu-darmstadt.de/ukp/research_6/research_areas/argumentation_mining, last accessed 2019/04/30.

[3] Potsdam corpus, http://angcl.ling.uni-potsdam.de/resources/argmicro.html, last accessed 2019/04/30.

2 Related Works

Discourse markers (discourse connectives) are usually considered as key indicators of discourse structure. They have been studied from various research perspectives. One of them is represented in Penn Discourse Treebank where discourse connectives are viewed as binary predicates that convey certain semantic relations and take propositions, events and states as their arguments PDTB [6]. PDTB annotation covers traditional functional words and phrases such as subordinating conjunctions (e.g. *when, because, as soon as*), coordinating conjunctions (*and, but, or*), adverbs (e.g. *instead, therefore*), prepositional phrases (e.g. *on the other hand*), etc.

T. van Dijk proposed classifying discourse connectives according to the type of relation they label: pragmatic connectives express the relation between speech acts, semantic connectives manifest the relations between the facts indicated in the text [7]. This difference corresponds to the opposition of subject matter and presentational relations in the Rhetorical structure theory [8]. Presentational rhetorical relations whose intended effect is to increase some inclination in the reader, such as the desire to act or the degree of positive regard for, belief in, or acceptance of the nucleus, overlap with argumentative discourse relations. The mapping of rhetorical discourse relations onto argumentative relations carried out in [9] confirms this pragmatic similarity. No wonder that first experiments in argumentation mining use the traditional functional lexicons as lexical indicators.

Stab and Gurevych [10] experimented with different types of features, including discourse markers from the PDTB annotation guidelines, to classify text units into the classes non-argumentative, major claim, claim, and premise. The PDTB markers appeared to be not helpful for discriminating between argumentative and non-argumentative text units, but they were useful to distinguish between the classes premise and claim. Eckle-Kohler et al. [11] present a study on the role of discourse markers in argumentative discourse on the material of German corpus, with arguments annotated according to the common claim-premise model of argumentation. They performed various statistical analyses regarding the discriminative nature of discourse markers for claims and premises. The experiments show that particular semantic groups of discourse markers are indicative of either claims or premises and constitute highly predictive features for discriminating between them.

The investigation of discourse relation signals given in [12] is more extensive, as it takes into account not only traditional discourse markers (e.g., *although, because, since, thus*), but also signals such as tense, lexical chains or punctuation, and their combinations. The authors of the project to create a corpus of rhetorical structures on the material of the Russian language[4] also consider a wide class of language expressions, including lexical items irrespective of their part of speech that can signal the presence of a rhetorical relation. Toldova et al. [13] consider not only functional words to be rhetoric relation markers. The markers include punctuation marks, prepositions, pronouns, speech verbs, etc. In the development of this approach on the example of causal relation indicators in [14] it is shown that, in addition to traditional functional

---

[4] Russian RST Discourse Treebank, https://linghub.ru/ru-rstreebank, last accessed 2019/04/30.

words, relation indicators are constructions based on the content words and provide informal specifications of some patterns that can be used for mining indicators in non-annotated text.

With regard to the indicators of the argumentation, the possibility of considering a wide class of language expressions that signal the use of specific reasoning schemes is demonstrated in the theoretical study [5], which also goes far beyond the functional classes of words. Considering the indicators of argumentation by analogy, the authors cite as an example constructions with significant words meaning analogy, comparison, similarity, and parallelism: *X can be compared to Z; X is similar to Z; X is the equivalent of Z; there are parallels (to be drawn) between X and Z; X reminds someone of Z.*

3 Information Model of Argument Annotation

An argument is a set of related statements used to prove a final statement (thesis, or conclusion). The structure of the argument highlights the statement-premise and the statement-conclusion connected by typed relations.

The structure of the argument can be represented as follows:

Argument = (Premise, Premise, ..., Conclusion, Weight)
Conclusion = (Statement | Argument, Support | Attack, Weight)
Premise = (Statement, Role, Weight)
Statement = (Utterance, Source *, impl. | expl.)

The type of argumentation relation expresses whether a given argument is evidence (*Support*) or refutation (*Attack*) of a thesis-conclusion. The conclusion can be either an explicitly expressed statement or some other argument. Related statements may serve as premises, where each premise plays a specific *Role* in a typical reasoning scheme.

A statement represents a natural language formulated proposition (*Utterance*), which the annotator (expert) associates with the *Source* that is a text fragment. Usually the statement coincides with the source, except for the existing anaphoric references and ellipsis recovered by the annotator from the context. Thus, a statement is an interpretation of a text fragment. However, it is possible that the necessary statement-premise is not explicitly specified in the text. In the case of implied premise, its statement can be formulated by the expert on the basis of extratextual knowledge.

All elements in the structure of the argument are supplied with *Weight* – a measure of the persuasiveness of the proof given, which allows us to ultimately assess the strength of the author's argument as a whole.

The given argument representation model corresponds to the AIF model [15], which is currently accepted as a standard in analyzing argumentative structures and, in particular, is used in the Carneades system [16]. Since in this study we focused on investigation of different types of indicators used in the texts for entering arguments and their structural components, the argument model was supplied with additional parameters for annotating the argumentation indicators in the text.

Indicator = (Source, Type, Definition, Frequency)

On discovering an indicator, the expert marks up a corresponding text fragment (*Source*) and points out which pragmatic aspect (*Type*) of the argument is signaled by the indicator. Based on the analysis of the selected fragment, the structural (grammatical) type of the indicator is determined and its lexical-syntactic *Definition* formed, which allows automatic search for the indicator in the texts. The *Frequency* parameter determines how discriminative this indicator is for the selected aspect of the argument. Frequency in the annotated text corpus is calculated automatically.

Additionally, the markup system implements the requirement of maximum "similarity" between the statement and the source. To this end, the following recommendations were developed for experts who carry out annotation of argumentation.

When annotating an *Argument*, text fragments corresponding to the explicitly presented statements are marked up first. Each fragment can be a chain of sentences, a single sentence, clause or nominalization. Every fragment is regarded as if all its anaphoric references (including ellipses) were resolved. In case of anaphoric nominalization of a whole statement within the Argument, an antecedent statement is marked up. Then, a suitable type of reasoning scheme (argumentation scheme) is chosen, the selected statements are linked into a single Argument, and the necessary parameters of the premises and a conclusion are indicated in accordance with the specified scheme. If necessary, implicit statements are introduced.

Let's give an example of the Argument marked up in the text[5]:

(in Russian) *По-французски любовь – atour, что тоже имеет тайный смысл. [Звукосочетание "mr" в индоевропейском праязыке соответствовало всему, что связано со смертью.] [Звук 'a' до сих пор во многих языках употребляется как противопоставление.]* **Поэтому** [*«atour» – противопоставление смерти, то есть жизнь!*]//text 21

In French love - amour, which also has a secret meaning. [The sound combination "mr" in the Indo-European proto-language corresponded to everything connected with death.] [The sound 'a' is still used as an opposition in many languages.] **Therefore** [*«amour» is the opposition of death, that is, life!*]

In this example, the Argument consists of two premises and a conclusion. The word *поэтому* '*therefore*' is an indicator of the conclusion of the Argument and of entire inference relation.

Note that the Argument does not always correspond to a continuous text fragment: between the conclusion and the premise there may be discourse units that are not related to this Argument (for example, Premise that supports the same Conclusion independently within another Argument), or irrelevant for argumentation (for example, explanations).

---

[5] Statements in the structure of the argument are presented in square brackets. The statement that presents the conclusion of the argument is underlined. Indicators are bold italic. After the fragment the source text is given.

4 Classification of Argumentation Indicators

Indicators of argumentation can be classified from different points of view: the pragmatic aspects of argumentation, the degree of grammaticalization, the semantics of the indicator's core word, the type of construction.

1. Pragmatic aspects of argumentation signaled by the indicator.

- opinion and strength of the argument (degree of confidence);
- inference relation between two statements;
- role of the statement in the inference relation (Premise vs. Conclusion);
- type of argumentative relation (Support vs. Attack);
- structure of the argumentation (Multiple vs. Serial argumentation);
- semantic-ontological relation which the typical reasoning scheme used in this case is based on.

In the following examples (1) and (2), the indicators *по-видимому* 'seemingly' and *специалисты предполагают, что* 'experts suggest that' present statements of the premise (2) and conclusion (1) as opinions with a certain weight. Indicators *поскольку* 'since' and *поэтому* 'therefore' with causal semantics explicitly indicate the presence of a relation of inference. In this case, the position of the marker in the segment indicates the role of the corresponding statement: *поскольку* introduces the Premise in (1), and *поэтому* introduces the Conclusion in (2). In both cases, the type of relation is Support. In (3) and (4), the indicators are based on predicates with the semantics of mental impact, *опровергать* 'refute' and *подтверждение* 'confirmation', here the distribution of roles in the inference move is identified by the actant position.

(1) **Поскольку** [*в языках сибирских народов все еще сохранилась четкая связь с индейскими наречиями*], **специалисты предполагают, что** [*многие мигранты возвращались из Америки назад, в Сибирь*.]//text 02

Since [*in the languages of the Siberian peoples there is still a clear connection with Indian dialects*], **experts suggest** that [*many migrants returned from America back to Siberia.*]

In the example (1), the opinion of specialists expressed in the conclusion and marked by an indicator of opinion, which corresponds to a not very high weight (the degree of confidence of the mental predicate is relatively low), is supported by the premise marked by the indicator of the basis of the conclusion.

(2) [*Осознание своей идентичности, в том числе и языковой, по-видимому, является важным компонентом душевного равновесия.*] Именно **поэтому** [*всегда находятся те, кто наперекор современным тенденциям, а то и инстинкту самосохранения поддерживает и сохраняет языки.*] **Тем более что** [*знание родного языка совершенно не означает отказа от других, более востребованных.*]//text 68.

[*Awareness of one's identity, including linguistic identity, is* **probably** *an important component of mental equilibrium.*] Just **for that reason** [*there are always those who, contrary to modern trends and even to the instinct of self-preservation, maintain and preserve languages.*] **All the more so that** [*knowledge of the mother language does not mean refusal to speak other, more popular ones.*]

In the example (2), two arguments are shown that prove the same thesis independently of each other, while the indicator *тем более что* '*all the more so that*' marks the second premise in the structure of Multiple argumentation.

(3) *Например, **поговаривают, что** [русских научили материться татары и монголы, а до ига, якобы, не знали на Руси ни одного ругательства.] **Однако** есть несколько **фактов, опровергающих это**. Во-первых, [у кочевников не было обычая сквернословить.]//*text 29.

*For example, **they say that** [the Tatars and the Mongols taught Russians how to swear and before the yoke, allegedly, they did not know a single curse in Russia.] **However**, there are several **facts that refute this**. First, [nomads didn't have the habit of foul language.]*

(4) *Во-первых, [у кочевников не было обычая сквернословить.] **В подтверждение этому** — [записи итальянского путешественника Плано Карпини, посетившего центральную азию. Он отмечал, что у них бранные слова вообще отсутствуют в словаре.]//*text 29.

*First, [the nomads did not have the habit of foul language.] **In confirmation of this** — [the records of the Italian traveler Plano Carpini, who visited Central Asia. He noted that swear words were absent in their lexicon.]*

Examples (3) and (4) demonstrate Serial argumentation. In (3) an opinion is refuted by the following premise (Attack relation), and in (4) this premise is supported by the reasoning corresponding to the typical scheme "From the Knower": the subject makes a statement relating to the domain he is familiar with - therefore, this statement is true.

2. Primary and secondary indicators.
Toldova et al. in [14] proposed to divide the indicators of a causal rhetorical relation into two classes (primary vs. secondary) according to the degree of their grammaticalization: the primary connectors are functional words (including multi-word units) fixed in grammars and dictionaries, and the secondary ones are less studied constructions based on content lexemes of causal semantics. Examples from the corpus of popular science texts make it possible to draw similar conclusions regarding argumentation indicators. We consider two classes of language means used as indicators of argumentation:

– discursive connectors are well-known functional units, including multi-word units (prepositions, conjunctions, introductory words): *поэтому* '*that is why*', *поскольку* '*since*', *следовательно* '*consequently*', *так как* '*as*', *значит* '*hence*', *тем более что* '*all the more so that*', *например* '*for example*', *в частности* '*in particular*', etc.;
– content words and indicator constructions including these words as their core components (see examples below).

3. Classification of indicators according to the semantics of the core content word.
Up to now the list of annotated content words which can serve as indicators or core words of indicator constructions is heterogeneous and far from complete. These words are mainly verbs and nouns of the following lexical-semantic classes:

• **mental state** *считать* '*to believe*', *предполагать* '*to suppose*', *убежден* '*be convinced*', *мнение* '*opinion*', *точка зрения* '*viewpoint*';

- **mental impact** *доказывать* 'to prove', *опровергать* 'to refute',*подтверждать* 'to confirm', *свидетельствовать* 'to indicate';
- **inference** *следовать* 'to follow/result', *получается* 'it follows that', *выходит* 'it follows that', *выходить* 'to follow/result', *получаться* 'to follow/result', *выводить* 'to conclude/infer', *следствие* 'consequence', *вывод* 'conclusion';
- **conflict** *противоречить* 'to contradict', *противоречие* 'controversy';
- **intellectual** *activity обнаружить* 'to discover', *выяснить* 'to find out', *выявить* 'to reveal';
- **speech activity** *говорить* 'to talk', *сообщать* 'to report', *утверждать* 'to state';
- **justification** *аргумент* 'argument', *доказательство* 'proof', *обоснование* 'basis', *свидетельство* 'evidence', *подтверждение* 'confirmation';
- **information** *факт* 'fact', *пример* 'example';
- **intellectual product** *тезис* 'thesis', *гипотеза* 'hypothesis', *теория* 'theory';
- **speech product** *сообщение* 'message', *слово* 'word';
- **expert** *ученый* 'scientist', *специалист* 'specialist', *лингвист* 'linguist', *философ* 'philosopher'.

4. Types of constructions for secondary indicators.

On the basis of speech and mental predicates, predicates of inference and mental impact, complex indicators of argumentation are formed. In addition to the core word, they can include markers of actant positions, for example, the conjunction *что* 'that' and the correlative pronoun construction *то, что* 'the fact that' for sentential actants, anaphoric and cataphoric elements such as the demonstrative pronoun *это/этот* 'this', adverb *отсюда* 'hence', the relative pronoun that 'what'. Examples of constructions under consideration are as follows:

- constructions with verbs of inference and mental impact
  из...следует, что 'from... it follows that'
  это...доказывает, что 'this... proves that'
  эти...свидетельствуют о том, что 'these... indicate that'
- verbal constructions of direct or indirect speech or opinion with the speech or mental verb and the «expert» class word in the subject position
  ученые... утверждают: "..." 'scientists...assert: "..." '
  литератор... заметил, что 'literary scholar...noted that'
- light verb constructions with nouns
  примером...является 'example ...is'
  аргумент был такой 'argument...was as follows'
  приводит... аргумент в пользу этого, что 'give an argument in favour of this'
  отсюда ... сделан... вывод о том, что 'come to a conclusion that'
- prepositional noun phrases
  в подтверждение этому 'in confirmation of this'
  на этом/таком основании 'on this/that basis'
  на следующем основании 'on the following ground'
  по мнению/словам 'according to smb'

5 Technological Aspects of Building a Lexicon of Argumentation Indicators

To support the development of lexicon of indicators, it is essential to provide the researcher with the necessary automation tools. In Fig. 1 the main stages of the process of creating and researching indicators are presented.

It is assumed that the process of argument annotation is accompanied by marking up argumentation indicators found out by the annotator. After a text fragment associated with the indicator is selected, a formal description of the indicator is automatically generated and added to the lexicon. This description is presented to the expert for validation and correction. Automated procedures carried out by the expert are supported by the appropriate software components.

Consider this process in more detail.

1. Selection of a text fragment corresponding to the indicator occurs together with annotation of the argument and its components. Analysis of the structure of the argument and the role of the indicator within this structure complement each other and facilitate annotator's work. The indicator annotation involves specification of the fragment boundaries (possibly with gaps) and selection of the argumentation aspect(s) signaled by the indicator.

2. Based on the selected fragment, it is necessary to specify a formal representation of the indicator in order to ensure automatic search of the indicator in the text, taking into account the variability of its presentation. At this stage, the text fragment is divided into elementary components (graphematic analysis), words are lemmatized, word combinations (phrases) are generated and normalized.

3. As the examples in paragraph 4 show, indicators are not only lexical units (single- or multi-word units), but also constructions, which can be formally represented by means of lexical-grammatical patterns. Automatically generated pattern allows for the lexical composition of the construction (lexical units in the normalized form), punctuation marks, gaps, and the boundaries of the indicator.

4. At the next stage, the obtained formal description is matched against the corpus and search results are displayed in the form of a concordance. Based on the study of the indicator's occurrences, the expert concludes whether the formal description is correct.

5. The expert can correct indicator description as appropriate: generalize individual lexical units to lexical-semantic classes, resolve ambiguities, specify grammatical features of words and phrases within structures (to ensure coordination or government), create lists of alternatives and indicate the boundaries of the construction.

6. The resulting lexical units and patterns approved by the expert are supplied with the necessary grammatical and argumentative features and introduced into the information retrieval lexicon, which provides search and automatic annotation of indicators in the texts of the corpus. This, on the one hand, removes the need to re-annotate indicators manually, and, on the other hand, signals the possible presence of argumentation in unannotated texts or the need to refine previously marked up arguments.

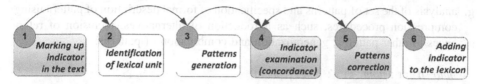

Fig. 1. The main stages of the development of lexicon of indicators (blocks with a light background correspond to fully automatic procedures, blocks with a dark background represent procedures carried out by an expert).

5.1   Indicator Pattern Generation

Indicators of argumentation can be classified from different points of view: the pragmatic aspects of argumentation, the degree of grammaticalization, the semantics of the indicator's core word, the type of construction.

The analysis of text fragments marked up as indicators is carried out using the Klan system [17]. Extraction of lexical units from a text fragment is not as obvious a task as it might seem. The paper [18] describes the emerging problems and gives a linguistic classification of errors. Most of the errors in the extraction of lexical units are related to the ambiguity and/or incorrect prediction of single words and the incorrectness and/ or incompleteness of the construction of word combinations.

The process of indicator pattern generation includes the following steps:

a. graphematic analysis, which provides for tokenization and selection of non-textual elements (numerical data, symbols, etc.),
b. lexical and morphological analysis (lemmatization, determination of lexical and grammatical features, paradigm representation, normalization),
c. identification of word combinations (based on predefined grammatical models and normalization),
d. generation of template (s) with a simple structure in the form of a chain of lexical units and punctuation marks:

так, например 'thus, for example': [*так*, s/, , *например*]

e. for discontinuous fragments, introduction of structural constraints into the pattern description (distant context and pattern boundaries)

если ..., то 'if...then': [begin: *если*, s/, , end: *то*]

f. analysis of pattern composition and ascription of grammatical features (for example, if the form of the indicator is fixed during annotation):

в подтверждение 'in confirmation': [*в*, *подтверждение* <acc, nom, sing>]

g. analysis of the set of patterns and specification of formal description of pattern using compression procedures, such as introduction of alternatives, inclusion of references to other patterns, generalization and combination of patterns:

это '*it*' or *этот* '*this*': [*это* | *этот*]

Thus, several types of structural organization of the formal description of indicators and their components can be distinguished.

Indicators with a simple structure include single- or multi-word functional and content units (inference predicates, speech and mental predicates, etc.).

Complex constructs described using patterns include simple chains (a chain of lexemes and punctuation marks), chains with grammatical constraints (prepositional phrases, verbal constructions, etc.) and discontinuous constructions.

Among the indicators with complex structural organization are the following:

– constructs combining distant context and grammatical constraints, for example, prepositional noun phrases

на ... основании '*on...ground*'
[begin: *на*, end: *основание* <gen,sing>]

including auxiliary constructs with imposed grammatical constraints

согласно... теории/исследованиям/гипотезе
'*according to...theory/research/ hypothesis*'
research_group = [*исследование* | *теория* | *гипотеза*]
[begin: *согласно*, end: research_group<dat>]

– constructs with elements defined by their lexical-semantic classes:

это...доказывает, что '*this... proves that*'
mental_impact_that = [w/<Sem:mental_impact>, s/, , *что*]
[begin: *это*, end: mental_impact_that]
из ...следует, что '*from... it follows that*'
inference_ that = [w/<Sem:inference>, s/, , *что*]
[begin: *из*, end: inference_that]
'*литератор... заметил, что*' '*literary scholar...noted that*'
speech_activity_that = [w/<Sem:speech_activity>, s/, , *что*]
[begin: <Sem:expert>, end: speech_activity_that]

– constructs with multiple gaps (distant contexts):

из... сделан... вывод о том, что '*from...come to ...conclusion that*'
concl_that = [*вывод, о, том*, s/, , *что*]
[begin: *из*, w/<Sem:light_verb>, end: concl_that]

Correct and complete description of indicator in accordance with annotated fragment is not always obtained as a result of automatic template generation. The same goes for lexical-semantic class identification in case of generalization. Manual correction and adjustment of the formal representation of indicator is required based on the examination of its contexts and use in various types of arguments.

5.2 Analysis of Indicator Structure

The traditional tool for the study of linguistic phenomena is concordance, which displays a listing of immediate and extended contexts of lexical units in the text corpus. The advanced implementation of searching and concordancing, in addition to lexical units, provides contexts of pattern descriptions, with support for output filtering in accordance with specified criteria (for example, argumentation features). This functionality greatly increases the possibilities for research.

The goal of indicator examination carried out by an expert is to ensure the accuracy of the generated formal descriptions, as well as to expand the lexicon by identifying and merging indicators similar in structure and generalizing lexical units to lexical-semantic classes. The pattern description language has the necessary capabilities, such as means for representing grammatical and semantic constraints, nested constructs, alternatives, and discontinuity.

Let us consider the process of indicator patterns on the example of the "From the Expert" reasoning scheme commonly used in the popular science texts.

[[«*Достичь этого помогают гласные*»], - *добавляет канадский исследователь Сэм Мэглио (Sam Maglio)*], *один из авторов новой работы.*//text 01

[["*Vowels help achieve this* "] adds Canadian researcher Sam Maglio], one of the authors of the new work.

In this example, the construction of direct speech is used, with the speech predicate and the «expert» class word in the subject position. This construction is generally recognized as a sign of argumentation. Thus, the annotator marked up the following text fragment as an indicator:

« ... » .. *добавляет* .. *исследователь* '« ... » .. adds .. researcher'

Based on this fragment, it is necessary to create a formal representation of the indicator. When generating a pattern, you can apply different strategies for forming its composition. For example, in this case the following pattern variants will be automatically generated:

– presentation of exact wordform with the help of grammatical features:

x = [begin: «, end: »]

y1 = [begin: x, *добавлять*<act,3pers,pres,sing>, end: *исследователь*<nom, sing>]

– presentation of all forms (normalization):

y2 = [begin: x, *добавлять*, end: *исследователь*]

– generation by grammatical model:

y3 = [begin: x, *добавлять*, end: *исследователь* <nom>]
y4 = [begin: x, *исследователь*<nom>, end: *добавлять*]

– specification of lexical-semantic class (with or without grammatical features):

y5 = [begin: x, w/<Sem: speech_activity>, end: w/<Sem: expert>], etc.

Determining the best strategy for each specific several types of indicator is one of the objectives of the study.

To expand and generalize the lexical composition of the generated pattern, the expert performs the following steps:

- considers the possibility of generalization of the core words by specifying their lexical-semantic classes,
- creates auxiliary patterns with alternatives,
- checks the generalization hypothesis using concordance,
- corrects and validates the indicator by checking all its occurrences in the corpus.

There are more than 300 occurrences of the «expert» class words: *исследователь* *'researcher'* (40), *ученый* *'scientist'* (119), *специалист* *'specialist'* (17), *эксперт* *'expert'* (6), *лингвист* *'linguist'* (98), *филолог* *'philologist'* (7), *антрополог* *'anthropologist'* (2), *археолог* *'archeologist'* (8), *профессор* *'professor'* (15), *физик* *'physicist'* (3), etc. The concordance listing shows that contexts of these words include the following lexical markers of argumentation: *добавлять* *'add'*, *пояснять* *'explain'*, *признавать* *'admit'*, *отмечать* *'note'*, *сообщать* *'report'*, *подытоживать* *'summarize'*, *резюмировать* *'sum up'*, etc. These words were grouped into the lexical-semantic class «speech_activity» to be used in final patterns.

As a result of the correction carried out by the expert, there are patterns that describe a whole class of situations:

quote_l = [“|«] quote_r = [”|»] DS = [begin: quote_l, end: quote_r]
Expert = [w/<expert>] | [ph/<expert>]
DSC1 = [begin: DS, w/<speech><V, past|pres>, end: Expert<N, nom>]
DSC2 = [begin: Expert<N, nom>, w/<speech><V, past|pres>, end: DS]

Search in the corpus shows that the construction corresponding to this pattern appears 7 times and 6 of these occurrences indicate the presence of the "From the Expert" argumentation.

Another example of a complex pattern corresponds to the indicator used in the "From the Sign" argumentation scheme. The pattern represents a construction with verb of mental impact and anaphoric element in the actant position.

Это *открытие также* **доказывает, что** [*переселение народов из центральной Азии в северную Америку 13 000 лет назад, возможно, было не окончательным.*]/*text 02

This *discovery also* **proves that** [*the migration of peoples from Central Asia to North America 13,000 years ago may not have been final.*]

to_chto = [s/ ,, что] | [то, s/, , что] | [того, s/, , что]
anaph_this = [это | этот | такой]
Proof = [begin: anaph_this, w/<caus_ment><V, pres>, end: to_chto]

The above examples demonstrate the technique of developing formal descriptions of indicators, including automatic generation and manual correction procedures.

6   Conclusion

The paper presents the results of a preliminary analysis of the argumentation indicators observed in the process of annotation of popular science texts in Russian. Corpus examples show main pragmatic aspects of the argumentation signaled by discursive indicators. Along with pragmatic meaning, the classification of indicators takes into account the type of language means used. Special attention is paid to insufficiently studied indicator constructions and classes of their core content words. We consider constructions with verbs and nouns of mental state, speech, inference, and mental impact.

The argumentation indicators are presented in the form of lexical units and lexical-grammatical patterns, which are automatically generated from annotated text fragments and can be manually corrected by the expert. The lexicon of indicators is planned to be used for automatic annotation of argument indicators in unannotated text, as well as for experiments in argument mining.

The process of argumentative annotation of the popular science corpus is ongoing. Upon completion of the work, the pilot version of the annotated corpus will be available in the open access. We assume that in the future the scope of the research will expand and cover new classes of content words and corresponding constructions. In particular, one can expect a significant expansion of the spectrum of indicators due to the semantic-ontological relations on which typical argumentation schemes are based.

Acknowledgments. The research has been supported by Russian Foundation for Basic Research (Grant No. 18-00-01376 (18-00-00889)).

References

1. Reed, C., Mochales Palau, R., Rowe, G., Moens, M.F.: Language resources for studying argument. In: Proceedings of the 6th Conference on Language Resources and Evaluation (LREC 2008), pp. 91–100 (2008)
2. Stab, C., Gurevych, I.: Annotating argument components and relations in persuasive essays. In: Proceedings of the 25th International Conference on Computational Linguistics (COLING 2014), pp. 1501–1510 (2014)
3. Peldszus, A., Stede, M.: An annotated corpus of argumentative microtexts. In: First European Conference on Argumentation: Argumentation and Reasoned Action, Portugal, Lisbon (2015)
4. Walton, D., Reed, C., Macagno, F.: Argumentation Schemes. Cambridge University Press, Cambridge (2008)
5. Van Eemeren, F.H., Houtlosser, P., Snoeck Henkemans, F.: Argumentative Indicators in Discourse: A Pragma-Dialectical Study. Argumentation Library, vol. 12. Springer, Dordrecht (2007). https://doi.org/10.1007/978-1-4020-6244-5
6. Prasad, R., et al.: The Penn Discourse Treebank 2.0 Annotation Manual. Technical report 203, Institute for Research in Cognitive Science, University of Pennsylvania (2007)
7. Van Dejk, T.: Text and Context: Explorations in the Semantics and Pragmatics of Discourse. Longman, London (1977)

8. Mann, W.C., Thompson, S.A.: Rhetorical structure theory: toward a functional theory of text organization. Text **8**(3), 243–281 (1988)
9. Stede, M., Afantenos, S.D., Peldszus, A., Asher, N., Perret, J.: Parallel discourse annotations on a corpus of short texts. In: Proceedings of the International Conference on Language Resources and Evaluation (LREC), Portoroz (2016)
10. Stab, C., Gurevych, I.: Identifying argumentative discourse structures in persuasive essays. In: Conference on Empirical Methods in Natural Language Processing (EMNLP), Doha, Qatar, pp. 46–56 (2014)
11. Eckle-Kohler, J., Kluge, R., Gurevych, I.: On the role of discourse markers for discriminating claims and premises in argumentative discourse. In: Proceedings of the Conference on Empirical Methods in Natural Language Processing (EMNLP), pp. 2236–2242 (2015)
12. Taboada, M., Das, D.: Annotation upon annotation: adding signalling information to a corpus of discourse relations. Dialogue Discourse **4**(2), 249–281 (2013)
13. Toldova, S., et al.: Rhetorical structure markers in Russian RST Treebank. In: Proceedings of the 6th Workshop on Recent Advances in RST and Related Formalisms, pp. 29–33 (2017)
14. Toldova, S., Pisarevskaya, D., Vasilyeva, M., Kobozeva, M.: The cues for rhetorical relations in Russian: "Cause-Effect" relation in Russian Rhetorical Structure Treebank. In: Computational Linguistics and Intellectual Technologies, Papers from the Annual International Conference "Dialogue", pp. 747–761 (2018)
15. Rahwan, I., Reed, C.: The argument interchange format. In: Simari, G., Rahwan, I. (eds.) Argumentation in Artificial Intelligence. Springer, Boston (2009). https://doi.org/10.1007/978-0-387-98197-0_19
16. Gordon, T.F., Walton, D.: The Carneades argumentation framework–using presumptions and exceptions to model critical questions. In: 6th Computational Models of Natural Argument Workshop (CMNA), European Conference on Artificial Intelligence (ECAI), vol. 6, pp. 5–13 (2006)
17. Sidorova, E.A.: Multipurpose dictionary subsystem for extraction of subject lexicon. In: Proceedings of the International Conference "Computational Linguistics and Intellectual Technologies" (Dialogue-2008), pp. 475–481 (2008). (in Russian)
18. Kononenko, I., Ahmadeeva, I., Sidorova, E., Shestakov, V.: Problems of extracting terminological core of the subject domain from electronic encyclopedic dictionaries. Syst. Inform. **13**, 49–76 (2018). (in Russian)

A Technique to Pre-trained Neural Network Language Model Customization to Software Development Domain

Pavel V. Dudarin[✉], Vadim G. Tronin, and Kirill V. Svyatov

Ulyanovsk State Technical University, Ulyanovsk, Russia
{p.dudarin,v.tronin,k.svyatov}@ulstu.ru

Abstract. According to the CHAOS report from Standish Group during 1992–2017, the degree of success of projects in the development of software intensive systems (Software Intensive Systems, SIS) has changed insignificantly, remaining at the level of 50% inconsistency with the initial requirements (finance, time and functionality) for medium-sized projects. The annual financial losses in the world due to the total failures are of the order of hundreds of billion dollars. The majority of information about software projects has textual representation. Analysis of this information is vital for project status understanding, revealing problems on the early stage. Nowadays the majority of tasks in NLP field are solved by means of neural network language models. These models already have shown state-of-the-art results in classification, translation, named entity recognition, and so on. Pre-trained models are accessible in the internet, but the real life problem domain could differ from the origin domain where the network was learned. In this paper an approach to vocabulary expansion for neural network language model by means of hierarchical clustering is presented. This technique allows one to adopt pre-trained language model to a different domain.

Keywords: NLP · Language model · Neural network · RNN ·
ULMFiT · Transfer learning · Clustering · Fuzzy graph clustering ·
Word-to-vec

1 Introduction

Code production is a complex and expensive process. Many resources are spent to get instruments of monitoring, control and prediction software development results. Many papers are dedicated to this theme, e.g., in [20] an approach to project architecture analysis is proposed. Besides the code itself there are a lot of information produced during the software development process. For example, tasks are tracked in a task tracking system, where each issue could be commented and discussed by team members. During the code review phase the content is discussed by developers. All this information is textual, thus NLP methods are

© Springer Nature Switzerland AG 2019
S. O. Kuznetsov and A. I. Panov (Eds.): RCAI 2019, CCIS 1093, pp. 169–176, 2019.
https://doi.org/10.1007/978-3-030-30763-9_14

required to analyze it and extract knowledge about the effectiveness of communication among team members, about emotional condition of the team, specific relations between colleagues. This knowledge could be used to monitor software development process, predict quality and timing, and reveal conflicts on the early stages.

Mostly the information generated during software process is presented as short sentences and short dialogues. Processing short texts is becoming a trend [15] in information retrieval [14]. Since a text rarely has external information, it is more challenging to process it than a document [17]. To coupe with this task different clustering techniques are used [18,19]. Each clustering procedure needs a similarity measure [4], and the most used technique to obtain this measure in NLP tasks is word2vec [13].

Although the word embedding approach has shown good efficiency [3], lately an approach of construction neural network language models is getting a leading position in NLP benchmarks [16], almost every state-of-the-art results are obtained by means of neural networks. But the process of neural network learning is quite long and computationally expensive.

Besides there are a lot of task in specific domains where there is no opportunity to teach special neural network. In this case the idea of transfer learning [9] looks very promising. Authors of ULMFiT propose to use their universal architecture to train language model and then to tune them for specific NLP tasks. However, in ULMFit the tokens list is limited, authors recommend using up to 60 000 tokens. And as long as different word forms are treated as different tokens, ULMFiTs vocabulary is even more limited. On the contrary, modern word embedding models [5] have 250–400 thousand of lemmas. Word embedding technique being combined with thesaurus could demonstrate even higher performance [2]. In case of Russian language with its huge possible word forms, the language model approach allows one to construct general purpose neural networks like casual phases generator only. The model does not allow including specific terms, neologism, swear words, rare used words and so on. In ELMo [7] and BERT [8] words are split into parts and then fed to neural network. But these models take a lot of calculation resources and could be afforded by huge corporations like Google. There are some multilingual pre-trained ELMo [6] and BERT models. But as for now they demonstrate very poor performance for Russian language. For example, 'happy birthday to' is a common phrase without double meaning, which could not be continued correctly by available models.

In this paper an approach to customization of pre-trained neural network language model to specific domain is proposed. This technique allows processing word outside the tokens list and thus to get benefits from transfer learning.

The rest of this paper is organized as follows. In Sect. 2 the detailed technique description is presented. Section 3 presents experimental results, and Sect. 4 concludes the paper.

2 Language Model Customization

The general idea of the proposed approach is to add an extra layer of words pre-processing before the neural network language model (Fig. 1).

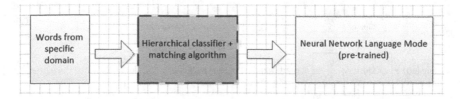

Fig. 1. Additional pre-processing layer

This layer consists of two parts: hierarchical classifier that groups words from neural network vocabulary and matching algorithm that matches new words to linear combination of words from vocabulary $new\_word = weight_1 * word_1 + ... + weight_N * word_N$.

2.1 Tokens Hierarchical Clustering

The first layer of neural network language model is an embedding layer which transforms one-hot encoded vectors into n-dimensional vectors of the embedding vectors space. Each coordinate of one-hot vector refers to a word in a vocabulary of language model.

Let us define W_{lm}, a set of words included in tokens list of neural network. The task is to organize words from tokens list into a tree, where leaf nodes contain single word $w_i \in W_{lm}$, and other nodes are clusters that include all the words below in the hierarchy $w_{kj} \in C_k \subset W_{lm}$. $|W_{lm}| = N$.

This task could be completed by performing procedure which is a hierarchical modification [10] of $\epsilon - clustering$ [11,12]. This procedure needs to be provided with a similarity measure for objects, let denote it by μ. There are a lot of pre-trained word embedding models for each language. This model provides a vector for each word and than the Euclidean or Manhattan distance could be calculated. In this paper the '$ruwikiruscorpora\_upos\_skipgram\_300\_2\_2019$'[1].

One of the main advantages of graph based approach is its ability to be interpreted by human. The classifier could be easily modified by experts to add information domain specifics [1]. At least all the words that are not from domain vocabulary could be cut off by the classifier. On the Fig. 2 a part of sample classifier is shown. This sub-tree consists of two main branches dedicated to software and hardware installation process. Each level has a number (ϵ) that indicates the step of hierarchical clustering procedure when these level was obtained and it means that all the branches on this level has mutual similarity less than ϵ.

Thus a hierarchical classifier with additional layer information could be obtained.

---

[1] The model was downloaded from open resource https://rusvectores.org/ru/models.

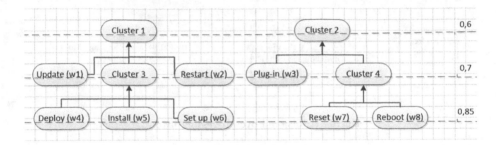

Fig. 2. Hierarchical clustering sub-tree sample

2.2 Specific Domain Words Matching

The task of the matching step is to construct vectors for words from specific domain so that they could be processed by a pre-trained neural network. These vectors should have N components, where N equals to the amount of inputs of neural network $N = |W_{lm}|$.

For each word w there are two possible cases. The word is already included into the language model tokens list $w = w_i \in W_{lm}$ and in this case the corresponding vector is $v = (0, 0, ..., 1, 0, ..., 0)$, where component with 1 has index i. Another case is where word $w \notin W_{lm}$. In this case there are some possible strategies to get a vector form. The first one, and the most evident, is to replace a given word with the most similar one according to similarity measure μ. This means to choose i, $\mu(w, w_i) = max(w, w_j) \forall j \in [1, N]$. This strategy does not require any classifier, but it is not efficient when there are some equidistant words in the tokens list, especially when they significantly differ in their semantic meaning. In order to have an alternative way of matching, the first strategy is also considered in the experimental part.

In the general case the proposed technique is as following:

1. If $max(w, w_j) = \mu(w, w_i) > 0, 9^2$ $\forall j \in [1, N]$ then $v = (0, 0, ..., 1, 0, ..., 0)$, with 1 on the i-th place.
2. Start with $\epsilon = 0, 9$ and find all the words $W_{nn} = \{w_j | \mu(w, w_j) >= \epsilon, j \in [1, N]\}$. If $|W_{nn}| = 0$ then set $\epsilon = \epsilon - \delta_\epsilon$. In this paper $\delta_\epsilon = 0, 05$, according to hierarchical clustering procedure specifics.
3. Get all the clusters $C_{nn} = \{c_j | \exists i\, w_i \in W_{nn}\}$ i.e. all the parent nodes in classifier for leaf nodes in W_{nn}.
4. Start with layer $l = 0, 9$ and get all nodes from this layer $L_l = \{c_j | c_j \in C_{nn}\, \&\, layer(c_j) = l\}$. If $|L_l| > 2^3$ then the change $l = l + \delta_l$ and move it to the previous step. In this paper δ_l has been chosen as $0,05$, according to hierarchical clustering procedure specifics.

---

[2] The value $\epsilon = 0, 9$ was obtained by experimental way and could differ from model to model.

[3] This threshold is heuristic and needs to be surveyed more thoroughly in future studies.

5. For each node (cluster) we define a weight according to the distance of the cluster center. $weight = \mu(w, cluster\,center_i) \,/\, |\sum_{j \in L_l} \mu(w, cluster\,center_j)|$
6. For each child node define weight in the same way as at the previous step and multiply by the parent's weight $weight = parent\,weight * children\,weight$.
7. Stop when all the leaf nodes get weights. All the other weights are set to 0 $weight_i = 0 \,\forall i \notin W_{nn}$ As a result $v = (weight_1, weight_2, weight_3, ..., weight_N)$

This algorithm is illustrated in Fig. 3. First, the similarity of word 'mount' to other words is calculated. The most similar words are 'install', 'set up' and 'plug-in' were detected. Then parent nodes are detected layer by layer from the bottom to the top, until only 2 nodes are left. Next, top-to-bottom process starts. Based on the distance to the cluster centers (0.8 and 0.71), the node weights are calculated as 0.53 and 0.47 respectively. And finally, the weights for children nodes of 'cluster 3' are calculated. Thus, a vector for word 'mount' will be (0, 0, 0.53, 0, 0.24, 0.23, 0, 0, ...).

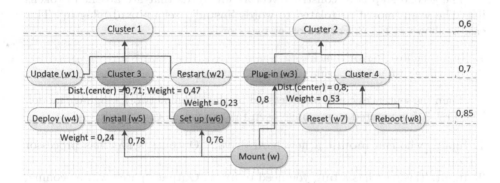

Fig. 3. Matching process sample for word 'mount'

Thus each word from the domain is converted into vectors in N-dimensional vector space.

Besides the words that are present in the language model the token list can be re-matched to other words or sets of words. This could be useful in case where word's meaning is changed significantly in the domain. For example: 'mount', 'branch', 'bug' in the software development domain.

3 Experimental Results

For experimental purposes pre-trained neural network language model for Russian language with architecture ULMFiT has been chosen[4]. This model has been trained on news portal (lenta.ru) and has perplexity 36,23.

---

[4] https://github.com/ppleskov/Russian-Language-Model.

All the most popular neural network language models take as an input sequence of words, to be more specific, sequence of words indexes in the tokens list. This make it difficult to use custom input vectors with pre-trained neural network. In this paper a hard code solution was used: the 'fastai' library has been modified to change not used input components into hard coded vectors.

To show the technique some common phrases from developers chats is used:

1. 'who can **mount** a new hard drive?'
2. 'this part has a **bug** you need to fix it'
3. 'this abstract class does not satisfy to this **interface**'

The chosen language model includes 'mount', 'bug' in common meaning and does not include word 'interface' in its tokens list. The aim is to be able to proceed this sentences with pre-trained neural network.

The first step is to construct a hierarchical classifier. The input layer of the current network has 60 000 neurons. The resulting hierarchy has about 80 000 nodes, 60 levels. The part of hierarchy is shown on Fig. 2.

The second step is to construct vectors for words that are absent in tokens list. The word 'mount' is related to words 'install', 'set up' and 'plug-in'. This case is shown in Fig. 3. For the other two words:

1. 'bug': 'failure', 'error', 'lack'
2. 'interface': 'structure', 'rule', 'protocol'

Then the sentences could be processed by the neural network language model. The first 3–5 generated words have been taken as an output result:

1. Input: 'who can **mount** a new hard drive?'. Output: 'server has processor core'
2. Input: 'this part has a **bug** you need to fix it'. Output: 'patch will be coming soon'
3. Input: 'this class could not be inherited from this **interface**'. Output: 'protocol is failed'

The results below were generated when one of the most similar words has been used instead of vector calculation.

1. Input: 'who can **mount** a new hard drive?'. Output: 'trip will be long and pleasant'
2. Input: 'this part has a **bug** you need to fix it'. Output: 'anti insect service'
3. Input: 'this class could not be inherited from this **interface**'. Output: 'the whole building is a heritage'

The neural network output in first two cases uses the common word meanings and produces wrong context. In the last case the word 'interface' was just ignored and the context produced was based on the word 'inherited' only.

4   Conclusion

In this paper an attempt to apply transfer learning technique to special domains was made. The proposed approach allows one to use not learned words with pre-trained neural network language model. It is important in domains with insufficient amount of texts to train custom language model or when the calculation resources are limited. This technique can also be used to prototype and check ideas (hypothesis) before starting to teach custom language model.

The results show effectiveness of proposed approach by more wide experiments need to be done. In the further study we will compare different neural network architectures within the proposed approach, searching a way of fine tuning the language model and comparison of effectiveness in different NLP benchmarks. It is important to develop extension to existing neural network frameworks to support not only the custom head, but also the custom tails.

Acknowledgements. The study was funded by Russian Foundation for Basic Research, research project no. 18-47-732005 and by the government of Ulyanovsk region, research project no. 18-47-732004.

References

1. Dudarin, P., Samokhvalov, M., Yarushkina, N.: An approach to feature space construction from clustering feature tree. In: Kuznetsov, S.O., Osipov, G.S., Stefanuk, V.L. (eds.) RCAI 2018. CCIS, vol. 934, pp. 176–189. Springer, Cham (2018). https://doi.org/10.1007/978-3-030-00617-4_17

2. Loukachevitch, N., Parkhomenko, E.: Recognition of multiword expressions using word embeddings. In: Kuznetsov, S.O., Osipov, G.S., Stefanuk, V.L. (eds.) RCAI 2018. CCIS, vol. 934, pp. 112–124. Springer, Cham (2018). https://doi.org/10.1007/978-3-030-00617-4_11

3. Arefyev, N., Ermolaev, P., Panchenko, A.: How much does a word weigh? Weighting word embeddings for word sense induction. CoRR, abs/1805.09209 (2018)

4. Panchenko, A., et al.: Serelex: search and visualization of semantically related words. In: Serdyukov, P., et al. (eds.) ECIR 2013. LNCS, vol. 7814, pp. 837–840. Springer, Heidelberg (2013). https://doi.org/10.1007/978-3-642-36973-5_97

5. Kutuzov, A., Kuzmenko, E.: WebVectors: a toolkit for building web interfaces for vector semantic models. In: Ignatov, D.I., et al. (eds.) AIST 2016. CCIS, vol. 661, pp. 155–161. Springer, Cham (2017). https://doi.org/10.1007/978-3-319-52920-2_15

6. Fares, M., Kutuzov, A., Oepen, S., Velldal, E.: Word vectors, reuse, and replicability: towards a community repository of large-text resources. In: Proceedings of the 21st Nordic Conference on Computational Linguistics, pp. 271–276 (2017)

7. Che, W., Liu, Y., Wang, Y., Zheng, B., Liu, T.: Towards better UD parsing: deep contextualized word embeddings, ensemble, and treebank concatenation. In: Proceedings of the CoNLL 2018 Shared Task: Multilingual Parsing from Raw Text to Universal Dependencies, pp. 55–64 (2018)

8. Devlin, J., Chang, M.-W., Lee, K., Toutanova, K.: BERT: pre-training of deep bidirectional transformers for language understanding. arXiv preprint arXiv:1810.04805 (2018)

9. Howard, J., Ruder, S.: Universal language model fine-tuning for text classification. In: Proceedings of the 56th Annual Meeting of the Association for Computational Linguistics (Volume 1: Long Papers), pp. 328–339 (2018)
10. Dudarin, P.V., Yarushkina, N.G.: An approach to fuzzy hierarchical clustering of short text fragments based on fuzzy graph clustering. In: Abraham, A., Kovalev, S., Tarassov, V., Snasel, V., Vasileva, M., Sukhanov, A. (eds.) IITI 2017. AISC, vol. 679, pp. 295–304. Springer, Cham (2018). https://doi.org/10.1007/978-3-319-68321-8_30
11. Yeh, R.T., Bang, S.Y.: Fuzzy relation, fuzzy graphs and their applications to clustering analysis. In: Fuzzy Sets and Their Applications to Cognitive and Decision Processes, pp. 125–149. Academic Press (1975)
12. Rosenfeld, A.: Fuzzy graphs. In: Fuzzy Sets and Their Applications to Cognitive and Decision Processes, pp. 77–95. Academic Press, New York (1975)
13. Tomas, M., Chen, K., Gregory, S.C., Jeffrey, D.: Efficient estimation of word representations in vector space. CoRR, abs/1301.3781 (2013)
14. Manning, C.D., Raghavan, P., Schütze, H.: Introduction to Information Retrieval. Cambridge University Press, New York (2008)
15. Dudarin, P., Pinkov, A., Yarushkina, N.: Methodology and the algorithm for clustering economic analytics object. Autom. Control Processes **47**(1), 591–604 (2017)
16. Jiaming, X., Bo, X., Zheng, S., Tian, G., Zhao, J.: Self-taught convolutional neural networks for short text clustering. Neural Netw. Official J. Int. Neural Netw. Soc. **88**, 22–31 (2017)
17. Tang, J., Wang, X., Gao, H., Hu, X., Liu, H.: Enriching short text representation in microblog for clustering. Front. Comput. Sci. **6**(1), 88–101 (2012). https://doi.org/10.1007/s11704-011-1167-7
18. Zhao, Q., Rezaei, M., Chen, H., Franti, P: Keyword clustering for automatic categorization. In: 2012 21st International Conference on Pattern Recognition (ICPR). IEEE (2012)
19. Pinto, D., Jiménez-Salazar, H., Rosso, P.: Clustering abstracts of scientific texts using the transition point technique. In: Gelbukh, A. (ed.) CICLing 2006. LNCS, vol. 3878, pp. 536–546. Springer, Heidelberg (2006). https://doi.org/10.1007/11671299_55
20. Nadezhda, Y., Gleb, G., Pavel, D., Vladimir, S.: An approach to similar software projects searching and architecture analysis based on artificial intelligence methods. In: Abraham, A., Kovalev, S., Tarassov, V., Snasel, V., Sukhanov, A. (eds.) IITI'18 2018. AISC, vol. 874, pp. 341–352. Springer, Cham (2019). https://doi.org/10.1007/978-3-030-01818-4_34

Predicting Personality Traits from Social Network Profiles

Maxim Stankevich[1]([✉]), Andrey Latyshev[2], Natalia Kiselnikova[3], and Ivan Smirnov[1,4]

[1] Federal Research Center "Computer Science and Control", RAS, Moscow, Russia
{stankevich,ivs}@isa.ru
[2] Limited Liability Company "RI Technologies", Moscow, Russia
andrey.latyshev@gmail.com
[3] Psychological Institute, Russian Academy of Education, Moscow, Russia
nv.pirao@gmail.com
[4] Peoples' Friendship University of Russia (RUDN University), Moscow, Russia

Abstract. Early detection of mental disorders risk is an important task for modern society. A large set of clinical works showed that five-factor personality traits model (Big Five) can predict mental disorders. In this paper, we consider the problem of automatic detection of personality traits from user profiles of Russian social network VKontakte. We describe the preparation of user profiles dataset, propose several features sets and evaluate machine learning methods for predicting personality traits. The results of experiments show that different features set demonstrate promising results on the task of a personality prediction.

Keywords: Personality traits · Social media · Machine learning

1 Introduction

Early detection of people with mental disorders risk is an important task for modern society. With a high availability of preventive methods, early detection can provide opportunity for preventive care in time and reduce the number of people who need treatment.

A large set of studies showed that five-factor personality traits model (Big Five) and its dispositions (extroversion, agreeableness, conscientiousness, neuroticism, openness to experience) predict and/or correlate with mental disorders [1]. In [2] T.A. Widiger and S.N. Mullins-Sweatt showed that the "Big Five" personality traits can be used for effective diagnostics of mental disorders. A number of studies [3–7] propose that it is possible to integrate the Big Five model with psychiatric models of disorders.

The development of machine learning methods and an increased amount of available social media data provided a lot of opportunities for researchers to build models that can reveal user personality using information from a personal profile. Moreover, social media data are a suitable tool for the investigation of human

S. O. Kuznetsov and A. I. Panov (Eds.): RCAI 2019, CCIS 1093, pp. 177–188, 2019.
https://doi.org/10.1007/978-3-030-30763-9_15

personality and behavior since it allows to make the process of data collection much easier and effective in comparison to manual offline methods [8, 9].

This paper describes the task of predicting the Big Five personality traits of Vkontakte users using textual and non-textual features extracted from 1020 personal profiles. In Sect. 2 we provide insight on related works; in Sect. 3 we present a dataset of Vkontakte profiles that we collected for this research; Sect. 4 describes our methods and feature engineering; the last section presents the results of experiments and discussion.

2 Related Works

Recent studies describe a range of methods that are focused on the identification of personality traits by analyzing text, images, video, and audio content posted by users on social networks.

Yarkoni et al. [10] conducted a large-scale analysis of identity using language analysis. They showed that using some specific groups of terms is related to the personality of the authors. Iacobelli et al. [11] used blogs texts to categorize author personalities and demonstrated that the structure of the text is also an important characteristic that can help to assess the author's personality. Oberlander et al. [12] studied how to make a conclusion about the personality of the blog authors by analyzing their text messages. They asked 71 different users to answer questionnaires to identify personality traits and then apply n-grams features with SVM-based classifier to reveal personality.

Golbeck et al. [13] showed that Twitter users can be assessed by their tweets using information about the number of subscribers, mentions, and words in a tweet. Souri et al. [14] collected information about the personal characteristics of volunteers and their Facebook profiles to address the personality prediction task. They suggested that it is possible to identify personality by analyzing the activity of users on a social network. The authors utilized the results of 100 questionnaires completed by Facebook users and performed various data mining methods to perform on the task. The result showed that it is possible to recognize the user's personality by profile analysis with a decent prediction accuracy.

Schwartz et al. performed an in-depth analysis of relations between social media language and personality traits [15]. The authors processed the personality traits data of 75,000 volunteers from Facebook and analyzed 700 million words, phrases, and topic instances. The proposed method of open-vocabulary analysis was utilized to discover language features that can be used to distinguish demographic and psychological attributes of Facebook users. They applied open-vocabulary approach and LIWC features [16] to perform the task of personality traits prediction and reported 65% to 79% classification accuracy across different personality traits.

However, the content of social networks includes graphic content as well as texts and information about likes, subscribers, etc. The development of methods and tools of machine learning made it possible to conduct personality studies by analyzing images.

Steele et al. in 2009 [17] studied the characteristics of profile images and their connection with the opinion of other users about the personality of image owners.

In their work, they asked users to complete the sentence "I see a person as someone who…" by looking at the images. The results showed that the more personal information contained in the photo, the greater was the level of agreement on the personality characteristics. However, the work did not indicate which personal characteristics were attributed to users. Cristani et al. [18] proved that there are visual patterns that correlate with the personality traits of 300 Flickr users. They also showed that information about images that users like correlates with users' personal traits, such as self-esteem. The higher the correlation between "real self" and "ideal self", the more accurately you can determine the user's identity by the posts that he or she liked. In their work, they showed that such personality traits as extraversion and conscience are most accurately identified. The results for defining neuroticism and agreeableness were also satisfactory.

Segalin et al. [19] researched images to identify the personality of the user who liked this image. They proposed a new set of functions that can encode information about these images better. They described each image by 82 different functions divided into four main categories: color, composition, textural properties, and faces. Their method is suitable for comparing images with personality traits, but it works better for attributive personality traits than for self-assessment. In their other work, Segalin et al. [20] proved the possibility of deep learning to explore the characteristics of personal qualities in images automatically. They determined the profile of the "Big Five" personal characteristics of each user in two ways: first, using a questionnaire, then using an assessment by a group of experts (they assessed the user's personal qualities based on his images). The convolutional neural network (CNN) based binary classifier model was then trained to evaluate each of the Big Five's traits.

Cucurull et al. [21] proposed a new methodology based on deep learning. Their goal was to create a combined model of personality traits based on images and text. They used images placed together with certain words that are considered to be closely related to a particular personality trait. The authors determined that there is a correlation between the posted images and their accompanying texts, which can be successfully modeled using deep neural networks to assess personality.

At present, research of the connection between the personality traits of users and social networking content is mainly conducted on English-language content. Studies of Russian-language content are just starting to develop [8, 9]. Our work studies personality traits using the analysis of activity and texts taken from the Russian social network VKontakte.

3   Dataset

We asked volunteers from Vkontakte to take part in our psychological research and complete "Big Five" NEO-FFI questionnaire [22]. Before answering questions, users provided access to their public pages under privacy constraints via Vkontakte application. We automatically collected all available information from public personal profile pages using Vkontakte API for the users who completed the questionnaire. Posts, comments, information about communities, friends, etc. were collected from January 2017 to April 2019 for each user. Overall, information from 1020 profiles was assembled to compile our dataset. All of the personal information that can reveal the identity of persons were removed from data collection.

Like in our previous paper [23] we divided the initial NEO-FFI score scale (0–48) of each personality trait as following labels: *low level* (0–20), *medium level* (21–32) and *high level* (33–48). However, in this work, we decided to transform the task to the binary classification by removing *medium level* scores.

The dataset for this research and described task is novel for the Russian-speaking social networks and we provide detailed statistics on the data in this section. Overall, the collected data contains the following types of information about 1020 users:

- **NEO-FFI questionnaires scores.** Scores for extroversion, agreeableness, conscientiousness, neuroticism, and openness to experience.
- **General information from personal pages.** Any available information from social media profiles including the number of friends, number of followers, number of follows, number of groups, age, gender, answers on predefined Vkontakte profile questions, profile visibility settings, number of photos, and information about relations, etc.
- **User messages in personal profiles.** All available textual information authored by users.
- **Commentaries.** Vkontakte API also provides an opportunity to collect commentaries that linked to the user's messages.
- **Reposts.** The major volume of content in users' profiles is reposting. Reposts are the usual posts which represent content that provided by other social media entities (other persons and groups) and retranslated by users on their personal pages.

The NEO-FFI scores distribution on the entire data is presented in Fig. 1. It can be seen from the data that all personal traits normally distributed with a mean value placed in the *medium level* interval. The mean score for the neuroticism biased to the *high level* and extroversion and conscientiousness scores biased to the *low level*.

The statistics on the gender and age in our dataset is presented in Fig. 2. The mean age is 24.82 with the standard deviation equal to 6.24. The gender ratio is unbalanced with a majority of females (69% females and 31% males). Some statistics on information retrieved for personal pages are presented in Table 1.

Table 1. Information from user's profiles

Value	Mean ± std	Min	Max
Number of friends	175.38 ± 176.85	0	2752
Number of followers	138.07 ± 242.78	0	2411
Number of authored posts	66.04 ± 108.48	0	1352
Number of reposts	92.39 ± 192.61	0	2483
Number of groups	526.37 ± 1029.38	0	5000

We found that collected data is extremely noisy. Some of the profiles are missing almost any information about their owners. Another drawback consists of the fact that we planned to analyze textual messages, but it is not possible when people do not

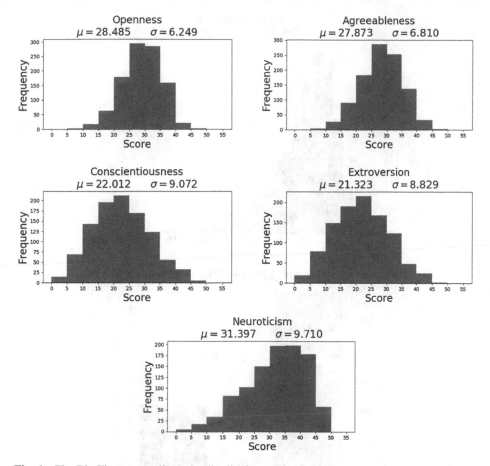

Fig. 1. The Big Five personality traits distribution on the data. μ corresponds to mean value; σ corresponds to the standard deviation.

provide any textual information. To make it possible to process the text data we performed the following actions:

1. Concatenate users post collections with commentaries authored by them.
2. Remove all characters which are not alphabet or standard punctuation marks from user's texts using regular expression;
3. Remove all posts with more than 2000 characters. The manual analysis of big posts revealed that they are usually not authored by user's themselves;
4. Set constraint 100 on the maximum number of posts per user;
5. Remove all users with less than 10 posts provided or with a total number of characters more than 40000.

Performing these actions on the raw data yielded the set of 632 users which we annotated as a *text-based set*. The general statistics on text information provided by users is presented in Table 2.

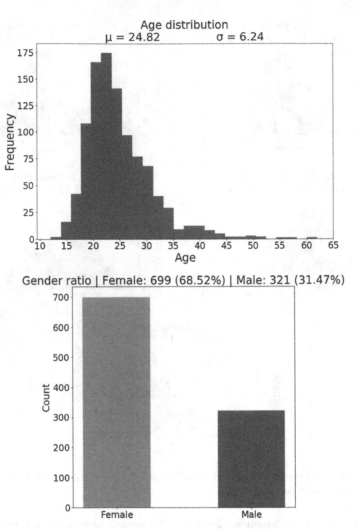

Fig. 2. Age distribution and gender partition on the data. μ corresponds to mean value; σ corresponds to the standard deviation.

Table 2. Statistics on the text-based set.

Value	Mean ± std	Min	Max
Posts per user	64.52 ± 33.63	10	100
Sentences per user	144.40 ± 105.04	10	732
Words per user	1369.86 ± 1299.53	51	7295
Avg. sentences per post	2.13 ± 0.98	1	9.67
Avg. words per sentence	8.56 ± 2.81	3.02	19.95
Avg. words per post	19.95 ± 14.56	3.22	117.35

4 Features and Methods

We used two types of features for predicting personal traits from social networks data. The first group includes meta-information from the user's profile and information about reposts. The second group of features focused on linguistic information from textual messages and includes morphological, syntactic, and psycholinguistic characteristics of the text.

- **Psycholinguistic characteristics.** Psycholinguistic characteristics are linguistic features which are based on morphological and syntactic information that represent psychological peculiarities of the author. We used more than 30 psycholinguistic features such as POS-tag ratio, Trager coefficient, the mean number of words per sentence, mean number of characters per word, average syntax tree depth, pronouns frequency, sentiment rate, different verbs forms usage, unique words ratio, etc. These features are described in more details in our other work that is related to the prediction of depression from essays in Russian [24]. We also extended this set with counts of uppercase characters, hashtags, exclamation marks, smiles, and links.
- **N-grams.** The n-grams features are a very popular and effective tool for various natural language processing task. We computed unigrams and bigrams sets of features using tf-idf values of words from users' messages.
- **Dictionaries.** We utilized dictionaries described in [25] which were used for the task of detection verbal aggression in social media writings. These dictionaries contain the following word groups: negative emotional words, lexis of suffering, positive emotional words, absolute and intensifying terms, motivation and stressful words, invectives, etc.
- **Profile information.** These simple features were leveraged from the general information about user's profiles: number of friends, number of followers, number of groups, number of posts, number of likes on posts, post/repost ratio. We utilized information about profile visibility settings as binary features. Different binary features were computed using information about some predefined Vkontakte questions which can be fulfilled by profile owner but also can remain empty (e.g. favorite books and movies, religious beliefs, relations, relatives, university, school, attitudes toward smoking and alcohol, etc.);
- **Repost matrix.** We found that one of the main activities in the users' profile is reposting of the content authored by groups/communities and other people. Some of these sources are very popular and followed by millions of people. We have analyzed the approach described in [26] where Facebook user likes were used to predicted personality. The information about repost sources was processed to form the repost matrix in the way similar to calculating bag-of-words but using repost sources as vocabulary and number of reposts from these sources as a word's usage count.

As it was mentioned before, we transformed our initial task of predicting personality traits to binary classification by excluding medium scores for each trait and leaving only *low* (0-20 on the NEO-FFI scale) and *high* (33-48 on the NEO-FFI scale) scores. We believe that high and low levels of personal traits are much more valuable for our research purposes described in the first section of this work.

The described features were calculated for 632 users that provided, at last, any amount of text. However, we decided to examine how profile information and repost matrix features will work on the full set of 1020 users because these features are not depending on the text volume. We want to outline the feature set labels that we used to demonstrate the classification report:

- **PC** – psycholinguistic characteristics;
- **UG** – unigrams;
- **BG** – bigrams;
- **D** – dictionaries;
- **PI** – profile information;
- **RM** – repost matrix.

5   Results of Experiments

To perform on the task, we utilized the scikit-learn machine learning library [27]. Random forest and support vector machine (SVM) models were used to perform an evaluation of the data. All of the feature's sets were normalized and scaled. Hyperparameters of the classification algorithms were tuned by grid-search runs.

Two different experiments were computed to evaluate the classification performance of retrieved features and models. First, we ran a binary classification using the information about 632 Vkontakte users who provided enough text volume to retrieve linguistic features from posts (text-based set). Secondly, we ran a binary classification task using only profile related features on the full data with 1020 samples (full data). To evaluate and compare performance we used ROC AUC score, since accuracy is not viable in our case because the *high level* and *low level* classes are not balanced. We included results of random-based dummy classifier in our classification report since the described task was not previously tested on Russian-speaking social network data. The classification report for text-based set presented in Table 3 and the classification report for full data presented in Table 4. The performance demonstrated as averaged ROC AUC score and standard deviation for 5 cross-validations run with 4-folds.

The outline of best classification performances per personality trait for the text-based set is the following. The combination of psycholinguistic characteristics and profile information feature sets (PC+PI) with Random Forest classifier yielded the best ROC AUC score for neuroticism and extraversion. It can be said that these personality traits predicted better than other traits in our experiments which is also correlated with results presented in related studies [10–18]. For agreeableness, the best result (69.71) was obtained using the PC indicator (Psycholinguistic characteristics). Surprisingly, repost matrix features (RM) demonstrated best predictions for openness to experience with SVM, but in general results for this trait, as well as for conscientiousness (highest ROC AUC – 63.97 with unigram features), are worst in comparison with other traits.

We found that psycholinguistic characteristics yielding good results on a personality prediction task. The simple profile information features also performed well on the

Table 3 Classification report for the *text-based set*. Personality trait labels are the following: **N** – neuroticism; **O** – openness to experience; **A** – agreeableness, **C** – conscientiousness, **E** – extroversion. Classification results demonstrated as averaged ROC AUC score ± standard deviation.

Number of samples					
Count	N	O	A	C	E
Low level	105	69	73	284	268
High level	318	225	225	110	102
SVC					
PC	68.07 ± 6.34	58.44 ± 8.87	64.63 ± 6.10	62.94 ± 2.88	71.15 ± 3.83
UG	64.11 ± 11.21	63.62 ± 7.06	63.21 ± 6.02	**63.97 ± 3.72**	69.58 ± 7.82
BG	65.11 ± 10.21	62.76 ± 6.91	61.54 ± 5.35	62.45 ± 3.20	69.68 ± 6.55
D	61.43 ± 3.88	51.72 ± 9.56	57.58 ± 8.01	52.47 ± 6.18	65.37 ± 5.27
PI	64.72 ± 2.58	61.15 ± 3.76	60.22 ± 5.14	57.76 ± 2.87	71.46 ± 2.91
RM	58.13 ± 5.75	**64.12 ± 6.02**	50.17 ± 4.28	58.06 ± 6.62	67.86 ± 7.52
PC + PI	65.45 ± 5.68	55.9 ± 2.48	62.26 ± 5.19	58.48 ± 6.28	72.97 ± 3.16
Random forest					
PC	68.48 ± 6.91	57.29 ± 7.44	**69.71 ± 3.56**	61.12 ± 2.01	73.55 ± 4.38
UG	62.31 ± 5.99	63.29 ± 7.07	61.7 ± 3.14	58.05 ± 6.34	71.40 ± 6.25
BG	62.33 ± 6.10	61.64 ± 5.61	61.98 ± 6.24	56.96 ± 6.68	70.25 ± 4.26
D	61.79 ± 4.64	55.87 ± 9.44	58.12 ± 6.21	56.10 ± 2.96	65.66 ± 4.53
PI	67.27 ± 1.65	52.87 ± 4.45	60.32 ± 7.56	62.37 ± 7.13	75.04 ± 4.52
RM	67.46 ± 3.88	60.28 ± 5.05	61.87 ± 11.49	59.38 ± 4.05	63.74 ± 4.62
PC + PI	**70.99 ± 5.97**	59.34 ± 7.29	69.60 ± 4.19	63.78 ± 3.72	**76.88 ± 2.53**
Dummy classifier					
–	46.9 ± 4.99	50.96 ± 8.76	51.12 ± 4.93	44.78 ± 2.74	46.92 ± 3.85

data, which is confirmed by results demonstrated in Table 4. The highest ROC AUC score for neuroticism achieved by PI set with Random Forest on full data. Our experiments showed that the n-gram based model demonstrate relatively poor results. We assume that this is related to the great amount of noise in the text data. The total amount of posts/words per users significantly vary from user to user and social media lexicon contains a lot of slang. We examined the same problem with dictionary-based features. It is clear that we can apply more limitations on the user's text, but these steps will reduce our text-based set even more. It is also true for profile information based features since some of the user's personal pages are completely empty. Some of these obstacles can be negotiated by extending data volume. In the other hand, data collection process is slow and require a lot of effort. However, on the current state of our research, we assume that it is not strictly necessary to impose a strong limitation on the data, even if our classification results are far from perfect.

To compare our performance with a result of personality prediction presented in [15], we ran several additional experiments: we classified people as being high or low in each trait by using top and bottom quartiles of personality scores. The results of a similar experiment in related work are ranged from 65% to 79% of classification

Table 4 Classification report for the *full data*. Personality traits labels are the following: **N** – neuroticism; **O** – openness to experience; **A** – agreeableness, **C** – conscientiousness, **E** – extroversion. The results demonstrated as averaged ROC AUC score ± standard deviation.

Number of samples					
Count	N	O	A	C	E
Low level	157	110	155	468	484
High level	557	346	316	166	145
SVC					
PI	69.78 ± 2.32	55.79 ± 1.95	66.42 ± 2.79	59.49 ± 4.46	71.01 ± 2.62
RM	56.62 ± 2.03	**63.35 ± 2.92**	55.7 ± 4.53	56.68 ± 4.54	60.06 ± 6.06
Random forest					
PI	**71.36 ± 2.70**	55.01 ± 2.3	**67.48 ± 4.69**	**64.39 ± 5.87**	**74.83 ± 3.83**
RM	62.41 ± 5.96	57.31 ± 5.36	64.35 ± 3.85	53.73 ± 4.28	57.66 ± 3.26
Dummy classifier					
–	49.67 ± 5.85	50.59 ± 3.34	50.61 ± 2.78	50.64 ± 3.86	48.55 ± 2.59

accuracy. In our experiment, classification accuracy ranged between 62% and 74% across personality traits. With a given volume of data, which is currently much smaller, our models demonstrate a slightly worse, but comparable performance.

6   Conclusion

In this study, we performed the task of predicting personality traits form social network profiles using data about 1020 users from Russian-speaking social network Vkontakte. We founded that social media texts are extremely noisy and require a lot of normalization. Providing that, we prepared the data and processed user's messages and personal profiles to form several sets of features: psycholinguistic characteristics, dictionaries, n-grams, profile information, and repost matrix. Our experiments were represented as a binary classification task by separating NEO-FFI questionnaire personality trait scores to high and low levels.

The various sets of features and classification algorithms were evaluated on the data revealing that psycholinguistic characteristics and profile information features yield good results on the task. In contrast, the results demonstrated that dictionary features achieved poor results on the data and should be modified. Due to the big amount of noise in the social media texts n-grams models did not work as well as we expected, but we are planning to adjust these models and overcome these limitations. We believe that repost matrix features have great potential and will demonstrate good results on a larger dataset. We are also planning to apply neural network based models to the personality prediction task.

To sum up, the proposed methods for identifying the personality traits of the Big Five model through analysis of text and user behavior parameters collected from social network demonstrate some positive results. On their basis, personality traits can be predicted with varying degrees of confidence. Thus, neuroticism and extraversion are best predicted on the basis of a model that uses psycholinguistic characteristics and information from a profile. The results show the possibility of identifying personality traits through the analysis of users' social network data. As a consequence, it is also possible to apply the proposed methods for identifying personal-related disorders.

Acknowledgments. This work was financially supported by the Ministry of Education and Science of the Russian Federation. Grant No. 14.604.21.0194 (Unique Project Identifier RFMEFI60417X0194).

References

1. Widiger, T.A., Costa Jr., P.T.: Personality and personality disorders. J. Abnormal Psychol. **103**(1), 78 (1994)
2. Widiger, T.A., Mullins-Sweatt, S.N.: Clinical utility of a dimensional model of personality disorder. Prof. Psychol. Res. Pract. **41**(6), 488 (2010)
3. Widiger, T.A., Costa Jr, P.T.: Personality Disorders and the Five-Factor Model of Personality. American Psychological Association, Washington (2013)
4. Widiger, T.A., Costa Jr, P.T., McCrae, R.R.: A proposal for Axis II: diagnosing personality disorders using the five-factor model (2002)
5. Wiggins, J.S., Pincus, A.L.: Conceptions of personality disorders and dimensions of personality. Psychol. Assess. J. Consult. Clin. Psychol. **1**(4), 305 (1989)
6. Piedmont, R.L., Sherman, M.F., Sherman, N.C., Dy-Liacco, G.S., Williams, J.E.: Using the five-factor model to identify a new personality disorder domain: the case for experiential permeability. J. Pers. Soc. Psychol. **96**(6), 1245 (2009)
7. Ozer, D.J., Benet-Martinez, V.: Personality and the prediction of consequential outcomes. Annu. Rev. Psychol. **57**, 401–421 (2006)
8. Panicheva, P., Bogolyubova, O., Ledovaya, Y.: Revealing interpetable content correlates of the dark triad personality traits. In: RUSSIR-2016. Springer (2016)
9. Ledovaya, Y.A., Tikhonov, R.V., Bogolyubova, O.N.: Social networks as a new environment for interdisciplinary studies of human behavior (2017)
10. Yarkoni, T.: Personality in 100,000 words: a large-scale analysis of personality and word use among bloggers. J. Res. Pers. **44**(3), 363–373 (2010)
11. Iacobelli, F., Gill, A.J., Nowson, S., Oberlander, J.: Large scale personality classification of bloggers. In: D'Mello, S., Graesser, A., Schuller, B., Martin, J.-C. (eds.) ACII 2011. LNCS, vol. 6975, pp. 568–577. Springer, Heidelberg (2011). https://doi.org/10.1007/978-3-642-24571-8_71
12. Oberlander, J., Nowson, S.: Whose thumb is it anyway? Classifying author personality from weblog text. In: Proceedings of the COLING/ACL 2006 Main Conference Poster Sessions, pp. 627–634, July 2006
13. Golbeck, J., Robles, C., Edmondson, M., Turner, K.: Predicting personality from twitter. In: 2011 IEEE Third International Conference on Privacy, Security, Risk and Trust and 2011 IEEE Third International Conference on Social Computing, pp. 149–156. IEEE, October 2011
14. Souri, A., Hosseinpour, S., Rahmani, A.M.: Personality classification based on profiles of social networks' users and the five-factor model of personality. Hum.-Centric Comput. Inf. Sci. **8**(1), 24 (2018)
15. Schwartz, H.A., et al.: Personality, gender, and age in the language of social media: the open-vocabulary approach. PloS one **8**(9), e73791 (2013)

16. Tausczik, Y.R., Pennebaker, J.W.: The psychological meaning of words: LIWC and computerized text analysis methods. J. Lang. Soc. Psychol. **29**(1), 24–54 (2010)
17. Fitzgerald Steele, J., Evans, D.C., Green, R.K.: Is your profile picture worth 1000 words? Photo characteristics associated with personality impression agreement. In: Third International AAAI Conference on Weblogs and Social Media, March 2009
18. Cristani, M., Vinciarelli, A., Segalin, C., Perina, A.: Unveiling the multimedia unconscious: implicit cognitive processes and multimedia content analysis. In: Proceedings of the 21st ACM International Conference on Multimedia, pp. 213–222. ACM, October 2013
19. Segalin, C., Perina, A., Cristani, M., Vinciarelli, A.: The pictures we like are our image: continuous mapping of favorite pictures into self-assessed and attributed personality traits. IEEE Trans. Affect. Comput. **8**(2), 268–285 (2016)
20. Segalin, C., Cheng, D.S., Cristani, M.: Social profiling through image understanding: personality inference using convolutional neural networks. Comput. Vis. Image Underst. **156**, 34–50 (2017)
21. Cucurull, G., Rodríguez, P., Yazici, V.O., Gonfaus, J.M., Roca, F.X., Gonzàlez, J.: Deep inference of personality traits by integrating image and word use in social networks. arXiv preprint arXiv:1802.06757 (2018)
22. Costa, P.T., McCrae, R.R.: Normal personality assessment in clinical practice: the NEO Personality Inventory. Psychol. Assess. **4**(1), 5 (1992)
23. Stankevich, M., Smirnov, I., Ignatiev, N., Grigoryev, O., Kiselnikova, N.: Analysis of big five personality traits by processing of social media users activity features. In: DAMDID/RCDL, pp. 162–166, October 2018
24. Stankevich, M., Smirnov, I., Kuznetsova, Y., Kiselnikova, N., Enikolopov, S.: Predicting depression from essays in Russian. In: Computational Linguistics and Intellectual Technologies, DIALOGUE, vol. 18, pp. 637–647 (2019)
25. Devyatkin, D., Kuznetsova, Y., Chudova, N., Shvets, A.: Intellectual analysis of the manifestations of verbal aggressiveness in the texts of network communities (Intellektuanyj analiz proyavlenij verbalnoj agressivnosti v tekstah setevyh soobshchestv). Artif. Intell. Decis. Making **2**, 27–41 (2014)
26. Kosinski, M., Stillwell, D., Graepel, T.: Private traits and attributes are predictable from digital records of human behavior. Proc. Natl. Acad. Sci. **110**(15), 5802–5805 (2013)
27. Pedregosa, F., et al.: Scikit-learn: machine learning in Python. J. Mach. Learn. Res. **12**, 2825–2830 (2011)

Extraction of Cognitive Operations from Scientific Texts

Dmitry Devyatkin[✉]

Federal Research Centre "Computer Science and Control" RAS, Moscow, Russia
devyatkin@isa.ru

Abstract. Rhetorical structure theory defines the relations between predicates and larger discourse units, but it does not consider the extralinguistic nature of text-writing at all. However, the text-writing process is totally related to the particular targeted activity. This paper presents a new approach that does not model a text as a result of a researcher's cognitive activity embodied in it, but it models cognitive activity reflected in the scientific text. We also propose and evaluate a framework for detection of text fragments, which is related to cognitive operations in scientific texts. The obtained results confirm the usefulness of the suggested set of cognitive operations for the analysis of scientific texts. Moreover, these results justify the applicability of the proposed framework to cognitive operation extraction from scientific texts in Russian.

Keywords: Cognitive operations · Argument mining · Sequence labeling · Random forest · Long-short term memory

1 Introduction

Scientific communication differs from the other forms of communication in many aspects determined by the essence of scientific knowledge. In process of writing, an author realizes a series of cognitive operations which is reflected in the scientific text in presenting results, as well as the steps of theoretical and empirical research where the results were obtained. Because of this, if a tool for cognitive operation extraction was developed, a scientific text could be considered as a "road map" that allows tracking the main steps of any research, evaluating its compliance with principles of scientific knowledge, as well as reliability and originality of the automatically obtained results.

Among the studies devoted to the text mining, we consider the rhetoric structure theory [1, 2] as one of the most relevant in the study of cognitive operations in scientific texts. Let us briefly describe some concepts of this theory used today in computer modelling of language communication.

The main subject of the discourse analysis is rhetorical, or functional-semantic, relations which link discursive units of different sizes. Elementary discursive units are clauses. They are included in the composition of ever larger units, up to the direct components of the text. In rhetorical relations, discourse units can act as a core or a

The paper is supported by Russian Foundation For Basic Research (grant 17-29-07049 ofi_m).

S. O. Kuznetsov and A. I. Panov (Eds.): RCAI 2019, CCIS 1093, pp. 189–200, 2019.
https://doi.org/10.1007/978-3-030-30763-9_16

satellite. These relations can be asymmetric (core-satellite) or symmetric (core-core), binary or multicomponent. There are object and presentation rhetorical relations. The first ones define the state of affairs in the real world. Object relations help a reader to recognize the attitude. The second ones represent the events in the discourse. The effect of their expression is to enhance the positive attitude of the reader to the reported information.

The set of rhetorical relationships is the same for any units. The list of these relations is obtained as a result of analyzing a large number of texts related to various genres (advertisements, personal letters, political essays, scientific essays, etc.). This list is not closed and can be expanded and refined when referring to texts which have not been taken into account yet.

The main "object" relations are "elaboration", "circumstance", "solution", "volitional cause", "volitional result", "non-volitional cause", "non-volitional result", "purpose", "condition", "otherwise", "interpretation", "evaluation", "restatement", "summary", "sequence", "contrast".

The main "presentation" relations are "motivation", "antithesis", "background", "enablement", "evidence", "justify", "concession," and some others.

The rhetorical relations between discourse units can often be interpreted in different ways. Thus, several options are possible in the construction of the graph. In most cases there are no language forms for marking particular relationships. This ambiguity is the source of significant difficulties for automatic argument extraction. It is easy to see that the main focus in this framework lies in the structure of discourse.

However, the text-writing process is inextricably related to the particular activity for which it is held. While discourse theory defines the rhetorical (semantic) relations between predicates and larger discourse units it does not consider the extralinguistic nature of text-writing at all.

The genre-based theory [3] is more suited to the representation of cognitive processes. This theory and similar ones are widely used in the tools for automatic text annotation [4]. However, they describe only particular parts of a scientific publication. A more complete theory for cognitive operations, which appeared in scientific papers, was suggested in [5].

This paper proposes an original approach that does not model a text like a result of a researcher cognitive activity embodied in it, but it models cognitive activity itself that is reflected in the scientific text. We also propose and evaluate the framework for detection of text fragments related to cognitive operations in scientific texts.

2   Related Work

The related works are devoted to argument mining. Currently, there are plenty of approaches and tag schemas that differ in conceptualization, scope and degree of refinement [5]. All these schemas consider quite formal texts, such as research papers, news articles, patents, etc., because arbitrary machine-learning model needs particular linguistic clues to detect the arguments in texts.

Teufel et al. proposed Argument zoning schema in [6]. Argument zoning provides an analysis of the rhetorical progression of the scientific arguments following the knowledge claims, such as "aim", "textual", "basis", "contrast", "background", "other", and "own". Ibekwe-SanJuan presented a similar schema in [7]. The proposed argumentative roles are "objective", "new thing", "related work", "result", "hypothesis", and "future work". The aim of that research was to develop automatic annotation methods for the argumentative role of sentences in scientific abstracts. They tested two different feature sets, which are superficial linguistic cues (lexis, pos-tags, the position of a token, etc.) and positional heuristics. They performed experiments on paper abstracts and found out that positional heuristics perform better than the linguistic cues because these cues do not always discriminate clauses from different argumentative zones. Another annotation schema for contemporary science, engineering, and sociology was introduced in [8]. This schema is aimed to represent relations among concepts in research papers, such as techniques, resources, and effects. The main goal of the provided schema is representing the semantics of research papers for intelligent search systems. The proposed tag set contains 16 relation types (such as "apply to", "subconcept", "result", "condition", "evaluation", etc.) and three entity types (such as "object", "measure", "term").

Paper [9] presents a tag-set, manually labelled corpora and machine learning models for argumentation mining in Portuguese news articles. The researchers provided a critical analysis of the obtained results. They conclude that simple lexical and syntactic-based features are not enough to successfully extract argumentation zones. The topic of the paper [10] is slightly different; namely, they consider arguments in political debates. In these two papers above, they applied Support Vector Machines for structured outputs (structured-SVM) [11] as the machine learning model. The similar machine-learning approach is presented in [12] The researchers proposed the following tags: "measure", "term", "topic", "method", and "experiment". The extraction process contains five steps: tagset design, semi-automatic annotation tool, annotation data construction, structural SVMs based entity recognition. Simple features such as lemmas, suffixes, word positions, part of speech tags etc. were used, like in other works. They also compared Conditional Random Fields [13] and structural SVM machine learning models and found out that the structural SVM outperforms the CRFs in both speed and precision.

The paper [14] provides an entirely different approach to argument mining in biomedical texts. The first step would be to extract high-level features, such as named entities and domain-specific relations between them. Also, a certain amount of domain knowledge would be required, for example, for the relations "similar" and "difference", which could be acquired from a domain ontology or domain experts. Therefore, they fulfil a knowledge base. After that, the argument scheme rules described in the preceding section would be applied to the knowledge base to recognize the premises, conclusion, and argumentation scheme of each argument in the text. Unfortunately, they do not provide any experimental results for this approach. This paper also highlights an important problem with mining arguments in scientific documents with only superficial text features rather than semantic ones. Namely, argument components may not occur through the text. The content of an argument may be widely separated, or the content of two arguments may be interleaved at the level of text.

Niculae et al. proposed a model and an approach to fit jointly clause classification and argumentative relation prediction [15] Moreover, the proposed composed approach with both SVM and RNN, which can enforce structure constraints (for example, transitivity), and can express dependencies between adjacent relations and propositions.

It is also worth to note end-to-end approaches based on deep neural networks. For example, in [16], in contrast to models that operate on the argument component level, the authors find that framing argument mining as dependency parsing leads to better performance. Namely, less complicated tagging models based on Bidirectional Long-Short Memory architecture (BiLSTM) [17] perform robustly across classification, being able to catch long-range dependencies inherent to the argument-mining problem [18]. In [19], this method was developed. The researchers proposed inner-attention BiLSTM with topic similarity features which deal better with long-term dependences.

The common problem mentioned in the most papers devoted to this topic is the lack of large labelled corpora applicable for training complex models with lots of features, such as neural networks. Some researchers apply the active learning approach to tackle this problem. However, the corpora creation remains a challenging and time consuming job even in this case. Another useful solution, in this case, might be to construct a strict feature set using linguistic knowledge about how cognitive operations expressed in the texts of the particular genre. This allows creating a simpler model which does not overfit on small datasets. In this study, we follow this assumption.

To sum up the review, several necessary conditions should be respected for the analysis of cognitive operations in texts.

1. The tag set should be genre-specific. It should reflect features of the cognitive activities specific for text-writing in a particular genre.
2. Deep multi-level linguistic features are needed because fragments related to different operations cannot be discriminated with superficial features.
3. Context and positions of the text units are crucial for cognitive operation extraction too.

3   Tag Set

In this research, we try to follow a cognitive approach to the analysis of scientific texts [20]. The cornerstone of this approach is the fact that cognitive activity is strongly related to scientific text writing.

Cognitive activity is a way to satisfy the needs, and it is comprised of some particular operations, which are the ways to achieve a required goal. Each operation can be considered as a way to meet the conditions in which the goal is represented. The conditions are considered both as internal (psycho- and neurophysiological) mechanisms, and external circumstances that have their subject logic, among the latter language is with its general structural and national-specific features. In contrast to the approaches mentioned above, this one implies that analysis for a particular genre should begin with the observing of social needs realized with the text writing.

This research is based on the tag set for a scientific text proposed in [5]. The main idea behind this tag set is that the cognitive operations play a particular role in scientific texts and the multilevel linguistic features are crucial for distinguishing them. This made it possible to highlight textual fragments in a scientific paper that are related to the goals of cognitive operations.

This tag set is more complicated than the ones which were mentioned above. It consists of several categories, related to the specific tasks of research. Each category can be implemented with broad set of cognitive operations. The set of universal categories include:

1. Description of a new phenomenon;
2. Presentation of empirical law of cause-and-effect type;
3. Critical analysis of existent theoretical knowledge;
4. Definition of principles of the theory developed;
5. Experimental testing of theory;
6. Presentation of experimental results.

Due to technical reasons, we focused in this study on two categories only. Let consider them in more detail (here we hold to the numeration suggested in [5]).

1. Description of a new phenomenon. This category contains a message about the discovery of a new object and its place among the known phenomena. The category can be implemented with the following operations.
   1.1. Description of a new object's properties. The goal is to record the results of observation. An object can be described in each specific case in accordance with a particular program inherent in a given discipline or scientific field. Therefore, when describing, the various object features can be distinguished - qualitative, quantitative, structural-morphological, functional, genetic, etc.
   1.2. Description of the most essential differential features of the new object.
   1.3. Determining the location of a new object in a system of known phenomena. Information that a new object belongs to a particular class implies an indication of the similarities and differences between this object and others.
   1.4. Description of the location and distribution of a new phenomenon.
2. Presentation of empirical law of cause-and-effect type. This category contains the system of cognitive operations aimed at discovering the empirical law. Empirical law can be presented to the reader in the form of a conclusion, as well as prospectively, as a hypothesis, confirmed by the facts presented in the text. The description of the object properties in different conditions of experiment can be not only verbal but also tabular or graphical. This category can be implemented with the following operations.
   2.1. Fixing experience data in different conditions. Most often it is related to describing the experiment results.
   2.2. Comparison and preliminary grouping of experimental data, by comparison, an indication of similarities and differences in experimental data.
   2.3. Representation of the established causal dependence during the ranking of experimental data; if the indicators are quantitative, they are grouped into rows in ascending or descending order of the trait;
   2.4. Empirical dependence which is revealed with the processing of experimental data.

2.5. Revealing the conditions which allow the phenomenon to give the best practical result.

2.6. A possible explanation of the established pattern by a more general pattern, i.e., the disclosure of the "mechanism" of a phenomenon, process, etc.

4 Tagging Framework

The proposed framework is presented in Fig. 1. Due to the small size of the training corpora, it is impossible to use end-to-end machine learning models that allow analyzing objects characterized by high-dimensional feature sets. Therefore, we separate the extraction of cognitive operations into several following steps: the extraction of linguistic features for clauses, applying the patterns to form high-level feature set with a smaller dimension, fitting a machine learning model to sequence labelling with this reduced feature set, applying the patterns to disambiguate clauses with multiple labels.

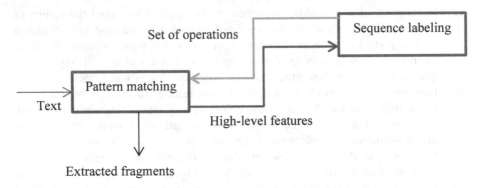

Fig. 1. Tagging Framework for cognitive operations extraction

At the first step, we apply MyStem [21] and SyntaxNet [22] to extract lexical, morphological features and syntactic dependencies in the clauses. Then semantic role labelling is performed with the analyzer created at the FRC CS&C RAS [23]. As a model for formal representation of the extracted linguistic features, we use heterogeneous semantic network constructed with the relational-situational model. This model includes nodes (syntaxemes) and links which reflect the syntactic and semantic dependencies between these syntaxemes [24].

The second step consists in matching these network models (for each clause) with context-free pat-terns, which contain a formalized description for multi-level linguistic features. The patterns reflect linguistic features corresponding to particular cognitive operations. They were designed in such a way to achieve rather high recall than precision (Because it is not possible for any context-free approach). To sum up, there are 36 distinct patterns for 10 cognitive operations. The patterns for the tag set are based on descriptions which were proposed by philologists and presented in [25].

Each pattern is a fragment of a heterogeneous semantic network. Nodes and relations in these fragments can be defined incompletely (e.g., a node description can have part of speech or lexeme list only). Examples of these patterns are presented in Table 1. This way each high-level feature vector encodes if a clause matches to some patterns.

Table 1. Examples of the patterns for high-level features

Cognitive operation	Examples of the patterns
1.1	{POS(NOUN)+Case(Nom)}<-*<- {POS(PASS_PART)}
1.1	{POS(ADJ)+ Case(Nom)}<-*<-{Case(Nom)+POS(NOUN)}
1.4	{Case(Nom)+POS(NOUN)}<-*<-{POS(PASS_PART)+L: ["*обнару-жить*","*найти*","*отметить*","*зафиксировать*", "*установить*"]}
2.1	{POS(NUM)}<-*<-{ POS(VERB)}
2.3	{IS_PRED(True)+L:["*расти*","*возрастать*","*увеличиваться*","*уменьшатьс я*","*усиливаться*","*сокращаться*","*падать*"]}
2.4	{Case(Acc)+POS(NOUN)}<=CAUS=>{Case(Nom)+POS(NOUN)}<-{IS_PRED(True)+L:["*вести*","*приводить*","*зависеть*","*определять*","*обусл овливать*","*детерминировать*","*вызывать*","*порождать*","*влечь*"]}
Description: "POS" – part of speech, "Case" – grammar case, "L" – lexeme,"IS_PRED" – whether a syntaxeme is a predicate word, "*" – any node, "<-" – syntax relation (child <- parent), "<=SEM_TYPE=>" – semantic relation.	

At the third step, we apply machine learning models that take into account the context of the analyzed objects to classify the clauses. Since a single clause can contain several cognitive operations at once, the problem of multi-output classification is solved. We have tested the following classification models for the sequence labelling:

1. Models based on compositions of decision trees with a sliding window, such as a random forest [26] and gradient boosting [27]. We applied window size from 1 to 3 clauses for these classifiers. A larger window result in overfitting.
2. The hypothesis inferred with AQ+JSM inductive method with a sliding window [28].
3. Recurrent neural networks LSTM (Long-Short Term Memory) [17] and GRU (Gated Recurrent Unit) [29] with a self-attention layer. We applied quite small networks (up to 16 recurrent cells) with dropout and examined one and bidirectional implementations.
4. Conditional Random Fields (CRF) [13].

We tested the last two model types on sequences up to 10 clauses. Since approaches 1, 2 and 4 are single-output classifiers, we trained an independent model for each output.

All hyperparameters for the classifiers above were revealed with grid search cross-validation. Apart from neural networks, these are quite simple models designed to deal with small datasets. To implement those methods, we used the Scikit-learn [30], TensorFlow [31] and CRFSuite [32] software libraries.

The last step consists of applying a set of patterns, similar to ones from step 2 to disambiguate clauses, which were labelled with several classes. More precisely, these patterns refer tokens from the clauses to distinct cognitive operations. This step has not been implemented yet.

5 Experimental Corpora

The experimental corpora consists of two parts[1]. The first one is devoted to test patterns and the second one is used to test the whole framework. Table 2 shows statistics for the corpora.

1. Corpus for pattern evaluation contains more than 400 small independent scientific text fragments (1–10 sentences, 10–100 tokens) in Russian related to particular cognitive operations and more than 100 fragments which do not belong to any considered category.
2. Corpus for sequence labelling evaluation contains about 200 manually labelled fragments (10–50 sentences, 50–1000 tokens) of scientific papers in Russian from different research directions (Biology, Math, Geology, etc.) written by various authors within different research groups. During the experiment we considered clause-level classification. Some clauses from the corpora were labelled by several classes, because these clauses contain several distinct cognitive operations.

Table 2. Experimental Corpora statistics (count of fragments)

Operation code	Pattern evaluation dataset		Sequence labeling evaluation dataset
	Positive	Negative	
1.1	40	56	48
1.2	5		6
1.3	32		17
1.4	18		13
2.2	23	44	31
2.3	156		40
2.4	103		10
2.5	12		17
2.6	39		20

6 Experimental Results

Tables 3 and 4 present the results of the comparison of linguistic features of clauses with the patterns (the codes for the operations are the same as in Sect. 3). Table 3 contains estimates of the quality of detection of text fragments containing cognitive operations. High recall ($R > 0.76$) shows that the proposed patterns almost always

---

[1] http://nlp.isa.ru/mental_actions.

allow detecting text fragments corresponding to the considered cognitive operations. The relatively low precision value (P) is because the patterns used are context-free.

Table 3. Results for the patterns evaluation

Operation code	P	R	F_1-macro
1.1	0.97	0.95	0.96
1.2	0.83	0.84	0.83
1.3	0.96	0.97	0.96
1.4	0.64	0.85	0.73
2.2	0.68	0.92	0.78
2.3	0.88	0.76	0.82
2.4	0.84	0.97	0.90
2.5	0.86	1.0	0.93
2.6	0.85	0.98	0.91

Table 4 presents the error rates associated with incorrect selection of a particular cognitive operation within the category (we used the same patterns for operations 1.1 and 1.2, so we did not compare them). It shows that in general the patterns allow quite accurate determining the correspondence of a specific cognitive operation to a particular textual fragment. Most of the errors, as in the previous case, are due to the context-free implementation of the patterns.

Table 4. Confusion matrices for the patterns evaluation

	1.1	1.2	1.3	1.4		2.2	2.3	2.4	2.5	2.6
1.1	-	-	0.03	0.06	2.2	-	**0.27**	0.08	0.02	0.21
1.2	-	-	0.05	0.16	2.3	0.18	-	**0.25**	0.23	0.01
1.3	0.04	0.06	-	0.03	2.4	0.14	0.19	-	0.05	0.07
1.4	0.18	**0.30**	0.02	-	2.5	0.22	0.03	0.07	-	0.11
					2.6	0.12	0.08	0.11	0.20	-

Table 5 presents the evaluation of the quality of detection of cognitive operations in step 3. The scores were calculated with the statistical procedure of 5-fold cross-validation on the labelled corpus [33]. The highest quality of extraction of cognitive operations from texts was attained with a method based on random forests, which may be due to the relatively small size of the training corpus.

Table 5. Results for the framework evaluation

Classifier	P	R	F_1-micro
LSTM+self-attention	0.59 ± 0.07	0.68 ± 0.08	0.62 ± 0.02
GRU+self-attention	0.63 ± 0.06	0.65 ± 0.09	0.63 ± 0.05
Random forest	**0.75 ± 0.09**	**0.69 ± 0.07**	**0.71 ± 0.07**
Gradient boosting	0.72 ± 0.10	0.63 ± 0.07	0.67 ± 0.09
AQ+JSM	**0.78 ± 0.06**	0.60 ± 0.07	0.68 ± 0.06
CRF	0.70 ± 0.09	**0.68 ± 0.05**	0.69 ± 0.09

7 Conclusion and Future Work

The obtained results confirm that the suggested set of cognitive operations is useful for the analysis of scientific texts. The results justify the applicability of the proposed framework to the cognitive operation extraction from scientific texts in Russian. The next steps of this research are the development of patterns and experimental evaluation for the last step of the proposed framework (disambiguation for clauses labelled with several classes). The labelled corpora and pattern set are going to be completed to cover the full tagging schema proposed in [5]. The proposed framework can be useful for solving applied problems related to science development. These problems include detection of promising research areas, subject and methodological gaps, and denoting interdisciplinary interests.

References

1. Mann, W.C., Matthiessen, C.M.I.M., Thompson, S.A.: Rhetorical Structure: Theory and Text Analysis, pp. 1–60. Information Sciences Institute, Marina del Rey (1989)
2. Kibrik, A.A.: Discourse Analysis in a Cognitive Perspective: Dr-Sci Thesis. In the form of Scientific Report. Dr. Phil. Sciences. http://www.philol.msu.ru/~otipl/new/main/people/kibrikaa/s_publications-ru.html. Accessed 10 Nov 2018
3. Swales, J.: Research Genres: Explorations and Applications. Cambridge University Press, Cambridge (2004)
4. Teufel, S.: Scientific argumentation detection as limited-domain intention recognition. In: Proceedings of Workshop for Frontiers and Connections between Argumentation Theory and Natural Language, p. 9 (2014)
5. Salimovsky, V.A.: Speech genres in functional and stylistic perspective (scientific academic text). Perm State University, Perm (2002)
6. Teufel, S., Moens, M.: Summarizing scientific articles: experiments with relevance and rhetorical status. Comput. Linguist. **28**, 409–445 (2002)
7. Ibekwe-SanJuan, F.: Semantic metadata annotation: tagging medline abstracts for enhanced information access. Aslib Proc. **62**, 476–488 (2010)
8. Tateisi, Y., Shidahara, Y., Miyao, Y., Aizawa, A.: Annotation of computer science papers for semantic relation extraction. In: Proceedings of the 9th International Conference on Language Resources and Evaluation, pp. 1423–1429 (2014)

9. Rocha, G., Lopes, C.H., Teixeira, J.: ArgMine: a framework for argumentation mining. In: 12th International Conference on Computational Processing of the Portuguese Language, PROPOR, pp. 13–15 (2016)
10. Lippi, M., Torroni, P.: Argument mining from speech: detecting claims in political debates. In: Thirtieth AAAI Conference on Artificial Intelligence, pp. 2979–2985 (2016)
11. Joachims, T., Finley, T., Yu, C.N.J.: Cutting-plane training of structural SVMs. Mach. Learn. 1(77), 27–59 (2009)
12. Jung, Y.: A semantic annotation framework for scientific publications. Qual. Quant. 3(51), 1009–1025 (2017)
13. Lafferty, J., McCallum, A., Pereira, F.C.N.: Conditional random fields: probabilistic models for segmenting and labeling sequence data (2001)
14. Green, N.L.: Towards mining scientific discourse using argumentation schemes. Argum. Comput. 9(2), 121–135 (2018)
15. Niculae, V., Park, J., Cardie, C.: Argument mining with structured SVMs and RNNs. arXiv preprint: arXiv:1704.06869 (2017)
16. Eger, S., Daxenberger, J., Gurevych, I.: Neural end-to-end learning for computational argumentation mining. In: Proceedings of the 55th Annual Meeting of the Association for Computational Linguistics, Vancouver, Canada, 30 July–4 August 2017, pp. 11–22 (2017)
17. Hochreiter, S., Schmidhuber, J.: Long short-term memory. Neural Comput. 8(9), 1735–1780 (1997)
18. Qi, L., Tianshi, L., Baobao, C.: Discourse parsing with attention-based hierarchical neural networks. In: Proceedings of the 2016 Conference on Empirical Methods in Natural Language Processing, pp. 362–371. Association for Computational Linguistics. https://aclweb.org/anthology/D16-1035. Accessed 29 July 2019
19. Stab, C., Miller, T., Gurevych, I.: Cross-topic argument mining from heterogeneous sources using attention-based neural networks. arXiv preprint: arXiv:1802.05758 (2018)
20. Giere, R.N.: Explaining Science: A Cognitive Approach. University of Chicago Press, Chicago (2010)
21. Mystem analyzer. https://tech.yandex.ru/mystem/doc/index-docpage. Accessed 28 July 2019
22. Andor, D., et al: Globally normalized transition-based neural networks. arXiv preprint: arXiv:1603.06042 (2016)
23. Shelmanov, A.O., Smirnov, I.V.: Methods for semantic role labeling of Russian texts. In: Proceedings of the International Conference Dialogue, Computational Linguistics and Intellectual Technologies, vol. 20(13), pp. 607–620 (2014)
24. Osipov, G.S., Smirnov, I.V., Tikhomirov, I.A.: Relational and situational method of search and analysis of texts and its application. Artif. Intell. Decis. Mak. 2(2), 3–10 (2008)
25. Devyatkin, D.A., Kadzhaya, L.A., Salimovsky, V.A.: Speech genres as an object of computer analysis (based on academic texts). Speech Genres 2(22) (2019). (in Russian)
26. Breiman, L.: Random forests. Mach. Learn. 1(45), 5–32 (2001)
27. Friedman, J.H.: Greedy function approximation: a gradient boosting machine. Ann. Stat. 29(5), 1189–1232 (2001)
28. Panov, A.I.: Extraction of cause-effect relationships from psychological test data using logical methods. Sci. Tech. Inf. Process. 5(41), 275–282 (2014)
29. Chung, J., et al.: Empirical evaluation of recurrent neural networks on-line modeling. arXiv preprint: arXiv:1412.3555 (2014)
30. Pedregosa, F., et al.: Scikit-learn: machine learning in Python. J. Mach. Learn. Res. 12, 2825–2830 (2011)

31. Abadi, M., et al.: TensorFlow: a system for large-scale machine learning. In: 12th USENIX Symposium on Operating Systems Design and Implementation (OSDI 2016), pp. 265–283 (2016)
32. Okazaki, N.: CRFSuite: a fast implementation of conditional random fields (CRFs) (2007)
33. Flach, P.: Machine Learning: The Art and Science of Algorithms That Make Sense of Data. Cambridge University Press, Cambridge (2012)

Fuzzy Models and Soft Computing

Evolutionary Design of Fuzzy Systems Based on Multi-objective Optimization and Dempster-Shafer Schemes

Alexander I. Dolgiy[1], Sergey M. Kovalev[1], Anna E. Kolodenkova[2], and Andrey V. Sukhanov[1(✉)]

[1] Rostov Branch JSC NIIAS, Rostov-on-Don, Russia
{ksm,a.suhanov}@rfniias.ru
[2] Samara State Technical University, Samara, Russia
anna82_42@mail.ru

Abstract. The paper considers a novel intelligent approach to the design of fuzzy systems based on Multi-Objective Evolutionary Fuzzy Systems (MOEFSs) theory. The presented approach is based on the principle of Pareto optimality using evidence combination schemes of Dempster-Shafer. The evidence combination scheme is used in evolutionary operators of search algorithms during implementation of fitness assignment and solution selection. The paper proposes new representation forms for integral and vector criteria reflecting not only accuracy and complexity of multi-objective fuzzy systems, but also their interpretability characterizing readability of fuzzy-rule base and semantic consistency. The main advantage of the considered MOEFSs is that they satisfy to many criteria simultaneously, which include interpretability properties of fuzzy systems, such as compact description, readability, semantic consistency and description completeness. The novel technique of solution selection and combination based on fusion of fitness estimations from several individuals using Dempster-Shafer theory is proposed. Here, Dempster-Shafer theory allows to select those solutions from Pareto-optimal ones, which are most satisfactory in multi-objective design terms. Solution selection and combination based on probability theory of evidence combination increase objectivity of the best solution selection in evolutionary algorithms. The novel techniques of fitness ranging in evolutionary algorithms and expert preferences integration into MOEFSs design based on Dempster-Shafer modified network models are proposed. The comparison results of MOEFSs design using several evolutionary algorithms are shown in the example of railway task decision. These results prove that the proposed evolutionary design provides a better compromise between accuracy and interpretability in comparison with conventional algorithms.

Keywords: Multi-objective fuzzy systems ·
Evidence combination schemes of Dempster-Shafer · Multicriteriality

The work was supported by RFBR grants No. 19-07-00263, 19-07-00195 and 19-08-00152.

S. O. Kuznetsov and A. I. Panov (Eds.): RCAI 2019, CCIS 1093, pp. 203–217, 2019.
https://doi.org/10.1007/978-3-030-30763-9_17

1 Introduction

In recent decades, fuzzy systems (FS) attract a lot of attention in many areas of implementation due to their universal approximation properties and ability to process the uncertainties and inaccuracies in behavior of complex systems without any accurate mathematical modeling. However, fuzzy systems design is complicated because enough complete expert information about the modeled object is missed and fuzzy model construction requires the automatic design based on experimental data [1, 2].

Modern approaches to automatic design of FS are based on evolutionary and genetic algorithms due to their universalism, their ability of task solution without accurate description of conditions and possibility to process big search spaces [3–5]. The hybridization of FS and genetic algorithms resulted in creation of new class of evolutionary FS.

It should be noted that evolutionary FS do not completely implement all abilities of FS in real-world task decisions, particularly, in those, which are connected with multicriteriality. Major areas, such as Data Mining, Multi-Objective design, regression analysis require FS to satisfy many criteria simultaneously. These criteria of modeling must reflect not only accuracy, but also knowledge base complexity together with interpretability characterizing compactness and readability of rule base. In such conditions, an improvement of a criterion often results in degradation of other ones. This issue requires development of new multi-objective approach to fuzzy system design. Because of this, last years, evolutionary FS is being expanded due to attracting the Multi-Objective Evolutionary Algorithms (MOEAs), which consider not single, but multiple conflicting criteria. MOEFSs, which are hybrid of FS and MOEAs, allow to satisfying multiple objectives of the FS design in new practical implementations of fuzzy logic [8, 9].

Real-world implementations of MOEFSs give rise to problems connected with heterogeneity of search spaces, presence of specific criteria for interpretability, necessity of selection based on multi-criteria features, necessity of expert preferences integration into the design, etc. [10].

In this paper, a new evolutionary approach is proposed for the MOEFSs design. The approach is based on utilization of Pareto optimality in formation of search spaces attracting probabilistic schemes of Dempster-Shafer for evidence combination to select evolutionary solutions by multi-criteria features.

The paper is organized as follows. In Sect. 2, state-of-the-art in multi-objective evolutionary design is considered. Section 3 formalizes the problem statement of evolutionary approach to multi-objective design for fuzzy systems. Section 4 provides the aims of FS design, which are objectives for the developed framework. Section 5 describes the way of solution suitability assessment. Section 6 proves the choice of the method for the decision assessment. In Sect. 7, the chosen approach based on Dempster-Shafer theory is formally described. Section 8 provides the proposed decisions for multi-objective evolutionary search. The computational experiments and their analysis are shown in Sects. 9 and 10, respectively. Finally, in Sect. 11, conclusion is given.

2 Multi-objective Evolutionary Design

The rising interest to MOEAs in FS design can be described by the wish of the specialists to obtain the models, which can satisfy many criteria reflecting, for example, such properties as accuracy, complexity and interpretability of fuzzy systems [1, 2]. MOEASs allow obtaining various types of fuzzy systems, satisfying various criteria with different degree [7], which are able to generate fuzzy models, where the compromise between interpretability and accuracy is reached. In the literature, the systems obtained as a result of the evolutionary optimization are called as Multi-Objective Evolutionary Fuzzy Systems (MOEFSs) [8, 9].

It is considered that MOEA is firstly developed by David Shafer, who proposed Vector Evaluated Genetic Algorithm (VEGA) [6]. VEGA is based on the simple genetic algorithm with slightly changed solution selection engine. The main disadvantage of the algorithm is that it cannot vary solutions during search. As well, it has no engine, which can adequately select non-dominated solutions in future generations. Shafer ideas were developed in the following works, in particular, the Non-Dominated Genetic Sorting Algorithm was proposed in [11], Niched Pareto Genetic Algorithm was proposed in [12] and Multi-Objective Genetic Algorithm was proposed in [13].

Thereafter, the development of work in this area took the path of increasing the elitism of the solutions selected in the population, which was, in fact, a kind of theoretical justification and requirement for ensuring the convergence of algorithms. The most representative algorithms among them are Strength Pareto Evolutionary Algorithm 2 (SPEA2) [3], Non-dominated Sorting Genetic Algorithm II (NSGA II) [4] and Pareto Archived Evolution Strategy (PAES) [5].

Nowadays, the most advanced ones among MOEAs are NSGA, SPEA and their modifications [14] due to the efficient fitness computation using estimations of solutions density and diversity support engine allowing to obtain wide range of Pareto-optimal solutions, which satisfy multi-objective design terms. It should be noted that the most of works dedicated to MOEAs is referred to synthesis of Mamdani fuzzy models [15], which are more interpretable, than Sugeno ones [16].

The team of H. Ishibuchi achieves good results in development of FS oriented on compromise between accuracy and interpretability. Their early researches [17] were dedicated to the application of simple MOEAs for fuzzy rules search in classification tasks considering two-objective goal (accuracy and number of rules). Then, the third objective considering minimization of rule length using additional training was proposed [18]. In [19], the modification of MOEA was proposed for three-objective optimization. The team also proposed NSGA-II for the rule selection [20] and rule generation goals considering three criteria [21]. The works of other scientific teams dedicated to the considered topic can be also found. For example, in [22], MOEA is used for simultaneous selection and training of fuzzy rules considering two criteria.

It should be noted that above mentioned approaches, which became the conventional ones in the area of multi-objective evolutionary modeling, are very common and do not consider the specifications of FS as a design object. These specifications are connected with heterogeneity of search space, the diversity of formalization way of semantic and interpretability criteria and necessity of integration of expert preferences together with testing procedures into evolutionary algorithm. These issues lead to necessity of new MOEFSs development. Although this area of research has not been systematically developed, a number of publications can be found in the review [10].

3 Evolutionary Approach to Multi-objective Design of FS

The developed framework is based on search techniques of multi-criteria optimization. Evolutionary search is an iterative process of forming a sequence of decision populations by alternating two stages. At the first stage, the fitness for each potential solution in the population is calculated, on the basis of which the probabilities of inclusion of certain chromosomes in subsequent stages of evolution are determined. At the second stage, solutions are selected and the genetic material of individuals of the population is exchanged using a crossover operator in order to form a new child population. The process continues until the termination criterion is fulfilled.

The main advantage of MOEAs lies in their ability to work with sets of potential solutions that are optimal in different contexts, thereby obtaining the possibility of studying a multi-modal environment. Multi-objective optimization is based on the Pareto principle.

In the common case, multi-objective optimization considers a potential solution in the form of vector $x = (x_1, x_2, \ldots, x_m)$ in feature space $X = X_1 \times X_2 \times \ldots \times X_m$. The optimization task considers minimization of $F: X \rightarrow Y$, which estimates the quality of a partial solution x by assigning goal vector $y = (f_1(x), f_2(x), \ldots, f_n(x))$ in multi-objective goal space $Y = Y_1 \times Y_2 \times \ldots \times Y_n$. It is considered that solution vector $a \in X$ dominates over solution vector $b \in Y$ (denoted by $a < b$) if

$$\forall i = 1, 2, \ldots, n \ f_i(a) \leq f_i(b);$$
$$\exists j = 1, 2, \ldots, n \ f_j(a) < f_j(b).$$

A solution vector is called Pareto optimal if it is not dominated in the above sense by any other particular solution in the whole parameter space X. The set of Pareto-optimal solutions in the solution space is called Pareto set, and its image in the target space is called the Pareto-front.

4 Design Criteria of MOEFs

MOEFs' optimization includes two main stages: the fuzzy rules selection and the membership functions (MF) tuning. Within the proposed approach, the selection of rules and tuning of the MF are carried out simultaneously with the coding rules and parameters in a single chromosome, thereby ensuring synergy of the selection and tuning.

In the developed MOEA, each chromosome is associated with a 3-D target vector, whose elements express the degree of fulfillment of the main design goals:

1. Error minimization (mean-squared error, MSE);
2. Complexity minimization (number of rules, NR);

3. Semantic interpretability (SI) maximization.

MSE is defined as follows:

$$MSE = \frac{1}{2|D|} \sum_{l=1}^{|D|} (F(x^l) - y^l)^2,$$

where D is the test data, $F(x^l)$ is the fuzzy system output at l-th sample, y^l is the known desired output.

Complexity index NR_g of a fuzzy system is expressed in terms of the geometric mean between the total number of knowledge base rules and the average length of a single fuzzy rule (the average number of fuzzy antecedents found in a rule):

$$NR_g = \frac{\sum_{i=1}^{m} A(r_i)}{m} / A_{\max},$$

where $A(r_i)$ is the number of variables at i-th rule, m is the number of rules, $A_{\max}$ is the user-defined maximum rule length.

The semantic interpretability is proposed to be estimated using comparison of MFs of the researched FS with corresponded MFs of the FS, which is considered as ideal one from the interpretability point of view. MFs of the ideal FS induce fuzzy partition satisfying to the specific restrictions set, which provides hypothetically "best" semantic interpretability. According to the users and developers, MFs with the best interpretability satisfy to the following restrictions:

1. MF is normal and convex;
2. MF satisfies to the Ruspini restrictions [23]:

$$\forall A \in L, \ x \in [x_0^A, \ x_k^A], \ \sum_{a \in A} \mu_a(x) = 1,$$

where L is the set of linguistic variables (LV) of FS; a is the fuzzy term of A, $[x_0^A, \ x_k^A]$ is the discrete base scale of A, $\mu_a(x)$ is the MF of a.

Let the interpretability of A be estimated using deviation E_A of the fuzzy partition induced by A from the fuzzy partition induced by ideal LV with the same number of fuzzy terms. For A, E_A is computed as follows:

$$E_A = \frac{\sum_{x \in [x_0^A, x_k^A]} \left[1 - \sum_{j=1}^{k} \mu_{a_j}(x) \right]^2}{|[x_0^A, \ x_k^A]|},$$

where $|[x_0^A, \ x_k^A]|$ is the number of points at the discrete scale, a_j is the j-th fuzzy term of A, μ_{a_j} is the MF of a_j, k is the number of fuzzy terms in A. The value of E_A for the continuous base scale X is computed as:

$$E_A = \frac{\int_{x_0}^{x^k} \left[1 - \sum_{j=1}^{k} \mu_{a_j}(x) \right]^2}{x_k - x_0},$$

where x_0, x_k are the boundaries of the base scale.

It is obvious that the minimal value of $E_A = 0$ corresponds to the ideally interpreted A and the difference between real LV and ideal one is increased as E_A grows. Interpretability of the FS containing m LV is computed as mean error:

$$E_A = \frac{\sum_{j=1}^{j=m} E_{A_j}}{m}. \tag{1}$$

Semantic interpretability index SI of FS containing m LV is computed via (1):

$$SI = \frac{1}{E_A + 1}$$

It is obvious that SI lies between 0 and 1. The highest level of interpretability corresponds to $SI = 1$ and the lowest one corresponds to $SI \rightarrow 0$.

5 Estimation of Solution Suitability and Fitness Assignment in MOEAs

Multi-objective evolutionary algorithms pursue the set of goals choosing the way of fitness estimation. These goals are directed to the efficiency increment of the evolutionary process. Among them, the most important are:

1. Increasing the elitism of the generated solutions in order to ensure the convergence of the evolutionary process;
2. Increasing the diversity of solutions with the aim of a more complete formation of the Pareto-front;
3. Increasing the level of consistency of the decisions regarding the main design criteria in order to reduce the space of choice and simplify the process of making a single decision, if required by the condition of the problem.

The fitness estimation techniques implemented on the basis of SPEA and NSGA (and their modifications) [14, 24, 25] and proved their real-world applications' efficiency correspond to the goals of increasing the elitism and the diversity of solutions. Briefly, the idea is the following. For every individual, the power $S(x_i)$ is computed based on the number of solutions, where it dominates, i.e.:

$$S(x_i) = |\{x_j \in P | x_i < x_j\}|,$$

where $|\cdot|$ is the power of a set.

Fitness $Q(x_i)$ of individual x_i is computed as the sum over all individuals, which dominate over x:

$$Q_e(x_i) = \sum_{x_j|x_j < x_i} S(x_j). \tag{2}$$

To increase the diversity, the density information is included into (2). This information is computed via measure, which is reciprocal to mean distance $\Delta(x_i)$ between individual x_i and its k nearest neighbors in the goal space, i.e.

$$\Delta(x_i) = \frac{\sum\limits_{x_j \in E_i} R(x_i, y_j)}{|E_j| = k}, \quad E_i = \{x \in P | \forall y \in P \backslash E_i \quad R(x_i, x) \le R(x_i, y)\},$$

where $R(x, y)$ is the Euclid distance between x and y.

The final equation for calculating fitness, which simultaneously satisfies the goals of increasing the elitism and diversity of decisions, has the form:

$$Q_{e\Delta}(x_i) = \frac{1}{Q_e(x_i) + \frac{1}{\Delta(x_i)}}. \tag{3}$$

Semantically, Eq. (3) means that x_i, which has less number of dominators and lies farther from neighbors, has higher value of $Q_{e\Delta}(x_i)$.

6 Compromise Estimation Based on Dempster-Shafer Scheme in MOEAs

During the choice of fitness estimation in multi-objective evolutionary algorithms, one of the important goals is to increase the consistency (or compromise nature) of the solutions generated in the evolutionary process. Consistency reflects the rate of satisfaction of a solution to all global criteria simultaneously. The necessity to introduce a measure of consistency in the fitness estimation is aimed, on the one hand, at reducing the search space and, on the other hand, to increasing the efficiency of the decision-making mechanism. It should be done for the optimal solution to avoid "taking sides" of any particular criterion and do not obtain a "one-sided" solution. In most modern MOEAs, such fitness assessment is not performed.

To solve this problem, the approach to fitness assignment for solutions is proposed in this paper. This assignment must provide the best compromise between all criteria in a multi-objective task, based on the use of a probabilistic scheme of combining evidence from the Dempster-Shafer theory. In general, the approach is the following.

The current population of solutions is considered as a set of hypotheses about the belonging of each solution to a certain subset of hypothetically optimal solutions to a multi-objective task, and a set of criteria acts as evidences. On the basis of evidences, it is concluded that one or another solution belongs to a given optimal subset. Suitability estimations of the decisions on a particular criterion (particular fitness) act as the basic probabilities (probability masses) of the hypotheses in the evidence combination scheme. Then, based on the hypotheses combination according to all evidences (criteria) of Dempster-Shafer scheme [26], it is possible to obtain integral probabilistic estimates of hypotheses about the belonging of the corresponding solutions to the optimal class taking into account the entire set of criteria. The implementation of this approach with stricter positions is described below.

Let $P = \{x_1, \ldots, x_n\}$ denote the set of Pareto-optimal solutions obtained at i-th iteration of an algorithm and $Q = \{q_1, \ldots, q_k\}$ denote the criteria set of multi-objective task. Every solution x is mapped into goal vector $y(x_i) = (q_1(x_i), \ldots, q_k(x_i))$ ($q(x)$ is the efficiency estimation of x by particular criterion (particular fitness) q). Let the particular finesses be normalized without loss of generality (i.e. $q_j(x_i) \leq 1$ for all i and j). Let P^0 denote the hypothetical subset of solutions which are optimal in multi-objective task taking into account all criteria Q. Let every particular criterion q for every potential solution x be considered as some evidence according to the membership of x to P^0. Obviously, the higher is the efficiency estimate of particular criterion q_i the higher is the probability of x_i to belong to P^0. Therefore, probability $P(x_i \in P^0)$ is proportional to the value of particular fitness $q_j(x_i)$, and, therefore, $q_j(x_i)$, can be used as the estimation of basic probability $m_{q_j}(x_i)$ of hypothesis about the belonging of x_i to P^0 based on evidence q_j from probabilistic scheme of Dempster-Shafer [26].

For the subset P' of arbitrary independent solutions, basic probability $m_{q_j}(P')$ of the hypothesis about probability of belonging of P' to P^0 is computed based on evidence q_j as follows:

$$m_{q_j}(P') = \prod_{x_i \in P'} q_j(x_i).$$

Thus, the probabilistic scheme of Dempster-Shafer can be built using P, Q, and $m_{q_j}(P')$ ($P' \subset P$, $q_j \in Q$). In the scheme, P plays the role of hypotheses set, Q plays the role of evidences set, $q_j(x_i)$ plays the role of j-th probability mass. Based on the combination of all solutions by all particular criteria, the basic probability $m_\Sigma(x_i)$, which is the measure of compromise for the corresponding solution, is computed.

The following section presents equations of evidence combination for the calculations of compromise estimations and integration of the calculated estimations into resulting equation of fitness computation.

7   Probability Scheme of Dempster-Shafer

In the theory of evidence combination of Dempster-Shafer, the function of Basic Belief Assignment (BBA) is defined for finite hypotheses set Ω, which is called as analysis area, as $m: 2^\Omega \to [0, 1]$. BBA satisfies to the following conditions:

$$m(\varnothing) = 0, \sum_{A \subseteq \Omega} m(A) = 1.$$

Two following functions are connected with BBA: belief and plausibility:

$$pl(A) = \sum_{A \cap B \neq \varnothing} m(B), \; bel(A) = \sum_{B \subseteq A} m(B).$$

The combination rule allows to combine two independent evidences with basic probabilities m_1 and m_2 and obtain the resulting basic beliefs m based on these evidences as follows:

$$m(\varnothing) = 0, \; m(A) = \frac{\sum_{B \cap C = A} m_1(B) m_2(C)}{\sum_{B \cap C \neq \varnothing} m_1(B) m_2(C)}, \; A \neq \varnothing.$$

To simplify the calculations, non-normalized conjunction rule of combination $\cap$ proposed in [27] and defined for all $A \subseteq \Omega$ is used:

$$m = m_1 \cap m_2 \Leftrightarrow m(A) = \sum_{B \cap C = A} m_1(B) m_2(C), \; \forall A \subseteq \Omega,$$

where $m_1()$ and $m_2()$ are the BBA of combined evidences, $m()$ is the BBA of combined evidences.

The key question in the combined BBA usage for fitness assignment for potential solutions $x_i \in P$ is ranging of single hypotheses $\{x_i\}$ in complete set Ω. With this aim, pignistic Smets transformation is used [27]. This transformation satisfies to the elementary requirements to rationality, which means that the probabilistic mass of single solution $m_\Sigma(x_i)$ is distributed equally between all elements of $H \subseteq \Omega$. The pignistic transformation is defined for the single solution as follows:

$$m_\Sigma(x_i) = \sum_{H \subseteq \Omega, \, x_i \in H} \frac{m(x_i)}{|H|},$$

$m_\Sigma(x_i)$ is single solution estimation, which is obtained as combination using Dempster-Shafer theory.

The integration of compromise measure $m_\Sigma(x_i)$ into fitness estimation computed as (3) leads to resulting fitness computed as follows:

$$Q_{e\Delta m}(x_i) = \frac{m_\Sigma(x_i)}{Q_e(x_i) + \frac{1}{\Delta(x_i)}}. \tag{4}$$

Equation (4) is the resulting equation for fitness calculation in evolutionary algorithms reflecting measure of elitism, consistency, and density of solutions.

8 MOEA Based on Dempster-Shafer Scheme

The proposed algorithm ($MOEA_{DS}$) is a modification of the well-known evolutionary algorithms of the SPEA and NSGA series, which are based on the Pareto-optimality principle [28]. SPEA and NSGA are iterative algorithms for adaptive random search for Pareto-optimal solutions in multi-objective tasks. At each iteration, MOEA generates solution population P_t, which supply genetic material for generating solutions at subsequent iterations of the evolutionary process, and also replenishes the archive A_t previously obtained at previous iterations $t - 1$, $t - 2$, ... of non-dominated solutions. The initial population of solutions P_0 is formed randomly, and the initial state of the archive A_0 is assigned empty, $A_0 = \emptyset$. Then, a series of actions repeated at each iteration is performed.

Firstly, the archive is updated by copying all non-dominated solutions from P_t into it and deleting all dominated solutions from it. If the size of the updated archive exceeds the predefined limit, further members of the archive are removed by the clustering method, which preserves the characteristics of the non-dominated front. If the size of the updated archive becomes less than the limited, then it is supplemented to the limited size by the "best" dominated solutions from the current population, according to their suitability estimations.

Secondly, the fitness estimations for all members of P_t and A_t are calculated based on formula (4).

Thirdly, on the basis of the calculated fitness estimations, solutions selection is performed. During selection, pairs of individuals are selected from P_t and A_t for crossing using binary tournaments.

The final stage is the recombination and mutation of chromosomes using the appropriate evolutionary operators SPEA [14], where the old population is replaced by the new off-springs.

$MOEA_{DS}$ is the following.

Input: N is the population size, $\sim N$ is the archive size, T is the iteration threshold.
Output: A is the dominated solution set.
Step 1. *Initialization*: the initial set P_0 is generated and initial empty archive $A_0 = 0$ is created, $t = 0$.
Step 2. *Fitness assignment*: fitness is calculated for each individual in P_t and A_t using (4).
Step 3. *Selection*: all dominated individuals are copied from P_t into P_{t+1} and from A_t into A_{t+1}. If size of P_{t+1} does not equal to N then it is increased or decreased to N by the correction procedures from SPEA.
Step 4 *Conclusion*: if $t \geq T$ then A_t is output and algorithm is stopped. Otherwise, go to step 5.
Step 5. *Pairing*: n solution pairs are randomly generated and compete based on (4). The winners fulfill the pool of pairing W for crossover and mutation.
Step 6. *Crossover and mutation*: crossover and mutation are applied to form a new population. $T = t + 1$. Go to step 2.

The above described algorithm is the general scheme, where distinctive parts of presented technique are presented. In contrast to the well-known algorithms of the SPEA and NSGA series, MOEA$_{DS}$ algorithm uses a new fitness assignment strategy that takes into account the compromise degree of the generated solutions. This allows one to concentrate the search process in the local area of compromise solutions, from which the best are ultimately selected. Due to the narrowing of the search area, the convergence of the algorithm is accelerated.

9 Experiments

To assess the efficiency of the proposed approach and the practical utility of the developed MOEA$_{DS}$ algorithm, the series of experiments were performed. An application problem from the field of railway automation is considered. The problem is connected with the prediction of the rolling velocities of railway cuts during the marshaling process. The predicted velocity of a cut is one of the most important parameters, which is necessary for solving automatic control problem of the railway retarder.

Automatic control over retarders is carried out on the basis of the compositional model, where the fuzzy predictive model is included as one of the components. The components of the compositional model are intelligent models based on fuzzy rules. To construct and train these models, the expert knowledge is used. It requires coordinated actions of the developers and a common understanding of the fuzzy rules included in the model. Therefore, the knowledge base of a fuzzy compositional model must satisfy not only the accuracy requirements, but also have a clear interpretation that is understandable to various groups of specialists. The interpretability of the prognostic model will enable its integration with other types of models. Based on the above described, the design of a fuzzy predictive model was implemented using two criteria that reflect both the accuracy and interpretability properties of the model.

The inputs of the fuzzy predictive model are the initial velocity, the weight, the number of cars and the free path of a cut. As well a number of parameters for the rolling section are used. The output is the predicted velocity at the end of free path.

In the experiments, MOEA$_{DS}$, SPEA, SPEA2 and NSGA were compared. Since MOEA$_{DS}$ is based on the principles of SPEA and NSGA and incorporates all their advantages, the purpose of the experiment was to determine how much the proposed approach to evolutionary multi-objective design is better than conventional ones. All the algorithms participating in the experiment solved the same task of building a predictive model based on a single database collected during three months of a hump.

The research database (DB) contains 1000 transactions, which are equally divided into train set and test set. The initial population contains 200 randomly generated individuals and is uniform for all algorithms. The archive size is 50 individuals, the evolution time is 200k iterations, the mutation probability parameter is 0.2. Two criteria are considered: the accuracy of velocity prediction represented by the Root-Mean-Square Error (RMSE), and integral estimate reflecting the complexity and interpretability of fuzzy model. They are calculated as follows:

$$I = \sqrt{SI \cdot NR_g},$$

where SI and NR_g are the interpretability and complexity indexes defined in Sect. 4.

In rule selection and rule tuning, all algorithms use double coding (CS and CT). In the CS $\left(C_S^p = (c_{S_1}, \ldots, c_{S_m})\right)$ part, the coding scheme consists of binary-coded strings with the size of m (where m is the number of initial rules). In the CT part, a real coding is considered, where m^i the number of labels of each i-th variable from the database:

$$C_T^p = C_1 C_2 \ldots C_n, \ C_i = (a_1^i, \ b_1^i, \ c_1^i, \ldots, a_{m^i}^i, \ b_{m^i}^i, \ c_{m^i}^i), \ i = 1, \ldots, n.$$

The initial population is obtained with all individuals having all genes with value '1' in the CS part. In the CT part the initial population is obtained inside the random interval of parameter values.

10   Analysis of Results

The results obtained on the basis of the considered models are presented in Table 1, where 1 is integral criterion Complexity-Interpretability, MSE_{tr} and MSE_{tst} are the RMSEs on train and test sets, respectively.

The following results can be obtained from analysis of Table 1:

1. $MOEA_{DS}$ has better accuracy in comparison with SPEA and NSGA, but a little bit worse than SPEA2;
2. $MOEA_{DS}$ obtains better results by integral criterion;
3. $MOEA_{DS}$ has better approximation to ideal two-objective algorithm in terms of Euclid distance of their results from ideal values.

Table 1. Results obtained by the studied methods.

Method	I	MSE_{tra}	MSE_{tst}
$MOEA_{DS}$	15.2	0.11	0.15
NSG	20.1	0.15	0.21
SPEA	18	0.13	0.17
SPEA2	18	0.12	0.14

Figure 1 shows the approximation of Pareto-front evolution for the developed algorithm after 50k, 100k, 150k and 200k iterations. The last iterations show the construction of the Pareto-front.

Figure 2 shows the final approximations of the Pareto-fronts for the two best results obtained by the SPEA2 and $MOEA_{DS}$ algorithms.

As expected, the advantage of the developed $MOEA_{DS}$ algorithm is noticeable in the compromise zone, although it is inferior to the SPEA 2 algorithm in the zones of particular criteria.

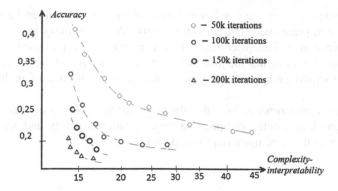

Fig. 1. Pareto-front evolution of MOEA$_{DS}$.

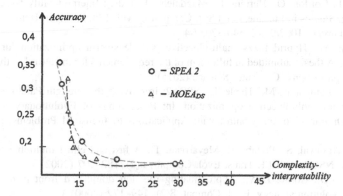

Fig. 2. Final approximations of Pareto-fronts for SPEA2 and MOEA$_{DS}$.

11 Conclusion

The paper proposes a new approach to the design of fuzzy systems based on the techniques of multi-objective evolutionary design, which allows to obtain multi-objective evolutionary fuzzy systems with different degrees satisfying different criteria. The approach also provides fuzzy systems that are best in satisfying the entire set of criteria. The main results of the study are as follows:

1. New forms of representation of integral and vector criteria are developed for the MOEFS reflecting both the accuracy and complexity properties of the fuzzy models, as well as interpretability properties that characterize the readability of the rule base, the completeness of the description, and semantic consistency.
2. A fundamentally new technique for determining solution fitness of multi-objective evolutionary algorithms based on the Dempster-Shafer theory of evidence, as well as a new method for selecting solutions based on merging the fitness estimates of several individuals using the Dempster-Schafer evidence combination scheme is proposed. The developed technique allows choosing from Pareto-optimal sets those solutions that meet at best the multi-objective design terms and increase the objectivity of the choice of the best solutions in multi-objective algorithms.

3. New techniques for ranging solution fitness of evolutionary algorithms and integrating expert preferences into a multi-objective design of fuzzy systems based on the combination of Dempster-Shafer evidence models are proposed. The Pareto-optimal solutions ranging for joint fitness provides the possibility of natural integration of expert preferences into the evolutionary algorithms of multi-objective design.

4. The results of experiments show that the proposed approach to the design of fuzzy systems provides a better compromise between interpretability and accuracy than the known methods of multi-objective design.

References

1. Casillas, J., Cordon, O., Herrera, F., Magdalena, L. (eds.): Interpretability Issues in Fuzzy Modeling. Studies in Fuzziness and Soft Computing, vol. 128. Springer, Heidelberg (2003). https://doi.org/10.1007/978-3-540-37057-4
2. Syafrullah, M.: Hybrid fuzzy multi-objective particle swarm optimization for taxonomy extraction. A thesis submitted in fulfilment of the requirements for the award of the degree of doctor of philosophy. Computer Science (2015)
3. Zitzler, E., Laumanns, M., Thiele, L.: SPEA2: improving the strength Pareto evolutionary algorithm for multiobjective optimization. In: Proceedings of Evolutionary Methods for Design, Optimization and Control with Applications to Industrial Problems, pp. 95–100 (2001)
4. Deb, K., Agrawal, S., Pratab, A., Meyarivan, T.: A fast and elitist multiobjective genetic algorithm: NSGA-II. IEEE Trans. Evol. Comput. 6(2), 182–197 (2002)
5. Knowles, J.D., Corne, D.W.: Approximating the non dominated front using the Pareto archived evolution strategy. Evol. Comput. 8(2), 149–172 (2000)
6. Schaffer, J.D.: Multiple objective optimization with vector evaluated genetic algorithms. In: Proceedings of the First International Conference on Genetic Algorithms, pp. 93–100 (1985)
7. Coello, C.A.C.: Multi-objective optimization. In: Martí, R., Panos, P., Resende, M. (eds.) Handbook of Heuristics, pp. 1–28. Springer, Cham (2018). https://doi.org/10.1007/978-3-319-07153-4_17-1
8. Coello, C.A.C., Lamont, G.B., Veldhuizen, D.A.V.: Evolutionary Algorithms for Solving Multi-Objective Problems. Springer, Boston (2007). https://doi.org/10.1007/978-0-387-36797-2
9. Deb, K.: Multi-Objective Optimization Using Evolutionary Algorithms, pp. 13–46. Wiley, Chichester (2001)
10. Elhag, S., Fernández, A., Alshomrani, S., Herrera, F.: Evolutionary fuzzy systems: a case study for intrusion detection systems. In: Bansal, J.C., Singh, P.K., Pal, Nikhil R. (eds.) Evolutionary and Swarm Intelligence Algorithms. SCI, vol. 779, pp. 169–190. Springer, Cham (2019). https://doi.org/10.1007/978-3-319-91341-4_9
11. Fonseca, C.M., Fleming, P.J.: Genetic algorithms for multi-objective optimization: formulation, discussion and generalization. In: Proceedings of the Fifth International Conference on Genetic Algorithms, pp. 416–423 (1993)
12. Horn, J., Nafpliotis, N., Goldberg, D.E.: A niched Pareto genetic algorithm for multiobjective optimization. In: Proceedings of the First IEEE Conference on Evolutionary Computation. IEEE World Congress on Computational Intelligence, vol. 1, pp. 82–87 (1994)

13. Srinivas, N., Deb, K.: Multiobjective optimization using nondominated sorting in genetic algorithms. Evol. Comput. **2**, 221–248 (1994)
14. Alcala, R., Gacto, M.J., Herrera, F., Alcalá-Fdez, J.: A multi-objective genetic algorithm for tuning and rule selection to obtain accurate and compact linguistic fuzzy rule-based systems. Int. J. Uncertainty Fuzz. Knowl. Based Syst. **15**, 539–557 (2007)
15. Mirjalili, S.: Genetic Algorithm. Evolutionary Algorithms and Neural Networks. SCI, vol. 780, pp. 43–55. Springer, Cham (2019). https://doi.org/10.1007/978-3-319-93025-1_4
16. Wang, Y., Dai, Y., Hirota, K.: Parameter optimization for intuitionistic trapezoidal fuzzy model using multiple objective programming method. In: Uncertainty Modelling in Knowledge Engineering and Decision Making, pp. 602–611 (2016)
17. Ishibuchi, H., Murata, T., Turksen, I.B.: Single objective and two-objective genetic algorithms for selecting linguistic rules for pattern classification problems. Fuzzy Sets Syst. **89**(2), 135–150 (1997)
18. Ishibuchi, H., Nakashima, T., Murata, T.: Three objective genetics-based machine learning for linguistic rule extraction. Inf. Sci. **136**, 109–133 (2001)
19. Ishibuchi, H., Yamamoto, T.: Fuzzy rule selection by multi-objective genetic local search algorithms and rule evaluation measures in data mining. Fuzzy Sets Syst. **141**(1), 59–88 (2004)
20. Narukawa, K., Nojima, Y., Ishibuchi, H.: Modification of evolutionary multiobjective optimization algorithms for multiobjective design of fuzzy rule-based classification systems. In: Proceedings of 2005 IEEE International Conference on Fuzzy Systems, pp. 809–814 (2005)
21. Ishibuchi, H., Nojima, Y.: Analysis of interpretability-accuracy tradeoff of fuzzy systems by multiobjective fuzzy genetics-based machine learning. Int. J. Approx. Reason. **44**(1), 4–31 (2007)
22. Cordon, O., Herrera, F., del Jesus, M.J., Villar, P.: A multiobjective genetic algorithm for feature selection and granularity learning in fuzzy-rule based classification systems. In: Proceedings of IX IFSA World Congress and XX NAFIPS International Conference, pp. 1253–1258 (2001)
23. Ruspini, E.H.: A new approach to clustering. Inf. Control **15**, 22–32 (1969)
24. Gacto, M.J., Alcala, R., Herrera, F.: Adaptation and application of multi-objective evolutionary algorithms for rule reduction and parameter tuning of fuzzy rule-based systems. Soft. Comput. **13**, 419–436 (2009)
25. Pulkkinen, P., Koivisto, H.: Fuzzy classifier identification using decision tree and multiobjective evolutionary algorithms. Int. J. Approx. Reason. **48**, 526–543 (2008)
26. Dempster, D., Shafer, G.: Upper and lower probabilities induced by a multi-valued mapping. Ann. Math. Stat. **38**, 325–339 (1967)
27. Smets, P.: The combination of evidence in the transferable belief model. IEEE Trans. Pattern Anal. Mach. Intell. **12**, 447–458 (1990)
28. Gohardani, S., Bagherian, M., Vaziri, H.: A multi-objective imperialist competitive algorithm for finding motifs in DNA sequences. Math. Biosci. Eng. **16**(3), 1576–1596 (2019)

Randomized General Indices for Evaluating Damage Through Malefactor Social Engineering Attacks

Artur Azarov[1(✉)], Olga Vasileva[2], and Tatiana Tulupyeva[1]

[1] SPIIRAS, St. Petersburg, Russia
artur-azarov@yandex.ru
[2] Saint Petersburg State University, St. Petersburg, Russia

Abstract. The paper is devoted to the application of the method of randomized general indices in assessing potential damage to a company if confidential information is leaked due to malefactor's social engineering attack. This assessment is used in a comparative analysis of the effectiveness of various measures aimed at increasing the level of user protection from the malefactor's social engineering attacks.

Keywords: Information security · Analysis of user protection level · Social engineering attacks · Method of randomized general indices

1 Introduction

Informatization of modern society affects all spheres of individual life and makes people use new technologies. The pace of life is rapidly growing, the need for quick access to information is becoming more important [20]. All these require non-trivial solutions in the field of information processing. In addition, it results in significant increase in the value of both corporate and personal information [5, 6]. Leakage of confidential information can ruin a business or a person's life [15]. That is why special attention is paid to the protection of confidential information [17]. The protection of such information itself consists of many components: from the protection of servers, communication systems, individual computers, to the protection of users of information systems [14, 17]. One of the methods of unlawful obtaining confidential information is the method of affecting users of information systems in which such information is stored, this influence is called impacts of social engineering attack of the malefactor. Some methods for analyzing the user's protection level from social engineering attack actions were developed earlier.

The next obvious step which goes after receiving estimates of the users' protection level from social engineering attacks, is the identification of a strategy to increase this protection level. In order to make a decision on the necessity of increasing user's

The results were partially supported by RFBR, project No. 18-37-00340, and Governmental contract (SPIIRAS) No. 0073-2019-0003.

S. O. Kuznetsov and A. I. Panov (Eds.): RCAI 2019, CCIS 1093, pp. 218–225, 2019.
https://doi.org/10.1007/978-3-030-30763-9_18

protection level, it seems necessary to carry out an assessment of the damage that can be inflicted on a company in case of a successful malefactor's social engineering attack actions. Due to the fact that the value of confidential data cannot always be established unambiguously, it is necessary to involve methods of working with such non-numeric, non-exact and non-complete expert knowledge (NNN-knowledge, NNN-information). It seems necessary to use the general indices method (GIM), particularly the randomized general indices method (RGIM), which allows working with fuzziness [7–12, 19, 23].

The article is devoted to the analysis of the possibility of using these mathematical methods to obtain estimates of the positional losses that can be inflicted on a company in case of successful malefactor's social engineering attacks.

2 Model Descriptions

To analyze the user's protection level some models have been developed. These models were presented in [1–3]. We give several models that are necessary to achieve the goal of this paper.

The extended user model that was presented in [1], includes user's vulnerabilities profile, which contains the severity of each vulnerability. Based on these indicators, the probabilities of the malefactor's social engineering attack impact success on specific users are obtained. The user model also includes links between users and critical documents contained in the information system. The parameter "link" is a loaded parameter, which also shows not only the existence of a link, but also the type of this link, i.e. the type of user access to the critical document (read, write, delete etc.). The user model can be represented as follows [1]:

$$U_i = \left(\left\{ V_j, V_j^i(D) \right\}_{j=1}^v ; \{Ac_j^i\}_{j=1}^k ; \{L_j^i\}_{j=1}^l \right),$$

where $\left\{ V_j, V_j^i(D) \right\}$ is user vulnerability profile, where V_j is j-th user vulnerability, and $V_j^i(D)$ is the degree of j-th vulnerability of i-th user, $\{Ac_j^i\}_{j=1}^k$ is the access of i-th user to the j-th critical document, $\{L_j^i\}_{j=1}^l$ is the type of the relationship between current user and the other users of informational system.

The model of critical documents, also presented in [1], contains an indicator of the value of the document. However, the assessment of the document's value may cause obvious difficulties in obtaining specific numerical values from experts. As usual approximate, interval, fuzzy estimates are much more convenient for experts [6, 7, 11].

Model of critical document can be described with the financial (or other) damage, that can be caused to the organization in case of unauthorized access to this document by the malefactor; and with the hosts, on which this critical document is being stored. This model can be represented as: $CD_i = \left(Dm^i; \left\{ H_j^i \right\}_{j=1}^k \right)$, where Dm^i financial (or other) damage that can be caused to the organization in case of unauthorized access to this document by the malefactor, and $\left\{H_j^i\right\}_{j=1}^k$ hosts, on which this critical document is being stored.

Relative assessments of the critical documents value can be obtained from experts and managers of the company, for which the protection level of users from social engineering attacks is assessed.

In other words, not an assessment of the form "document has value X", but "document A is more valuable than document B", which is much easier for experts to formulate [6–11]. Such information can be presented in the form of a system of inequalities and equalities for the weighting factors $OI = \{w_i > w_j, \ w_r = w_s, \ \ldots\}$ [3].

Interval (fuzzy) assessment of the critical document value may be another type of presentation of the source data. Such interval estimates can be represented as a system of inequalities that define the limits of the possible variation of the critical document value $II = \{a_i \leq w_i \leq b_i, \ \ldots\}$.

Afterwards, two situations that differ in the adequacy of the received information can be considered. The first case is that the combined information $I = OI \cup II$ is sufficient to unambiguously determine the value of critical information stored in the information system. In the second case, this information is not enough, then it can be argued that the information I is incomplete.

Thus, the problem in question may contain NNN-information I, due to the uncertainty of the assessed situation.

3 Application of RGIM

First of all, let consider GIM [7–12]. It can be presented as a sequence of such steps.

1. Forming vector of initial characteristics $x = (x_1, \ldots, x_n)$. This vector contains the characteristics that are necessary and sufficient for a comprehensive assessment of the studied quality of the object. In the considered task, the quality of an object means the damage that can be caused to a company in case of the leakage of certain critical documents, so each x_i is a certain critical document stored in the information system.

2. Forming a vector of individual indicators $q = (q_1, \ldots, q_m)$ representing the functions $q_i(x)$, $i = 1, \ldots, m$, of the original characteristics vector $x = (x_1, \ldots, x_n)$. In our case, each individual indicator q_i is a function of individual characteristic x_i: $q_i = q_i(x_i)$, $i = 1, \ldots, m = n$. Also considered indicators are polarized and normalized. To calculate the indicator $q_i(x)$, the approach presented in the article [4] is used, namely, the indicator is calculated as the total probability of access to it through at least one user of the information system. Such probability may be represented as $p_{\text{doc-acc}}^r = 1 - (1 - p_{\text{doc1}}^r) \ldots (1 - p_{\text{docN}}^r)$, where $p_{\text{doc1}}^r \ldots p_{\text{docN}}^r$ probabilities of access to critical documents doc1..docN. In turn, each p can be calculated as $\tilde{P}_{\text{sum}j} = 1 - \sum_{i=1}^{k} (\tilde{P}_i)$, where p is the full probability of achieving the by the malefactor in case of successful social engineering attack that has passed through all possible chains of users, the last users in which have access to a critical document. The probability of success of malefactor's social engineering attack through a chain of users can

be calculated as follows. Let P_i probability of success of malefactor's social engineering attack on an i-th employee. $P_{i,j}$ the probability of success of malefactor's social engineering attack on j-th user through the user i if the user i has already been successfully attacked. Then the probability of the path in the graph of relations from user m to user j through users i_k may be represented as:

$$\tilde{P}_{m-\ldots-i_k-\ldots-j} = P_m \prod_{k=1}^{n-1} (P_{i_k,i_{k+1}} P_{i_{k+1}}),$$

where $i_1 = m, i_n = j$.

3. Selecting a type of synthesizing function $Q(q)$. This function forms summary assessment characterizing the object under study as a whole from individual indicators $q = (q_1, \ldots, q_m)$, in our case we are talking about assessing the damage that a company can inflict if information leaks. It is obvious that this indicator will be probabilistic in nature due to the fact that each q_i is a probability. What is more, synthesizing function $Q(q)$ also depends on vector $w = (w_1, \ldots, w_m)$, which consists of non-negative parameters $w_1, \ldots, w_m$, which determines the significance of individual indicators $q_1, \ldots, q_m$. For this reason, for a summary assessment Q: $Q = Q(q) = Q(q; w)$. Under the significance of the individual indicator in the considered paradigm, the value i of the critical document is considered.

4. Determining the values of the vector parameters $w = (w_1, \ldots, w_m)$, $w_i \geq 0$.

It is the determination of the values of the vector's parameters that requires the use of the RGIM [12]. As we have mentioned earlier, there is no possibility to uniquely identify each variable w_i. As it was shown above, NNN-information I can be obtained from the managers of the company, for which the analysis of the user's protection level from social engineering attacks is carried out, due to the uncertainty of the situation being assessed. If the presence of NNN-information I about the value of certain critical documents allows reducing the set $W = \{w^\theta, \theta \in \Theta\}$ of all possible values of w_i to the set of all admissible values satisfying the strictly inclusion of sets $W(I) \subset W$, then this information is called nontrivial.

When forming the set of all admissible value vectors $W(I)$ it becomes possible to create a model of such an uncertainty of setting a value vector according to NNN-information I and to use a random value vector $\tilde{w}(I) = (\tilde{w}_1(I), \ldots, \tilde{w}_m(I))$ uniformly distributed on set $W(I)$. Randomizing $\tilde{w}(I) = (\tilde{w}_1(I), \ldots, \tilde{w}_m(I))$ of vector of possible values w_i $w = (w_1, \ldots, w_m)$ leads to the randomization $\tilde{Q}_+(q; I) = Q_+(q; \tilde{w}(I))$ of corresponding summary indicator $Q_+(q; w)$.

For random possible values of w_i $\tilde{w}_1(I), \ldots, \tilde{w}_m(I)$ it is natural to use for estimation mathematical expectations $\bar{w}_i(I) = E\tilde{w}_i(I)$, $i = 1, \ldots, m$. To measure the accuracy of estimates $\bar{w}_i(I)$ standard deviations $s_i(I) = \sqrt{D\tilde{w}_i(I)}$, can be used, where $D\tilde{w}_i(I)$ is a variance of the random coefficient $\tilde{w}_i(I)$. Expectation vector $\bar{w}(I) = (\bar{w}_1(I), \ldots, \bar{w}_m(I))$ may be implemented as a numeric image of NNN-information I.

Reliability of ordering randomized coefficients $\tilde{w}_r(I)$, $\tilde{w}_s(I)$ is determined by the probability $p(r, s; I)$ of stochastic inequality $\tilde{w}_r(I) > \tilde{w}_s(t)$.

For randomized cumulative score $Q_+(q; \tilde{w}(I))$ that synthesizes indicators $q_1, \ldots, q_m$ using NNN-information I, it becomes possible to calculate the average score $\bar{Q}_+(q; I) = E \, Q_+(q; \tilde{w}(I))$.

Standard deviation can be used to measure the accuracy of this estimate $S(q; I) = \sqrt{D\tilde{Q}_+(q; I)}$, where $D\tilde{Q}_+(q; I)$ is a random index variance of $\tilde{Q}_+(q; I) = Q_+(q; \tilde{w}(I))$. The reliability of the ordering of randomized evaluations $Q_+(q^{(j)}; \tilde{w}(I))$, $Q_+(q^{(l)}; \tilde{w}(I))$ may be estimated by the probability $P(j, l; I)$ of stochastic inequality $Q_+(q^{(j)}; \tilde{w}(I)) > Q_+(q^{(l)}; \tilde{w}(I))$. It is this average rating that can reflect the potential damage that a company can inflict in the event of a successful social engineering attack impact on users of this company.

4 Discussion

This section is devoted to the description of the use of damage assessment algorithm that can be inflicted on a company in case of successful malefactor's social engineering attack actions. As previously suggested, based on the analysis of user profiles in social networks [16, 18] and, if necessary, additional psychological testing of users, it is possible to construct users' vulnerabilities profiles. The user vulnerabilities profile contains the severity of individual user vulnerabilities. Based on the indicators of the severity of vulnerabilities according to [1–3], it is possible to create a probabilistic assessment of the resistance of a user's vulnerabilities to the malefactor social engineering attacks. A single aggregated indicator of user protection level or its inverse, the probability of success of the malefactor's social engineering attack actions [1–3], can also be obtained. Then, based on the matrix of users' access to critical documents, as well as on the user social relations graph, probabilistic estimates of the malefactor access to critical documents may be occurred, and an indicator of the overall protection level of the information system from the malefactor social engineering attack may be calculated (Fig. 1).

The next step is forming a strategy to increase the user protection level of protection from malefactor social engineering attacks. An assessment of the success of such a strategy can be obtained through indicators of the overall protection level of information system and an indicator of the potential loss of an organization that can be incurred in case of the loss of confidential data. The mathematical apparatus presented in this article can be used for assessing such possible losses. NNN-information about the value of critical documents that can be received from company executives and experts may be used for estimates of the potential loss of an organization from the leakage of confidential data both before and after the procedures to improve the user's protection level. In addition to the obvious advantages of this approach, i.e., the visual representation of changes in the user protection level, additional advantages are the ability to work with interval estimates of the value of critical documents. Hence, if necessary, it is possible to use this mathematical apparatus as algebraic Bayesian network of trust [13, 21, 22].

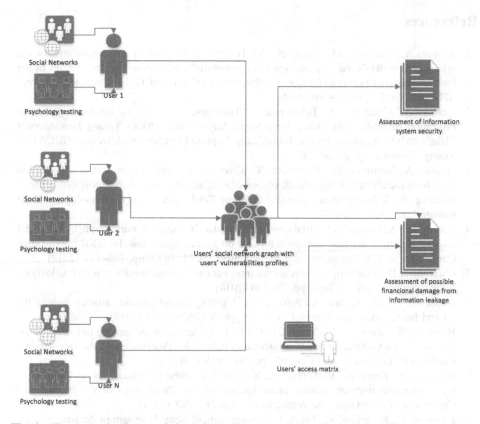

Fig. 1. The general scheme of the information system protection level analysis from social engineering attacks

5 Conclusion

The purpose of this article was to analyze the possibility of using RGIM to obtain estimates of the damage that can be inflicted on a company in case of successful malefactor social engineering attacks.

The article presented a mathematical apparatus that can be used when working with NNN-information on damage assessment. The use of RGIM seems appropriate due to the impossibility of unambiguously determining the value of certain critical documents that a malefactor can gain access to. Thus, this approach will significantly improve the accuracy of calculating the potential damage to the company from the malefactor social engineering attacks.

References

1. Azarov, A., Abramov, M., Tulupyev, A., Tulupyeva, T.: Models and algorithms for the information system's users' protection level probabilistic estimation. In: Proceedings of the First International Scientific Conference "Intelligent Information Technologies for Industry" (IITI 2016), vol. 2, pp. 39–46 (2016)
2. Azarov, A., Abramov, M., Tulupyeva, T., Tulupyev, A.: Users' of Information System Protection Analysis from Malefactor's Social Engineering Attacks Taking into Account Malefactor's Competence Profile. Biologically Inspired Cognitive Architectures (BICA) for Young Scientists, pp. 25–30 (2016)
3. Azarov, A., Suvorova, A., Tulupyeva, T.: Changing the information system's protection level from social engineering attacks, in case of reorganizing the information system's users' structure. In: II International Scientific-Practical Conference "Fuzzy Technologies in the Industry", pp. 56–62 (2018)
4. Azarov, A., Suvorova, A.: Sustainability of the user's social network graph to the social engineering attack actions: an approach based on genetic algorithms. In: XXII International Conference on Soft Computing and Measurement (SCM 2018), pp. 126–129 (2018)
5. Chereshkin, D.: Problemy obespecheniya informacionnoj bezopasnosti v novyh usloviyah. Informatizaciya i svyaz', № 3, pp. 99–106 (2014)
6. Gupta, B., Tewari, A., Jain, A., Agrawal, D.: Fighting against phishing attacks: state of the art and future challenges. Neural Comput. Appl. **28**, 3629–3654 (2017)
7. Hovanov, N., Kornikov, V., Seregin, I.: Qualitative information processing in DSS ASPID-3W for complex objects estimation under uncertainty. In: Proceedings of the International Conference "Informatics and Control", pp. 808–816 (1997)
8. Hovanov, N., Kornikov, V., Seregin, I.: Randomized synthesis of fuzzy sets as a technique for multicriteria decision making under uncertainty. In: Proceedings of the International Conference "Fuzzy Logic and Applications", pp. 281–288 (1997)
9. Hovanov, N., Kornikov, V., Tokin, I.: A mathematical methods system of decision making for developmental strategy under uncertainty. In: Global Environmental Change. Perspective of Remote Sensing and Geographic Information Systems, pp. 93–96 (1995)
10. Hovanov, N., Kolari, J.: Estimating the overall financial performance of Mexican banks using a new method for quantifying subjective information. J. Financ. Eng. **7**(1), 59–77 (1998)
11. Hovanov, N., Fedotov, Yu., Zakharov, V.: The making of index numbers under uncertainty. In: Environmental Indices: Systems Analysis Approach, pp. 83–99 (1999)
12. Hovanov, N.: Evaluation of complex objects in the context of lack of information. In: Proceedings of the 7th International Scientific School "Modeling and Analysis of Safety and Risk in Complex Systems", pp. 18–28 (2008)
13. Kharitonov, N., Maximov, A., Tulupyev, A.: Algebraic Bayesian networks: the use of parallel computing while maintaining various degrees of consistency. Stud. Syst. Decis. Control **199**, 696–704 (2019)
14. Kotenko, I., Chechulin, A., Branitskiy, A.: Generation of source data for experiments with network attack detection software. J. Phys. Conf. Ser. **820**, 12–33 (2017)
15. Schaik, P., Jeske, D., Onibokun, J., Coventry, L., Jansen, J., Kusev, P.: Risk perceptions of cyber-security and precautionary behavior. Comput. Hum. Behav. **62**, 5678–5693 (2017)
16. Shindarev, N., Bagretsov, G., Abramov, M., Tulupyeva, T., Suvorova, A.: Approach to identifying of employees profiles in websites of social networks aimed to analyze social engineering vulnerabilities. In: International Conference on Intelligent Information Technologies for Industry, pp. 441–447 (2017)

17. Struharik, R., Vukobratović, B.: A system for hardware aided decision tree ensemble evolution. J. Parallel Distrib. Comput. **112**, 67–83 (2018)
18. Suleimanov, A., Abramov, M., Tulupyev, A.: Modelling of the social engineering attacks based on social graph of employees communications analysis. In: 2018 IEEE Industrial Cyber-Physical Systems (ICPS), pp. 801–805 (2018)
19. Tarasov, V.: On granular structures of measurement in ambient intelligence systems: Vassiliev's and Belnap's sensors and their communication models. Inf. Meas. Control Syst. **5**, 65–74 (2013)
20. Terlizzi, M., Meirelles, F., Viegas Cortez da Cunha, M.: Behavior of Brazilian banks employees on Facebook and the cybersecurity governance. J. Appl. Secur. Res. **12**, 224–252 (2017)
21. Tulupyev, A., Kharitonov, N., Zolotin, A.: Algebraic Bayesian networks: consistent fusion of partially intersected knowledge systems. In: The Second International Scientific and Practical Conference "Fuzzy Technologies in the Industry – FTI 2018", pp. 109–115 (2018)
22. Vasileva, O., Kiyaev, V.: Monitoring and controlling the execution of the sea cargo port operation's schedule based on multi-agent technologies. In: CEUR Workshop Proceedings of the 2nd International Scientific and Practical Conference "Fuzzy Technologies in the Industry – FTI", vol. 2258, pp. 243–248 (2018)
23. Zadeh, L.: Toward a theory of fuzzy information granulation and its centrality in human reasoning and fuzzy logic. Fuzzy Sets Syst. **90**(2), 111–127 (1997)

Multiclass Classification Based on the Convolutional Fuzzy Neural Networks

V. V. Borisov$^{(\boxtimes)}$ ⓘ and K. P. Korshunova ⓘ

"Moscow Power Engineering Institute" in Smolensk, The Branch of National
Research University, Moscow, Russia
vbor67@mail.ru, ksenya-kor@mail.ru

Abstract. The paper presents a solution to the multiclass classification problem based on the Convolutional Fuzzy Neural Networks. The proposed model includes a fuzzy self-organization layer for data clustering (in addition to convolutional, pooling and fully-connected layers). The model combines the power of convolutional neural networks and fuzzy logic, it is capable of handling uncertainty and imprecision in the input pattern representation. The Convolutional Fuzzy Neural Networks could provide better accuracy in multiclass classification tasks when classified objects are often characterized by uncertainty and inaccuracy in their representation.

Keywords: Multiclass classification · Fuzzy clustering ·
Convolutional fuzzy neural networks

1 Introduction

Nowadays Convolutional Neural Networks (CNN) are one of the most powerful approaches to solving image classification problems. The CNN architectures make the explicit assumption that the inputs are images, which allows to encode certain abstract properties into the architecture.

However, it is still difficult to detect the boundaries between classes in the classification of images of complex objects or complex real-world scenes. These classification objects are often characterized by uncertainty and inaccuracy in its representation and have a complex structure with non-isolated, overlapping classes.

The fuzzy classification (unlike regular classification) means that neighboring classes have the continuous boundary with overlapping areas. The classified object is characterized by its degree of belonging to different classes. This approach is suitable for many applications and provides a simple representation of a complex feature space.

To enable a system to deal with cognitive uncertainties in a manner more like humans, one may incorporate the concept of fuzzy logic into the neural networks. The hybrid systems combine the capabilities of neural networks and fuzzy computations [1, 2]. For practical purposes, a fuzzy neural network is often more effective than just a fuzzy network or an ordinary (classical) neural network, as it allows indeterminate and inaccurate information processing.

Fuzzy logic and neural networks are combined in various ways. Fuzziness can be incorporated into different parts of traditional neural networks. One of the main way is

S. O. Kuznetsov and A. I. Panov (Eds.): RCAI 2019, CCIS 1093, pp. 226–233, 2019.
https://doi.org/10.1007/978-3-030-30763-9_19

to incorporates fuzziness into the structure of networks by adding fuzziness to the values of training examples, by "blurring" input data and obtaining output information in terms of fuzzy set theory [2–6].

Multiclass classification based on the model of Convolutional Fuzzy Neural Network (CFNN) for real world objects and scenes classification is proposed in the paper.

2 CFNN Architecture

The proposed CFNN model's architecture [7] is built up of three parts: encoder, classifier [8–10] and the self-organization layer (the fuzzy layer) between them. The structure of the proposed CFNN is presented in Fig. 1.

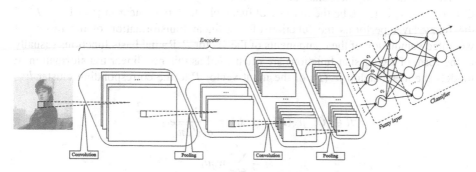

Fig. 1. The structure of the CFNN.

The first part is used as an image "encoder". The encoder is needed to convert the "raw" pixels of the input images into vectors of high level visual features. It is an ordinary CNN that consists of various combinations of convolutional and pooling layers.

The Convolutional layer is the core building block of a CNN that does most of the computational heavy lifting. To calculate the convolution, we swept the kernel (we should flip the kernel first and then do the convolution) on the image and at every single location we calculated the output that is a multiplication or other dot product. Each position results in an activation of the neuron and the output is collected in the feature map. The activation function is commonly a RELU layer. Each convolutional neuron processes data only for its receptive field.

Convolutional networks may include local or global pooling layers to streamline the underlying computation. Its function is to progressively reduce the spatial size of the representation to reduce the amount of parameters and computation in the network, and hence to control overfitting. Pooling layers reduce the dimensions of the data by combining the outputs of neuron clusters at one layer into a single neuron in the next layer. Local pooling combines small clusters, typically 2×2. Global pooling acts on all the neurons of the convolutional layer. Max pooling uses the maximum value from each of a cluster of neurons at the prior layer. In addition to max pooling, the pooling units can also perform other functions, such as average pooling or even L2-norm pooling.

The stack of convolutional and pooling layers convert an input image into a set of deep (or high-level) features that describe the image. Let these features be $P = (p_1, \ldots, p_J)$.

In the typical structure of a CNN P features become an input information for a classifier. It is one or more fully-connected layers (just regular multilayer perceptron). The output of the classifier (and the output of the whole CNN) is class scores for the input object.

In contrast to regular Convolutional Neural Network, the CFNN includes the self-organization layer (the fuzzy layer), which is a kind of preprocessor. It is situated between the convolutional network and the classifier (a kind of postprocessor).

In the CFNN architecture the features P become an input information for the self-organization layer (part 2).

The number of neurons of the fuzzy layer is the number of clusters $C = \{c_1, \ldots, c_L\}$. Let L be the number of fuzzy clusters. Each neuron $(l = 1, \ldots, L)$ of the fuzzy layer performs the function of non-linear transformation of the results of weighted summation of the components of the vector P. Radial basis functions (usually in the form of a Gaussian function) are often used as this non-linear transformation. It models the membership $\mu_{c_l}(P)$ of the input vector P to the corresponding cluster l:

$$\forall l \in |C| \quad \mu_{c_l}(P) = f(s_l) = \frac{1}{\sigma_l \sqrt{2\pi}} e^{-\frac{(s_l - m_l)^2}{2\sigma_l^2}},$$

$$s_l = \sum_{j=1}^{J} w_{lj} p_j.$$

Parameter m_l is the centroid of a cluster c_l, parameter σ_l is "blurring" of cluster c_l boundaries level (both are real values).

The fuzzy layer forms a vector consisting of the membership degrees of P w.r.t. the specific cluster centers: $\left(\mu_{c_1}(P), \ldots, \mu_{c_L}(P)\right)$. The components $\mu_{c_l}(P)$ are calculated to satisfy the normalization condition $\left(\sum_{l=1}^{L} \mu_{c_l}(P) = 1\right)$ for each training sample vector.

Note that these clusters are not equivalent to output classes and the number of clusters and target classes can differ. The outputs of neurons of the "fuzzy layer" are used as inputs of the classifier (a kind of postprocessor).

It is one or more fully-connected layers (just regular multilayer perceptron). The output of the classifier (and the output of the whole CNN) is class scores for the input object.

The structure of the fuzzy layer and the classifier is presented in Fig. 2.

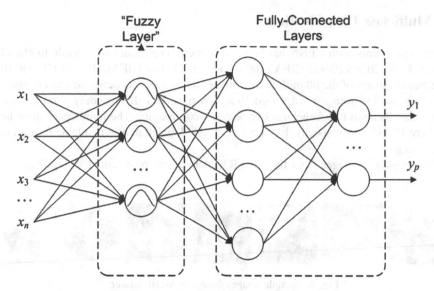

Fig. 2. The structure of the last CFNN layers.

3 CFNN Training

The training of the Convolutional Fuzzy Neural Network consists of three independent steps for three components of the net.

First of all we train the convolutional network (a regular CNN corresponding to the determinate CFNN) to form some abstract properties of the input image by back-propagation [10, 11]. Nowadays there are a lot of "pretrained" models that have been already trained on a large data sets from a related domain [12]. So we can skip this step of CFNN training.

The second part is the tuning of the fuzzy layer parameters, which is called self-organization. The fuzzy layer is self-organizing. It is trained in an unsupervised way using a competitive learning scheme. Self-organization of the fuzzy layer means choosing the positions of the cluster centers (choosing the parameters of the membership functions in the formula above). Various fuzzy clustering algorithms can be applied (C-means algorithm, Gustafson–Kessel algorithm [13]).

The third part is the classifier training. The parameters of the convolutional and fuzzy layers are stable. Only fully-connected layers weights are tuned. The classifier is trained by a standard backpropagation algorithm.

After completing the three parts of training, the CFNN becomes ready for work, when an image pixel array is fed to the CFNN input. The output of a network is a vector with components that characterize the belonging of the input image to each of the classes (class scores). The image is assigned to the class with the max score value.

The work of the CFNN is divided into three stages: the input pattern (image) comes through a series of transformations, as a result a vector of high-level characteristics is formed; further, fuzzy layer performs a preliminary distribution of the input data into fuzzy clusters; the last fully connected layers perform the classification, assigning the result class label to each group of clusters.

4   Multiclass Classification

Some experiments with CFNN has been performed. The model were made to classify images from CIFAR10 and CIFAR100 datasets [14]. The CIFAR-10 and CIFAR-100 are labeled subsets of the 80 million tiny images dataset. It was designed and created by the Canadian Institute for Advanced Research (CIFAR). It is widely used for easy image classification task/benchmark in research community. The numbers of classified label are 10 and 100, respectively. There are 50000 labeled photos available for training and testing.

Some sample images from the CIFAR10 dataset are represented in Fig. 3.

Fig. 3.   Sample images from CIFAR10 dataset.

As an encoder we use a CNN close to the VGG16 model [15] because it is simple but powerful neural network architecture.

The structure of the encoder is represented in Table 1.

Table 1.   The structure of the convolutional encoder

Layer number	Layer	Parameters
1	Convolutional Layer	896
2	Convolutional Layer	9248
3	Maxpooling Layer	
4	Dropout Layer	
5	Convolutional Layer	18496
6	Convolutional Layer	36928
7	Maxpooling Layer	
8	Dropout Layer [16]	

The Fuzzy Layer consists of 163 neurons (163 clusters). We have clustered the set of data (both CIFAR10 and CIFAR100 dataset) several times, with different numbers of clusters. Then we have chosen the number of clusters when the Fuzzy Partition Coefficient [16] is maximized (The FPC is defined on the range from 0 to 1, with 1 being the best. It is a metric that shows the cleanliness of data described by a certain clustering model).

The classifier includes 2 fully connected layers. They have 512 (as prototype VGG16 architecture has) and 10 or 100 neurons (for CIFAR10 and CIFAR100 dataset respectively).

We have had three independent stages to train the CFNN model.

Stage 1. Training the Encoder net to classify CIFAR images (method for stochastic optimization: Adam – Adaptive Moment Estimation [17]). The CNN training takes a lot of resources, so we could have only 10, 25 and 50 epochs.

Stage 2. Self-organization of the Fuzzy Layer (using fuzzy c-means clustering [18]).

Stage 3. The classifier training (method for stochastic optimization: Adam). Only weights of fully-connected layers were tuned while the parameters of the convolutional and fuzzy layers were stable, so we could have 100 epochs.

We use programming language Python and Keras deep learning library [19] for the CFNN implementation.

The results of the experiments comparing the proposed CFNN and the regular CNN (with VGG16 architecture shown in Table 1) are presented in Table 2.

They show that we can solve multiclass classification problem more effectively using the proposed CFNN model than using the regular prototype (for both CIFAR10 and CIFAR100 dataset).

Table 2. The results of the experiments

Training the encoder epochs	The regular CNN (VGG16 net) accuracy, %		The CFNN accuracy, %	
	CIFAR10	CIFAR100	CIFAR10	CIFAR100
10	61.36	59.22	72.52	62.3
25	67.28	63.41	75.36	67.52
50	76.14	68.19	83.96	72.3

Experimental results show that incorporation of the fuzzy layer into the CNN allows the quality of multiclass classification problem solution (accuracy) increase even when the corresponding regular CNN does not show high accuracy. It is right for both CIFAR10 and CIFAR100 datasets. After only 50 epochs of regular CNN training we add some epochs of c-means clustering and the classifier training (that takes much less time than 1 regular CNN training epoch) and can achieve 84% accuracy instead of 76% for CIFAR10 dataset and 72% accuracy instead of 68% for CIFAR100 dataset.

5 Conclusion

A solution to multiclass classification problem based on the CFNN was proposed. Fuzziness is incorporated into the structure of network in terms of fuzzy sets theory. The proposed model combines the power of convolutional neural networks and fuzzy logic and is capable of handling uncertainty and imprecision.

The training of the CFNN consists of three independent steps for three components of the net.

Some experimental work to measure the effectiveness of CFNN for multiclass image classification has been performed. These experiments shows that the CFNN could provide better accuracy for multiclass classification problems in less training time.

Acknowledgments. The work was supported by grant RFBR № 18-07-00928_a "Methods and technologies of intellectual support for research of complex hydro-mechanical processes in conditions of uncertainty on the convoluted neuro-fuzzy networks".

References

1. Fuler, R.: Neural Fuzzy Systems. Publishing House Abo Akademi University, Turku (1995)
2. Borisov, V.V.: Hybridization of intellectual technologies for analytical tasks of decision-making support. J. Comput. Eng. Inform. **2**(1), 148–156 (2014)
3. Keller, J.M., Hunt, D.J.: Incorporating fuzzy membership function into the perceptron algorithm. IEEE Trans. Pattern Anal. Mach. Intell. **7**(6), 693–699 (1985)
4. Mitra, S., Pal, S.K.: Fuzzy multi-layer perceptron, inferencing and rule generation. IEEE Trans. Neural Networks **6**, 51–63 (1995)
5. Mitra, S., Pal, S.K.: Fuzzy self organization, inferencing and rule generation. IEEE Trans. Syst. Man Cybern. Part A Syst. Hum. **26**(5), 608–620 (1996)
6. Pal, S.K., Mitra, S.: Multilayer perceptron, fuzzy sets and classification. IEEE Trans. Neural Networks **3**(5), 683–697 (1992)
7. Korshunova, K.P.: A convolutional fuzzy neural network for image classification. In: Proceedings 3rd Russian-Pacific Conference on Computer Technology and Applications (RPC), Vladivostok, Russia, pp. 1–4 (2018)
8. Le Cun, Y., et al.: Handwritten digit recognition with a back-propagation network. In: Advances in Neural Information Processing Systems 2 (NIPS), pp. 396–404 (1989)
9. Le Cun, Y., Bottou, L., Bengio, Y., Haffner, P.: Gradient-based learning applied to document recognition. Proc. IEEE **86**(11), 2278–2324 (1998)
10. Le Cun, Y., Bengio, Y., Hinton, G.: Deep learning. Nature **521**, 436–444 (2015)
11. Avedyan, E.D., Galushkin, A.I., Selivanov, S.A.: Comparative analysis of structures of fully connected neural networks and convolutional neural networks and their learning algorithms. Inf. Commun. **1**, 18–30 (2017). (in Russian)
12. Model Zoo. BVLC/caffe/. https://github.com/BVLC/caffe/wiki/Model-Zoo. Accessed 21 April 2019
13. Osovsky, S.: Neural Networks for Information Processing. Finansy i statistika Publ, Moscow (2002)
14. CIFAR-10 and CIFAR-100 datasets/Alex Krizhevsky's home page. https://www.cs.toronto.edu/~kriz/cifar.html. Accessed 06 April 2019
15. Simonyan, K., Zisserman, A.: Very deep convolutional networks for large-scale image recognition. In Proceedings International Conference on Learning Representations (2014). http://arxiv.org/abs/1409.1556

16. Hinton, G.E., Srivastava, N., Krizhevsky, A., Sutskever, I., Salakhutdinov, R.R.: Improving neural networks by preventing co-adaptation of feature detectors, arXiv.org (2012). https:// arxiv.org/abs/1207.0580. Accessed 01 May 2019
17. Diederik, K., Ba, J.A.: A method for stochastic optimization, arXiv.org (2014). https://arxiv. org/abs/1412.6980. Accessed 01 May 2019
18. Trauwaert, E.: On the meaning of Dunn's partition coefficient for fuzzy cluster. Fuzzy Sets Syst. **25**, 217–242 (1988)
19. Keras Documentation Keras: The Python Deep Learning library. https://keras.io. Accessed 06 April 2019

Algebraic Bayesian Networks: Naïve Frequentist Approach to Local Machine Learning Based on Imperfect Information from Social Media and Expert Estimates

Nikita A. Kharitonov[1,2], Anatoly G. Maximov[1,2(✉)],
and Alexander L. Tulupyev[1,2]

[1] St. Petersburg Institute for Informatics and Automation of the Russian Academy
of Sciences, St. Petersburg, Russia
maksimov.20.43@gmail.com
[2] St. Petersburg State University, St. Petersburg, Russia

Abstract. The task of model learning arises in algebraic Bayesian networks as one of the probabilistic graphical models. Several approaches to machine learning of algebraic Bayesian networks are known. This research is dedicated to the algorithm of machine learning of algebraic Bayesian network represented by a knowledge pattern on missing data. Besides this algorithm, some examples of machine learning on artificial and real data from social media are considered.

Keywords: Algebraic Bayesian network · Imperfect information · Missing data · Machine learning · Knowledge pattern · Social media · Machine learning algorithm

1 Introduction

The problem of learning a model on the available data [15,18] arises in algebraic Bayesian networks [20,21], which are probabilistic graphical models [3,4,19]. Knowledge patterns can be ideals of conjuncts, disjuncts, or quants with interval estimates of their probability.

Algebraic Bayesian networks can be trained on data with a large count of missing values [6,10,17]. Social media are one of the common source of imperfect information about opinions and events [1,13], which perfectly suite for network training.

One would like to build a network under assumption that there are events or statements which can be interpreted in binary semantics. Besides, information about events/statements from social media can be completed with expert

The research was carried out as part of the project according to the state task SPI-IRAS № 0073-2019-0003 as well as with particle financial support from the Russian Foundation for Basic Research, project № 18-01-00626.

knowledge. For example, "it is unlikely that x_1 entails x_2" or "it is probably that one of x_1 or x_2 will occur." Such information has no direct numeric data on probability of certain statements, but can significantly reduce the uncertainty of estimates, which are formed from contents of social media. Another point is the ability to store such information under the assumption that the estimates "unlikely"/"possibly"/"most likely" were given interpretation in the form of scalar or interval probability estimates.

The aim of the work is to create an algorithm for local training of algebraic Bayesian networks which are represented by knowledge patterns and demonstrate the results of its work on data from social media.

2   Related Works

Algebraic Bayesian networks belong to the class of probabilistic graphical model, as well as Belief Bayesian networks [9,22,24] and Markov fields [19]. They all belong to the machine learning models [15,18]. However, in contrast to Bayesian Belief networks, algebraic Bayesian networks make it possible to take into account imprecise, non-numeric, incomplete expert estimates, which are formally expressed in statements about the truth limits of individual network elements or the probabilities of some propositional formulas. There are publications in English [8,25,26] and in Russian [20,21] that are dedicated to Algebraic Bayesian networks. The logical-probabilistic inference has been formulated and developed, so there is a need to formalize and develop learning algorithms for Algebraic Bayesian networks, which consider

- the presence of missing values in the samples;
- non-numeric data coming from experts about the comparison of probability values;
- probabilities of propositional formulas with scalar or interval estimates, or relationship of order, which appear while interpreting expert statements.

The next works dedicated to the analysis of the data from social media [12,23].

To the authors knowledge there is no researches by the moment about training of algebraic Bayesian networks and using them to data analysis from social media.

3   Algebraic Bayesian Networks

Algebraic Bayesian networks belong to the class of probabilistic graphical models, to which belong Bayesian Belief networks and Markov networks [3,4,19]. Algebraic Bayesian networks are a collection of closely related assertions about the domain, called knowledge patterns. Knowledge is expressed as estimates of conjunct truth probabilities [20,21] (in addition, there are network models for quants and disjuncts, as well as methods for converting models), which can have both scalar and interval values. The knowledge pattern is the ideal of conjuncts over some small number of atoms in this paradigm. The combination of knowledge patterns (which can have and often have intersections) is an algebraic Bayesian network with several levels of network representation distinguished: secondary, tertiary, quaternary structures [5,14]. Figure 1 shows an example of a network over five knowledge patterns, and Fig. 2 shows an example of a knowledge pattern over three atoms.

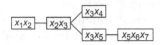

Fig. 1. Algebraic Bayesian network

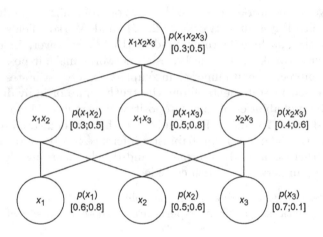

Fig. 2. Knowledge pattern

One of the most important tasks is to create and to study the network on some data set. At the same time, the data set may have missing values or inaccuracies (often arising during data collection) that must be taken into account and processed (the apparatus of algebraic Bayesian networks allows this). In addition, it may be necessary to formalize and process some expert statements or other restrictions on data. This study addresses the issue of learning a knowledge pattern.

The concept of consistency in algebraic Bayesian networks allows to verify the correctness of the estimates of the truth made in network. The concept of consistency is associated with the concept of *maintaining* consistency. As a result of maintaining consistency, one can either obtain consistent refined estimates of the probabilities of each element of the ideal, or recognize interval estimates of probabilities over the ideal as contradictory.

Since the concept of consistency will be used below, here are some theoretical considerations.

To maintain consistency in the knowledge pattern with interval estimates, it is necessary to solve a series of linear programming problems as follows:

$$p^-(f) = \min_{\mathcal{R}}\{p(f)\}$$

$$p^+(f) = \max_{\mathcal{R}}\{p(f)\}$$

for all formulas f from the conjunct ideal, where

$$\mathcal{R} = \mathcal{E} \cup \mathcal{D}$$

$$\mathcal{D} - \text{limits from subject matter}$$

$$\mathcal{R} - \text{limits from probability theory axioms}$$

The set of constraints $\mathcal{D}$ is

$$\mathcal{D}^{(n)} = \left\{ \begin{array}{l} p_0^-(x_1) \le p(x_1) \le p_0^+(x_1) \\ \vdots \\ p_0^-(x_1 x_2) \le p(x_1 x_2) \le p_0^+(x_1 x_2) \\ \vdots \\ p_0^-(x_1 x_2 \ldots x_n) \le p(x_1 x_2 \ldots x_n) \le p_0^+(x_1 x_2 \ldots x_n) \end{array} \right\}$$

The set of constraints $\mathcal{E}$ for x_1 and x_2 is

$$\mathcal{E}^{(2)} = \left\{ \begin{array}{l} p(x_1 x_2) \ge 0 \\ p(x_1) - p(x_1 x_2) \ge 0 \\ p(x_2) - p(x_1 x_2) \ge 0 \\ 1 - p(x_1) - p(x_2) + p(x_1 x_2) \ge 0 \end{array} \right\}$$

The book [20] shows how to effectively calculate $\mathcal{E}$ for $x_1, x_2 \ldots x_n$.

4   Learning a Knowledge Pattern

In the framework of this work, an assumption is made about the availability of data prepared for learning presented in the form of a set of atoms and their corresponding meanings. An example of such a data set for learning a knowledge pattern over two atoms is given in Table 1 (? stays for unknown, or missing value.)

Thus, the input is a set of meaning of atoms in knowledge pattern in the case of machine learning of algebraic Bayesian networks. In this case, some of the meanings can be omitted (including all, however, such a case will not allow to get any knowledge pattern that is useful for further use). The aim of machine learning is to obtain a consistent knowledge pattern based on this data set.

At the beginning, let us consider a data set without missing values. In this case, the probability of the truth of an atom is equal to the ratio of the number of true (1) value of its entries in the data to the data set size. An intuitive example is given in Table 2.

Table 1. Data set example. ?—missing values.

№	x_1	x_1	x_3
1	1	0	?
2	?	1	?
3	0	1	1
4	1	1	1
5	0	0	?
6	?	?	1
7	1	1	1
8	1	0	1
9	1	1	1
10	1	0	1

Table 2. Data set example without missing values. Probability of atoms.

№	x_1	x_1	x_3
1	1	0	0
2	0	1	0
3	0	1	0
4	1	1	1
5	1	1	0
6	1	0	0
7	0	1	0
8	1	1	1
9	1	1	0
10	1	1	1
Prob.	0.7	0.8	0.3

On the basis of the obtained probabilities of the truth of atoms, estimates of the probabilities of the truth of their conjuncts are obtained. In this case, two approaches are possible.

In the first case, for each input set, the probability of the remaining conjuncts is calculated (in this example, $x_1 x_2$). The calculation takes place according to the rules of strong logic of indeterminacy, introduced by S. Kleene [11]. If a conjunct contains at least one atom with a negative value, it is matched with 0, otherwise—1. Also if one of the atoms in the conjunct has an unknown estimate, the latter is matched to 0 or ? by a similar rule. Further, estimates of the probability of truth of conjuncts are obtained, similar to atoms.

In the second case, it is considered that a knowledge pattern has some prior probability distribution. For example, each element corresponds to the interval

$[0; 1]$ of the probability of its truth (with the exception of an empty conjunct, which is always true). In the process of learning, the estimates that are obtained from data are changed (the estimates of the probability of the truth of atoms), and then the consistency of the knowledge pattern is maintained (that is, the correctness of the distribution of the obtained estimates [7]).

In this study, the first method is used to skip maintaining the consistency of a knowledge pattern. This is explained by the fact that each of the complete sets of atomic definitions is a consistent knowledge pattern with scalar estimates, and the whole set is a linear combination of consistent knowledge patterns. According to Theorem 1 below, such a combination is a consistent knowledge pattern.

Theorem 1 [21]. A knowledge pattern, which is a linear combination of consistent knowledge patterns with interval estimates, is consistent.

Next, an example from Table 1 will be considered. Atoms with unknown meanings can have the value of both 0 and 1. It is logical to present the unknown values as an interval $[0; 1]$. In this case, the values that are known are easily representable as intervals $[0; 0]$ or $[1; 1]$. The next step is similar to working with data without missing values, with the difference that the left and right limits of truth intervals are considered separately. Result and produced conversions for the example from Table 1 are represented in Table 3.

Table 3. Data set example with missing values. Probability of atoms.

№	x_1	x_1	x_3
1	$[1; 1]$	$[0; 0]$	$[0; 1]$
2	$[0; 1]$	$[1; 1]$	$[0; 1]$
3	$[0; 0]$	$[1; 1]$	$[1; 1]$
4	$[1; 1]$	$[1; 1]$	$[1; 1]$
5	$[0; 0]$	$[0; 0]$	$[0; 1]$
6	$[0; 1]$	$[0; 1]$	$[1; 1]$
7	$[1; 1]$	$[1; 1]$	$[1; 1]$
8	$[1; 1]$	$[0; 0]$	$[1; 1]$
9	$[1; 1]$	$[1; 1]$	$[1; 1]$
10	$[1; 1]$	$[0; 0]$	$[1; 1]$
Prob.	$[0.6; 0.8]$	$[0.5; 0.6]$	$[0.7; 1]$

The final step of the learning process is obtaining an assessment of the truth values of various conjuncts obtained from these atoms, and their learning. The result is shown in Fig. 3.

An algorithm for learning a knowledge pattern on an existing set of prepared data will be formulated in the next section.

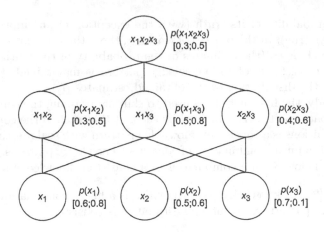

Fig. 3. Result of learning

4.1 A Naïve Frequentist Algorithm for Knowledge Pattern Machine Learning

The input of the algorithm is n, the number of atoms in the knowledge pattern and *input* is a list of arrays with length n, each of which contains value of atom i on the position i. The values are 0 (false), 1 (true), or ? (missing value).

The algorithm returns a consistent knowledge pattern KP learned on input data.

The process of the algorithm is described as follows. On the basis of *input* list *list* of arrays with length 2^n is created each of which contains conjunct values. In this case, the indexation is introduced as follows: at the position k there is a conjunct consisting of atoms with indices i, for which at the place i from the end in binary representation k is 1. For example, on place $5_{10} = 101_2$ there will be a conjunct $x_1 x_3$.

Next, two arrays with length 2^n are created, the first of which ($arrLB$) corresponds to the lower boundaries of the truth intervals of conjuncts, the second ($arrUB$) corresponds to the upper boundaries. Both are filled with zeros (except for the first position corresponding to the empty conjunct, it is 1 on it).

Next comes a cyclic round of the list items, arr, the current item. At each step, if $arr[i] = 1$, then values increase at $arrLB[i]$ and at $arrUB[i]$; if $arr[i] = ?$, then value increases at $arrUB[i]$; if $arr[i] = 0$, then the arrays do not change.

After passing the list normalization occurs: elements $arrLB$ and $arrUB$ divided by the number of elements in *list*.

At the final stage of the algorithm, a knowledge pattern is created with lower estimates of the probability of the truth of conjuncts from $arrLB$ and upper estimate from $arrUB$.

Here is the pseudo-code of the algorithm:

LearnKP(int n, List < byte[] > input){
create list;

```
create arrLB;
create arrUB;
for all arr ∈ input do
    Create tmpArr;
    //array of conjuncts probability value
    list.Add(tmpArr);
end for
for all arr ∈ list do
    for i = 1..2^n do
        if arr[i] = 1 then
            arrLB[i] + +;
            arrUB[i] + +;
        else
            if arr[i] =? then
                arrUB[i] + +;
            end if
        end if
    end for
end for
for i = 1..2^n do
    arrLB[i] = arrLB[i]/list.Length;
    arrUB[i] = arrLB[i]/list.Length;
end for
KP = CreateKP(arrLB, arrUB);
returnKP;
}
```

A situation is possible, when, besides data themselves, some truth estimates are known (for example, obtained from experts). For example, one expert stated: "It is very likely that x_1", and the second expert added: "And the probability of x_3 is less than x_1." In the framework of work with algebraic Bayesian networks, in particular, with knowledge patterns, these statements can be represented as interval estimates. So, the first phrase can be interpreted as follows: $p(x_1) \geq 0.75$, and make the appropriate changes in the knowledge pattern. The second phrase implies that the upper bound of the probability $x3$ cannot be greater than the upper bound of the probability $x1$. The knowledge pattern obtained after making changes is presented in Fig. 4. The final step in such a situation is the maintenance of consistency and obtaining a result (for this example, taking into account the expert opinion, the knowledge pattern remains consistent).

5 An Example of Learning a Knowledge Pattern on Data from Social Media

In this section we give a simple example of the use of machine learning of algebraic Bayesian networks based on real data from social media. Suppose that

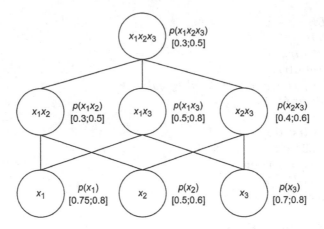

Fig. 4. After inserting expert values

we have two groups of VKontakte (social network in Russia), dedicated to different academic disciplines of one group of students, in which materials, tasks, and assessments are placed. The goal is to get the probability that the average participant in one group belongs the other one, and is also a current student of the Faculty of Mathematics and Mechanics of St. Petersburg State University (information taken based on the information on the user page). On the basis of these data, it will be possible to find out whether it is necessary to have better information about groups or not.

Input data contains 54 lines with three fields that have values of 1 (a person is in a group/is a student), 0 (not a member/is not) and ? if there is no information whether the person is a student or not. After processing and presentation in the form of a list of arrays, they are fed to the input of the method that produces the

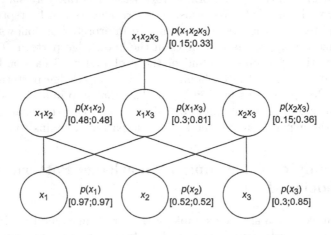

Fig. 5. Result of learning on real data

learning. The result is shown in Fig. 5, where x_1, x_2 are the probability of finding a participant in the first and second groups, respectively x_3 is the probability that the participant is a student.

Thus, the probability that a new member joins one group is 48%. In addition, a group member is a student with a probability from 30% to 81%, and at the same time all three conditions are fulfilled with a probability from 15% to 33%. It can be concluded that it is necessary to better inform students about groups.

6 Conclusion

The results obtained make it possible to study the use of algebraic Bayesian networks in the analysis of data from social media, for example, when investigating/estimating a level of user readiness to resist social engineering attacks [2, 16].

Our future work will be related to training of the entire algebraic Bayesian network. The problem of preparing data of various types for network training also remains open.

References

1. Abdel-Basset, M., Mohamed, M.: The role of single valued neutrosophic sets and rough sets in smart city: imperfect and incomplete information systems. Meas. J. Int. Meas. Confederation **124**, 47–55 (2018)
2. Abramov, M.V., Azarov, A.A.: Identifying user's of social networks psychological features on the basis of their musical preferences. In: Proceedings 20th IEEE International Conference on Soft Computing and Measurements (SCM), St Petersburg, Russia, pp. 90–92 (2017)
3. Azar, A., Dolatabad, K.M.: A method for modelling operational risk with fuzzy cognitive maps and Bayesian belief networks. Expert Syst. Appl. **115**, 607–617 (2019)
4. Baggenstoss, P.M.: On the duality between belief networks and feed-forward neural networks. IEEE Trans. Neural Networks Learn. Syst. **30**(1), 190–200 (2019)
5. Filchenkov, A.A., Tulupyev, A.L.: Coincidence of the sets of minimal and irreducible join graphs over primary structure of algebraic Bayesian networks. Vestnik St. Petersburg Univ. Math. **45**(2), 106–113 (2012)
6. Jiang, X., Zhang, L., Qiao, L.: Completing missing exam scores with structural information and beyond. J. Appl. Remote Sens. **13**(2), 022005-1–022005-11 (2018)
7. Kharitonov, N., Malchevskaia, E., Zolotin, A., Abramov, M.: External consistency maintenance algorithm for chain and stellate structures of algebraic bayesian networks: statistical experiments for running time analysis. Adv. Intell. Syst. Comput. **875**, 23–30 (2019)
8. Kharitonov, N.A., Tulupyev, A.L., Zolotin, A.A.: Software implementation of reconciliation algorithms in algebraic Bayesian networks. In: Proceedings 20th IEEE International Conference on Soft Computing and Measurements (SCM), St Petersburg, Russia, pp. 8–10 (2017)
9. Klepac, G., Kopal, R., Mršíc, L.: Predictive complex event processing based on evolving Bayesian networks. In: Hybrid Intelligence for Social Networks, pp. 25–45. Springer, Cham (2017)

10. Krause, R.W., Huisman, M., Steglich, C., Sniiders, T.A.: Missing network data a comparison of different imputation methods. In: Proceedings of the 2018 IEEE/ACM International Conference on Advances in Social Networks Analysis and Mining (ASONAM 2018), Barcelona, Spain, pp. 159–163 (2018)
11. Malinowski, G.: Kleene logic and inference. Bull. Sect. Logic **43**(1/2), 43–52 (2014)
12. Pandey, B., Bhanodia, P.K., Khamparia, A., Pandey, D.K.: A comprehensive survey of edge prediction in social networks: techniques, parameters and challenges. Expert Syst. Appl. **124**, 164–181 (2019)
13. Ren, B., Zhang, Y., Chen, J., Shen, L.: Efficient network disruption under imperfect information: the sharpening effect of network reconstruction with no prior knowledge. Physica A **520**, 196–207 (2019)
14. Romanov, A.V., Levenets, D.G., Zolotin, A.A., Tulupyev, A.L.: Incremental synthesis of the tertiary structure of algebraic Bayesian networks. In: Proceedings 19th IEEE International Conference on Soft Computing and Measurements (SCM), St Petersburg, Russia, pp. 28–30 (2016)
15. Sharifzadeh, M., Sikinioti-Lock, A., Shah, N.: Machine-learning methods for integrated renewable power generation: a comparative study of artificial neural networks, support vector regression, and Gaussian Process Regression. Renew. Sustain. Energy Rev. **108**, 513–538 (2019)
16. Shindarev, N., Bagretsov, G., Abramov, M., Tulupyeva, T., Suvorova, A.: Approach to identifying of employees profiles in websites of social networks aimed to analyze social engineering vulnerabilities. Adv. Intell. Syst. Comput. **679**, 441–447 (2018)
17. Singh, B., Toshniwal, D.: MOWM: Multiple Overlapping Window Method for RBF based missing value prediction on big data. Expert Syst. Appl. **122**, 303–318 (2019)
18. Su, H.P., Lian, C., Liu, J.C., Liu, Y.L.: Machine learning models for solvent effects on electric double layer capacitance. Chem. Eng. Sci. **202**, 186–193 (2019)
19. Suwanwimolkul, S., Zhang, L., Ranasinghe, D.C., Shi, Q.F.: One-step adaptive markov random field for structured compressive sensing. Signal Process. **156**, 116–144 (2019)
20. Tulupyev, A.L., Nikolenko, S.I., Sirotkin, A.V.: Bayesian Belief Networks: Probabilistic logic Approach. SPb.: Nauka, Saint-Petersburg (2006). (in Russian)
21. Tulupyev, A.L., Sirotkin, A.V., Nikolenko, S.I.: Bayesian Belief Networks. SPbSU Press, Saint-Petersburg (2009). (in Russian)
22. Varshney, D., Kumar, S., Gupta, V.: Predicting information diffusion probabilities in social networks: a Bayesian networks based approach. Knowl.-Based Syst. **133**, 66–76 (2017)
23. Vitoropoulou, M., Karyotis, V., Papavassiliou, S.: Sensing and monitoring of information diffusion in complex online social networks. Peer-to-peer Networking Appl. **12**(3), 604–619 (2019)
24. Wang, Y., Gaoand, H., Chen, G.: Predictive complex event processing based on evolving Bayesian networks. Pattern Recogn. Lett. **105**, 207–216 (2018)
25. Zolotin, A.A., Malchevskaya, E.A., Tulupyev, A.L., Sirotkin, A.V.: An approach to sensitivity analysis of inference equations in algebraic bayesian networks. Adv. Intell. Syst. Comput. **679**, 34–42 (2018)
26. Zolotin, A.A., Tulupyev, A.L.: Sensitivity statistical estimates for local a posteriori inference matrix-vector equations in algebraic Bayesian networks over quantum propositions. Vestnik St. Petersburg Univ. Math. **51**(1), 42–48 (2018)

Inference Methods for One Class of Systems with Many Fuzzy Inputs

Vasiliy Sinuk and Maxim Panchenko[✉]

Belgorod State Technological University named after V.G. Shukhov,
Belgorod, Russia
panchenko.maks@gmail.com

Abstract. The paper presents the inference methods for fuzzy systems of Mamdani type, which, for many fuzzy inputs and for any t-norms, are implemented with polynomial computational complexity. Center of sums and the discrete version of the center of gravity methods are applied for the rule base at the defuzzification stage. The network structures of the systems corresponding to these methods are given.

Keywords: Systems with fuzzy inputs · Fuzzy truth value ·
Mamdani inference method · Possibility measure

1 Introduction

In the absence of sufficiently accurate knowledge about the control object, traditional methods of solving control problems are ineffective or may not be applicable at all. In this case, you can build a fuzzy control system using the fuzzy sets theory and fuzzy logic. Fuzzy control based on fuzzy modeling, the types of which are determined by methods of fuzzy inference. The most popular in control is the inference method presented by Mamdani [1, 2].

In modern packages of fuzzy modeling [3], the inference is computed only at crisp values of the input variables of the control system. However, in some applications, input data may contain either non-numeric (linguistic) values [4, 5], or noisy input signals [6]. As in the first and in the second case, they are formalized by membership functions and are called fuzzy inputs.

Mamdani's approach is reduced to interpretation of expression «*if X is A, then Y is B*», where X and Y are linguistic variables, and A and B linguistic values of X and Y respectively. The source of uncertainty is that «*if X is A, then Y is B*» can be interpreted in two different ways. The first, and most obvious way, is to treat such an expression as «*if X is A, then Y is B*» or as «*(X, Y) is A × B*», where $A \times$ B is a Cartesian product of fuzzy sets A and B. So in this interpretation «*if X is A, then Y is B*» is a joint constraint on X and Y. An alternative way is understanding of «*if X is A, then Y is B*» as a conditional constraint or, equivalently, implication. This direction was investigated for systems with many fuzzy inputs into [7]. This paper is devoted to the development of the Mamdani approach.

© Springer Nature Switzerland AG 2019
S. O. Kuznetsov and A. I. Panov (Eds.): RCAI 2019, CCIS 1093, pp. 245–255, 2019.
https://doi.org/10.1007/978-3-030-30763-9_21

In [6], inference is considered for such systems with fuzzy inputs, which are based on operations of *max_min* or *max_product* composition with linear complexity. Operator *min* (taking the minimum) and *product* (arithmetic product) are *t*-norms [8] and correspond to Mamdani's [1] and Larsen's [9] inference rules. But for other *t*-norms, need to change of which occurs in the training of fuzzy systems, it is not possible to realize an inference with the polynomial computational complexity in systems with many fuzzy inputs. This article discusses methods that solve this problem regardless of the *t*-norms that are changed.

In the first section, the statement of the problem and the estimation of the complexity of fuzzy output for Mamdani-type control systems of the MISO structure at non-singleton inputs are performed. The second one considers the inference for one rule based on the fuzzy truth value. The third proves the theorem about decomposition of multidimensional membership function. The fourth and fifth sections show the inference for fuzzy rule base and construction of the corresponding network structures based on center of sums and center of gravity defuzzification methods.

2 Statement of the Problem

Define the linguistic model as a base of fuzzy rules R_k, $k = \overline{1, N}$:

$$R_k: \text{If } x_1 \text{ is } A_{1k} \# x_2 \text{ is } A_{2k} \# \ldots \# x_n \text{ is } A_{nk}, \text{then } y \text{ is } B_k, \tag{1.1}$$

where N is a number of fuzzy rules, $A_{ik} \subseteq X_i$, $i = \overline{1, n}$, $B_k \subseteq Y$ are fuzzy sets that are described by membership functions $\mu_{A_{ik}}(x_i)$ and $\mu_{B_k}(y)$ respectively. $x_1, x_2, \ldots, x_n$ are input variables of the linguistic model, and $[x_1, x_2, \ldots, x_n]^T = x \in X_1 \times X_2 \ldots \times X_n$. Characters X_i, $i = \overline{1, N}$ and Y denote domain range of the input and output variables, respectively. In (1.1), linguistic connections "AND" or "OR", are denoted by «#».

In following notation $X = X_1 \times X_2 \ldots \times X_n$ and $A_k = A_{1k} \times A_{2k} \times \ldots \times A_{nk}$, the rule (1.1) represented as a fuzzy implication

$$R_k: A_k \rightarrow B_k, k = \overline{1, N}.$$

R_k can be formalized as a fuzzy relation defined on a set $X \times Y$, that is $R_k \subseteq X \times Y$ is fuzzy set with membership function:

$$\mu_{R_k}(x, y) = \mu_{A_k \rightarrow B_k}(x, y).$$

The Mamdani model defines the function assignment like $\mu_{A_k \rightarrow B_k}(x, y)$ based on known membership functions $\mu_{A_k}(x)$ and $\mu_{B_k}(y)$ in the following way [2, 6]

$$\mu_{A_k \rightarrow B_k}(x, y) = T_1\left(\mu_{A_k}(x), \mu_{B_k}(y)\right) = \mu_{A_k}(x) \overset{T_1}{*} \mu_{B_k}(y), \tag{1.2}$$

where $\overset{T_1}{*}$ is an arbitrary *t*-norm that is used as a parameter.

The task is to determine the fuzzy inference $B'_k \subseteq Y$ for the system represented as (1.1), if the inputs are fuzzy sets $A' = A'_1 \times A'_2 \times \ldots \times A'_n \subseteq X$ or x_1 is A'_1 and x_2 is A'_2 and $\ldots$ and x_n is A'_n with the corresponding membership function $\mu_{A'}(x)$. In accordance with the generalized fuzzy rule modus ponens [4], fuzzy set B'_k determined by the composition of a fuzzy set A' and relation R_k, such

$$B'_k = A' \circ (A_k \rightarrow B_k)$$

or using the membership functions:

$$\mu_{B'_k}(y) = \sup_{x \in X} \left\{ \mu_{A'}(x) \overset{T_2}{*} \left(\mu_{A_k}(x) \overset{T_1}{*} \mu_{B_k}(y) \right) \right\}, \tag{1.3}$$

where $\overset{T_2}{*}$ can be any t-norm. Complexity of the expression (1.2) is $O(|X|^n \cdot |Y|)$.

3   Inference Method Based on Fuzzy Truth Value

For fuzzy systems with one input, following (1.2), the inference is described by the relation:

$$\mu_{B'_k}(y) = \sup_{x \in X} \left\{ \mu_{A'}(x) \overset{T_2}{*} \left(\mu_{A_k}(x) \overset{T_1}{*} \mu_{B_k}(y) \right) \right\} \tag{2.1}$$

Applying the rule of truth modification [5]:

$$\mu_{A'}(x) = \tau_{A_k/A'} \left(\mu_{A_k}(x) \right),$$

where $\tau_{A_k/A'}(\cdot)$ is a fuzzy truth value of a fuzzy set A_k in relation to A', representing the compatibility membership function $CP(A_k, A')$ A_k towards A', and A' is considered reliable [9]:

$$\tau_{A_k/A'}(v) = \mu_{CP(A_k, A')}(v) = \sup_{\substack{\mu_{A'}(x)=v \\ x \in X}} \left\{ \mu_{A_k}(x) \right\}, \quad v \in [0, 1]$$

Moving from variable x to variable v, denoting $\mu_{A_k}(x) = v$:

$$\mu_{A'}(x) = \tau_{\frac{A_k}{A'}} \left(\mu_{A_k}(x) \right) = \tau_{\frac{A_k}{A'}}(v) \tag{2.2}$$

Then the generalized Modus Ponens rule for systems with one input (2.1) can be written as follows:

$$\mu_{B'_k}(y) = \sup_{v \in [0,1]} \left\{ \tau_{\frac{A_k}{A'}}(v) \overset{T_2}{*} \left(v \overset{T_1}{*} \mu_{B_k}(y) \right) \right\} \tag{2.3}$$

4 The Decomposition Theorem of a Multidimensional Membership Function (1.2)

This theorem can be used under the condition that modeling the linguistic connective "AND" in the antecedent of rule (1.1) is used with t-norm "MIN", and for linguistic connective "OR" is used t-conorm "MAX".

Theorem 3.1
If $T(\mu_{A_{ik}}(x_i), \mu_B(y))$, $i = \overline{1,n}$ not increasing by argument $\mu_{A_{ik}}(x_i)$, then: in case of linguistic connective "AND":

$$T(\mu_{A_k}(x), \mu_B(y)) = T\left(\min_{i=\overline{1,n}}\{\mu_{A_{ik}}(x_i)\}, \mu_B(y)\right) = \min_{i=\overline{1,n}}\{T(\mu_{A_{ik}}(x_i), \mu_B(y))\},$$

in case of linguistic connective "OR":

$$T(\mu_{A_k}(x), \mu_B(y)) = T\left(\max_{i=\overline{1,n}}\{\mu_{A_{ik}}(x_i)\}, \mu_B(y)\right) = \max_{i=\overline{1,n}}\{T(\mu_{A_{ik}}(x_i), \mu_B(y))\}.$$

Proof
Consider the proof of property 1:

Function $T(\mu_{A_{ik}}(x_i), \mu_B(y))$ is non-decreasing in argument $\mu_{A_{ik}}(x_i)$, if $\forall \mu_B(y) \in [0, 1]$ from the condition $\mu_{A_{ik}}(x_i') \le \mu_{A_{ik}}(x_i'')$ follows inequality:

$$T(\mu_{A_{ik}}(x_i'), \mu_B(y)) \ge T(\mu_{A_{ik}}(x_i''), \mu_B(y)) \tag{3.1}$$

This property is valid for any t-norm, according to their definition [6]

Assume any of the values $\mu_B(y) \in [0, 1]$. Let also $(x_1, x_2, \ldots, x_n) \in X_1 \times X_2 \ldots \times X_n$ and define:

$$\mu_{A_{ik}}(x_e) = \min_{i=\overline{1,n}}\{\mu_{A_{ik}}(x_i)\}. \tag{3.2}$$

This implies: $\mu_{A_{ik}}(x_e) \le \mu_{A_{ik}}(x_i) \ \forall i = \overline{1,n}$, in accordance with (3.1):

$$T(\mu_{A_{ik}}(x_e), \mu_B(y)) \le T(\mu_{A_{ik}}(x_i), \mu_B(y)) \quad \forall i = \overline{1,n}, \tag{3.3}$$

then taking into account (3.2):

$$T(\mu_{A_{ik}}(x_e), \mu_B(y)) = \min_{i=\overline{1,n}}\{T(\mu_{A_{ik}}(x_i), \mu_B(y))\}. \tag{3.4}$$

Since $T(\mu_{A_{ik}}(x_e), \mu_B(y))$ exists at the right part of expression (3.4) and taking into

account (3.2): $T\left(\min_{i=\overline{1,n}}\{\mu_{A_{ik}}(x_i)\}, \mu_B(y)\right) = \min_{i=\overline{1,n}}\{T(\mu_{A_{ik}}(x_i), \mu_B(y))\}$

Property 1 of Theorem 3.1 is proved. Property 2 is proved similarly.

5 Calculation of an Output Value for the Rule Base Based on Center of Sums Defuzzification Method

When the condition of the Decomposition theorem of the multidimensional membership function (1.2) is satisfied and using the linguistic connection "AND", (1.3) takes the form:

$$\mu_{B'_k}(y) = \min_{i=\overline{1,n}}\left\{ \sup_{x_i \in X_i}\left\{ \mu_{A'_i}(x_i) \overset{T_2}{*} T_1\left(\mu_{A_{ik}}(x_i), \mu_{B_k}(y)\right)\right\}\right\}, \quad k = \overline{1,N} \qquad (4.1)$$

Expression (4.1) can be written through the fuzzy truth value as follows from (2.3), and (4.1) takes the form:

$$\mu_{B'_k}(y) = \min_{i=\overline{1,n}}\left\{ \sup_{v_i \in [0,1]}\left\{ \tau_{A_{ik}/A'_i}(v_i) \overset{T_2}{*}\left(v_i \overset{T_1}{*} \mu_{B_k}(y)\right)\right\}\right\}, \quad k = \overline{1,N} \qquad (4.2)$$

Expression (4.2) characterized by complexity of order $O(|v_i| \cdot |Y| \cdot n)$ and corresponds to a polynomial.

If $T_1 = T_2 = T$, then considering the t-norm property of associativity, (4.2) can be converted to:

$$
\begin{aligned}
\mu_{B'_k}(y) &= \min_{i=\overline{1,n}}\left\{ \sup_{v_i \in [0,1]}\left\{ \tau_{A_{ik}/A'_i}(v_i) \overset{T}{*}\left(v_i \overset{T}{*} \mu_{B_k}(y)\right)\right\}\right\} \\
&= \min_{i=\overline{1,n}}\left\{ \sup_{v_i \in [0,1]}\left\{ \left(\tau_{A_{ik}/A'_i}(v_i) \overset{T}{*} v_i\right) \overset{T}{*} \mu_{B_k}(y)\right\}\right\} \\
&= \min_{i=\overline{1,n}}\left\{ \sup_{v_i \in [0,1]}\left\{ \tau_{A_{ik}/A'_i}(v_i) \overset{T}{*} v_i\right\} \overset{T}{*} \mu_{B_k}(y)\right\} = \min_{i=\overline{1,n}}\left\{ \prod_{A_{ik}/A'_i} \overset{T}{*} \mu_{B_k}(y)\right\}, \\
k &= \overline{1,n},
\end{aligned}
\qquad (4.3)
$$

$$\prod_{A_{ik}/A'_i} = \sup_{v_i \in [0,1]}\left\{ \tau_{A_{ik}/A'_i}(v_i) \overset{T}{*} v_i\right\} \qquad (4.4)$$

$\prod_{A_{ik}/A'_i}$ is a scalar value, according to the definition [11] is a possibility measure of A_{ik} corresponds to the input A'_i [10].

Consider the fuzzy systems introduced in Sect. 2, and taking into account the above transformations, obtain a crisp output value using the center of sums defuzzification method [6]. In this case, the output value can be calculated as:

$$\bar{y} = \frac{\sum_{k=\overline{1,N}} \bar{y}_k \cdot \mu_{B'_k}(\bar{y}_k)}{\sum_{k=\overline{1,N}} \mu_{B'_k}(\bar{y}_k)}, \qquad (4.5)$$

where $\bar{y}$ is a crisp output value of system consisting of N rules (1.1); $\bar{y}_k$ are centers of membership functions $\mu_{B_k}(y)$, $k = \overline{1, N}$:

$$\mu_{B_k}(\bar{y}_k) = \sup_{y \in Y}\{\mu_{B_k}(y)\} = 1 \tag{4.6}$$

Following (4.2) and (4.5) we have

$$\bar{y} = \frac{\sum_{k=\overline{1,N}} \bar{y}_k \min_{i=\overline{1,n}}\left\{ \sup_{v_i \in [0,1]} \left\{ \tau_{A_{ik}/A_i'}(v_i) \overset{T_2}{*} \left(v_i \overset{T_1}{*} \mu_{B_k}(\bar{y}_k) \right) \right\} \right\}}{\sum_{k=\overline{1,N}} \min_{i=1,n}\left\{ \sup_{v_i \in [0,1]} \left\{ \tau_{A_{ik}/A_i'}(v_i) \overset{T_2}{*} \left(v_i \overset{T_1}{*} \mu_{B_k}(\bar{y}_k) \right) \right\} \right\}} \tag{4.7}$$

Considering (4.6) we obtain

$$\sup_{v_i \in [0,1]} \left\{ \tau_{A_{ik}/A_i'}(v_i) \overset{T_2}{*} \left(v_i \overset{T_1}{*} 1 \right) \right\} = \sup_{v_i \in [0,1]} \left\{ \tau_{A_{ik}/A_i'}(v_i) \overset{T_2}{*} v_i \right\}. \tag{4.8}$$

Since t-norms by definition satisfies the boundary condition $T(a; 1) = a$, then substituting (4.8) into (4.7) we obtain

$$\bar{y} = \frac{\sum_{k=\overline{1,N}} \bar{y}_k \cdot \min_{i=\overline{1,n}}\left\{ \prod_{A_{ik}/A_i'} \right\}}{\sum_{k=\overline{1,N}} \min_{i=\overline{1,n}}\left\{ \prod_{A_{ik}/A_i'} \right\}} \tag{4.9}$$

So the result $\bar{y}$ obtained using the center of sums defuzzification method with fuzzy inputs does not depend on t-norm T_1.

Consider inference when the input data is crisp [12]:

$\tau_{A_{ik}/A_i'}(v_i) = \delta(v_i) = \begin{cases} 1 \; if \; v_i = v_{ik} \\ 0 \; if \; v_i \neq v_{ik} \end{cases}$, where $v_{ik} = \mu_{A_{ik}}(\bar{x}_i)$, $k = \overline{1, N}$; $i = \overline{1, n}$; $\bar{x}_i$, $i = \overline{1, n}$ are crisp input values, then

$\prod_{A_{ik}/A_k'} = \sup_{v_i \in [0,1]} \left\{ \delta(v_i) \overset{T_2}{*} v_i \right\} = v_{ik}$ taking into account that $T_2(1; v_{ik}) = v_{ik}$.

As a result an output value is calculated as

$$\bar{y} = \frac{\sum_{k=\overline{1,N}} \bar{y}_k \cdot \min_{i=\overline{1,n}}\{v_{ik}\}}{\sum_{k=\overline{1,N}} \min_{i=\overline{1,n}}\{v_{ik}\}} \tag{4.10}$$

Thus, with crisp input data and the center of sums defuzzification method, the system output does not depend on t-norms T_1 and T_2. Obtained result (4.10) is consistent with well-known results in [13]. The structure of the fuzzy system, which is described by the relation (4.9), is shown in Fig. 1.

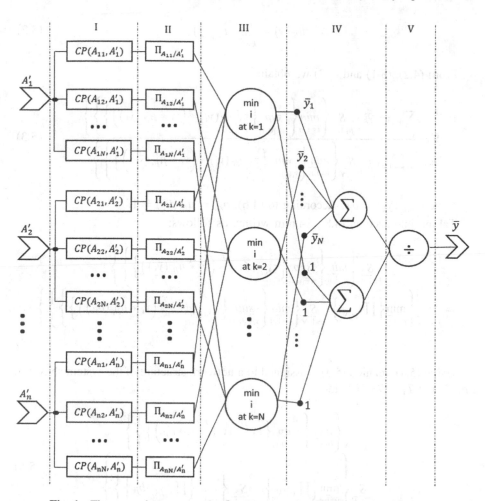

Fig. 1. The network structure of a fuzzy system described by expression (4.9)

6 Calculation of an Output Value for the Rule Base Based on the Center of Gravity Defuzzification Method

Consider a fuzzy system (4.2), the output of which is determined based on discrete version of the center-of-gravity defuzzification method [6]:

$$\bar{y} = \frac{\sum_{k=\overline{1,N}} \bar{y}_k \cdot \mu_{B'}(\bar{y}_k)}{\sum_{k=\overline{1,N}} \mu_{B'}(\bar{y}_k)}, \tag{5.1}$$

where $\bar{y}$ is a crisp output value; $\bar{y}_k$ are centers of membership functions $\mu_{B_k}(y), k = \overline{1,N}$, defined by (4.6). Fuzzy set B' for the Mamdani systems [2] is obtained as a result of combination of fuzzy sets B'_k, $k = \overline{1,N}$ using t-conorm or S-norm, i.e.

$$\mu_{B'}(y) = \mathop{S}_{k=\overline{1,N}} \mu_{B'_k}(y).$$ (5.2)

From (4.2), (5.1) and (5.2) we obtain

$$\bar{y} = \frac{\sum_{k=\overline{1,N}} \bar{y}_k \cdot \mathop{S}_{j=\overline{1,N}}\left\{\mathop{min}_{i=\overline{1,n}}\left\{\mathop{sup}_{v_i\in[0,1]}\left\{\tau_{A_{ij}/A'_i}(v_i) \overset{T_2}{*} \left(v_i \overset{T_1}{*} \mu_{B_k}(\bar{y}_k)\right)\right\}\right\}\right\}}{\sum_{k=\overline{1,N}} \mathop{S}_{j=\overline{1,N}}\left\{\mathop{min}_{i=\overline{1,n}}\left\{\mathop{sup}_{v_i\in[0,1]}\left\{\tau_{A_{ij}/A'_i}(v_i) \overset{T_2}{*} \left(v_i \overset{T_1}{*} \mu_{B_k}(\bar{y}_k)\right)\right\}\right\}\right\}}$$ (5.3)

Denote $\mu_{B_j}(\bar{y}_k) = b_{jk}$. According to (4.6), $b_{kk} = \mu_{B_k}(\bar{y}_k) = 1$.
Taking into account (4.8), S-norm written as follows:

$$\mathop{S}_{j=\overline{1,N}}\left\{\mathop{min}_{i=\overline{1,n}}\left\{\mathop{sup}_{v_i\in[0,1]}\left\{\tau_{A_{ij}/A'_i}(v_i) \overset{T_2}{*} \left(v_i \overset{T_1}{*} \mu_{B_k}(\bar{y}_k)\right)\right\}\right\}\right\}$$
$$= \mathop{S}_{j=\overline{1,N}}\left\{\mathop{min}_{i=\overline{1,n}}\left\{\prod_{A_{ij}/A'_i}\right\}, \mathop{S}_{j=\overline{1,N}}\left\{\mathop{min}_{i=\overline{1,n}}\left\{\mathop{sup}_{v_i\in[0,1]}\left\{\tau_{A_{ij}/A'_i}(v_i) \overset{T_2}{*} \left(v_i \overset{T_1}{*} \mu_{B_k}(b_{jk})\right)\right\}\right\}\right\}\right\}$$ (5.4)

Using (5.4), relation (5.3) is assigned to a network structure of the system shown in Fig. 2. Let $T_1 = T_2 = T$, then

$$\mathop{S}_{j=\overline{1,N}}\left\{\mathop{min}_{i=\overline{1,n}}\left\{\mathop{sup}_{v_i\in[0,1]}\left\{\tau_{A_{ij}/A'_i}(v_i) \overset{T}{*} \left(v_i \overset{T}{*} b_{jk}\right)\right\}\right\}\right\}$$
$$= \mathop{S}_{j=\overline{1,N}}\left\{\mathop{min}_{i=\overline{1,n}}\left\{\prod_{A_{ij}/A'_i}\right\}, \mathop{S}_{\substack{j=\overline{1,N}\\ j\neq k}}\left\{\mathop{min}_{i=\overline{1,n}}\left\{\prod_{A_{ij}/A'_i} \cdot b_{jk}\right\}\right\}\right\}$$ (5.5)

In this case, the network architecture of the system will take the form shown in Fig. 3.

$$\text{If } \quad b_{jk} = 0 \quad j,k = \overline{1,N} : j \neq k,$$ (5.6)

then (5.3), taking into account (5.4) and (5.5), will take the form of expression (4.9), and the network structure shown in Figs. 2 and 3, is reduced to the structure shown in Fig. 1. A special case of this inference is the singleton-type model [13].

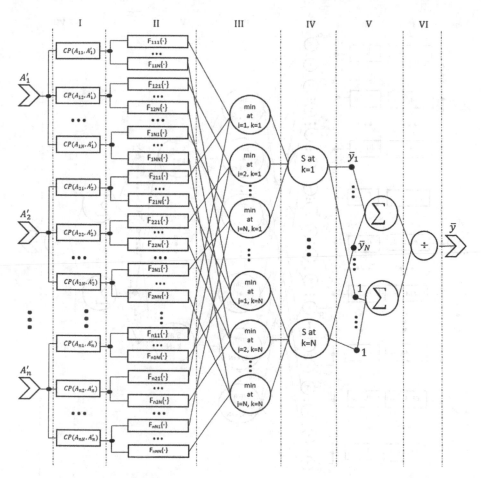

Fig. 2. The network structure of a fuzzy system described by expressions (5.3) and (5.4)

In Fig. 2, $F_{ijk}\{\cdot\} = \underset{v_i \in [0,1]}{sup} \left\{ \tau_{A_{ij}/A_i'}(v_i) \overset{T_2}{*} \left(v_i \overset{T_1}{*} \mu_{B_k}(\bar{y}_k) \right) \right\}$

For the fuzzy sets B_k, $k = \overline{1,4}$, shown in Fig. 4, condition (5.6) holds. In this case, with the same fuzzy input sets, the center of sums defuzzification method leads to the same result as when using the center of gravity defuzzification method (5.1).

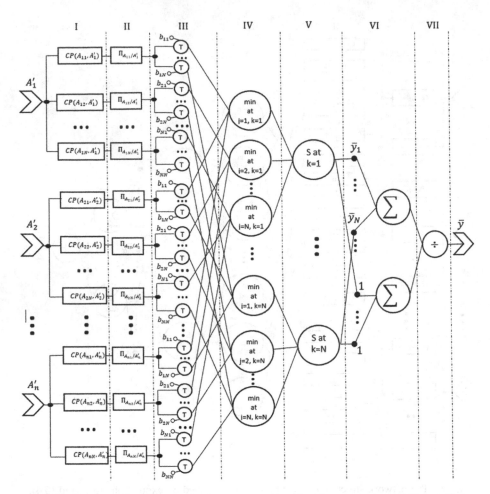

Fig. 3. The network structure of a fuzzy system described by expressions (5.3) and (5.5)

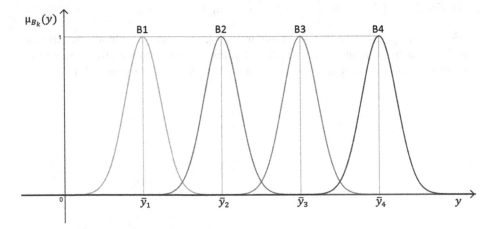

Fig. 4. Examples of fuzzy sets that satisfy to the (5.6) condition

7 Conclusion

Fuzzy inference based on the decomposition theorem makes it possible to propagate the Mamdani approach for systems with many fuzzy inputs with polynomial computational complexity, regardless of the used t-norms. The change of them can be used in teaching such systems. It is necessary to take into account that the decomposition theorem is performed under the condition that the modeling of the linguistic connective "AND" in the antecedent of rule (1.1) applies the t-norm "MIN", and for the linguistic connective "OR" the t-conorm "MAX" is used.

The obtained ratios of output values for Mamdani-type fuzzy systems use center of sums and center of gravity defuzzification methods. These relationships are applied to the construction of network structures and after the development of learning algorithms for their parameters will be transformed into neuro-fuzzy systems, which will be the goal of further research.

References

1. Mamdani, E.H.: Applications of fuzzy algorithm for control a simple dynamic plant. Proc. IEEE **121**(12), 1585–1588 (1974)
2. Pegat, A.: Fuzzy Modeling and Control. BINOM, Knowledge Lab, Moscow (2009)
3. Leonenkov, A.V.: Fuzzy modeling in MATLAB and fuzzyTECH. SPb: BHV – Petersburg (2003)
4. Zadeh, L.A.: Outline of a new approach to the analysis of complex systems and decision processes. IEEE Trans. Syst. Man Cybern. **SMC-3**(1), 28–44 (1973)
5. Borisov, A.N., Alekseev, A.V., Krumberg, O.A. et al. Decision-making models based on linguistic variable. Zinatne, Riga (1982)
6. Zadeh, L.A.: PRUF—a meaning representation language for natural languages Int. J. Man Mach. Stud. **10**, 395–460 (1978)
7. Sinuk, V.G., Panchenko, M.V.: Fuzzy inference method for one class of MISO-structured systems with fuzzy inputs. Artif. Intell. Decis. Making **4**, 33–39 (2017)
8. Alsina, C., Frank, M.J., Schweizer, B.: Associative Functions: Triangular Norms and Copulas. World Scientific, Singapore (2006)
9. Larsen, P.M.: Industrial applications of fuzzy logic control. Int. J. Man Mach. Stud. **12**, 3–10 (1980)
10. Dubois, D., Prade, A.: Possibility theory. Applications to the representation of knowledge in computer science. Radio and communication (1990)
11. Yager, R.R.: Some relationships between possibility, truth and certainty. Fuzzy Sets Syst. **11**, 151–156 (1983)
12. Kutsenko, D.A., Sinuk, V.G.: Indirect fuzzy inference method for multi-input production systems. Softw. Prod. Syst. **1**, 45–47 (2008)
13. Kruglov, V.V., Dli, M.I., Golunov, R.U.: Fuzzy logic and artificial neural networks. Fizmatlit (2001)

Intelligent Systems and Applications

Chaotic Phenomena in Collective Behavior

Vadim L. Stefanuk[1,2]([⊠]) and Tatjana O. Zemtsova[1]

[1] Peoples' Friendship University of Russia,
Miklucho-Maklaya str. 6, 117198 Moscow, Russia
zemcovato@yandex.ru
[2] Institute for Information Transmission Problems,
Bolshoi Karetny per. 19, 127051 Moscow, Russia
stefanuk@iitp.ru

Abstract. The paper is intended to discover a chaotic behavior in collective of a number of interacting dynamic systems with the goal oriented learning. Previously it was shown that these semi-independent systems are able to achieve their individual goals iff the vector of these goals belongs to a certain area $\Lambda^{(n)}$. We call this behavior pattern as collective automata behavior that maybe successful or not. Past research showed a similar property in collective of a pair of finite state automata that also have a similar restriction for successful behavior.

Computer experiments performed in this paper for case $n = 2$ have demonstrated that some chaos is present both outside of the area $\Lambda^{(n)}$, and within it. Analogous chaotic phenomena were not mentioned before in collective behavior of intelligent agents. However, these phenomena are undoubtedly important for practical applications where goals for intelligent dynamic systems either established from outside, or chosen by systems independently. They may produce some undesirable, even harmful global effects in implemented technical devices.

Keywords: Chaotic phenomena in dynamic systems · Technical systems · Intellectual dynamic · Collective behavior of intelligent systems · Chaotic behavior · Edge of chaos · Expedient behavior

1 Introduction

Lately there was a special interest to the Artificial Intelligence systems which, while solving a problem, are also able to explain in what way the solution is achieved and what is the reason for it [1]. Such an explanation is needed in the systems of the Deep Learning type. In this case it is especially important to convince the user that the solution found is correct.

Actually elements of the explanation were included in the classic Expert Systems, where the explanations were achieved by the tracing of knowledge used in the decision making. Obviously the ability of a system to convincingly explain to human user or

The research work was partially supported by Russian Fond for Basic Research, grants №18-07-00736A and №17-29-07053.

S. O. Kuznetsov and A. I. Panov (Eds.): RCAI 2019, CCIS 1093, pp. 259–270, 2019.
https://doi.org/10.1007/978-3-030-30763-9_22

another system why the result went wrong and what should be done to fix an error is important property.

In the present paper a stress was made on the fact that there can be some elements in a system which are beyond control of the system itself. These elements are not controlled with the logic that defines the performance of intelligent systems.

In this case it would not be enough to demonstrate the steps of system performance. Instead one needs to show the most important things with an explanation, why these phenomena do exist. This problem appears of course in Reinforced Learning [2, 3], especially when it is used jointly with Deep Learning Networks.

The content of the paper is devoted to phenomena of chaos that may arise in intelligent systems that are tuned to a logically justified learning. We study the behavior of a collective of two independently controlled systems with expedient learning.

This collective is described by a joint system of differential equations with the purpose to discover a non-standard behavior of its parts caused by interactions. Earlier for such a collective and its generalizations it was shown that the vector of the sub-system goals belongs to some area which breaks up into two regions. In the first of these regions the goals are achievable in accordance with the mentioned equations. In the present paper it is shown that in the second, supplemented region, where the selected objectives cannot be achieved, it is still possible to observe a collective behavior. Yet, the latter has some particular properties which are typical for chaotic phenomena.

These phenomena were not mentioned before in research on collective behavior, however it can be important for some practical applications as usually the goals for members of collective are established from outside, or independently chosen with subsystems.

There are some grounds to believe that in a similar way, i.e. with use of the chaos theory, the collective behavior of pair of learning finite state machines with intelligent behavior can also be described if one considers the subarea of phase space where successful joint behavior of such machines is unattainable.

The phenomena of chaos in dynamic systems have been mentioned in many areas, such as biology, or economic systems, explaining some uncontrollable various phenomena, such as crises in economic formations. The publication [4], in which the main characteristics leading to chaotic behavior are demonstrated, was one of the first scientific publications in the respective domain.

Chaotic phenomena undoubtedly may play significant role in the collective systems [5], but they have not been studied yet. The main reason for this is the fact that strict theoretical consideration of games or collective behavior of systems [2, 5–9, 12] from this point of view was not conducted until now.

In this research the behavior of two independently managed learning systems described with a joint set of two differential equations has been studied. It is easy to see that results obtained for a pair of subsystems may be extended to a general case, and it worthwhile to start with a pair.

There are reasons to believe that in a similar way the collective behavior of couple of learning finite state intelligent machines may be described in the same way within the area of phase space in which the successful joint behavior of automatic machines is unattainable.

As we mentioned above it is reasonable to begin such a research with a case of joint behavior of two subsystems that was typical for initial publications [5–8] and a recent paper [2].

The rest of the paper is organized as follows.

Some important facts from the theory of chaotic systems with a number of the evidences borrowed from literature are listed in Sect. 2 to demonstrate novelty and singularity of the research undertaken in the present work.

In Sect. 3 we present several known problems of collective behavior as examples that are used further for discussion and illustration. In Sect. 4 results of computer simulation of collective behavior of continuous intelligent systems are considered in detail.

Section 5 contains discussion of computer modeling and it compares analytic and simulation date with the purpose to describe so-called edge of the chaos. In Sect. 6 the obtained results of the research are summed up and the tasks demanding further research are mentioned.

2 Theory of Chaotic Systems

In modern technical systems unrepeated, irregular, unordered sequences of states are usually connected with the concept of chaos. The chaos theory is the area of mathematics focusing on behavior of dynamic systems that are especially sensitive to the initial conditions of a system starting points [10].

Chaos is a cross-disciplinary theory claiming that in seemingly random chaotic systems there are some basic models containing feedbacks, repetition, self-similarity, fractals, self-organization, and dependence on programming conditions at the starting point, i.e. a dependence on initial conditions [11].

2.1 To Definition of a Chaotic System

In this theory we are talking about deterministic systems, where the previous state determines the future ones. However, at the same time, the present state given in an approximate way, does not make it possible to determine the system future, even approximately[1].

Presently there is no established mathematical definition for the chaos. The used definition, which was originally formulated by Robert L. Devanay [11], tells the following. To treat some dynamic system as a chaotic one, the system should have the following properties:

1. The system should be sensitive to initial conditions.
2. It should be topologically intermixed.
3. It should have dense periodic orbits.

---

[1] "When the present determines the future, but the approximate present does not approximately determine the future" [4].

It was demonstrated in some cases that the last two properties from above follow from the property of the extreme sensibility to initial conditions. Some alternative definitions of chaos use only the first two properties from the ones stated above are listed in [10].

The extreme sensitivity to initial conditions in a dynamic system means that each point in a chaotic system approaches closely to other points with quite different future trajectories. In other words, small change of the current trajectory may result in significantly different behavior of the system in the future.

More exact mathematical conditions for the chaos are as follows: the system should have nonlinear characteristics, to be globally stable, but it should have at least one balance position of oscillatory type.

Only nonlinear systems can belong to the class of chaotic systems. According to the Poincaré-Bendixon theorem, a plane continuous dynamical system cannot be chaotic. Among continuous systems, only spatial systems may have chaotic behavior, for which the presence of at least three dimensions or non-Euclidean geometry is a prerequisite. However, a discrete dynamical system at some stage can exhibit chaotic behavior even in one-dimensional or two-dimensional space.

From the mathematical point of view, the behavior of a system at any time is fully determined if the conditions for the existence and uniqueness of the solution of the corresponding differential equation are satisfied. For long time it was assumed that in such certain (deterministic) systems, there can be no chaos: after all, the solution is a continuous and differentiable function. It was only on the border between 19th and 20th centuries Henri Poincare found that chaotic movements can appear even in some Hamiltonian mechanical system.

In this paper the chaotic phenomena are sought for systems of collective behavior, when the system consists from many intelligent subsystems. Each subsystem is able to learn reaching a goal, which is either established by the environment or has been chosen independently from the goals of other subsystems.

3 Machine Learning and Collective Behavior

In the 1960s in the USSR the school studying different behavior and learning models on the base of a basis of finite state machines was created. The interest of this school was concentrated on various ideas of behavior of living organisms, and have been based on the original researches and publications by Mikhail Tsetlin, professor of Moscow State University. His research was later covered in his book [8]. The combination of the deep mathematical analysis of the created constructions with their engineering implementation using electronic means of those days was one of the features of the approach by M.L. Tsetlin. These demonstrations allowed showing new opportunities to a wide audience.

In particular, M.L. Tsetlin invented an original new principle of learning of the finite state machine with memory by the way of a special organized change of internal states of the automaton on the base of input signals treated as encouragements or punishments for the actions performed by the machine. It was referred to as expedient learning leading to expedient behavior[2].

The construction of so-called intelligent machine with linear tactics having a certain depth of memory for each of its possible actions was offered by M.L. Tsetlin. This construction gave rise to a number of publications that described various other constructions of learning machines with Expedient Behavior in the USSR of that time. These constructions found a number of important applications in biology modeling, and in many technical systems [6]. One of the remarkable technical achievements was the use of ε-automata to control "with a thought of mind" a hand that was lost by a student due to some misfortune. Thus, at the end of 1950th a Moscow State University student Dima Kalinin was able to pick up objects with his artificial fingers.

It should be noted that a number of original developments on learning, pattern recognition and other systems connected with the organization of intellectual behavior was the main reason for the decision of Organizing Committee of IJCAI-1975 to hold this important international conference on Artificial Intelligence in the USSR. As a result, IJCAI-1975 took place in Georgia (USSR) on the premises of Institute of Cybernetics in Tbilisi.

3.1 Collective Behavior of Two Finite State Machines

The publication [5] was the first paper where the term "collective behavior of automata" was introduced. It was followed by a number of similar research in the field of collective behavior and games of the learning automatic machines.

The theory of collective behavior of automatic machines is still one of a few strict formal models of this sort of systems. In the publication [5] the collective (joint) behavior of two finite automata [6], namely two finite-states machines with linear tactics each having two actions in a certain random environment, was considered. This pair of automata was capable to perform 4 actions (1, 1), (1, 2), (2, 2), (2, 1). The problem of a possibility of achievement one certain action by the pair, e.g., action (1, 1) (see [6] and Fig. 1) was formulated.

By studying the corresponding Markov chains in the paper [5] it was shown that with the growth of memory of automatic machines, action (1, 1) is achievable not always, but only on the provision of an additional condition, namely $p_1 + p_2 < 1$, where p_1 is the probability of a penalty, which both automatic machines receive while

---

[2] RL is a theory of Reinforcement Learning with rewards of a general kind and arbitrary arranged discrete final states. Thus, the theory RL [2, 3] can be considered as a further formalization of Expedient Learning (EL) for the case when the reward rules are of a general kind. Expedient Learning, based on rewards and punishments, was first reported by M.L. Tsetlin in 1960. M.L. Tsetlin proposed several concrete constructions of expedient automata, such as Linear Tactic automaton. However, using Graph Theory and Markov Chains and Chains of Markov-Brouns [14], he proved in 1960 mathematically that a deep memory is obligatory for asymptotical optimality or expedient behavior. V.L. Stefanuk in 1962 introduced concept of collective behavior of automata, considering collective behavior of a pair of such automata. He obtained results described in [5, 6].

performing action (1, 1) at once, and p_2 is a probability of a penalty, for each other combinations of actions of automatic machines. (The probability of encouragements q_i is defined by the obvious relation $q_i = 1 - p_i, i = 1, \ldots, 4$.)

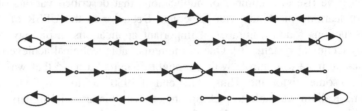

Fig. 1. The rules of changes of internal states of automata when receiving a penalty or reward for the first action (the left group of states) and for the second action (right-wing group of states).

According to the tradition of those days, V.L. Stefanuk built an electronic (with vacuum tubes) model showing the possibility of successful learning of the collective consisting of two learning machines on the premises of Department of Physics of Fluctuations of Physical Faculty of Moscow State University [5, 6] in 1968. Later a theoretical work was published [5] that contained the above mentioned important result for the collective of two automata with Expedient Behavior, that was described above.

3.2   Collective Behavior of Two Technical Systems with a Continuous Set of Statuses

The second example of collective behavior of technical systems will be considered in detail in this paper. It concerns the possibility of design of a broadband communication that became the predecessor for modern mobile communication. We proposed it in 1965, i.e. many years before modern communication systems came to operation.

Consider the following two connected devices of power control, used in a wideband mobile communicating systems [12], operating in continuous time.

$$
\begin{aligned}
\lambda_1^0 \frac{dP_1(t)}{dt} &= \sigma_1 P_1(t)[\lambda_1(t) - \lambda_1^0] \\
\lambda_2^0 \frac{dP_2(t)}{dt} &= \sigma_2 P_2(t)[\lambda_2(t) - \lambda_2^0]
\end{aligned}
\tag{1}
$$

In above equations the following parameters are used:

$$
\begin{aligned}
\lambda_1(t) &= \frac{N_1 + a_{12}P_2}{a_{11}P_1} \\
\lambda_2(t) &= \frac{N_2 + a_{21}P_1}{a_{22}P_2}
\end{aligned}
\tag{2}
$$

Here $\lambda_i(t)$ is the noise-to-signal ratio at the input of i-the device; N_i is an additive noise level at the input of this device; $p_i(t)$ is the power emitted by this device; σ_i is the parameter determining the speed of $\lambda_i(t)$ approaching to target value λ_i^0; t is time. Concerning the meaning of the positive parameters a_{ij} see the publications [3, 9].

4 Simulation Results for Collective Behavior of Continuous Learning Systems

Modeling was implemented with the help of programming system MatLAB created by MathWork Inc. (USA, Mr. Natick, State of Massachusetts).

System (1) with various initial conditions for λ_1^0 and λ_2^0 was tested for the following values of the parameters: $a_{ij} = 1$, $\sigma_i = 5$, $\forall i, j = 1, 2$; $N_1 = 1.9$, $N_2 = 2$ during time interval $t = [0, 20]$. As search of the chaotic phenomena was a research objective, some simple values for parameters have been used.

In paper [12] it was shown theoretically that in space of vectors $(\lambda_1, \ldots, \lambda_n)$ there exists area $\Lambda^{(n)}$ covering all achievable vectors. In our experiments we used $\Lambda^{(2)}$, which is defined with the following equation:

$$\lambda_1 \lambda_2 \geq \frac{a_{11} a_{22}}{a_{12} a_{21}}. \tag{3}$$

The area $\Lambda^{(2)}$ is graphically displayed in Fig. 2 for the case where all the values $a_{i,j} = 1$.

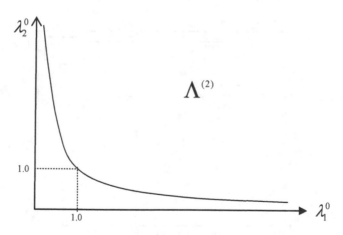

Fig. 2. The area of achievable pairs of values $(\lambda_1^0, \lambda_2^0)$

If $(\lambda_1^0, \lambda_2^0) \in \Lambda^{(2)}$, then such a vector is achievable. As shown analytically in [12], no problems arise in the sense that one has $\lambda_1(t) \to \lambda_1^0$ and $\lambda_2(t) \to \lambda_2^0$ while $t \to \infty$ in accordance with the set of equations (1) as it is shown in Fig. 3.

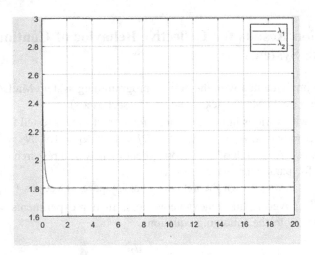

Fig. 3. An illustration of solution for the goal values $\lambda_1^0 = \lambda_2^0 = 1.8$.

In Fig. 4 it is shown how these results are achieved due to adequate change in time of the powers of each of the devices.

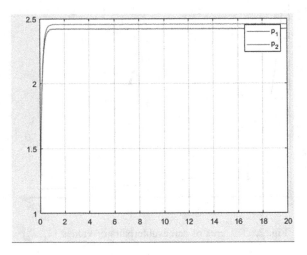

Fig. 4. Behavior of powers p_1 and p_2 allowing to achieve the $\lambda_1^0 = \lambda_2^0 = 1.8$

Please note that the data in Figs. 3 and 4 look like nice smooth curves. Yet, by the corresponding choice of the ordinate axes scale one may discover a chaotic behavior of these curves, which are reminiscent of a periodic random processes (Fig. 5).

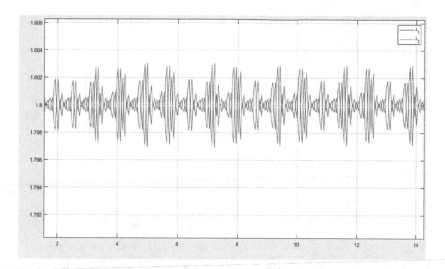

Fig. 5. Chaos behavior of a piece of the curves from Fig. 3.

The observed chaotic behavior may be either due to the properties of the system (1), or due to the chaotic property of computer modeling itself [4, 10] considered as some dynamic process.

The above chaotic behavior is observed under the condition $(\lambda_1^0, \lambda_2^0) \in \Lambda^{(2)}$ i.e. when the vector $(\lambda_1^0, \lambda_2^0)$ is achievable.

Quite a different behavior is observed when the vector $(\lambda_1^0, \lambda_2^0)$ is not achievable and one has $(\lambda_1^0, \lambda_2^0) \notin \Lambda^{(2)}$. In order to see the difference two concrete examples of computer simulation will be considered in the next section.

5 The Border of the Obtainable Values Area $\Lambda^{(2)}$ as the Edge of Chaos

The concept of edge of chaos is described in [13]. The edge of chaos is some point in phase space describing the trajectory of evolution of a certain dynamic system, which separates the area of ordered dynamic system behavior from the area characterized with its chaotic behavior. It was frequently observed that the close proximity of the trajectory to the edge of chaos is optimal for evolving of a dynamic system.

In this respect the area $\Lambda^{(2)}$ is the edge of chaos, as the smallest distance of the system (1) trajectory from the boarder of $\Lambda^{(2)}$ (from inside), the better is the situation for the users as they may achieve the small values for the quality of communication λ_i^0, which is desirable for the communication participants as shown in [6, 12]. However, right after crossing this boarder the system changes its behavior to the chaotic one.

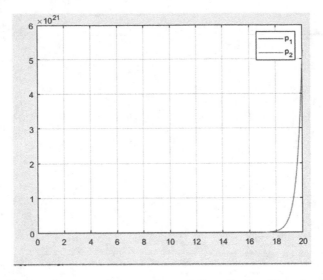

Fig. 6. The evolution of powers of the members of the collective (1) under the goal values $\lambda_1^0 = \lambda_2^0 = 095$

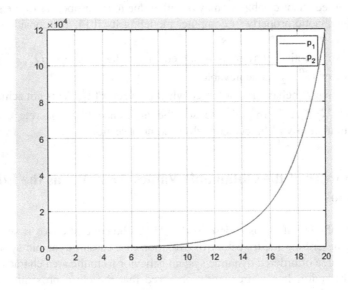

Fig. 7. The evolution of powers of the members of the collective (1) under the other goal values $\lambda_1^0 = \lambda_2^0 = 1.0$.

In result the evolution is characterized with uncontrollable growth of the required power that is not desirable. Actually, we have arrived to a classical definition for the chaos in the sense that the further system behavior turned out to be unpredictable. The increase of the power and its tempo are dependent on the value of change of the initial conditions, i.e. how far is the vector $(\lambda_1^0, \lambda_2^0)$ from the border $\Lambda^{(2)}$.

This property will be demonstrated in Figs. 6 and 7, where the uncontrollable growth of powers of each device (1), with its amount and its tempo dependant on the distances $(\lambda_1^0, \lambda_2^0)$ from the boarder of $\Lambda^{(2)}$.

6 Conclusion

Thus, the chaotic behavior in the considered cases is observed in accordance with the properties of chaotic systems in the usual sense. The first requirement of chaotic dependence – strong dependence on the selection of initial conditions – is obviously fulfilled. On the one hand, there exists area $\Lambda^{(2)}$ responsible for achievement of goals λ_1^0 and λ_2^0. If these values are achievable, then it is observed that $P_1(t)$ and $P_2(t)$ increase to their stable values exponentially as it was expected. On the other hand, namely in the area of unattainable values λ_1^0 and λ_2^0 some strong chaotic phenomena were noticed: either first algorithm from (1) or the second one is receiving the priority, which is of a chaotic character. In our experiments it was shown that it is impossible to predict, which of the learning devices would receive a priority.

The second property of chaos is a periodic phenomenon. It is easy to discover this property, that is typical for chaotic system, on the corresponding diagram when values of parameters λ_1^0 and λ_2^0 are equal to each other.

The carried-out modeling has proved that in collective behavior of the considered systems there are components of chaotic phenomena. By the way, some authors noted that chaotic properties of the *system itself used for modeling*. The MatLAB, in principle, can lead itself to chaotic distortions of the computer simulation results.

There is no doubt that designers of MatLAB somehow took care of it. However, to provide additional reliability of modeling we applied purely analytical result about existence of area $\Lambda^{(n)}$ within which the target vector of all components of collective is achievable, whereas the vector out of this area is unattainable. Thereby, we have obtained independent confirmation of computer simulation results.

Besides, some facts known from publications concerning the mobile communication area, which will not be discussed here in details, also demonstrate the existence of chaotic phenomena in behavior of technical systems with continuous sets of states, demonstrating important role of chaotic phenomena in practice.

The results obtained in this paper present evidences that in the systems of collective behavior one should expect chaotic phenomena in some cases despite the facts that all subsystems are deterministic and even having some intelligent properties. It seems to be inherent not only to particular locally organized intelligent systems. It might be typical also for many other types of complex systems, e.g., systems of economic development, or systems of local control of taxi service in a city, or systems controlling collective of drones that jointly solving a problem, and in many others cases.

We hope that the results of the present research may provide a general direction for studying new situations, where chaotic phenomena might be observed and may bring some unexpectedness to carefully planned locally organized Artificial Intelligence systems.

References

1. Fox, M., Long, D., Magazzeni, D.: Explainable planning. In: Proceedings of the IJCAI-17, Workshop on Explainable (2017)
2. Grau-Moya, A., Leibfried, F., Bou-Ammar, H.: Balancing two-player stochasic games with soft Q-learning. In: IJCAI-18, pp. 268–274 (2018)
3. Sutton, R., Barto, A.: Reinforsment Learning. MIT Press, Cambridge (1998)
4. Lorenz, E.N.: Deterministic non-periodic flow. J. Atmos. Sci. **20**(2), 130–141 (1963)
5. Stefanuk, V.L.: An example of collective behavior of two automata. Autom. Remote control **24**(6), 781–784 (1963)
6. Stefanuk, V.L.: Local organization of intelligent systems: models and applications, 328 p. Fizmatlit, Moscow (2004)
7. Tsetlin, M.L.: On finite automata behavior in random environments. Autom. Remote Control **22**(10), 1345–1354 (1961)
8. Tsetlin, M.L.: Automation Theory and Modeling of Biological Systems. Academic Press, New York (1973)
9. Williams, R.J.: A class of gradient-estimating algorithms for reinforcement learning in neural networks. In: Proceedings of the IEEE First International Conference on Neural Networks (1987)
10. https://en.wikipedia.org/wiki/Chaos_theory (2019)
11. Devaney, R.L.: An Introduction to Chaotic Dynamical Systems, 2nd edn. Addison-Wesley, Reading (1989)
12. Stefanuk, V.L., Tzetlin, M.L.: On power control in the collective of radio stations. Inf. Trans. Prob. **3**(4), 59–67 (1967)
13. https://en.wikipedia.org/wiki/Edge_of_chaos
14. Mnih, V., Kavukcuoglu, K., et al.: Human-level control through deep reinforcement learning. Nature **518**, 529–532 (2015)

Data Collection and Preparation of Training Samples for Problem Diagnosis of Vision Pathologies

Alexander P. Eremeev and Sergey A. Ivliev[⊠]

National Research University "MPEI", Moscow, Russia
eremeev@appmat.ru, siriusfrk@gmail.com

Abstract. The paper presents an approach and a methodology that were used to collect and store training samples. Preliminary processing in the decision support system for diagnosing complex vision pathologies is described. A training sample consists of various records of biopotentials obtained from a special medical device.

Keywords: Decision support · Diagnostics · Training sample · Tagged data · Digital signal processing · User interface

1 Introduction

Recently, methods using specialized diagnostic medical devices have gained popularity in the diagnostics of vision pathologies. Methods based on the electroretinography inspired search for new meaningful parameters of electroretinogram (ERG) and their subsequent analysis with techniques of artificial intelligence [1, 2, 4, 9]. Electroretinography is a method for assessing the functional state of the retina based on the recording of the biopotentials that occur in it during light stimulation. The result of electroretinography is an ERG, a graph (curve) that reflects the reaction of the eye to light flashes and consists of several waves. The main problem in the successful implementation of the developed methods was the absence of any significant and meaningful sample of available data.

The main difficulties that have arisen with data collection are the following:

- the absence of any informatization and automation of medical activities in the field of case management;
- use in the activities of related medical organizations of various medical devices with data recording, but without the possibility of their export to external systems;
- the noisiness of data received by medical diagnostic devices;
- errors during data collection.

All this has resulted in a state where formally there is a large amount of diagnostic data, but for the development of methods and high-quality diagnostic systems, it is necessary to carry out considerable preparatory work on preliminary data processing.

S. O. Kuznetsov and A. I. Panov (Eds.): RCAI 2019, CCIS 1093, pp. 271–282, 2019.
https://doi.org/10.1007/978-3-030-30763-9_23

General directions of this work:

- preparation of a unified data storage system (database) of patient examinations, which will also allow for the extraction of ERG data obtained by electrophysiological diagnostic devices [3];
- extraction of ERG data with its transformation into an intermediate export format for a unified storage system;
- ERG data preprocessing;
- consulting with an expert (physiologist) to formalize the subject area, determine the entities and the connections between them, i.e. formation of domain ontology;
- development of an interface for the work of an expert and a doctor, which would simplify the management of medical records and would contribute to the accumulation and preliminary processing of data in the data storage system.

As a result, a system of storage and analysis of specialized diagnostic data such as ERG will be developed. This allow for further integration of new data sources obtained from new devices (including from other institutions) and interaction with other experts in terms of creating promising intelligent decision support systems for the diagnosis of complex pathologies of vision with the use of new methods of ERG analysis [6, 8].

2 System for Storing and Retrieving Data from Medical Devices

The main approaches to the development of data storage systems were described by the authors in [3]. Several basic requirements for such a system and the corresponding database (storage) of data (hereinafter DB) are formulated:

- recording data on the results of biophysical studies (for example, ERG data);
- recording and storage of clinical patient data and medical examination data;
- adding additional data to research data (for example, measurement data obtained from other instruments, including graphically).

An important task turned out to be the task of extracting data from the medical apparatus for vision diagnostics. This device, called Tomey, is used in the Helmholtz Moscow Research Institute for Ophthalmology and allows one to accrue ERG. This unit comes with ready-made software, which was developed long ago, and it does not allow to export data to modern DBMS and convenient work formats. Next, we briefly consider the process of extracting data from the database of such an apparatus, since we had to solve the so-called problem of reverse development of the database [5], because the data in the Tomey database is stored as attached files, and for subsequent processing, building ontology and using the neural network to diagnose conversion to SQL format database.

The assumption was made about storing data files in the same directory as the database itself, which is justified by finding large files in the database directory, and also by the fact that the names of these files coincide with the names of the database tables.

The next step is to analyze these files for extracting informative data that can be used further for machine learning. It is established that the file consists of research records, which in turn consist of sequences of floating-point values, and that the database with the test dataset contains 3,934 research records. As a result, the analysis of the structures of the Tomey DB was performed, the results of which are presented in Fig. 1 and detailed below.

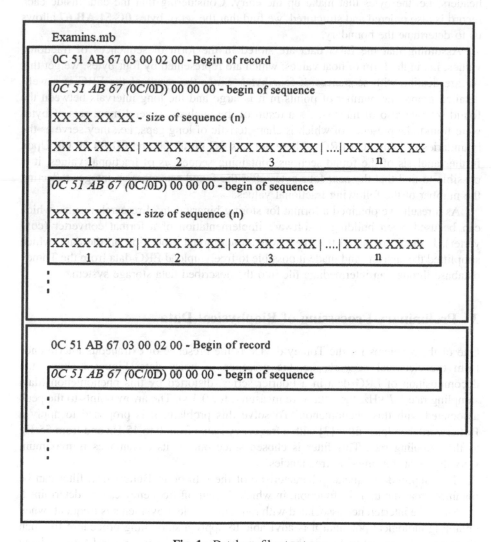

Fig. 1. Database file structure

The file is filled with information unevenly. "Empty" (non-informative, not of interest) sections alternate with sections containing information, which indicates the presence of some data alignment. Since we use the assumption that the file consists of records, we will try to isolate a certain sequence of bytes for all the informative sections, which may be the heading for all records about the research. As a result of experiments, it is possible to find such a sequence - **0C 51 AB 67 03 00 02 00**. The number of occurrences of this sequence corresponds to the number of research records in the database (3934). Since this sequence is at the beginning of each record, we will consider it as a header. Next, we will analyze the bytes located between the found headers, i.e. the bytes that make up the entry. Considering that the data inside each record is also ordered and structured, we find that the set of bytes **0C 51 AB 67** allows us to determine the boundary.

Assuming that the ERG data are stored in the form of sequences of fractional values, i.e. in the form of float values, which are represented by four bytes, we get that we are dealing with sequences of four bytes. Since the result of the ERG is a well-detailed graph, the number of points in it is large and the long intervals between the found sets are also of interest. As a result of the analysis, several more sets of bytes were found, the presence of which is characteristic of long gaps, i.e., they serve as the boundaries of individual ERGs. These are sets **0C 00 00 00** and **0D 00 00 00**. Upon further analysis of the found sections containing sequences of fractional values, it is possible to find that the next four bytes after the found sets store an integer reflecting the number of the following fractional values.

As a result, we obtained a format for storing binary data of research results, which can be used when building a software implementation of a format converter (converter). It should be noted that there was no additional protection on the data, which simplified the analysis and made it possible to freely upload ERG data from the Tomey database through an intermediate file into the described data storage system.

3   Preliminary Processing of Biophysical Data

One of the problems for the Tomey device is the presence of extraneous interference from the electrical network, i.e. the presence of noisy data. Figure 2 shows the decomposition of ERG data in a Fourier series, distorted by this phenomenon (data sampling rate 1.7 kHz, the data were measured for 0.3 s). The arrow points to the peak associated with this phenomenon. To solve this problem, it is proposed to apply a Butterworth bandpass filter [7] with a frequency range from 0 to 45 Hz and from 55 Hz to the sampling rate. This filter is chosen since one of its advantages is maximum smoothness at transmission frequencies.

The amplitude-frequency characteristic of the n-th order Butterworth filter can be obtained from the transfer function, in which the cut-off frequency can be determined.

Since the interference associated with random muscle movements is frequent, when obtaining biological potential it is advisable to apply a smoothing procedure for such situations. This is justified since the analysis is important for the general form of large fluctuations in the graph, and not for individual peaks. As a filtering method, Hamming window smoothing is used. The window size is set empirically to preserve the main features of ERG and is equal to 32.

Figure 3 presents an example of an ERG before filtering and smoothing and after them. It should be noted that since the raw data were used, the ordinal number of the reference for the signal discretization was plotted on the abscissa and the amplitude was plotted on the ordinate axis.

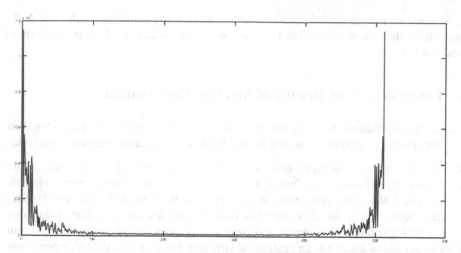

Fig. 2. Distortion of the ERG signal by electrical interference

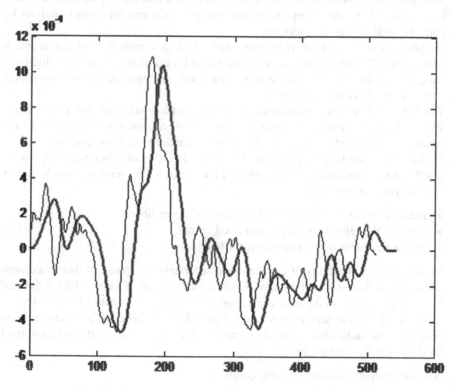

Fig. 3. Preprocessing result. Thin line – before, bold – after.

These two operations are not so important when using neural networks, but at the same time they have a significant impact on the performance of other methods of analysis [2].

4 Formalization of Results of Medical Examination

Based on consultations with experts, the main observable parameters were identified, the storage and processing of which is important for subsequent diagnostic analysis:

1. The optic nerve head (optic disc), i.e., the structure of the eye nerve itself. When considering the optic disc, first of all, it is paid attention to two factors: color and borders. Color: pale pink, pale, blanching from the temporal side, and borders: clear, indistinct. If the optic disc has clear boundaries and pale pink color, then everything is fine with this part of the nerve, any other indicators are not the norm.
2. The macula of the eye is an anatomical structure that provides the color perception of the visual image. On examination of the macula, the following main criteria are distinguished: without focal changes, the reflex is blurred, dystrophic foci, edema. It is also possible to obtain a photo of the macula of the eye for further analysis by convolutional neural networks [4].
3. Peripheral vision is visual perception, for which a certain part of the retina is responsible. The peripheral vision is responsible for the ability to see at twilight and dark time of the day. In addition to the state without features, it emits dystrophic changes and deposits of pigment.
4. The field of view is the angular space visible with a fixed view and a fixed head. When checking, central, absolute, relative, or other scotomas are isolated, and sometimes narrowed the field of view borders are noted in some patients.
5. Optical coherence tomography data. The method of optical coherence tomography (OCT) allows visualizing the structures of the eye in a transverse section. With this method you can determine:

   - reduced or not the thickness of the layer of nerve fibers;
   - whether the retinal contour is disturbed or not;
   - retinal thickness at the photoreceptor level.

6. Vision acuity is the ability of the eye to see separately two points at their maximum convergence. The size of the image depends on the angle of view, which is formed between the nodal point of the eye and the 2 extreme points of the object in question. The vision acuity takes values from 0.0 to 1.0, where 0.0 is the minimum possible value indicating the total absence of light perception, and 1.0 is a normal indicator for the average person.

   Standard patient statistics are also collected:

- Age;
- Gender;
- Postponed diseases;
- Bad habits (alcoholism, smoking, drug addiction).

It is worth noting that the OCT and photograph of the macula can be attached to the results of the analysis for further processing by neural networks.

There was also a large list of diagnoses that can be determined based on ERG data and clinical data collected above.

In the future, the formalization of the subject area will be further refined.

Based on these collected data, an ontological model of the formation of documents was built (Fig. 4.) and the following collections of documents for physical storage in the NoSQL database were identified:

- The Diagnosis collection is a collection containing all possible patient diagnoses.
- A collection of ClinicalData for information on different types of clinical data. It contains the name and possible values for this type.
- Patient collection that stores patient data. It contains the card number, the patient's full name, the intended diagnosis, the final diagnosis, the list of studies, all clinical data, doctor's notes, patient's complaints, and doctor's recommendations. This collection includes Exam and ClinicalDataValue attachments for storing examinations and clinical data.

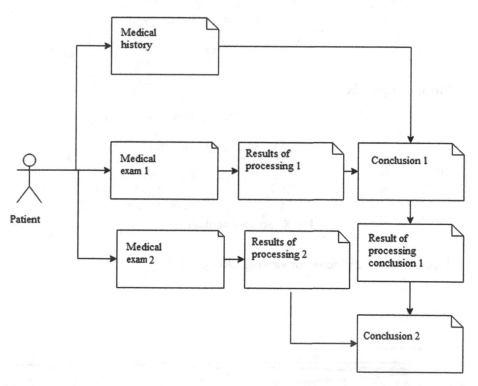

Fig. 4. The ontological model of the formation of documents and the extraction of knowledge from them.

5 Interface Development

As a result of discussion with an expert and analysis of general approaches to the design of human-machine interfaces, it was decided to develop a web application. As a server, the Flask microform in Python 3 was used. For the client-side, HTML, CSS framework Bootstrap 4 and JavaScript were used.

The interface developed with the use of the ontology is a set of screens-windows for working with different types of users: an expert physiologist, an ophthalmologist as a decision-maker, a young doctor (intern), for whom additional explanations are provided using cognitive graphics. An example of a screen for the formation of the diagnosis is presented in Fig. 5.

Diagnoses

Unconfirmed diagnosis

OU:	⇕	Input new diagnosis	Add
OS:	⇕	Input new diagnosis	Add
OD:	⇕	Input new diagnosis	Add

Final diagnosis

OU:	⇕	Input new diagnosis	Add
OS:	⇕	Input new diagnosis	Add
OD:	⇕	Input new diagnosis	Add

Fig. 5. Screen with diagnosis

Figure 6 shows a window for viewing ERG graphs.

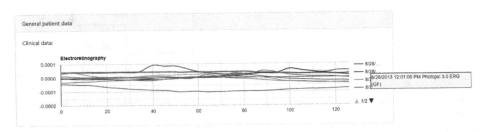

Fig. 6. Screen for viewing ERG charts

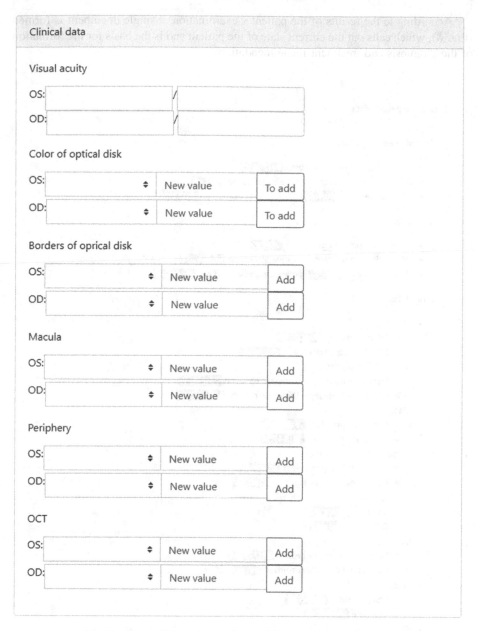

Fig. 7. Enter clinical data with the ability to add clarifications

The above clinical data are available for input in a single form, while the doctor may additionally indicate the specific values of clinical data (Fig. 7).

According to the results of the patient's examination, a single document is formed (Fig. 8), which calls out the current state of the patient and is the basis for the formation of the diagnosis and treatment recommendations.

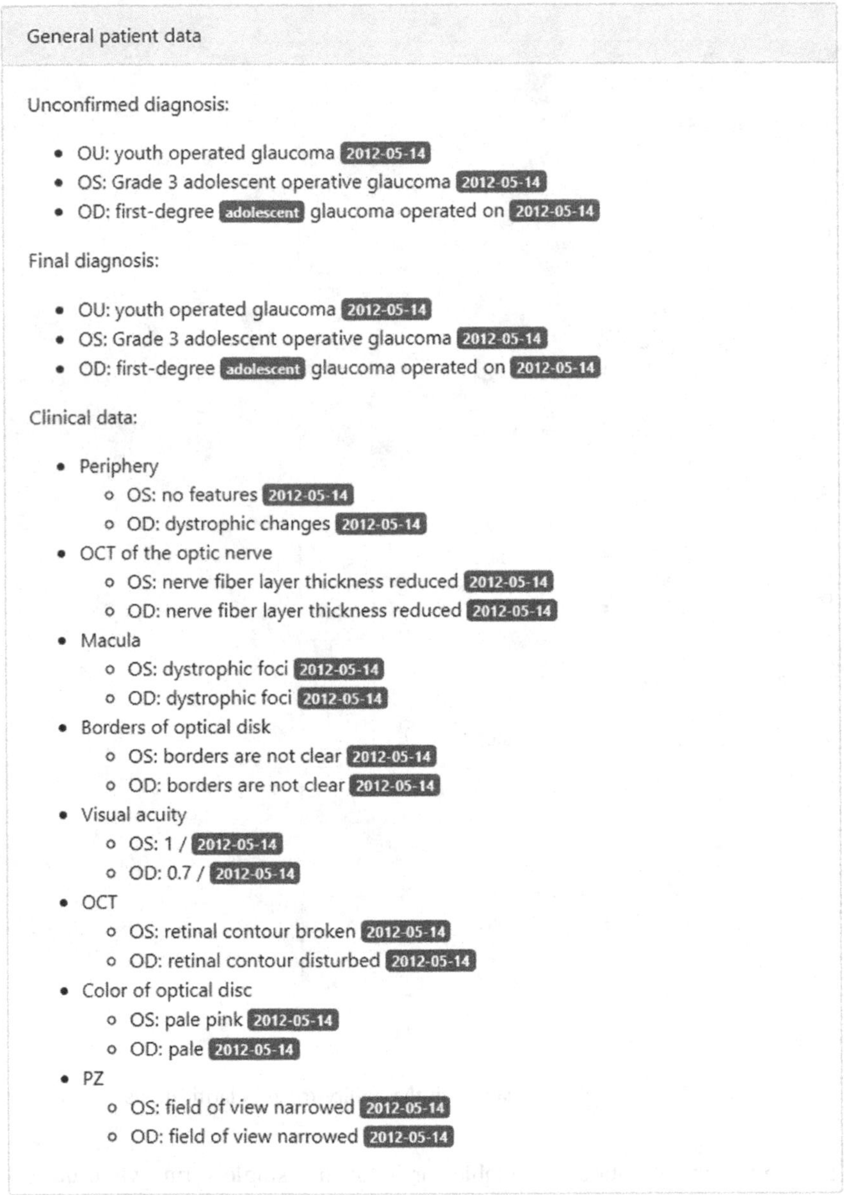

General patient data

Unconfirmed diagnosis:

- OU: youth operated glaucoma `2012-05-14`
- OS: Grade 3 adolescent operative glaucoma `2012-05-14`
- OD: first-degree `adolescent` glaucoma operated on `2012-05-14`

Final diagnosis:

- OU: youth operated glaucoma `2012-05-14`
- OS: Grade 3 adolescent operative glaucoma `2012-05-14`
- OD: first-degree `adolescent` glaucoma operated on `2012-05-14`

Clinical data:

- Periphery
  - OS: no features `2012-05-14`
  - OD: dystrophic changes `2012-05-14`
- OCT of the optic nerve
  - OS: nerve fiber layer thickness reduced `2012-05-14`
  - OD: nerve fiber layer thickness reduced `2012-05-14`
- Macula
  - OS: dystrophic foci `2012-05-14`
  - OD: dystrophic foci `2012-05-14`
- Borders of optical disk
  - OS: borders are not clear `2012-05-14`
  - OD: borders are not clear `2012-05-14`
- Visual acuity
  - OS: 1 / `2012-05-14`
  - OD: 0.7 / `2012-05-14`
- OCT
  - OS: retinal contour broken `2012-05-14`
  - OD: retinal contour disturbed `2012-05-14`
- Color of optical disc
  - OS: pale pink `2012-05-14`
  - OD: pale `2012-05-14`
- PZ
  - OS: field of view narrowed `2012-05-14`
  - OD: field of view narrowed `2012-05-14`

Fig. 8. Screen with the results of the examination of the patient

6 Conclusion

Several issues related to the preliminary processing and analysis of data from specialized medical devices in terms of the implementation of intelligent decision support systems for the diagnosis of complex eye pathologies, as well as for training young doctors (residents) are considered.

The focus was on solving the following tasks:

- Development of a convenient form of data storage and their preliminary processing in terms of subsequent use in intelligent decision support systems;
- Formalization and creation of ontology;
- Building a user interface designed for different types of users (experts, doctors, residents).

Further research directions and objectives are as follows:

- Improving the user interface, especially cognitive graphics;
- Integration with previously developed software [2, 4, 9];
- Integration with new tools (including hardware) and methods for diagnosing complex eye pathologies.

The results obtained and the software based on them make it possible to collect and store complex patient data in a simple and convenient form for subsequent analysis and diagnosis, which, in turn, simplifies the work of experts and practitioners and makes a better diagnosis (which is especially important in the early stages of the disease).

In conclusion, we note that the obtained results can also be applied to other subject problem areas (for example, when analyzing cardiograms), where there are also huge data arrays that require conversion and storage in a format convenient for subsequent analysis with the possibility of applying modern research methods of diagnostics, including methods of artificial intelligence, such as data mining.

Acknowledgment. The work was supported by Russian Foundation for Basic Research, project no. 17-07-00553, 18-29-03088.

References

1. Anisimov, D.N., Vershinin, D.V., Kolosov, O.S., Zueva, M.V., Tsapenko, I.V.: Diagnostics of the current state of dynamic objects and systems of complex structure using fuzzy logic methods using simulation models. Artif. Intell. Decis. Making **3**, 39–50 (2012). (in Russian)
2. Eremeev, A.P., Ivliev, S.A.: Analysis and diagnosis of complex pathologies of vision based on wavelet transformations and the neural network approach. In: Proceedings of the VIII International Scientific and Technical Conference "Integrated Models and Soft Computing in Artificial Intelligence", Kolomna, 18–20 May 2015, vol. 2, pp. 589–595 (2015). (in Russian)
3. Eremeev, A.P., et al.: Using NoSQL databases and machine learning for implementation of intelligent decision system in complex vision patalogies. In: 2018 3rd Russian-Pacific Conference on Computer Technology and Applications (RPC), pp. 1–4 (2018)

4. Eremeev, A., Ivliev, S.: Using convolutional neural networks for the analysis of nonstationary signals on the problem diagnostics vision pathologies. In: Kuznetsov, Sergei O., Osipov, Gennady S., Stefanuk, Vadim L. (eds.) RCAI 2018. CCIS, vol. 934, pp. 164–175. Springer, Cham (2018). https://doi.org/10.1007/978-3-030-00617-4_16
5. Basilea, C., Canavesea, D., Reganoa, L., Falcarinb, P., De Sutterc, B.: A meta-model for software protections and reverse engineering attacks. J. Syst. Softw. **150**, 3–21 (2019)
6. Barraco, R., et al.: A comparison among different techniques for human ERG signals processing and classification. Physica Med.: Eur. J. Med. Phys. **30**(1), 86–95 (2013)
7. Khodyko, D.L., Salomatin, S.B.: Adaptive filtering of a nonstationary structural signal. Reports of BSUIR. № 4 (66) (2012). (in Russian)
8. Tsapenko, I.V.: Electrophysiological studies in the diagnosis of diseases of the retina and optic nerve (I). Federal State Institution "Institute of Eye Diseases. G. Helmholtz of the Ministry of Health of Russia" (2017). (in Russian)
9. Korolenkova, V.A., Pronin, A.D., Kolosov, O.S.: The construction of the amplitude-frequency characteristics of the retina and the formalization of their parameters for use in diagnostic systems. In: Intelligent Systems, Control and Mechatronics - 2017: Materials of the All-Russian Scientific-Technical. Conference, Sevastopol, 18–20 September, pp. 175–178 (2017). (in Russian)

Using Ontology Engineering Methods for Organizing the Information Interaction Between Relational Databases

Nadezhda Yarushkina[ID], Anton Romanov[(✉)][ID], and Aleksey Filippov[ID]

Ulyanovsk State Technical University, Street Severny Venets 32,
432027 Ulyanovsk, Russian Federation
{jng,al.filippov}@ulstu.ru, romanov73@gmail.com
http://ulstu.ru

Abstract. The article describes an example of data consolidation between two relational databases (RDB). The proposed approach involves using of ontological engineering methods for extracting ontologies from RDB data models. The merging of the resulting ontologies is used to organize the information interaction between the RDB. The difference between the traditional and the proposed data consolidation algorithms is shown, their advantages and disadvantages are considered.

Keywords: Relational databases · Metaontology · Ontology · Ontology merging · Data consolidation

1 Introduction

A lot of enterprise information systems (IS) [1,2] use relational databases (RDB) for data storage. However, the task of storing data in such systems is partially solved when:

- the data has closed formats;
- the data stored in external files;
- automated processes do not require features implemented in the RDB.

In another case, all processed data are stored in the RDB, and all automated processes are used features of RDB when the RDB is the primary external data storage of the information system.

The problem of organizing information interaction between various ISs has appeared in the process of creating the system for balancing the production capacity of a large aircraft factory.

Large factories usually have many ISs that use different approaches and technologies based on various data models [3–8]. The main points of the development of methods for information interaction between ISs at the aircraft factory and the system for balancing the production capacity are:

© Springer Nature Switzerland AG 2019
S. O. Kuznetsov and A. I. Panov (Eds.): RCAI 2019, CCIS 1093, pp. 283–297, 2019.
https://doi.org/10.1007/978-3-030-30763-9_24

- reducing the count of manually entered data;
- reducing the time of consolidated reports generation;
- reducing data inconsistency in different ISs;
- increasing the metasystem flexibility.

2 State of the Art

The following possible methods of organizing information interaction between ISs at the aircraft factory and the system for balancing the production capacity are [3–8]:

1. Direct exchange;
2. File sharing;
3. Web services.

When the information interaction is organized by the direct exchange, the source and the target systems use the same RDB. The advantages of the direct exchange method are high speed and simple organization of interaction. The disadvantages of the direct exchange method are the lack of data protection from unauthorized access, binding to specific RBD management system or technology, and difficult support of interaction configurations.

The following steps are necessary to implement the direct exchange method:

1. Developing information interaction configurations;
2. Developing rules for mutation of the source data models into the target data models;
3. Developing a mechanisms for populating and updating the direct exchange data model on the data source side.
4. Developing a mechanism for accessing the data source and converting received data to the target data models on the data target side.
5. Developing a mechanism for checking the integrity and the correctness of data in the direct exchange process.

When the information interaction between the ISs organized by the file sharing method the information interaction is based on writing and reading data from a file with a specific structure. The advantages of the file sharing method are simple implementation, and many existing information systems support this method. The disadvantages of the file sharing method are the fundamental complexity of the binary files transfer and large number of encodings of text data, which is an outdated technology.

The implementation steps of the file sharing method are identical to the steps of the direct-exchange method, but the file sharing does not require compatibility of the data sources. However, the file format specification should clearly describe the structure of the file, the set of fields and data types, flags or conditions for fields population, and sets of possible values for enumerations. The rules for processing records from the shared file should include descriptions of algorithms for data processing, especially if the target RDB executes business methods after data insertion. Unobvious actions should also be described. It is necessary to provide a mechanism for checking a downloaded data with the possibility of feedback between source and target RDBs.

The service-oriented approach (SOA) can be used to organize information interaction in a decentralized information environment. The advantage of the SOA is self-documenting standard protocols which reduce the complexity of the information interaction organization. The disadvantages of the SOA are the lack of standards for message formats describing, and highly skilled analysts and developers are required.

The following steps are necessary to solve the problem of organizing information interaction based on the SOA:

1. Define the technology to access the web service.
2. Define the technology and rules to realize authorization and authentication processes.
3. Define the mechanism of maintaining web service versioning.
4. Define a set of web service methods.
5. Define the technology and process of binary files exchange.

The easiest way to organize the information interaction between several RDBs is the development of the system (the metasystem) that will execute SQL queries to source RDBs on a schedule and will save data to RDB of the target metasystem. The main disadvantage of this approach is the need to maintain correspondence between SQL queries for data extraction and RDB data models of a large number of data sources. In our case, data sources are RDBs of the aircraft factory ISs. The data models of RDBs may change in the process of their operation and development.

Thus, the technical problems of organizing information interaction between ISs are as follows:

1. Possible failures in data networks leading to delays and loss of information;
2. The heterogeneous nature of ISs at the aircraft factory;
3. Gaining access to the RDB data model of ISs at the aircraft factory;
4. The need to support and adapt the integration solution.

Data integration systems can provide data integration at the physical, logical, and semantic level. Each level of the data integration process has its own issues, which must be solved [3–8]:

– various data representation formats can be used at the physical level;
– heterogeneity of the used models and/or data models for different RDBs may take place at the logical level;
– different data domains or domain fragments with various set of concepts may be contained in different RDBs at the semantic level.

The types of data model inconsistencies are heterogeneity conflicts, naming conflicts, semantic conflicts, and structural conflicts. Also, the types of data inconsistencies are different data formats, different representation of values, loss of data relevance by one of the RDBs, operator input errors in some data sources, and the difficulty of entities identification because of data distortions.

Some of the methodological problems arise in the process of organizing the information interaction are as follows [3–8]:

1. Development of the architecture of the data integration system;
2. Creating a metaontology as the basis of a single user interface in the integration system;
3. Development of methods for mapping data models;
4. Development of methods for building mappings into the metaontology for specific models of separate RDBs;
5. Integration of metadata used in the data integration system;
6. Removing heterogeneity of data sources.
7. Development of mechanisms for semantic integration of RDBs.

It was decided to use data consolidation based on the direct exchange method as the primary approach for organizing the information interaction between the production capacity balancing system and ISs at the aircraft factory. Consolidation of data is the data extraction from source RDBs and data recording to the primary storage (target RDB).

The consolidation process involves the implementation of three stages (ETL): extraction, transformation, and loading [3–8]. Usually, the ETL process is called "data integration". In the process of consolidation the data are transferred from several RDBs to the primary storage. There is some delay between the moment of updating information in the sources and the time when these changes are updated in the primary source.

The process of developing the consolidation mechanism includes

1. Extracting metadata (the ontological representation) in the form of OWL/XML ontology from RDB data model of each integrated IS;
2. Ontology merging for metaonology creation.

At the moment, a lot of researchers use the ontological approach for extracting metadata from the RDB data model:

1. The Relational.OWL [10] currently supporting only MySQL and DB2 database management systems (DBMS). The generated ontology contains classes: Database, Table, Column, and PrimaryKey, and properties: has, hasTable, hasColumn, isIndentifiedBy, references, scale, length. The main disadvantage of ontology generated by Relational.OWL is the presence of limited coverage of the domain, not considering for instances, data types, foreign keys, and constraints.
2. The OWL-RDBO [11, 12] currently supporting only MySQL, PostgreSQL and DB2 DBMSs. The generated ontology contains classes: DatabaseName, RelationList, Relation, AttributeList, Attribute, and the following properties: hasRelations, hasType, referenceAttribute, referenceRelation. The main disadvantage of ontology generated by OWL-RDBO is the presence of concepts external to the domain, such as RelationList to group a set of Relation, and AttributeList to group a set of attributes.

3. Other approaches, such as [13, 14] extract the real world relations from the RDB data model, and unable to reconstruct the original RDB data model.

Ontology-Based Data Access (OBDA) is a popular approach for building a conceptual layer over data sources in the form of an ontology that hides the structure of that data sources [15, 16]. The OBDA allow to execute unified semantic queries (SPARQL, Web-PDDL and others) to this conceptual view, and the users no longer need understanding of the data sources models (relations between RDB entities, differences between data types and data encodings). The OBDA system translates semantic user queries into queries over various integrated data sources. The ontology is connected to the data sources through a declarative specification given in metaontology that relates the ontology classes and properties to SQL views over data. However, the primary purpose of the ODBA is querying data from several data sources with semantic user queries, and this is not data consolidation.

Thus, it is necessary to develop a method for data consolidation based on ontology merging of metadata extracted from the RDB data model of several ISs of the aircraft factory. The main problems that need to be solved are:

1. Providing data to users in a unified form. Data obtained from various RDBs is converted into a specific unified presentation format in the process of data consolidation at the physical level. The primary storage is used as a single entry point to obtain data located in different RDBs at the logical level. A single representation of the data is used for taking into account semantics of the data at the semantic level.
2. Corresponding data models. The metaontology is the data consolidation settings contains correspondences between data models (tables and columns) of integrated ISs.
3. Combining interfaces and data types. Integration avoids duplicate data entry, which reduces the burden on operators. Such integration will transparent for people who work with the system for balancing the production capacity.

3   Ontological Representation of the RDB Data Model

The proposed data consolidation algorithm consists of the following steps:

1. Extracting metadata from the RDB data model for automatic generation of ontologies for the source and target RBDs.
2. Creation of the metaontology. Ontology merging to configure correspondences between objects, attributes, and relationships of integrated ISs.
3. Using the metaontology to perform the consolidation procedure on a schedule.

Ontology is a model of knowledge representation for a specific problem area [9]. An ontology contains a set of classes, individuals, properties, and relations between them. An ontology is based on the dictionary of terms which reflecting the concepts of a problem area. Also, the dictionary contains a set of rules (axioms). The terms can be combined to construct a set of statements about the state of the problem area based on a set of axioms.

The relational data model can be represented as the following expression:

$$RDM = \langle E, H, R \rangle, \tag{1}$$

where $E = \{E_1, E_2, \ldots, E_p\}$ is a set of RDB entities (tables);
$E_i = (name, Row, Col)$ is the i-th RDB entity that contains the name, set of rows Row and columns Col;
$Col_j = (name, type, constraints)$ is the j-th column of the i-th RDB entity that contains the following properties: the name, the type, and set of constraints;
$H = \{H_1, H_2, \ldots, H_q\}$ is a hierarchy of RDB entities in the case of using the table inheritance function:

$$H_j = E_i D(x) E_k, \tag{2}$$

where E_i and E_k are RDB entities;
$D(x)$ is a 'parent-child' relation between E_i and E_k;
$R = \{R_1, R_2, \ldots, R_r\}$ is a set of RDB relations:

$$R_l = E_i \frac{F(x)}{G(x)} E_k, \tag{3}$$

where $F(x)$ is an RDB relation between E_i and E_k;
$G(x)$ is an RDB relation between E_k and E_i.

Functions $F(x)$ and $G(x)$ can take values: U is a single relation and N stays for multiple relations.

The ontological representation of the RDB data model is as follows:

$$O = \langle C, P, L, R \rangle, \tag{4}$$

where $C = \{C_1, C_2, \ldots, C_n\}$ is a set of data model ontology classes;
$P = \{P_1, P_2, \ldots, P_m\}$ is a set of properties of data model ontology classes;
$L = \{L_1, L_2, \ldots, L_o\}$ is a set of data model ontology constraints;
R is a set of data model ontology relations:

$$R = \{R_C, R_P, R_L\}, \tag{5}$$

where R_C is a set of relations defining the hierarchy of data model ontology classes;
R_P is a set of relations defining the 'class-property' data model ontology ties;
R_L is a set of relations defining the 'property-constraint' data model ontology ties.

The following function is used to map the RDB structure (Eq. 1) to the ontological representation (Eq. 4):

$$F(RDM, O) : \{E^{RDM}, H^{RDM}, R^{RDM}\} \longrightarrow \{C^O, P^O, L^O, R^O\}, \tag{6}$$

where $\{E^{RDM}, H^{RDM}, R^{RDM}\}$ is a set of RDB entities and relations between them (Eq. 1);

$\{C^O, P^O, L^O, R^O\}$ is a set of ontology entities (Eq. 4).

The process of mapping the RDB structure into an ontological representation contains several steps:

1. *Formation of ontological representation classes.*

   A set of ontological representation classes C is formed using the set of RDB entities C $E_i \rightarrow C_i$. The number of classes of the ontological representation must be equal to the number of RDB entities;

2. *Formation of properties of ontological representation classes.*

   A set of properties P of the i-th ontological representation class C_i is formed using the set of columns Col of the i-th RDB entity E_i $Col_j \rightarrow P_j$. The number of properties of the i-th ontological representation class C_i must be equal to the number of columns of the i-th RDB entity E_i. The name of the j-th property P_j is the name of the j-th column Col_j of the RDB entity;

3. *Formation of ontological representation constraints.*

   A set of constraints L of the properties of the i-th ontological representation class C_i is formed based on the set of columns Col of the i-th RDB entity E_i $Col_k \rightarrow \hat{L}$. The number of constraints of the i-th ontological representation class C_i must be equal to the number of constraints of the i-th RDB entity E_i. However, there are limitations to this approach due to the difficulty of mapping constraints if they have triggers or stored procedures;

4. *Formation hierarchy of ontological representation classes.*

   It is necessary to form a set of ontology relationships R_C between all the child and parent classes corresponding to the hierarchy of RDB entities if table inheritance uses in RDB $H \rightarrow R_C$. The domain of the j-th ontological representation relationship R_{Cj} is indicated by the reference to the parent class C_{parent}. The range of the j-th ontological representation relationship R_{Cj} is indicated by the reference to the child (or a set) class C_{child}.

5. *Formation of relations between classes and properties of classes of ontological representation.*

   The set of ontological representation relationships R_P is based on the set of columns Col of the i-th RDB entity E_i and the set of RDB relations R. Two types of relationships are formed for each j-th ontological representation property P_j:

   (a) The relationship 'class-property'. The domain of the ontological representation relationship is indicated by the reference to the i-th class C_i to which the j-th property belongs, and the range belongs to the j-th property reference P_j.

   (b) The relationship 'property-data type class'. The domain of the k-th ontological representation relationship is indicated by the reference to the j-th property P_j. The range is indicated by the reference to the l-th class C_l corresponding to the l-th RBD entity E_l, or the reference to the m-th ontology class C_m corresponding to the data type of the j-th RBD column Col_j.

6. *Formation of relations between properties of classes and constraints of properties of classes of ontological representation.*

   The set of relations R_L of ontological representation is based on the set of columns Col of the i-th RDB entity. The domain of the j-th ontological representation relationship R_{Lj} is indicated by the reference to the k-th property P_k. The range of the j-th ontological representation relationship R_{LJ} is indicated by the reference to the k-th constraint $Col \rightarrow R_L$.

   It is necessary to form a metaontology based on the ontological representations that is obtained after mapping the RDB structure of each of the integrated information systems to the ontological representation.

4   Creation of the Metaontlogy

The definition of an ontological system is used as a formal representation of a metaontology:

$$\overset{O}{\sum} = \langle O^{META}, O^{IS}, M \rangle, \tag{7}$$

where O^{META} is the metaontology;

$O^{IS} = \{O_1^{IS}, O_2^{IS}, \ldots, O_g^{IS}\}$ is a set of ontological representations of RDB data models that must be integrated;

M is a model of reasoner.

   The following steps are necessary to form a metaontology based on the set of ontological representations of the RDB data models that must be integrated:

1. *Formation of the universal concept dictionary for the current domain.*

   The process of formation of a metaontology O^{META} is based on the common terminology. Ontological representations of all RDB data models that must be integrated O^{IS} should be built from a single concept dictionary. The concept dictionary is formed by the expert based on the analysis of the obtained ontological representations.

2. *Formation of a metaontology O^{META}.*

   At this step, the set of top-level classes C^{META} are added to the metaontology O^{META}. The set of top-level classes C^{META} describes systems that must be integrated, and it is used as the basis for ontology merging.

3. *Formation of class hierarchy of metaontology O^{META}.*

   At this step, the metaontology establishes a correspondence between the class hierarchies $C^{O_i^{IS}}$ of ontological representations O^{IS} of RDB data models that must be integrated.

4. *Formation of class properties of the metaontology O^{META}.*

   At this step, the metaontology establishes a correspondence between the properties $P^{O_i^{IS}}$ of ontological representations O^{IS} of RDB data models that must be integrated. The expert decides which class properties of ontological representations O^{IS} should be included in the metaontology O^{META}.

5. *The formation of axioms of classes and properties, checking the metaontology O^{META} for consistency.*

At this step, constraints $L^{O^{IS}}$ are applied to the properties $P^{O^{IS}}$ and classes $C^{O^{IS}}$ of the metaontology O^{META} based on the constraints of the ontological representations O^{IS}. After that, the resulting metaontology O^{META} should be checked for internal consistency using the reasoner M. However, the development of methods for checking the conditions of constraints is required, since the existing reasoners do not support working with such objects.

Let us see the following example of the metaontology creation. Some aircraft factory IS is the source RDB, and the production capacity planning system is the target RDB.

Table 1 shows the structure of the "Equipment and Tools" table of the aircraft factory IS.

The "Equipment and Tools" entity of the target RDB consists from several tables:

1. Tools (Table 2).
2. Tool types (Table 3).
3. Tool parameters (Table 3).
4. Table "Tools + Tool parameters" (Table 4) for organizing many to many relation between "Tools" and "Tool parameters" tables.

Thus, the ontological representation of the "Equipment and Tools" entity (Table 1) of the source RDB can be represented as:
$$O^S = \langle$$
$\quad C^S = \{$ Equipment and Tools (E&T), CHAR, NUMBER, BLOB, DATE $\}$,
$\quad P^S = \{$ t2_ob, t2_ng , t2_nn, ..., t2_dc, t2_vid, t2_doc, t2_prim, t2_yyyy $\}$
$\quad L^S = \{$ nullable, $\langle$ length, 2 $\rangle$, ..., $\langle$ precision, 5 $\rangle$, $\langle$ precision, 6 $\rangle$ $\}$
$\quad R_P^S = \{$ $\langle$ E&T, t2_ob, CHAR $\rangle$, $\langle$ E&T, t2_ng, NUMBER $\rangle$, ...,
$\quad\quad \langle$ E&T, t2_yyyy, CHAR $\rangle$ $\}$
$\quad R_L^S = \{$ $\langle$ E&T, t2_ob, $\langle$ length, 200 $\rangle$ $\rangle$, ..., $\langle$ E&T, t2_doc,
$\quad\quad \langle$ length, 100 $\rangle$ $\rangle$ $\}$ $\rangle$,

where C^S is a set of the ontological representation classes;
P^S is a set of the ontological representation properties;
L^S is a set of the ontological representation constraints;
R_P^S is a set of relations between classes and properties of the ontological representation;
R_L^S is a set of relations between properties and constraints of the ontological representation.

The ontological representation of the "Equipment and Tools" entity (Tables 2, 3 and 4) of the target RDB can be represented as:
$$O^T = \langle$$
$\quad C^T = \{$ Tools (T), Tool types (TT), Tool parameters (TP),
$\quad\quad$ Tools + Tool parameters (TTP), INTEGER, VARCHAR, DATE $\}$,
$\quad P^T = \{$ T_id, T_name, T_serial_number, ..., TTP_value $\}$,
$\quad L^T = \{$ nullable, $\langle$ length, 255 $\rangle$ $\}$,

Table 1. The "Equipment and Tools" table of the aircraft factory IS

Column	Data type	Description
t2_ob	CHAR(200)	Name
t2_ng	NUMBER(5)	Group
t2_nn	NUMBER(6)	Position
t2_r1	CHAR	Type #1
t2_r2	CHAR	Type #2
t2_r3	CHAR	Type #3
t2_p1	CHAR(2) nullable	Parameter #1
t2_z1	CHAR(8) nullable	Parameter #1 value
t2_p2	CHAR(2) nullable	Parameter #2
t2_z2	CHAR(8) nullable	Parameter #2 value
t2_p3	CHAR(2) nullable	Parameter #3
t2_z3	CHAR(8) nullable	Parameter #3 value
t2_gm	BLOB	Geometric model
up_dt	DATE	Date of last update
up_us	CHAR(32)	User
t2_dc	BLOB	Attachment
t2_vid	CHAR(4)	Tooling type
t2_doc	CHAR(100)	Document name
t2_prim	CHAR(100) nullable	Notes
t2_yyyy	CHAR(4)	Production date

Table 2. The "Tools" table of the production capacity planning system

Column	Data type	Description
id	INTEGER	Primary key
name	VARCHAR(255)	Name
serial_number	VARCHAR(255) nullable	Serial number
inventory_number	VARCHAR(255)	Inventory number
production_date	DATE	Production date
tool_types_id	INTEGER	Link to "Tool type" table (foreign key)

Table 3. The "Tool types" and "Tool parameters" tables of the production capacity planning system

Column	Data type	Description
id	INTEGER	Primary key
name	VARCHAR(255)	Name

Table 4. The "Tools + Tool parameters" table of the production capacity planning system

Column	Data type	Description
tool_id	INTEGER	Link to "Tools" table (foreign key)
tool_parameter_id	INTEGER	Link to "Tool parameters" table (foreign key)
value	VARCHAR(255)	Parameter value

$R_P^T = \{ \ \langle \ T, \ T\_id, \ INTEGER \ \rangle, \dots, \langle \ TTP, \ TTP\_value, \ VARCHAR \ \rangle \ \}$

$R_L^S = \{ \ \langle \ T, \ T\_name, \ \langle \ length, \ 255 \ \rangle \ \rangle, \dots, \langle \ TTP, \ TTP\_value,$
$\qquad \langle \ length, \ 255 \ \rangle \ \rangle \ \} \ \rangle.$

Consider the example of the metaontology O^{Meta} formation for ontological representations O^S and O^T:

Step 1. Formation of the universal concept dictionary for the current domain.

– Term "Position" (Table 1) of source same as term "Primary key" (Table 2) of the target.
– Term "Notes" (Table 1) of source same as term "Inventory number" (Table 2) of the target.

Step 2. Formation of a metaontology.
$C^{Meta} = \{ \ \langle \ Source, \ Oracle, \ Settings1 \ \rangle, \langle \ Target, \ PostgreSQL, \ Settings2 \ \rangle \ \}$

Step 3. Formation of class hierarchy of the metaontology.
$R_C^{Meta} = \{ \ \langle \ Source, \ Equipment \ and \ Tools \ \rangle, \langle \ Target, \ Tools \ \rangle, \dots,$
$\qquad \langle \ Target, \ Tools \ + \ Tool \ Parameters \ \rangle \ \}$

Step 4. Formation of class properties of the metaontology.
$R_P^{Meta} = \{ \ \langle \ \langle \ Source, \ t2\_nn \ \rangle, \ t2\_nn\_T\_id, \ \langle \ Target, \ T\_id \ \rangle \ \rangle, \dots,$
$\qquad \langle \ \langle \ Source, \ t2\_z3 \ \rangle, \ t2\_z3\_TTP\_value, \ \langle \ Target, \ TTP\_value \ \rangle \ \rangle \ \}$

Step 4. Formation of axioms of classes and properties, checking the metaontology for consistency.
$R_L^{Meta} = \{ \ \langle \ t2\_ob\_T\_name, \ \langle \ Source, \ \langle \ length, \ 200 \ \rangle \ \rangle, \langle \ Target,$
$\qquad \langle \ length, \ 255 \ \rangle \ \rangle, \dots, \langle \ t2\_z3\_TTP\_value, \ \langle \ Source, \ nullable,$
$\qquad \langle \ length, \ 8 \ \rangle \ \rangle, \langle \ Target, \ \langle \ length, \ 255 \ \rangle \ \rangle \ \}$

The proposed method is allowed to configure the correspondence between tables and fields of two RDBs. The main problem is the need for ontology merging. However, this problem can be solved by the use of specialized tools to automate the ontology merging process. Also, specialized tools allow dividing the developer and domain expert roles. The main advantage of the proposed method is the ability to dynamically generate the necessary SQL queries to select and insert data from/to the RBD based on metaontology.

5   Experiments

Consider the software component that implements the proposed method for organizing the information exchange between ISs. The following experiment demonstrates the high speed of generation of the ontological representation of the RDB data model in the OWL/XML format. Figure 1 presents a screen form for configuring parameters for connecting to the RBDs of two integrated ISs.

Source   **Target**

DBMS   DBMS

PostgreSQL ▾   PostgreSQL ▾

URL   URL

jdbc:postgresql://loc   jdbc:postgresql://loc

Login   Login

postgres   postgres

Password   Password

•••••••   •••••••

Connect   Connect

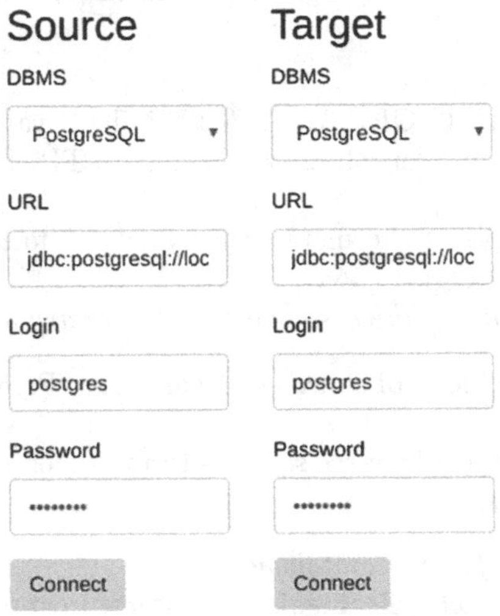

Fig. 1. Screen form for configuring parameters of connection to the RBDs of two integrated ISs

The average time of the OWL ontology generation for RDB, which contains 5 tables, 26 columns, and 8 restrictions, is 558 ms.

The average time of the OWL ontology generation for RBD, which contains 38 tables, 195 columns, and 88 restrictions, is 822 ms.

Figure 2 shows the screen form for ontology merging of ontological representations of the RDB data models of two integrated ISs.

The resulting metaontology is passed to the data exchange component. Also, the data exchange component contains the reasoner, which allows checking:

– the correctness of the processed ontological representations;
– the ability to convert data types;
– the restrictions of columns of integrated tables.

An informational message containing the details is displayed if an error occurs. For example, if the value in the column with the nullable restriction is null, the following message is displayed *nullable columns are not populated: tool.unit_id.*

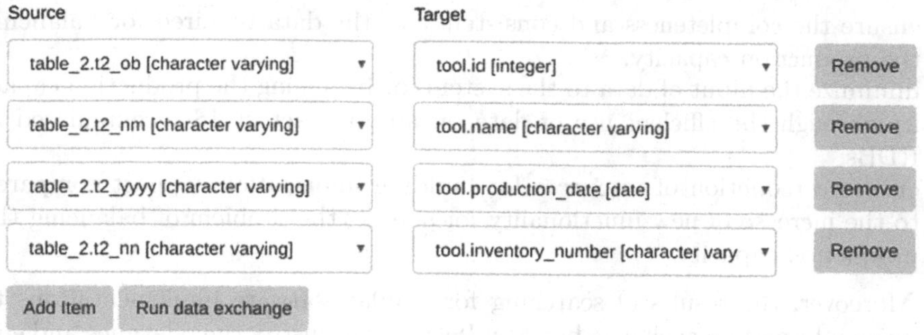

Source		Target		
table_2.t2_ob [character varying]	▾	tool.id [integer]	▾	Remove
table_2.t2_nm [character varying]	▾	tool.name [character varying]	▾	Remove
table_2.t2_yyyy [character varying]	▾	tool.production_date [date]	▾	Remove
table_2.t2_nn [character varying]	▾	tool.inventory_number [character vary	▾	Remove

Add Item   Run data exchange

Fig. 2. Screen form for ontology merging of ontological representations of the RDB data models of two integrated ISs

The set of SQL queries to select data from the source RDB and to insert data to the target RDB are generated if the metaontology is correct. For example, SQL query for selecting data from source RDB

SELECT tab0.t9 _ki AS id, tab0.t9 _nm AS name FROM table _9 AS tab0
and SQL queries for insert data to target RDB
INSERT INTO product (id, name)
VALUES (TO _NUMBER (: id, '99999999'),: name).

As you can see from this example, the data type of the source column is converted to the data type of the target column, if necessary. The execution of generated queries allows for organizing information interaction between the two ISs.

The proposed method allows organizing information interaction without the participation of developers in contrast to the traditional approach of consolidation based on the method of direct data exchange. The only requirement of the proposed method is the presence of a metaontology. The disadvantages of the current implementation of the proposed method are:

1. The need for implementation of the data type casting algorithms in case of their mismatch, for each DBMS.
2. The need for adapting the proposed method implementation to the SQL dialect of DBMS involved in the exchange process. Random DBMS cannot be supported by this implementation.

6   Conclusion

The proposed approach – based on ontology engineering methods – for organizing the information interaction between RDB in the task of balancing the production capacity of the aircraft factory allows to:

– ensure the completeness and consistency of the data required for balancing the production capacity;
– minimize the input of data to the system for balancing the production capacity through the efficient use of data on aircraft factory ISs accumulated in RDBs;
– ensure a reduction of resources for building information support compared to the increase of new functionality for solving the problem of balancing the production capacity.

Moreover, the results of searching for similar software implementations to organize information exchange between ISs allow to justify the relevance and efficiency of the proposed approach. The proposed method allows organizing information interaction between ISs without the participation of developers, which helps to increase the flexibility and efficiency of data consolidation.

Acknowledgments. The study was supported by:
– the Ministry of Science and Higher Education of the Russian Federation in framework of projects 2.4760.2017/8.9 and 2.1182.2017/4.6;
– the Russian Foundation for Basic Research (Grants No. 18-47-732016 and 18-47-730022).

References

1. Supported Database Systems (Overview). SAP Help Portal (2019). https://help.sap.com/viewer/d77277f42c0b469db8794645abd954ea/8.0/en-US/64f4ef081ed74836b570b56d7bcb4527.html. Accessed 23 Jul 2019
2. 1C Developer Network. Database management system (2019). https://1c-dn.com/1c_enterprise/database_management_system/. Accessed 23 Jul 2019
3. Clark, T., Barn, B.S., Oussena, S.: A method for enterprise architecture alignment. In: Proper, E., Gaaloul, K., Harmsen, F., Wrycza, S. (eds.) PRET 2012. LNBIP, vol. 120, pp. 48–76. Springer, Heidelberg (2012). https://doi.org/10.1007/978-3-642-31134-5_3
4. Rouhani, D.B., et al.: A systematic literature review on enterprise arquitecture implementation methhodologies. Inf. Softw. Technol. **62**, 1–20 (2015)
5. Medini, K., Bourey, J.P.: SCOR-based enterprise architecture methodology. Int. J. Comput. Integrat. Manuf. **25**, 594–607 (2012)
6. Poduval, A., et al.: Do more with SOA Integration: Best of Packt (2011)
7. Caselli, V., Binildas, C., Barai, M.: The Mantra of SOA. Service Oriented Architecture with Java. Birmingham, UK (2008)
8. Berna-Martinez, V.J., et al.: Method for the Integration of Applications Based on Enterprise Service Bus Technologies (2018)
9. Gruber, T. Ontology. http://tomgruber.org/writing/ontology-in-encyclopedia-of-dbs.pdf. Accessed 23 Jul 2019
10. de Laborda, C.P., Conrad, S.: Relational.owl: a data and schema representation format based on owl. In Proceedings of the 2nd Asia-Pacific Conference on Conceptual modelling-Volume 43, pp. 89–96. Australian Computer Society Inc. (2005)
11. Trinh, Q., Barker, K., Alhajj, R.: RDB2ONT: a tool for generating owl ontologies from relational database systems. In Telecommunications. In: International Conference on Internet and Web Applications and Services/Advanced International Conference on AICT-ICIW 2006, pp. 170–170. IEEE (2006)

12. Trinh, Q., Barker, K., Alhajj, R.: Semantic interoperability between relational database systems. In: IDEAS 2007 11th International Database Engineering and Applications Symposium, pp. 208–215. IEEE (2007)
13. Barrett, T., et al.: RDF representation of metadata for semantic integration of corporate information resources. In: International Workshop Real World and Semantic Web Applications, vol. 2002. Citeseer (2002)
14. Bizer, C.: D2R MAP - A Database to RDF Mapping Language. In: Proceedings of the 12th International World Wide Web Conference - Posters (2003)
15. Dou, D., LePendu, P.: Ontology-based integration for relational databases. In: Proceedings of the 2006 ACM symposium on Applied computing, pp. 461–466. ACM (2006)
16. Calvanese, D., et al.: Ontop: answering SPARQL queries over relational databases. Semantic Web J. **8**, 471–487 (2017)

Technology of Personalized Preventive Recommendation Formation Based on Disease Risk Assessment

Oleg G. Grigoriev[1] and Alexey I. Molodchenkov[1,2(✉)]

[1] Federal Research Center "Computer Science and Control" of RAS,
Vavilova str. 44, kor. 2, Moscow 119333, Russian Federation
oleggpolikvart@yandex.ru, aim@tesyan.ru
[2] RUDN University, Miklukho-Maklaya str. 6, Moscow 117198
Russian Federation

Abstract. The paper describes the technology of forming a list of personalized preventive recommendations. The technology consists of the following main components: human health state, data acquisition module, database, knowledge base, and solver with output explanation. In the version presented, this technology allows one to assess the risks of stroke, myocardial infarction and depression, contains more than two hundred risk factors for these diseases and more than twenty preventive recommendations. Training for this version was based on automated analysis of a large number of publications and expert knowledge.

Keywords: Health optimization · Risk factors · Artificial intelligence · Knowledge base · Heterogeneous semantic network · P4 medicine · Predictive medicine · Risk factors assessment

1 Introduction

P4 medicine, which focuses on services for the improvement and preservation of health, is currently being developed around the world. Technologies that collect and analyze information from various devices (bracelets, watches, smartphones, scales, etc.), show the dynamics of changes in this information and provide analysis results along with the simplest recommendations, are undergoing active development. Software solutions and cloud services, which process data from various sources, carry out an in-depth assessment of users health status and issue a list of preventive recommendations for improving people's health, are actively developing too. As an example, one can bring such services as Welltok [1] and Welltory [2]. In the course of work, a number of tasks are solved, and the first of them is to collect all possible person's data, including information from various gadgets, user surveys, electronic medical records, and social networks. The task of collecting information from diverse sources, starting

This work was supported by Ministry of Education and Science of the Russian Federation, grant no. 14.604.21.0194 (Unique Project Identifier RFMEFI60417X0194).

S. O. Kuznetsov and A. I. Panov (Eds.): RCAI 2019, CCIS 1093, pp. 298–309, 2019.
https://doi.org/10.1007/978-3-030-30763-9_25

with ordinary bracelets, smartphones and ending with information from medical information networks, has been worked out fairly well.

After processing the collected information a specialist, usually referred to as a Health Manager, carries out assessment of human health state. In order to assess the risks of diseases, it is necessary to analyze a large amount of heterogeneous information, preferably including information about a person's genetic predisposition to various diseases. [3–5]. It is necessary to quickly process and analyze large volumes of the information received and build up a ranking list of preventive recommendations, which will then be transferred to a Health Manager. Since such an analysis goes far beyond the limits of conventional statistical analysis, it is practically impossible for a person to perform it without the use of technologies of Artificial Intelligence (AI). The use of AI technologies allows organizing a continuous process of data collection, dynamic people's health changes assessment, issuing recommendations to them, testing their use, and, accordingly, assessing the effect of the recommendations used. Human health assessing automation in the area of health optimization is complicated by the fact that there are no clearly allocated features by which we can estimate the probability of the disease and often lack the necessary data. This leads to the fact that modern methods of machine learning are inappropriate here, in contrast to the diagnosis of diseases.

The article describes a technology that allows for a comprehensive risk assessment of diseases based on the data collected, identification of risk factors for these diseases and the development of preventive recommendations aimed at reducing the impact of those risk factors that can be affected by prevention. The proposed technology is currently tested on three diseases: stroke, myocardial infarction, and depression.

2 Technology Description

The main components of the technology are:

- module for obtaining human health state data;
- data base;
- knowledge base;
- solver with an explanation module.

The data collection module contains a number of services for collecting medical data that operate in different modes. The first service allows you to receive data from external applications using the REST API technology [6]. This service contains a batch API that allows you to transfer several values of a number of parameters collected over a certain period from several users in a single request. Parameter transfer is initiated by the sending application.

In addition, this module contains a number of applications that collect information on a given user, if he agrees, constantly and without his participation. Information is collected from sources such as Google Fit, Apple Health, social networks [7] and is a set of parameter values that characterize a user and his risk factors for certain diseases. The information collected depends on the sources to which access is granted. This technology allows you to connect various sources and methods of data collection, including the Internet of Things technology.

Collected values are stored in a database, which is designed so that the list of parameters necessary for assessing the diseases risks and building a list of preventive recommendations can be supplemented or modified without changing the structure of the tables or the structure of the database itself.

The main component of the diseases risk assessment and the preventive recommendations selection is the knowledge base. The knowledge base is implemented in the form of a heterogeneous semantic network [8, 9], further HSN, and consists of sections, HSN nodes, node properties, and links between nodes.

HSN nodes form the main part of the knowledge base. Nodes can represent disease risk factors, lifestyle facts, personal factors, specific statements, events, observations results, user's condition characteristics, recommendations for prevention. Examples of nodes are "Overweight", "Stress frequency once a day", "Young age", "Alcohol abuse", "Male", "Female", "Smoking", "Duration of smoking up to 5 years, "Strokes in old age among relatives of the 1-st degree kinship", "Insomnia", "High sense of loneliness", etc. Experts group the nodes into sections according to their meaning in the system. There are following sections in the system knowledge base: "Risk factors", "Hidden characteristics", "Disease risks", "Preventive recommendations", "user's life events", etc. Below we provide explanations for some node sections.

There are two node categories in the knowledge base. The first category includes nodes that reflect health and lifestyle knowledge, which determine the course of reasoning: node-data; the second includes nodes that participate in the solutions formation: nodes-hypotheses. In the knowledge base of the system, the risk factors, user's life events, user characteristics act as data nodes, and the disease risks and preventive health-improving recommendations - as hypotheses nodes.

Links between nodes in the knowledge base show the impact of the node on the generation or exclusion of others. Links are possible between any two nodes, although the most important ones are between the data nodes and the hypothesis nodes.

Knowledge base fragments are presented in Figs. 1 and 2. The structure of the knowledge base is described in more detail in [10, 11].

As it was mentioned, it is impossible to train such systems using only machine learning technologies due to the lack of most data and the lack of links certainty. Machine learning and data analysis technologies can be applied to the processing of such data as genomic, to assess a person's susceptibility to certain diseases.

It is well known that data sets are not the only source of knowledge for building intelligent systems. Other sources include texts and expert knowledge. It is these knowledge sources were used for the training of the system's first version. Using technologies developed at the Institute of Systems Analysis of the Russian Academy of Sciences (in 2015, admitted to the Federal Research Center "Computer Science and Control" of RAS) to analyze large text volumes, experts were able to identify more than 200 risk factors for such diseases as stroke, myocardial infarction and depression. These risk factors include not only person's physiological characteristics, but also his lifestyle features, the way he works, feels, what he eats, what medications he takes, etc. As a result, all parameters that can lead to the risk factors of the diseases above can be divided into the following sections:

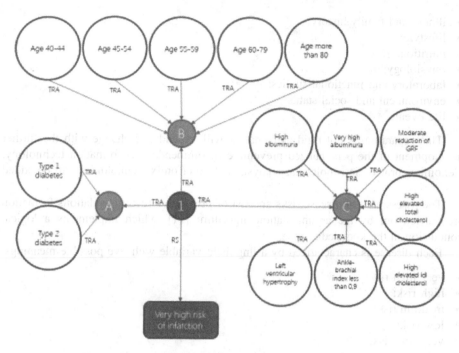

Fig. 1. Knowledge base fragment for myocardial infarction.

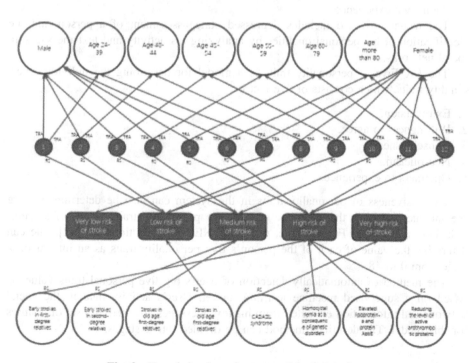

Fig. 2. Knowledge base fragment of the for stroke.

- illness and family history;
- lifestyle;
- nutrition;
- physiology;
- laboratory and functional studies;
- environment and social status;
- life events.

This separation is not rigid and final; it will expand and change with the further development of the personalized preventive recommendations formation technology. Genomics, proteomics, molecular analysis and other omix technologies will be added too.

The assessment of disease risks and list of preventive recommendations formation are carried out by the argumentation algorithm [11], which implements a logical conclusion in the knowledge base.

Each disease is characterized by a linguistic variable with five possible meanings:

- very high risk;
- high risk;
- medium risk;
- low risk;
- very low risk.

Such leveling was chosen by experts based on automated analysis of publications and their own experience.

The technology also includes depressed state assessment of a person and the identification of his personal qualities by analyzing his activity and text messages in social networks.

The Big Five of personality traits is a model for describing the individual personality traits, which consists of five factors:

1. Extraversion.
2. Willingness to agree.
3. Consciousness.
4. Neuroticism.
5. Openness to experience.

Expressiveness of personality traits in the system can also be determined using special questionnaires that calculate each of the personality traits values of an individual on a set scale. For example, using the NEO-FFI questionnaire [12], one can determine the value of each of the person's five personality traits as an integer on a scale from 0 to 48.

The method of automatically detection of user's big five personal traits values is based on a supervised machine learning model. User's activity data in the social network and information extracted from his text messages are used as a set of features for this model. The described method can be divided into 2 stages:

1. Selection of personality traits expression informative features based on machine learning.
2. Identifying social network user personality traits.

As a result, a person's depressed state assessment and each of his personality traits assessment are determined.

After diseases risk assessing, a selection of preventive recommendations aimed at reducing the number of risk factors and/or their effect on diseases is carried out.

Recommendations selection, including lifestyle changes, is carried out on the basis of the obtained values of diseases risk factors analysis for a specific user. Each recommendation is associated with a number of risk factors and is aimed at optimizing their impact. For the recommendations selection, an argumentation algorithm is used, which makes this choice depending on the current indicators of health, lifestyle, problem areas and individual human characteristics. The algorithm is based on the inference from the knowledge base, which results in a list of recommendations, ranked by decreasing the appropriate level of risk and the number of risk factors affecting the disease risk. For each recommendations list, one can get an explanation of its output.

The last technology component is the task of drawing up a plan of preventive measures. This plan includes many preventive procedures, examinations, tests, etc., applied to the calendar grid. Health Manager formes it manually for each individual user on the basis of the plan of preventive measures of Ministry of Health and recommendations issued by the system. The end user can see his personal preventive plan formed by the Health Manager.

While personalized plan of preventive measures forming, health state, lifestyle, problem areas and individual characteristics of a person are taken into account.

The main purpose of the personalized plan of preventive measures forming method is to build an ordered list of preventive measures, both clinical and non-clinical. The Health Manager then creates a plan for the patient based on the preventive measures ordered list.

Health Manager is responsible for the formation of the complete plan of preventive measures. Some of the preventive measures are not related to risk factors. They serve rather to collect relevant information about human health. It is not necessary to perform all preventive measures, and the process of incorporating them into the plan can be automated.

Thus, the algorithm of a personalized plan of preventive measures forming method consists of the following steps:

1. request to the database for information to form a list of preventive measures;
2. launching the procedure for forming a preventive measures list;
3. sending a preventive measures list to the Health Manager to form a plan.

The algorithm is illustrated in Fig. 3.

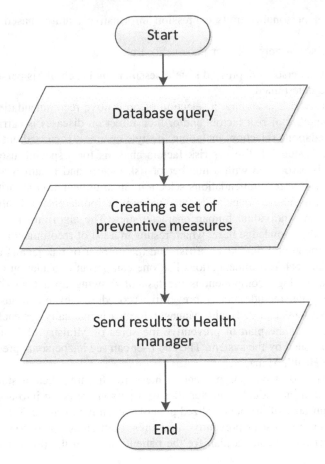

Fig. 3. The algorithm of the personalized plan of preventive measures forming method.

The inference is performed in accordance with the adapted algorithm described in the work [13]. Further, the Health Manager makes the final decision on the selection and placement of preventive measures, taking into account the time of their implementation.

The Health Manager may also assign any preventive measures from the list approved by the Ministry of Health, or appoint additional measures required by this user.

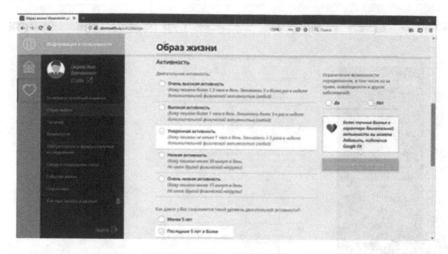

Fig. 4. Lifestyle Questionnaire.

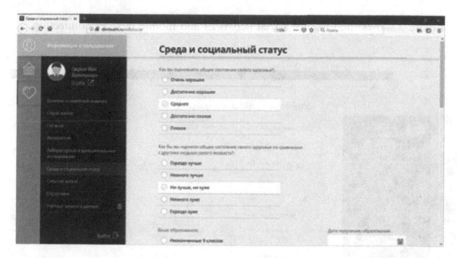

Fig. 5. Questionnaire about the environment and social status of the user. Psychological questionnaires are in a separate section.

The technology is currently undergoing comprehensive testing. Testing of individual software modules was carried out, and testing of the operation of all modules in the complex is currently being conducted. For this, an appropriate interface was developed. Now it is used to test the full cycle of the entire technology. The main interface fragments are presented in Figs. 4, 5, 6, 7, 8, 9 and 10.

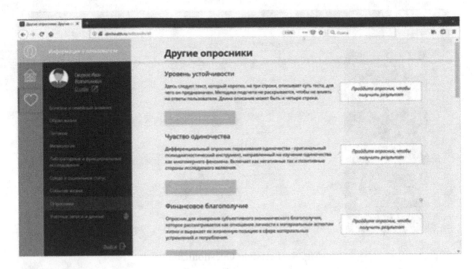

Fig. 6. Selecting questionnaires.

Figure 7 shows the form for social networks and mobile devices connecting.

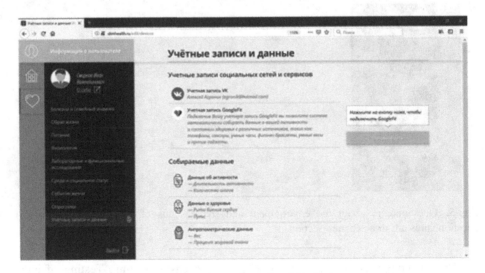

Fig. 7. Forms for social networks and mobile devices connecting.

Figures 8, 9 and 10 depict the forms of the risk assessment results and of the preventive recommendations choice.

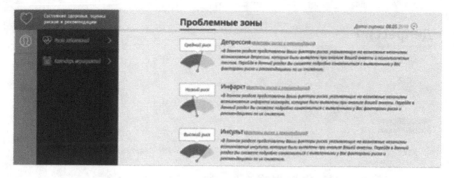

Fig. 8. Disease risk assessment.

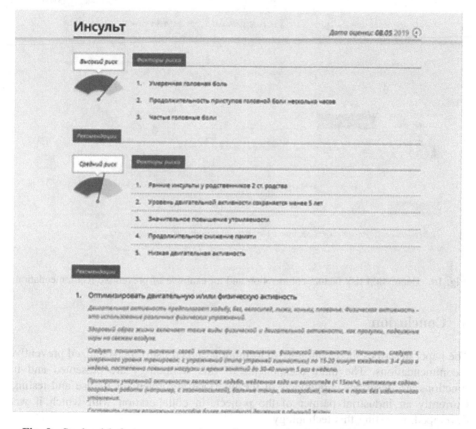

Fig. 9. Stroke risk factors enumeration and an example of preventive recommendation.

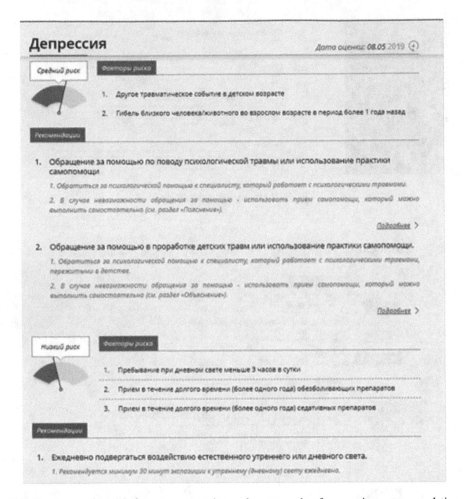

Fig. 10. Depression risk factors enumeration and an example of preventive recommendation.

3   Conclusion

The paper describes the technology of forming a ranked list of personalized preventive recommendations. The main components of this technology are presented and its functions are described. Fragments of the interface are given for its use and testing. Currently an industrial partner of the project, in collaboration with which it was developed, is testing this technology.

References

1. Welltok. https://www.welltok.com/
2. Welltory. https://welltory.com/ru/how-it-works/

3. Prins, B.P., et al.: Genome-wide analysis of health-related biomarkers in the UK household longitudinal study reveals novel associations. Sci. Rep. **7**(1), 11008 (2017)
4. Wigmore, E.M., et al.: Genome-wide association study of antidepressant treatment resistance in a population-based cohort using health service prescription data and meta-analysis with GENDEP. Pharmacogenomics J. 1 (2019)
5. Narasimhan, V.M., et al.: Health and population effects of rare gene knockouts in adult humans with related parents. Science **352**(6284), 474–477 (2016)
6. REST API. https://www.restapitutorial.com/
7. Danina, M.M., Kiselnikova, N.V., Smirnov, I.V.: Development of a method for assessing personalized risks of depression. In: The European Proceedings of Social & Behavioural Sciences EpSBS, vol. XLIX, pp. 181–189 (2018)
8. Osipov, G.S.: Formulation of Subject domain models: part I. Heterogeneous semantic nets. J. Comput. Syst. Sci. Int. **30**(5), 1–12 (1992)
9. Makarov, D.A., Molodchenkov, A.I.: Creation of systems of acquisition of knowledge for construction of medical expert systems on the basis of a kernel of software MedExp. J. Inf. Meas. Control Syst. **7**(12), 86–89 (2009)
10. Grigoriev, O.G., Kobrinskii, B.A., Osipov, G.S., Molodchenkov, A.I., Smirnov, I.V.: Health management system knowledge base for formation and support of a preventive measures plan. Procedia Comput. Sci. **145**, 238–241 (2018)
11. Grigoriev, O.G., Molodchenkov, A.I.: Risk health evaluation and selection of preventive measures plan with the help of argumental algorithm. In: Kuznetsov, S.O., Osipov, G.S., Stefanuk, V.L. (eds.) RCAI 2018. CCIS, vol. 934, pp. 280–290. Springer, Cham (2018). https://doi.org/10.1007/978-3-030-00617-4_26
12. Costa, P.T., McCrae, R.R.: NEO Five-Factor Inventory (NEO-FFI). Psychological Assessment Resources, Odessa (1989)
13. Osipov, G.S.: Methods for Artificial Intelligence, 2nd edn, p. 296. Fizmatlit, Moscow (2016)

Constructing Features of Competence-Oriented Specialist Models Based on Tutoring Integrated Expert Systems Technology

Galina V. Rybina(✉), Andrey Y. Nikiforov,
Elena S. Fontalina, and Ilya A. Sorokin

National Research Nuclear University MEPhI, Moscow, Russia
galina@ailab.mephi.ru

Abstract. The scientific and technological experience of the development and use of tutoring integrated expert systems and the creation of a single ontological space of knowledge and skills for the automated construction of competence-oriented models of specialists in the field of methods and technologies of artificial intelligence in the direction of training "Software engineering" obtained at the Department of Cybernetics of NRNU MEPhI is analyzed.

Keywords: Artificial intelligence · Tutoring integrated expert systems ·
Problem-oriented methodology · Intelligent software environment ·
AT-TECHNOLOGY workbench · Intellectual tutoring · Software engineering ·
Knowledge engineer · Student model · Competence-oriented specialist model ·
Ontology of courses/disciplines · Professional competences

1 Introduction

Historically, the priority research areas of the Department of Cybernetics of the National Research Nuclear University MEPhI and the basic fundamentals of training of engineers-mathematicians in the fields of Artificial Intelligence Systems, Computer Software, Information and Mathematical Systems of the Automated Control System, within the specialty Applied Mathematics, were closely related in the early 1970s in the scientific school of L.T. Kuzin in the field of artificial intelligence (AI). The main provisions of the scientific school of L.T. Kuzin and the research program until the mid-1980s were focused on the creation and evolutionary development of cybernetic models associated with the arrival of the new area of knowledge engineering, AI, and the development and research of a wide range of models and knowledge representation languages in the context of intellectual databanks.

A new stage in the formation of the scientific and educational appearance of the department in the field of AI began at the turn of the 1970s and 1980s, when several various areas related to the development of methods for constructing intelligent systems of various architectural typologies as the main products of AI emerged from the cybernetic scientific school of L.T. Kuzin. At the same time there appeared respective software, which took into account the need of training system programmers and specialists in programming technology.

S. O. Kuznetsov and A. I. Panov (Eds.): RCAI 2019, CCIS 1093, pp. 310–319, 2019.
https://doi.org/10.1007/978-3-030-30763-9_26

Therefore, for the educational process, in conjunction with courses on methods and technologies of AI, there were developed and tested at the base enterprises (NICEVT, INEUM, Keldysh Institute of Applied Mathematics, etc.) and in the educational and scientific laboratories of the department specialized courses on programming languages, fundamentals of translators, programming technology, modern software development tools, software verification and certification, basic systems modeling, etc. Basic education of programming and programming technology has become an integral part of training specialists in AI and a "calling card" of the graduates of the department.

Thus, the presence of a strong programming school at the Department of Cybernetics, long-term traditions of training specialists in the field of system software, and the influence of the works that have dominated in the domestic practice in the field of programming and design automation have allowed the full-fledged training of qualified specialists in methods and technologies for building a broad class of intelligent systems (static, dynamic and integrated expert systems, intelligent dialog systems, intelligent tutoring systems, intelligent agents and multi-agent systems, etc.), as well as to focus attention on the issues of the creation of various software tools to automate the process of designing and developing these classes of systems.

For the educational process, author's courses and programs were developed, original textbooks and tutorials on the basics of designing and programming technology of intelligent systems of various architectural typologies, studying problem-and subject-oriented languages for AI (PROLOGUE, LISP), as well as specialized tools (INTER-EXPERT, ECO, Level 5 Object, G2, AT-TECHNOLOGY, etc.).

In general, the formation of the modern scientific and educational appearance of the department in the field of artificial intelligence is naturally associated with the historical, conceptual and technological integration of all three of the above specializations within the basic specialty "Applied Mathematics", and the creation and active formation refers to the periods of 1971–1990 and 1991–2014. The current stage of development, starting in 2015, has been continuing in the framework of the direction of training "Software Engineering" (bachelor and magistrate programs).

It is important to note here that according to many experts, for example [1] and others, the area of "Software Engineering" is a natural development of programming technology, and the modern understanding of this area was formed much later than the appearance in our country of the term "programming technology"(only in 2004 in the SWEBOK knowledge core (Software Engineering Body of Knowledge), and in 2014 SWEBOK v. 3.0 was published, which received international recognition as ISO/IEC Technical Report 197596: 2015).

Consider some modern innovations in the field of AI technologies that are currently used for the practical implementation of the educational process at the Department of Cybernetics. A new approach is the development and use of tutoring integrated expert systems (IES) and the creation of a single ontological space of knowledge and skills for the automated construction of competence-oriented models of specialists in the field of AI in the area of "Software Engineering".

2   Features of Development and Use of Tutoring Integrated Expert Systems in the Educational Process of NRNU MEPhI

The use of the most modern scientific results in the field of AI, including teachers and staff of the Department is a long-term tradition of the organization of educational process on methods and technologies of AI at the Department of Cybernetics. In this case, we are talking about the theory and technology of construction of IES of different architectural typology, based on problem-oriented methodology [2] and intelligent software environment of the AT-TECHNOLOGY workbench [3, 4], providing a total automated support of the processes of development and maintenance of a wide class of static and dynamic IES, including tutoring IES and tutoring web-oriented IES (web-IES).

The problems related to the application of problem-oriented methodology and tools of the AT-TECHNOLOGY tutoring for the purposes of *intellectual tutoring* [3] through the development of intelligent tutoring systems (ITS), created on the basis of the architecture of tutoring IES and web-IES, were widely covered in the press of different years, for example [5–7], etc.

Currently, the possibility of effective practical implementation of such an approach to the construction of ITS is provided by two factors.

1. Active development of the conceptual foundations of the problem-oriented methodology, which allows on the basis of *scalable* architecture of IES [2] to implement a fairly powerful functionality necessary for modern ITS (construction of developed student models, adaptive tutoring models, models of problem areas, models of explanation, teacher models, models of applied ontologies of courses/disciplines/specialties, etc.).

2. The use of intelligent software technology (based on the means of the AT-TECHNOLOGY workbench) for automated support of the processes of constructing IES at all stages of the life cycle, providing archiving of the unique expert-methodological experience of subject teachers, reducing the intellectual load on knowledge engineers (knowledge analysts), reducing the development time of tutoring IES and web-IES [5, 6].

Since 2008, tutoring IES and web-IES, developed in the Intellectual Systems and Technologies laboratory of the Department of Cybernetics of the National Research Nuclear University MEPhI, have been actively used for automated support of basic courses/disciplines in the field of training of Applied Mathematics and Informatics and Software Engineering including: Introduction to Intelligent Systems, Models and Methods of Knowledge Representation and Processing, Intelligent Dialog Systems, Dynamic Intelligent Systems, Designing the Knowledge-Based Cybernetic Systems, Modern Intelligent System Architectures, Intelligent Simulation Modeling Tools, Intelligent Information Systems and etc. For all these courses and disciplines, using the basic tools of the AT-TECHNOLOGY workbench, the applied ontologies [3] are implemented and dynamically developed, which together form the "Intelligent Systems and Technologies" generalized ontology, which allowed to create a single ontological space of knowledge and skills through integration with ontologies of basic courses/disciplines on programming technology and to implement, practically, a full set of functional tasks typical of intelligent technology, including [3, 5]:

- *Individual planning* of the methodology for studying a specific training course (specifying on the basis of ontologies of courses/disciplines of a personal trajectory/tutoring strategy, individual control and identification of "problem areas" in students' knowledge and skills, optimization of individual learning, taking into account the psychological portrait of the learner, etc.);
- *Intelligent analysis* of learning tasks (modeling the reasoning of students solving learning tasks of various types, including using non-formalized methods, identifying types of errors and causes of their manifestation in knowledge and skills instead of their finding, feedback through dynamic updating of students' knowledge and skills, forecast grades on exams, etc.);
- *Intelligent decision support* (using technology of traditional expert systems (ES) and IES for intellectual assistance at each stage of solving educational problems, including extended explanations like "how?" and "why?", the choice of solutions, a hint of the next stage of the decision, etc.).

These capabilities of tutoring IES and web-IES fully correspond to the functional and technological aspects of modern foreign ITS, in particular [8–10], and adaptive tutoring systems [11], and also create prerequisites for further research on the implementation of promising approaches in the form of intelligent monitoring and intelligent collective tutoring, as well as for the semantic integration of individual tutoring IES with their parallel use in the educational process.

In modern conditions, the implementation of effective practical implementation and further functioning of the ITS of any architectural complexity is impossible without instrumental software support for the design and maintenance of the ITS at all stages of the life cycle. However, currently there is no accepted standard technology for the development of intelligent systems, including ITS. Therefore, for these purposes, either general-purpose tools and platforms are used, or specialized tools are created.

For example, the concept and general architecture of the Internet complex IACPaaS (Intelligent Application, Control and Platform as a Service) [12] is aimed at supporting common technological principles of development and use of applied and instrumental intelligent systems and their management. Based on this project, the cloud platform IACPaaS [13] is designed to support the development, management and remote use of application and instrumental multi-agent cloud services and their components for various subject areas. The IACPaaS platform is an example of a cloud platform for the implementation of programs that process information in the form of hierarchical homogeneous semantic networks, in particular, on its basis, an intelligent learning environment for the diagnosis of acute chronic diseases was implemented [14].

At the same time, the increasing number of international studies are focused on creating problem-oriented tools and technologies for the development of intelligent systems of different classes, for example [15, 16]. Interesting projects and approaches are also presented in domestic works [17, 18], etc.

The conceptual basis of the new approach used for instrumental support of problem-oriented methodology of construction of IES is the concept of the "intelligent environment model" [2], on the basis of which is currently implemented, experimentally investigated and actively used, including to support the educational process at the Department of Cybernetics and other universities, intelligent software engineering of automated construction of IES, combining approaches of knowledge engineering, ontological engineering, intelligent planning, and traditional programming [4, 19].

3 Ontological Approach to the Dynamic Formation of Competence-Oriented Models of Specialists

The ontology model in accordance with [3] is presented in the form of a semantic network in which vertices reflect various elements of courses/disciplines (sections, topics, subtopics, definitions, etc.), including a model of targeted competencies and a set of models of various learning influences on the identification of knowledge and the skills of the students. The edges of the network show different types of connections (relationships) between course elements, competencies, and learning influences.

Automated support for the construction of applied ontologies for each course/discipline based on this model is carried out using special tools that function as part of the AT-TECHNOLOGY workbench, closely described in [6, 19] and other works.

From a methodological point of view, it is important to note that by creating the ontology "Intelligent Systems and Technologies" (which has currently about 900 vertices from 8 courses/disciplines) it was possible to build a single ontological knowledge and skills space, which allows to

- implement the training cycle in accordance with [20], the curriculum and teaching materials (lectures, practical exercises, etc.);
- provide a fully functional construction of competence-oriented students models for the entire period of study (bachelor, master), and as a final result the formation of models of future professionals, including individual psychological portraits);
- compare the current competencies of the students with the target ones, identify the so-called "problem areas" in knowledge and plan the training effects in the form of solving specific practical tasks for each student in order to achieve a higher level of competencies, etc.;
- show great intelligent learning opportunities, namely: individual planning of the methodology for studying specific training courses; intellectual analysis of learning tasks; intellectual decision support, etc.

As a basic information and methodological resource for building models of professional competencies, in particular, for such professions as "software engineer", "system analyst", "IT system specialist", "software architect", etc. the professional standards for the Information Technology industry [21] were used quite effectively.

The main focus is traditionally placed on the ontologies of such disciplines as "Cybernetic Systems Programming Technology (Software Project Management)", "Software Systems Design and Architecture", "Designing of systems based on knowledge", "Dynamic Intelligent Systems", etc., within which students receive basic theoretical knowledge and practical techniques, typically for the development of traditional software systems and intellectual systems of various architectural typologies, including: life cycle and methodology design and development of software systems; various software system architectures; modeling in languages such as UML, testing, verification and certification of software; CASE-tools, workbench-systems and other types of tools that allow to automate the process of developing software systems, etc.

At present, there is no universal classification of competencies, however, the generally accepted point of view is the allocation of professional and universal competencies. Further specification depends on the specifics of the profession, the traditions of the university that trains specialists in this field, and other feature.

In this case, taking into account the long-term traditions of the Department of Cybernetics of NRNU MEPhI, it is, in fact, the integration of system and software engineering with methods and technologies of AI, so according to the Federal State Educational Standard 3+ [20], the two following competencies are used as the base ones for training knowledge engineers: *the formalization capacity in his or her subject area, with the view to the limitations on study methods in use; the ability to use methods and instrumental means of study of professional business items.*

The achievement of these target competencies is facilitated by the common ontological space of knowledge and skills, which is formed by the applied ontologies of courses/disciplines of several tutoring IES and web-IES. It is important to note that the general competency model, which is a component of the ontology base model in the form of a semantic network, is used in applied ontologies of courses/disciplines as a hierarchy of subject/problem-oriented private competences (with weights) reflecting the methodology of teaching specific courses.

As for the information necessary for the formation of social and personal competences (from the group of universal competences), taking into account the personal characteristics of the students, here you can partially use the information presented in the professional standards in the job description "self-development" for each specialty [20]. In addition, to identify personal characteristics, there are a large number of psychological tests, surveys, special sites, etc. For example, in the context of tutoring IES and web-IES [3, 5] for building models of students, the possibility of identifying about 20 personal characteristics and their correlation with an individual learning model. The main problem here is the search and selective selection of expert information, signaling the degree of manifestation of specific competence for each of the personal characteristics.

As the experience of the development and use of tutoring IES and web-IES in the educational process showed, the main problems in the formation of professional and universal competences are:

- Selection at each stage of training (bachelor, master) of the knowledge, skills and abilities that students should acquire (applied ontologies of courses/disciplines, generalized ontologies of individual areas of training are used);
- Improvement of methods of control and testing, conducted both with the purpose of forming current competence-oriented models of students, and upon completion of training (using the web-testing of students with the generation of variants based on a genetic algorithm);

- Effective account of the personal characteristics of students when selecting and shaping learning strategies and influences, including the development of special corrective learning influences aimed at developing individual student personal characteristics (the results of psychological tests of students are used together with various types of learning interactions);
- The use of additional (repeated) training on the basis of the identified gaps in knowledge and skills, etc. (the sets of learning interactions are used for different clusters of students).

In general, based on the experience of building competence-oriented models of graduates (bachelors and masters) in the field of Software Engineering, it is necessary to provide solutions to the following important tasks in the organization of the modern educational process:

- conceptual understanding of the programming process and instilling computational and logical thinking skills for the implementation of specific tasks in the form of a program and/or a software system;
- selection and use of various programming paradigms, including OO-oriented, functional, logical, environment-oriented, and various types of programming languages, as well as the development of competence in the use of a particular language;
- application of new approaches from the field of AI by presenting typical knowledge from the field of programming in the form of plans for solutions [9], to help students who have difficulty in moving from a method or algorithm for solving a problem to its software implementation.

An example of the implementation of the processes of automated construction of competence-oriented models of specialists in the field of knowledge engineering based on the ontology "Intelligent Systems and Technologies" is given in [7].

4   Review of the Monitoring of Tutoring IES Functioning Processes for the Dynamic Design of Competence-Oriented Models for Future Professionals

The monitoring of the functioning of tutoring IES and web-IES in this case is associated with "tracking" and analyzing all the processes of building for each student and personalized model of the student in the relevant discipline by identifying the current level of knowledge/skills using web testing and other methods, as well as the formation of a psychological portrait of the student's personality as an important component of the student model.

It should be noted that, in accordance with the problem-oriented methodology, the basis of the approach for constructing the current competence-based model of the student is a dynamic comparison of the results of web testing with the corresponding fragment of the applied ontology of the course/discipline. The result is the so-called "problematic areas" [3] in the knowledge of students in individual sections/subsections and the construction of current competencies, jointly reflecting the state of the student model not only in terms of knowledge level, but also providing a conceptual and technological connection with the processes of identifying skills solve some types of educational non-formalized tasks recommended in [3] or training in knowledge engineering.

It is also necessary to form lists of students (contingents) with high and/or low indicators of knowledge/skills, conduct systematic statistical data processing, as well as ensure the generation of current and final reports (statements) for departments and deans.

The final term logs that reflect the students the competence-oriented students models contain complete information about the students - assessments obtained during the control measures related to the identification of knowledge and skills, the current level of professional competence, information about passing psychological testing, information about independent work, the final forecast grades, as well as a real grade obtained in the exam (statements are formed for all students enrolled in a particular course/discipline).

An important place in the formation of the future specialist's model is given to the analytical and statistical processing of the results of the use of tutoring IES. By introducing special parameters that characterize both the individual learner and a specific contingent (cluster) of students. These parameters were formulated by an expert on the basis of an analysis of a fairly representative amount of data (about 2000 student models) and focused primarily on the basic structure of the student model [2], the components of which are: the student knowledge model, the student skills model, psychological portrait, model competences and other components).

Our experience has shown that the parameters (indicators) formed as a result of [6, 7] were the most popular from the point of view of building competence-oriented models of future specialists:

- analysis of the "problematic areas" of each student in specific courses/disciplines and their clustering;
- individual training planning (typology and sequence of learning influences, the influence of learning influences to increase the level of knowledge, the search for the most effective training impacts);
- calculating the correlation between current levels of knowledge and skills on relevant topics of the course/discipline;
- taking into account the psychological portrait of the student (personal degree of achievement of the target competencies for specific courses/disciplines, etc.);
- forecast assessment on the exam according to the results of the semester (analysis of reasoning in solving specific training problems).

A number of parameters are used to process information for the entire contingent of students (group, stream, etc.), namely: the cumulative analysis of "problem areas" for specific courses/disciplines and their clustering; assessment and clustering of individual training plans for specific courses/disciplines; forecast of the results of the examination session (connection of levels of knowledge and skills and assessment for the exam in the context of the course, analysis and clustering of psycho-types of students, etc.).

5 Conclusion

Thus, the methodical and technological experience in the domain of automated design using IES and web-IES of competence-oriented models of specialists in the domain of methods and technologies of AI shows big modern opportunities to promptly and efficiently review, adjust (focusing on the most modern innovations in the professional sphere), and predict the level and quality of the graduate cohort of professionals. This approach helps to establish relations both with employers and potential customers, and allows to plan targeted training of specialists in various areas, starting with junior courses.

Acknowledgements. The work was performed with the Russian Foundation for Basic Research support (Project No. 18-01-00457).

References

1. Lavrishcheva, E.M.: Software Engineering. Paradigms, Technologies and CASE-tools. Textbook for Universities. Yurayt Publishing House, Moscow (2016)
2. Rybina, G.V.: The Theory and Technology of Integrated Expert Systems Construction. Nauchtekhlitizdat, Moscow (2008)
3. Rybina, G.V.: Intellectual Systems: From A to Z: A Series of Monographs in Three Books. b.1: Knowledge-based Systems. Integrated Expert Systems. Nauchtekhlitizdat, Moscow (2014)
4. Rybina, G.V., Blokhin, Y.: Methods and software for intelligent planning for the construction of integrated expert systems. Artif. Intell. Decis. Mak. **1**, 12–28 (2018)
5. Rybina, G.V.: Intellectual technology of construction of training integrated expert systems: new opportunities. Open Educ. **21**(4), 43–57 (2017)
6. Rybina, G.V., Rybin, V.M., Blokhin, Y.M., Sergienko, E.S.: Intelligent support of educational process basing on ontological approach with use of tutoring integrated expert systems. In: Abraham, A., Kovalev, S., Tarassov, V., Snasel, V., Vasileva, M., Sukhanov, A. (eds.) IITI 2017. AISC, vol. 680, pp. 11–20. Springer, Cham (2018). https://doi.org/10.1007/978-3-319-68324-9_2
7. Rybina, G.V., Fontalina, E.S.: Automated construction of young specialists models with the use of tutoring integrated expert systems. In: Proceedings of IV International Conference on Information Technologies in Engineering Education, pp. 41–44 (2018)
8. Nye, B.D.: Intelligent tutoring systems by and for the developing world: a review of trends and approaches for educational technology in a global context. Int. J. Artif. Intell. Educ. **25**, 177–203 (2015)
9. Bonner, D., Walton, J., Dorneich, M.C., Gilbert, S.B., Winer, E., Sottilare, R.A.: The development of a testbed to assess an intelligent tutoring system for teams. In: Workshops at the 17th International Conference on Artificial Intelligence in Education, AIED-WS 2015, CEUR Workshop Proceedings (2015)
10. Rahman, A.A., Abdullah, M., Alias, S.H.: The architecture of agent-based intelligent tutoring system for the learning of software engineering function point metrics. In: 2nd International Symposium on Agent, Multi-Agent Systems and Robotics, ISAMSR 2016, pp. 139–144 (2016)

11. Sosnovsky, S., Mitrovic, A., Lee, D., Brusilovsky, P., Yudelson, M.: Ontology-based integration of adaptive educational systems. In: 16th International Conference on Computers in Education (ICCE 2008), pp. 11–18 (2008)
12. Gribova, V.V., Kleshchev, A.S., Krylov, D.A., Moskalenko, F.M., et al.: Complex for intelligent systems based on cloud computing. In: Artificial Intelligence and Decision-Making, no. 1, pp. 27–35 (2011)
13. Gribova, V.V., Kleshchev, A.S., Krylov, D.A., Moskalenko, F.M., et al.: Basic technology for the development of intelligent services on the cloud platform IACPaaS. Part 1. Development of knowledge base and problem solver. In: Software Engineering, no. 12, pp. 3–11 (2015)
14. Gribova, V.V., Ostrovsky G.E.: Intellectual learning environment for the diagnosis of acute chronic diseases. In: Fifteenth National Conference on Artificial Intelligence with International Participation of CII-2016. Proceedings of the Conference, pp. 171–179. T3. Universum, Smolensk (2016)
15. Burita, L.: Intelligent software ATOM for knowledge systems development. In: Proceedings of the IADIS International Conference Intelligent Systems and Agents 2013, ISA 2013, Proceedings of the IADIS European Conference on Data Mining 2013, ECDM 2013 (2013)
16. Gharaibeh, N., Soud, S.A.: Software development methodology for building intelligent decision support systems. In: Doctoral Consortium on Software and Data Technologies – Proceedings of the Doctoral Consortium on Software and Data Technologies, DCSOFT 2008; In Conjunction with ICSOFT 2008, pp. 3–14 (2008)
17. Telnov, Yu.F., Kazakov, V.A.: Ontological modeling of network interactions of organizations in the information and educational space. In: Fifteenth National Conference on Artificial Intelligence With International Participation of CII-2016. Proceedings of the Conference, pp. 106–114. T1. Universum, Smolensk (2016)
18. Trembach, V.M.: Systems of management of databases of the evolving knowledge for the solution of problems of continuous education. MESI, Moscow (2013)
19. Rybina, G.V., Blokhin, Y., Tarakchyan, L.S.: Intelligent planning and control of integrated expert systems development process. Adv. Intell. Syst. Comput. **848**, 266–271 (2018)
20. The portal of the Federal state educational standards of higher education. www.fgosvo.ru
21. Development of professional standards for the information technology industry. The Committee on education in the IT field. The website APIT. http://www.apkit.ru/default.asp?artID=5573

UAV Trajectory Tracking Based on Local Interpolating Splines and Optimal Choice of Knots

Mikhail Khachumov[1,2]($\boxtimes$) ⓘ and Vyacheslav Khachumov[1,2] ⓘ

[1] Federal Research Center "Computer Science and Control" of the Russian Academy of Sciences, Vavilova str. 44/2, 119333 Moscow, Russia
khmike@inbox.ru
[2] RUDN University, Miklukho-Maklaya str. 6, 117198 Moscow, Russia

Abstract. We consider trajectory-tracking problem for an unmanned aerial vehicle (UAV) based on optimal choice of knots of the interpolating spline. As examples, we use typical second-order curves: ellipses, parabolas, hyperbolas, obtained by cutting a cone with planes. The rules are proposed for rational placement of a given number of knots for curves given in parametric form. The use of spline interpolation methods opens the way to developing mathematical tools for tracking complex trajectories, storing geometrical information in a compact form and reproducing trajectories with a predetermined accuracy on a general basis. The research is focused on parametric cubic Hermite spline and Bezier curves, which are characterized by simplicity of computational implementation. We have conducted experimental studies to search for the optimal allocation of knots. The problem of moving along the route represented by a parabola has been investigated under wind loads taking into account the mathematical model of the aerial vehicle. We consider an approach to dynamic motion planning based on strategies and rules that imitate actions of a pilot when rapid actions are needed.

Keywords: UAV · Motion trajectory · Modeling · Conic sections · Hermite local spline · Bezier curve · Interpolation nodes · Optimization

1 Introduction

1.1 Motivation

When reproducing complex trajectories and performing trajectory tracking for robotic systems, in particular, unmanned aerial vehicles (UAVs), one can use methods of pointwise and analytical descriptions of curves. The analytical description gives a more compact representation, which simplifies the processes of transformation and outputting of information. However, special algorithms to rational output calculated values are necessary, providing, on the one hand, the required quality, which means the accuracy of reproduction, and, on the other hand, the computational efficiency of output tools, i.e. their versatility and speed.

S. O. Kuznetsov and A. I. Panov (Eds.): RCAI 2019, CCIS 1093, pp. 320–334, 2019.
https://doi.org/10.1007/978-3-030-30763-9_27

The method of so-called piecewise conic approximation is often used in aerospace applications. Here, the combination of rectilinear and conic segments (ellipses, parabolas, hyperbolas) is applied to modeling complex motions. Such a representation is used, for example, in the task of planning the landing process of unmanned aerial vehicles on the surface of the moving platform [1]. In this case, a UAV trajectory consists of four sections containing (1) two circular arc sections, (2) a linear section connecting the points of two circular maneuvers, (3) a landing section, which in turn consists of parabolic and linear segments. The disadvantage of piecewise conic approximation is the lack of a universal method that combine motion and control planning. The complexity of the problem is due to the fact that the coordinates of the joint points are not strictly defined, which leads to the need of using numerical methods to obtaining motion parameters.

The well-known method of constructing typical curves (ellipses, parabolas, hyperbolas) using equal-perimeter lengths [2] gives, with a sufficient number of points, good quality, but it is time-consuming and redundant in terms of the number of knots. Special algorithms designed to create certain curves are not applicable for creating unified output tools. Spline interpolation approach provides universality of computational procedures for reproducing various curves and allows one to develop mathematical software on a unified methodological basis and reproduce curves with predetermined accuracy. Local splines are of considerable interest and characterized by simplicity of computational implementation [3]. There is a strong need to investigate applicability of local splines, in particular Hermite splines and Bezier curves, to support trajectory tracking for robotic systems.

1.2   Related Works

The analysis of state-of-the-art research papers shows the expediency and relevance of using spline functions to solve complex problems of trajectory planning and tracking for autonomous aerial vehicles. In paper [4], to model UAV trajectories the authors propose to use quadratic Bezier curves due to their simplicity and the fact that the first derivative at any point on the curve can be easily computed. The method of Bezier curves allows for quick computation of curvature, reduces the number of state variables and simplifies calculation of certain flight constraints, such as minimum turn radius. Paper [5] concerns constructing a trajectory based on Bezier curves for visiting a given set of points in the shortest time possible by an unmanned flight vehicle. The waypoints to be visited can be at different altitudes, and the addressed problem is to find a fast and smooth 3-D trajectory that allows UAV to capture all areas of interest. The proposed solution is based on machine learning herewith the requested trajectory is determined as a sequence of Bézier curves. The obtained results confirm feasibility of the proposed approach which has also been experimentally verified with a real UAV. Paper [6] considers finding a feasible trajectory for a UAV that should pass through a set of given points, where the starting and ending points are known. The maximum flight time serves as a limiting factor for a number of points that can be visited. To generate smooth trajectories for a UAV the author use Hermite splines. The minimal time of flight estimate for a given Hermite spline is calculated using known motion model of the UAV limited by maximum velocity and acceleration. Paper [7] is devoted to path planning and tracking for robotic systems in real time using cubic Hermite splines. The velocity profile of the obtained trajectory is determined in order to achieve smooth movement within given physical constraints. One of the modern approaches for UAVs trajectory planning is to use B-splines [8, 9]. In contrast to linear and polynomial interpolations, one of the positive points of B-splines is high interactivity which enables to rationally modify the shape of the curve. If the order of the B-spline curve is equal to the number of control points, it reduces to a Bezier curve.

1.3   Main Contributions

This paper deals with the problem of generating complex UAV trajectories based on optimal choice of knots of the interpolating spline. As movement trajectories we use typical second-order curves: ellipses, parabolas, hyperbolas, obtained by cutting a cone with planes. The problem of optimal choice of knots for local interpolating splines is considered, and the rules are proposed for the placement of a given number of knots for curves defined in a parametric form. As local splines we use Hermite parametric cubic spline and Bezier curves (four-point and five-point), which are characterized by simplicity of computational implementation. Experimental studies have been conducted to find optimal knots for a parametric cubic Hermite spline. A method is proposed that allows one to construct a Bezier curve exactly passing through preselected points. The problem of moving along a route represented by a parabola was experimentally simulated under wind perturbations. The developed software contains an intelligent control module able to quickly respond to changes in external conditions taking into account mathematical models of wind loads and aerial vehicles.

2   Finding the Parameters of Typical Curves Defined by Conic Sections

We first determine the parameters of second-order curves: ellipses, parabolas, and hyperbolas, obtained by cutting a cone with planes. Next, we find dependencies between the parameters of the curve, the cone, and the cutting plane P.

1. An ellipse defined as $\frac{x^2}{a^2} + \frac{y^2}{b^2} = 1$ is formed as a result of cutting a cone with a plane P that is perpendicular to its axis and not parallel to any of its generating lines. Semi-axis values (a, b) are ones of its general parameters. Let the cone be defined, for example, by the value of the its half-base A and an angle of generating line β, and the section is specified by an angle α and the anchor point, which is moved from the point of intersection of the cone axis with its base by value B. The problem has a solution if $\alpha < \beta$ and $A < B$. The parameters of the ellipse are calculated as follows:

$$a = (A - B)tg(\beta)^2(\cos(\alpha)/(\cos(\alpha)^2 tg(\beta)^2 - \sin(\alpha)^2),$$
$$b = A - Btg(\alpha)/tg(\beta) + (A - B)/(ctg(\alpha)^2 tg(\beta)^2 - 1).$$

2. A parabola is obtained when a secant plane P passes perpendicular to XOY plane and parallel to one of the generating lines of the cone (at an angle β). A parabola is given by the equation $y^2 = 2px$. One of its major parameters is the focal length $a = p/2$. We assume that its anchor point is moved from the generator along the OX axis by a value X_1 $(0 < X_1 < 2A)$. After transformations we get

$$p = X_1 \cos(\beta), \ a = 1/2X_1 \cos(\beta).$$

3. A hyperbola is defined as a result of cutting a cone with the plane P perpendicular to XOY plane and parallel to OX axis. A hyperbola is described by an equation $\frac{x^2}{a^2} - \frac{y^2}{b^2} = 1$ in the coordinate system defined on the plane P. As in the previous case, the anchor point of the section plane is defined by value X_1, $0 < X_1 < A$. We obtain:

$$a = (A - X_1)tg(\beta)), \ b = aY_B/\sqrt{X_B^2 - a^2},$$

where $X_B = Atg(\beta)$, $Y_B = \sqrt{A^2 - (A - X_1)^2} = \sqrt{X_1(2A - X_1)}$.

Thus, we determined dependencies between the parameters of conic sections.

3 Formulation of the Problem

We propose a combined approach to specify a UAV trajectory based on spline interpolation apparatus implementing trajectories represented by a combination of conic segments.

The general formulation of the problem contains the following subtasks:

1. Construct the trajectory using the piecewise conic approximation method.
2. For each analytically defined conic segment $y = f(x)$, $x = [a, b]$ construct the spline $d(x)$, which coincides in the reference nodes of the grid with the function $f(x)$.
3. Find optimal location of knots in accordance with a given quality criterion.
4. Perform flight simulations, taking into account the mathematical models of a UAV and wind loads in the MATLAB system.

This paper solves the problems of constructing and modeling motion trajectory of an aircraft-type UAV in accordance with the proposed criterion that evaluate deviation from the conical sections interpolated by a cubic Hermite spline.

4 Optimal Choice of Knots of the Interpolating Spline

The choice of interpolation knots is an essential problem that depend on the required accuracy of trajectory reproduction. Let $S(x, t)$, $S(y, t)$ determine interpolating spline. We introduce a parameter $\theta = \theta$ (i, t) characterizing the angle of inclination of the vector drawn from the origin for an ellipse, or from a focal point for a parabola and a hyperbola, and passing through the point $p'(S(x, t), S(y, t))$ to its intersection with the interpolating curve in point p. Then the relative deviation of the radius-vectors of points p and p' with the same value of the angular parameter θ is equal to

$$\delta(\theta) = \frac{\left| R_{p'}(\theta) - R_p(\theta) \right|}{R_{p'}(\theta)},$$

where

$R_{p'}(\theta) = \sqrt{(S(x,\theta) - \alpha)^2 + S(y,\theta)^2}$ is the radius-vector of point p',

$R_p(\theta) = \sqrt{(x(\theta) - \alpha)^2 + y(\theta)^2}$ is the radius-vector of point p on the interpolating curve.

Given the symmetry of the contours of sections, we get the following relations: for an ellipse:

$$\alpha = 0, \ x(\theta) = \frac{ab}{\sqrt{a^2 k^2 + b^2}}, \ y(\theta) = \frac{b}{a}\sqrt{a^2 - x^2(\theta)}, \ k = \frac{S(y,\theta)}{S(x,\theta)}, \ \theta_{max} = \frac{\pi}{2};$$

for a parabola:

$$\alpha = a, \ x(\theta) = a + \frac{2a}{k^2}\left(1 + sign(S(x,\theta) - a)\sqrt{1 + k^2}\right),$$

$$y(\theta) = 2\sqrt{ax(\theta)}, \ k = \frac{S(y,\theta)}{S(x,\theta) - a}, \ \theta_{max} = \sqrt{\frac{X}{a}},$$

where X is the parameter defining the constraint for OX axis;

for a hyperbola:

$$\alpha = c, \ x(\theta) = \frac{1}{a^2 k^2 - b^2}\left(a^2 k^2 c + sign(S(x,\theta) - c)ab^2\sqrt{1 + k^2}\right),$$

$$y(\theta) = \frac{b}{a}\sqrt{x(\theta)^2 - a^2}, k = \frac{S(y,\theta)}{S(x,\theta) - c}, \theta_{max} = arcch\left(\frac{X}{a}\right),$$

where a, b, c, X are the parameters of the sections,

$$sign(x) = \begin{cases} 1, & x > 0 \\ -1, & x < 0. \end{cases}$$

The problem of optimal approximation of the contour of a conic section is formulated as follows: find knots, such that

$$\max_{\theta \in [0, \theta_{max}]} \delta(\theta) \to \min. \tag{1}$$

Theoretically, the problem of optimal choice of knots for interpolating local splines was considered, for example, in [10], where the authors obtained an expression for the asymptotically best location of nodes for $N \to \infty$. However, the practical application of the results obtained in the paper is rather complex. In the present work, to obtain knots we use special algorithms [2], designed to draw ellipses, parabolas and hyperbolas, and allowing to place points on a curve in a certain rational way.

The rules for allocation of a given number of knots for curves defined in a parametric form are associated with setting equal angular increments $d\theta$. Recurrent expressions for allocation of points for the first quadrant are as follows:

for a circle:

$$x(\theta)_{n+1} = x(\theta)_n \cos(d\theta) - y(\theta)_n \sin(d\theta),$$

$$y(\theta)_{n+1} = x(\theta)_n \sin(d\theta) + y(\theta)_n \cos(d\theta), \ d\theta = \frac{\pi}{N-1};$$

for an ellipse:

$$x(\theta)_{n+1} = x(\theta)_n - a\sin(\theta)d\theta, \ y(\theta)_{n+1} = y(\theta)_n + b\cos(\theta)d\theta, \ d\theta = \frac{\pi}{N-1};$$

for a parabola:

$$x(\theta)_{n+1} = x(\theta)_n + y(\theta)_n d\theta + a(d\theta)^2,$$

$$y(\theta)_{n+1} = y(\theta)_n + 2a(d\theta), \ d\theta = \frac{\theta_{max}}{N-1}, \ \theta_{max} = \sqrt{\frac{X}{a}};$$

for a hyperbole:

$$x(\theta)_{n+1} = x(\theta)_n ch(d\theta) + \frac{a}{b} y(\theta)_n sh(d\theta),$$

$$y(\theta)_{n+1} = \frac{b}{a} x(\theta)_n sh(d\theta) + y(\theta)_n ch(d\theta), \ d\theta = \frac{\theta_{max}}{N-1}, \ \theta_{max} = arcch\left(\frac{X}{a}\right).$$

5   Approximation of a Conic Section by a Bezier Curve

The Bezier curve is a very convenient and widely used tool for generating smooth curves. One of the curve feature is that its shape is completely determined by a polygon defined for a set of given points, and it directly passes only through the first and ending points. A polygon uniquely defines the shape of a curve [3]. The first and last vertices lie on a curve, while other vertices determine the derivatives, the order and the type of the curve. This method allows modifying the shape and order of the curve by changing the number of points until you reach the desired result. A method is proposed that allows one to draw a Bezier curve passing exactly through pre-selected points.

The Bezier curve is described by a polynomial function:

$$P(t) = \sum_{i=0}^{n} P_i J_{n,i}(t),$$

where $J_{n,i}(t)$ is a basic function of the form:

$$J_{n,i}(t) = \frac{n!}{i!(n-i)!} t^i (1-t)^{n-i}.$$

Here $t = 0, \ldots, 1$ is a parameter, $i = 0, \ldots, n$ is a point number. Thus, the Bezier curve is determined by $(n+1)$ points of the polygon.

5.1   Four-Point Bezier Curve

For a four-point curve, we get the following third-order polynomial [3]:

$$P(t) = P_0 J_{3,0}(t) + P_1 J_{3,1}(t) + P_2 J_{3,2}(t) + P_3 J_{3,3}(t),$$

where $J_{3,0}(t) = (1-t)^3, J_{3,1}(t) = 3t(1-t)^2, J_{3,2}(t) = 3t^2(1-t), J_{3,3}(t) = t^3$; and P_0, P_1, P_2, P_3 are the coordinates of given points.

To draw a four-point Bezier curve passing exactly through points $P_0 = (x_0, y_0), P_1 = (x_1, y_1), P_2 = (x_2, y_2), P_3 = (x_3, y_3)$, one should replace points P_1, P_2 by points $P_1^* = (x_1^*, y_1^*)$, $P_2^* = (x_2^*, y_2^*)$. The Bezier curve is described in this case by the following equations:

$$x(t) = x_0(1-t)^3 + x_1^* \cdot 3t(1-t)^2 + x_2^* \cdot 3t^2(1-t) + x_3 t^3,$$
$$y(t) = y_0(1-t)^3 + y_1^* \cdot 3t(1-t)^2 + y_2^* \cdot 3t^2(1-t) + y_3 t^3.$$

Suppose that if $t = t_1$, then takes place $x(t_1) = x_1, y(t_1) = y_1$ and if $t = t_2$ then takes place $x(t_2) = x_2, y(t_2) = y_2$. We obtain:

$$x_1^* = \frac{x_1 - x_0(1-t_1)^3 - x_3 t_1^3}{3t_1(1-t_1)^2} - \frac{x_2^* t_1}{1-t_1}, \quad x_2^* = \frac{A_x}{B},$$

where:

$$A_x = x_2 - x_0(1 - t_2)^3 - \frac{(x_1 - x_0(1 - t_1)^3 - x_3 t_1^3)t_2(1 - t_2)^2}{t_1(1 - t_1)^2} - x_3 t_2^3,$$

$$B = 3t_2^2(1 - t_2) - \frac{3t_1 t_2(1 - t_2)^2}{1 - t_1}.$$

Formulas for calculating variables y_1^*, y_2^* are similar. To determine values t_1, t_2 we use the following approximate method. As an intermediate parameter, we use the length of the polyline formed by the segments connecting successively the points (x_0, y_0), (x_1, y_1), (x_2, y_2), (x_3, y_3). Let D be equal to $d_1 + d_2 + d_3$ where d_i, $i = (1,2,3)$ be the distance between points (x_{i-1}, y_{i-1}), (x_i, y_i). Then, approximately, we get: $t_1 = d_1/D$, $t_2 = (d_1 + d_2)/D$. Thus, all the parameters necessary for calculating (x_1^*, y_1^*), (x_2^*, y_2^*) are determined.

To draw a Bezier curve passing through the points (x_0, y_0), (x_1, y_1), (x_2, y_2), (x_3, y_3) it is necessary and sufficient that the following system of equations is valid:

$$x_1 = x_0(1 - t_1)^3 + x_{11}3t_1(1 - t_1)^2 + x_{21}3t_1^2(1 - t_1) + x_3 t_1^3 \tag{2}$$

$$x_2 = x_0(1 - t_2)^3 + x_{11}3t_2(1 - t_2)^2 + x_{21}3t_2^2(1 - t_2) + x_3 t_2^3 \tag{3}$$

$$y_1 = y_0(1 - t_1)^3 + y_{11}3t_1(1 - t_1)^2 + y_{21}3t_1^2(1 - t_1) + y_3 t_1^3 \tag{4}$$

$$y_2 = y_0(1 - t_2)^3 + y_{11}3t_2(1 - t_2)^2 + y_{21}3t_2^2(1 - t_2) + y_3 t_2^3 \tag{5}$$

Here, t_1, t_2 are the values of parameter t ($0 \le t \le 1$) at the points (x_1, y_1), (x_2, y_2); (x_{11}, y_{11}), (x_{21}, y_{21}) are two additional points that, jointly with (x_0, y_0) and (x_3, y_3), define the desired polygon setting the required curve. Since the curve has a parametric form, the equations for x and y coordinates are identical, what allows us to operate with a single coordinate while performing transformations. From (2) we obtain:

$$x_{11} = (x_1 - x_0(1 - t_1)^3 - x_3 t_1^3)/(3t_1(1 - t_1)^2) - x_{21}t_1/(1 - t_1).$$

We substitute the value of x_{11} into (3), and after the corresponding transformations, obtain $x_{21} = A_x/B_x$, where

$$A_x = x_2 - x_0(1 - t_2)^3 - (x_1 - x_0(1 - t_1)^3 - x_3 t_1^3)t_2(1 - t_2)^2/(t_1(1 - t_1)^2) - x_3 t_2^3,$$
$$B_x = 3t_2^2(1 - t_2) - 3t_1 t_2(1 - t_2)^2/(1 - t_1).$$

Formulas for calculating variables y_{11}, y_{21} are similar. Thus, all the parameters necessary for calculating (x_{11}, x_{21}) and (y_{11}, y_{21}) are determined and we can construct the curve by the formulas:

$$x(t) = x_0(1-t)^3 + x_{11}3t(1-t)^2 + x_{21}3t_1^2(1-t) + x_3t^3,$$
$$y(t) = y_0(1-t)^3 + y_{11}3t(1-t)^2 + y_{21}3t_1^2(1-t) + y_3t^3.$$

The curve has interpolation properties since it passes through all given points. Figure 1 shows the typical and interpolating Bezier curves, as well as the original and calculated (external) polygons that define the shape of the typical and interpolating Bezier curve, respectively.

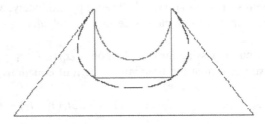

Fig. 1. Construction of typical and interpolating four-point Bezier curves

The proposed approach of using the Bezier curve allows one to expand the possibilities of interpolation for smooth motion trajectories of robotic systems.

5.2 Five-Point Bezier Curve

It is advisable to apply a similar approach to a five-point Bezier curve, since it allows, under certain conditions, to draw ellipsoids and circles. Here, 3 additional points (x_{11}, y_{11}), (x_{21}, y_{21}), (x_{31}, y_{31}) are to be determined, which ensure the curve to pass through the given five points. A five-point Bezier curve is defined by the following equations:

$$x(t) = x_0(1-t)^4 + x_{11}4t(1-t)^3 + x_{21}6t^2(1-t)^2 + x_{31}4t^3(1-t) + x_4t^4,$$
$$y(t) = y_0(1-t)^4 + y_{11}4t(1-t)^3 + y_{21}6t^2(1-t)^2 + y_{31}4t^3(1-t) + y_4t^4.$$

An example of constructing five-point Bezier curves is presented in Fig. 2

As one can see from the figure, the curve does not pass through inner points of the polygon.

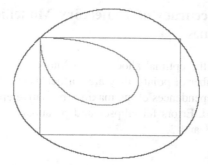

Fig. 2. Construction of typical and interpolating five-point Bezier curves

6 Approximation of a Conic Section by a Hermite Spline

The expression for the local cubic Hermite spline has the following form [3]:

$$
\begin{aligned}
S(x,t) &= x_i(1 - 3t^2 + 2t^3) + x_{i+1}(3t^2 - 2t^3) + x_i'd_i(t - 2t^2 + t^3) - x_{i+1}'d_i(t^2 - t^3), \\
S(y,t) &= y_i(1 - 3t^2 + 2t^3) + y_{i+1}(3t^2 - 2t^3) + y_i'd_i(t - 2t^2 + t^3) - y_{i+1}'d_i(t^2 - t^3).
\end{aligned}
\tag{6}
$$

Here, (x_i, y_i) are the coordinates of the i–th knot, d_i is the distance between knots $(x_i\ y_i)$, (x_{i+1}, y_{i+1}), x_i', y_i' are the approximate values of the derivatives at the i–th knot; $i = 0,1,...,N$; N is the number of knots; the parameter t varies within $(0,1)$.

For convenience, a spline can be represented in another form. For example, after opening the brackets and regrouping (6), we get:

$$
S(x,t) = x_i + t(C_i + t(B_i + tA_i)),
\tag{7}
$$

where

$$
C_i = x_i'd_i, \quad A_i = 2D_i + C_i + x_{i+1}'d_i, \quad D_i = x_i - x_{i+1}, \quad B_i = -(A_i + C_i + D_i),
$$

The resulting expression for the spline (7) contains only the multiplication and addition operations, what simplifies its hardware implementation [11]. Another representation according to Horner's scheme is as follows:

$$
(((((((((x_i - x_{i+1})\frac{2}{d_i} + x_i)t + x_{i+1}') - x_i')\frac{2d_i}{3} - x_i) + x_{i+1})\frac{3}{d_i} - x_{i+1}')t + x_i')d_i t + x_i.
\tag{8}
$$

Expressions (7), (8) are executed repeatedly for all t and can be effectively implemented in a conveyor-type processor.

7 Studies of the Accuracy of Trajectory Modelling by Hermite Splines

Experimental studies of the optimal allocation of knots have been carried out. After allocating the given number of points, they are further used as knots for interpolation with Hermite splines. Dependences of the maximum relative error $\delta\%$ and the number of knots N were obtained. Errors for ellipses and parabolas with different parameters are presented in Tables 1 and 2.

Table 1. Relative error of ellipse generation

N	b/a parameter									
	0.1	0.2	0.3	0.4	0.5	0.6	0.7	0.8	0.9	1.0
7	13	12	10	8	6	5	4.5	4.0	3.2	2.5
9	7.5	6.6	5.2	4.0	3.0	2.8	2.2	1.8	1.2	1.0
11	5.8	4.6	3.5	2.5	2.2	2.0	1.8	1.5	1.0	0.6
13	4.3	3.2	2.5	1.8	1.5	1.2	0.9	0.8	0.2	0.2
15	3.5	2.6	1.8	1.2	0.9	0.7	0.2	0.2	0.2	0.2
17	3.0	2.2	1.2	1.0	0.8	0.2	0.2	0.2	0.2	0.2
19	2.4	1.6	1.2	0.8	0.7	0.2	0.2	0.2	0.2	0.2

Table 2. Relative error of parabola generation

N	b/a parameter					
	1	2	3	4	5	6
3	1.8	4.8	8.4	12.0	16.5	20.8
4	0.5	1.8	2.6	4.2	5.6	7.2
5	0.4	1.6	1.2	1.8	2.5	3.2
6	0.2	0.4	0.8	1.0	1.2	1.8
7	0.2	0.3	0.3	0.5	0.9	1.2
8	0.2	0.2	0.2	0.3	0.8	1.0
9	0.2	0.2	0.2	0.2	0.2	0.5

Information about the type of conic section and its parameters allows us to obtain necessary dependencies and choose the number of knots. Calculation of δ is time-consuming and therefore the data establishing the relationship between the type of the curve, the accuracy and the number of knots should be stored in the database in advance. Table 3 shows trajectories of the various curves constructed by Hermite splines when knots are given and the dependence of the error on the curve parameters.

Table 3. Examples of generated curves

Typical parameters	Visualization

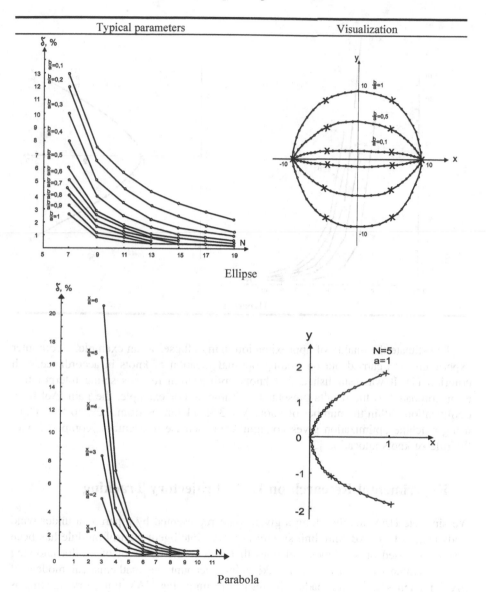

Ellipse

Parabola

(*continued*)

Table 3. (*continued*)

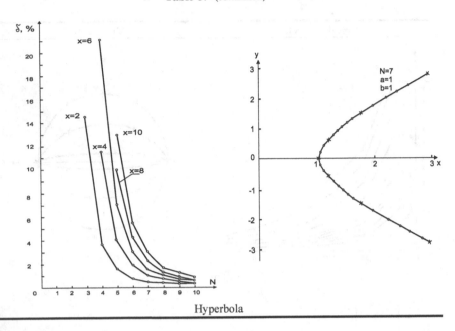

Hyperbola

To estimate the quality of approximation using ellipses as an example, a computer experiment was carried out on finding optimal location of knots in accordance with criterion (1). It was established that knots optimization reduces spline interpolation error compared to the results presented in Table 1. For example, the gain $|\Delta\delta|$ from optimization within the number of knots $N = 3 \div 11$ ranges from 0.2% to 5%. Thus, using machine optimization gives no significant increase in accuracy, compared with the rule of knots allocation [2].

8   Experimental Research on UAV Trajectory Tracking

We simulate UAV motion along a given route represented by a parabola under wind loads using MATLAB Simulink system [12]. An intelligent control module has been developed based on strategies and rules that imitate the behavior of a pilot allowing quickly synthesize control actions taking into account the mathematical models of UAV dynamics and wind loads. The result of simulating UAV trajectory tracking is shown in Fig. 3.

At first, we solve the problem of optimizing the location of interpolation knots (red markers) with the proposed method. Next, we solve the problems of interpolating a trajectory with the Hermite spline and selecting additional reference points (gray markers).

A series of carried out experiments and the obtained results confirm the feasibility of interpolating UAV trajectories by local splines, in particular Hermite spline and Bezier curve.

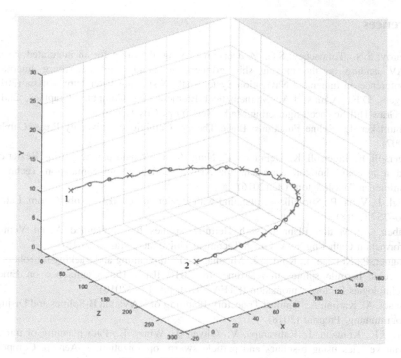

Fig. 3. UAV trajectory tracking

9 Conclusion

The analysis of state-of-the-art papers showed the demand for using spline functions in solving complex problems of trajectory planning and tracking for UAVs. To generate the required trajectory we propose to use Hermite splines and Bezier curves as local parametric interpolating splines. A method is proposed that allows one to draw a Bezier curve passing directly through selected points.

The considered algorithms for generating knots of typical conic sections and the subsequent interpolation of curves using local parametric splines are characterized by simple implementation and versatility. A solution to the problem of optimizing the location of Hermite spline knots is proposed. Experimental studies have shown that local splines provide an acceptable accuracy of curve interpolation, and can be recommended for practical use in the problems of trajectory planning and tracking for robotic systems.

Acknowledgement. This research was supported by the Russian Science Foundation (Project No. 16-11-00048).

References

1. Sharov, S.N., Tolmachev, S.G.: A decision making algorithm for an integrated system of UAV landing on the moving ship gripper. In: 22nd Saint Petersburg International Conference on Integrated Navigation Systems (ICINS), Saint Petersburg, Russia (2015)
2. Rogers, D.F., Adams, J.A.: Mathematical Elements for Computer Graphics, 2nd edn. McGraw-Hill Science/Engineering/Math, New York City (1989)
3. Schumaker, L.: Spline Functions: Basic Theory. Cambridge University Press, Cambridge (2007)
4. Ingersoll, B., Ingersoll, K., DeFranco, P., Ning, A.: UAV path-planning using Bezier curves and a receding horizon approach. In: AIAA Modeling and Simulation Technologies Conference, Washington, DC (2016)
5. Faigl, J., Váňa, P.: Surveillance planning with Bézier curves. IEEE Rob. Autom. Lett. **3**(2), 750–757 (2018)
6. Duben, A.: Motion Planning with Hermite Splines for Unmanned Aerial Vehicle in Information Gathering Task. Czech Technical University, Prague (2018)
7. Wagner, P., Kotzian, J., Kordas, J., Michna, V.: Path planning and tracking for robots based on cubic hermite splines in real-time. In: 2010 IEEE 15th Conference on Emerging Technologies Factory Automation (ETFA 2010), pp. 1–8 (2010)
8. Babaei, A., Karimi, A.: Optimal Trajectory-Planning of UAVs via B-Splines and Disjunctive Programming. Preprint (2018)
9. Foo, J.L., Knutzon, J., Kalivarapu, V., Oliver, J., Winer, E.: Path planning of unmanned aerial vehicles using b-splines and particle swarm optimization. J. Aerosp. Comput. Inf. Commun. **6**(4), 271–290 (2009)
10. Ligun, A.A., StorChai, V.F.: On optimal choice of knots for Hermite spline interpolation of functions. Anal. Math. **2**, 267–275 (1976)
11. Khachumov, M.V., Khachumov, V.M.: The architecture and mathematical support of an intelligent control system for a small UAV. In: Proceedings of the 2019 International Conference on Industrial Engineering (ICIE-2019), Sochi, Russia, pp. 1–6 (2019)
12. Khachumov, M.V.: Problems of group pursuit of a target in a perturbed environment. Sci. Tech. Inf. Process. **44**(5), 357–364 (2017)

Spatial Clustering Based on Analysis of Big Data in Digital Marketing

Anton Ivaschenko[1]([✉]) [iD], Anastasia Stolbova[2] [iD],
and Oleg Golovnin[2] [iD]

[1] Samara State Technical University,
Molodogvardeyskaya 244, 443100 Samara, Russia
anton.ivashenko@gmail.com
[2] Samara University, Moskovskoye shosse 34, 443086 Samara, Russia
anastasiya.stolbova@bk.ru

Abstract. Analysis and visualization of large volumes of semi-structured information (Big Data) in decision-making support is an important and urgent problem of the digital economy. This article is devoted to solving this problem in the field of digital marketing, e.g. distributing outlets and service centers in the city. We propose a technology of adaptive formation of spatial segments of an urbanized territory based on the analysis of supply and demand areas and their visualization on an electronic map. The proposed approach to matching supply and demand includes 3 stages: semantic-statistical analysis, which allows building dependencies between objects generating demand, automated search for a balance between supply and demand, and visualization of solution options. An original concept of data organization using multiple layer including digital map, semantic web (knowledge base) and overlay network was developed on the basis of the introduced spatial clustering model. The proposed technology, being implemented by an intelligent software solution of a situational center for automated decision-making support, can be used to solve problems of optimization of networks of medical institutions, retail and cultural centers, and social services. Some examples given in this paper illustrate possible benefits of its practical use.

Keywords: Segmentation · Clustering · Big Data · Geo marketing · Digital economy

1 Introduction

The problem of coordination of supply and demand is one of the most challenging for various areas of modern society. The spatial distribution of organizations and enterprises providing services to the population in an urbanized area is one of the most important tasks for the state, business, and society. Uncontrolled development of supply leads to a decrease in the level of service and causes financial losses. Expanding of the proposal in places that do not meet current requirements becomes unacceptable in modern realities.

S. O. Kuznetsov and A. I. Panov (Eds.): RCAI 2019, CCIS 1093, pp. 335–347, 2019.
https://doi.org/10.1007/978-3-030-30763-9_28

In order to improve the efficiency of decision-making support of managing of supply and demand modern technologies of Big Data analysis can be applied. This approach becomes possible due to the implementation of modern technologies for Big Data processing and visualization (Surnin et al. 2017; Mooi et al. 2018), which allows us to dynamically simulate the relationship between supply and demand in the required amount of computation.

Application of geomarketing technology to knowledge management being extracted from Big Data provides the formation of spatial clusters to meet spatially distributed needs at different points in time in the present and in the future.

Using these technologies, in this paper we propose spatial clustering for adaptive analysis of demand and supply, development of their equilibrium and providing decision-making support using Big Data processing to derive spatial segments on an electronic map of an urbanized territory.

2   State of the Art in Cluster Analysis and Geomarketing

To identify and localize supply and demand zones, it is necessary to apply cluster analysis, which is a widely used method of unsupervised learning (Ivaschenko et al. 2019). The main feature of supply and demand zones is that the data characterizing them is geo-spatial. We considered various approaches to cluster analysis of data: probabilistic, graph, hierarchical, among which the most well-known are the algorithms DBSCAN, CURE, k-means or the method of averages, and spectral clustering (Stamp 2018).

The DBSCAN algorithm (Density-based spatial clustering of applications with noise) proposed in (Ester et al. 1996), is one of the most studied and efficient algorithms in the field of clustering (Scitovski and Sabo 2019). This algorithm makes it possible to find groups of arbitrary shape and is able to isolate noise from the rest of the data in the clustering process (Kassambara 2017), which distinguishes it from such popular algorithms as k-means and SLINK (Monalisa and Kurnia 2019). However, the considered algorithm has a significant drawback: complexity and long execution when working with Big Data (Luchi et al. 2019).

The k-means algorithm is popular and one of the simplest clustering algorithms (Friggstad et al. 2019), however it has such disadvantages as sensitivity to the choice of the starting point (Jeong et al. 2018), has no concept of noise, and also allows you to define only spherical clusters (Wang et al. 2019).

Also a significant drawback is the need to know the resulting number of clusters. There are various improvements to the k-means algorithm, for example, k-means++, aimed at solving the problem of determining optimal cluster centers, which affects the efficiency of clustering (Yang and Zhu 2018; Zhao et al. 2018).

Spectral clustering is a method based on the connectedness of objects with each other, when objects are represented by nodes of graphs (Shaham et al. 2018). This clustering method is highly accurate and simple to implement, but becomes inefficient when working with Big Data due to the high computational complexity (Shastri et al. 2019).

The CURE algorithm (Clustering Using REpresentatives) is intended for clustering large data sets (Cai and Liang 2018), is effective for low-dimensional data, allows for detecting clusters of complex shapes and is resistant to choices, but works only on numerical data (Aparajita et al. 2018).

As a result of the analysis of data clustering algorithms, it was revealed that when clustering geospatial data, the DBSCAN algorithm (Xia and Shen 2018; Perumal and Velumani 2018; Kuo et al. 2018) showed itself most efficiently.

The results of cluster analysis of supply and demand are linked to spatial data, which, when planning to achieve an equilibrium between supply and demand, is the task of geomarketing (Ramadani et al. 2018). Geomarketing is widespread in the field of health (Khalili Moghaddam and Lowe 2019), retail (Zaim et al. 2018), and banking (Kaar and Stary 2018).

In solving the problems of matching supply and demand, the main directions of geomarketing analysis is the selection and determination of the optimal location and characteristics of the objects of supply and demand.

Digital geo-marketing methods are used to analyze the development of the economy of urban space, which allows you to study the competitive environment of a city, form and visualize coverage areas for supply and demand, study business opportunities and make it possible to justify a strategy for locating various enterprises (Yarosh 2019). The problem of large scale commercial data processing and analysis to improve decision-making are studied in (Rivera and Burnaev 2017).

The mentioned above algorithms can form a full-functional toolset used to develop clusters of digital marketing. Nevertheless, their practical implementation is concerned with a necessity to visualize the process of decision-making in order to make the logic clear and confident for the users. In order to reach this goal on the basis of some experience in automated decision-making support (Ivaschenko et al. 2016, 2017) a solution described below was developed.

3 Spatial Clustering Model and Problem Statement

Let us specify the problem to be solved as follows: it is necessary to carry out an analysis of supply and demand dynamics in order to achieve equilibrium. For this purpose, on the electronic map of some territory we mark the area of demand and the area of supply by segments, in the simplest case having the form of a circle or polygon.

When managing various activities, it is necessary to combine or make the supply and demand areas as close as possible. At the same time, the supply area can cover several demand areas at once.

Thus, in order to manage the objects that form the supply, in order to optimally locate them relative to the areas of demand, it is necessary to solve the following tasks:

- selection of the best gravity centers of demand areas;
- clustering of demand points;
- selection of the best centers of supply areas;
- clustering of supply points;
- determination of the radii of action of the areas of supply;

- definition of management strategy.

The basis of the organization of effective management of supply and demand is the analysis of the main objects generating supply and demand: territorially-distributed organizations and enterprises and their customers, including potential ones.

So, all objects of demand have the following general characteristics: the spatial location of $L = \{l_k\}$ and parameters $D = \{d_k\}$. The parameters are characterized by the area of distribution depending on various factors. Thus, in a simplified form, the territory S_d, covered by the factor d_k, is determined by a circle with center L and radius R (see Fig. 1):

$$S_d = (L, R). \tag{1}$$

The objects of the supply h have the following main characteristics considered in this work: spatial location of L^*, resources N_h, financing B_h and equipment E_h. The criteria for equipping the objects of the proposal is the availability of personnel M_e, equipment M_c and capacity M_v:

$$E_h = \{M_e, M_c, M_v\}. \tag{2}$$

The set of characteristics of the object of the proposal determines the effective scope of its operation S_h:

$$S_h(N_h, B_h, E_h) = (L^*, R^*). \tag{3}$$

The proposed approach to matching supply and demand includes the following steps:

- Semantic-statistical analysis, which allows to build dependencies between objects that generate demand:
  - clustering of demand objects by parameters $D = \{d_k\}$;
  - cross-correlation analysis, evaluating the influence of some parameters $D = \{d_k\}$ on others $D = \{d_k\}$.
- Decision-making support, in which, based on the results obtained in the first and second stages, various domain tasks are solved:
  - determination of demand for the offer;
  - development of recommendations on the redistribution of resources;
  - development of recommendations on the spatial location of new objects that form the proposal;
  - determination of the cost of redistribution of resources;
  - calculation of the cost of the proposal.

4 Management Strategies

When managing supply and demand, one can determine the following leverage:

- financial management: reducing or increasing the price of the offer;
- resource management: installation of new equipment, redistribution of existing equipment, personnel management;
- demand management: creating conditions that increase demand.

Depending on the specific situation, it is possible to control various parameters. So, supply points can compete with each other, and then the development strategy is price management to attract demand. Some areas of demand may not be covered by supply, and then the main development strategy is to create new areas of supply, or to reallocate resources in existing areas.

To determine the management strategy, the following model is proposed (see Fig. 1):

$$R^*(t) = F\left(K_{ij}, B_{ij}, E_{ij}, N_{ij}\right),\tag{4}$$

where i is resource;
j is resource instance (part);
$K_{ij}(t)$ is the number of demand objects that require part of the resource;
$E_h(t)$ is infrastructural equipment;
$B_h(t)$ is financing;
$N_{ij}(t)$ is the number of supply objects located nearby.

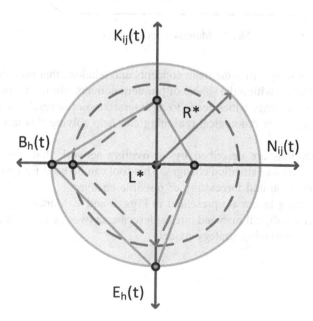

Fig. 1. Decision-making strategy model.

The task of defining a management strategy in this case is reduced to finding the optimal values for changing parameters so that the range of the object of supply is maximum and covers most of the demand. In this case, the scope of the various objects of the proposal must have minimal intersection.

5 Multiple Layers Concept of Data Analysis

Using the introduced spatial clustering model we propose an original concept of data organization, which allows formalization and analysis of various dependencies. The concept is illustrated in Fig. 2. For a digital map, which remains the main component of a geo information system, there are introduced two additional layers of data.

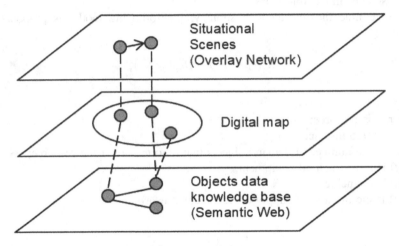

Fig. 2. Multiple data layers concept.

Knowledge base specifies the main concepts and relations that provide interpreting of digital map objects within the sphere of problem domain. Multiple problem domains can refer to a single map, which leads to an intersection of several knowledge bases. Modern technologies of ontological reasoning can help solving this task on technical level.

Various situations are described by an overlay network that specifies real and virtual scenes describing situation changes. This tool can be used for either analysis of real data or simulation and forecasting of possible changes.

Spatial clustering layers are presented in Figs. 3 and 4. Markers represent objects distribution over the digital map and circles describe an overlay network built using an introduced decision-making strategy model.

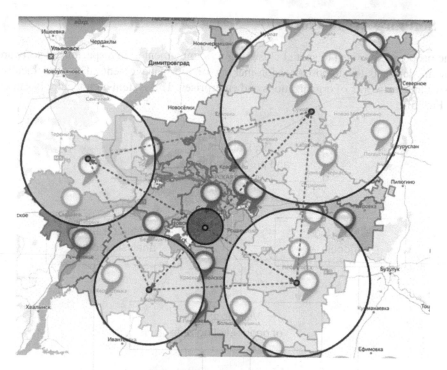

Fig. 3. Objects and data overlay placed on a digital map.

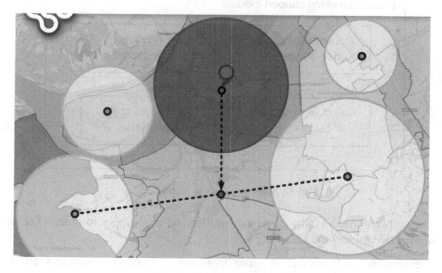

Fig. 4. Proposed decision.

6   Software Architecture

The proposed approach to spatial clustering was implemented in a specialized software system designed to support decision-making of top-management of geographically-distributed networks of organizations and enterprises. The system architecture is shown in Fig. 5.

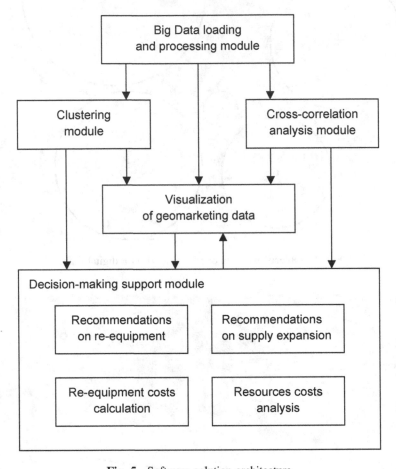

Fig. 5. Software solution architecture.

The software system allows analytics on demand and supply in order to achieve equilibrium by solving the following tasks:

- determination and analysis of qualitative and quantitative parameters affecting supply and demand according to various criteria;
- building an interactive map with the possibility of grouping by relay indicators;
- assessment of the possibility and need for the redistribution of resources: funds, personnel, equipment, etc.;
- assessment of the cost of ongoing changes.

The system implements the following main functions:

- creating and downloading data on the network of organizations and enterprises;
- work with individual enterprises and organizations and their indicators;
- cross-correlation analysis of the demand for services and institutions for individual criteria;
- recommendations on the most profitable redistribution of resources between organizations and enterprises;
- analysis of the cost value of the redistribution of resources;
- visualization on an interactive digital map;
- capturing the formal description of a problem domain in the form of ontology;
- simulation and modeling of possible situation changes.

7 Implementation and Probation Results

The proposed approach and software for Big Data processing and visualization can be used to solve problems of optimization of networks in various problem domains, e.g. retail industry, banking acquiring, social services development, etc. One of the challenging areas of its effective practical implementation is health care. Medical services nowadays require innovative high technology equipment, which efficient application is determined by patients demand. Therefore medical services development becomes one of the promising areas of spatial clustering application in practice.

Modern methods of data analysis and decision-making support for the development of medical services should take into account the ontological features of the healthcare field. In particular, the methods of managing medical institutions should consider geo-referencing and provide an opportunity to analyze the need for additional funding, re-development of institutions depending on the prevalence of diseases and the needs of the population in different regions.

Multiple layers concept allows specifying basic relations between medical institutions and their equipment, diseases and nosologies, categories of the population, and financing of medical institutions. This data was used to calculate the cost of services, re-equipment, taking into account individual characteristics of medical institutions, and the demand for the population with geographic reference to specified territories.

The main object of the provision of medical services are medical institutions intended for the diagnosis, treatment and rehabilitation of people.

The analysis of the subject area made it possible to determine the expected sources of the initial data for the developed system: medical institutions, the federal state statistics service, data of the mass media, social networks. From such sources it is possible to obtain data such as population size, age composition of the population, number of hospital beds, capacity of outpatient polyclinic diseases, number of doctors by specialties, incidence.

For the correlation analysis of the demand by patients for medical services and institutions for individual nosologies, independent filters are used:

- population categories: gender, age range, the scope of work;
- types of medical institutions:
  - hospital,
  - clinic,
  - private medical institution;
- nosology: types;
- disease: ICD-10, stage.

As a result of applying filters, the correlation between them is displayed on the map using the following layers:

- medical institutions that provide services in the chosen direction are displayed on the map with points with a radius of effective action;
- the type of point (circle, square, triangle) determines the type of medical institution: clinic, hospital, private medical institution;
- the color of the dot determines the presence of compartments for working with the selected nosology;
- the prevalence of diseases for the selected categories of the population are displayed on the map by areas that are filled with color, the shades of which correspond to the density of the population with the selected disease.

Thus, comparing on the interactive map (see Fig. 6) the area of action of medical institutions and the epicenters of diseases, it is possible to assess the effectiveness of the use of the institution.

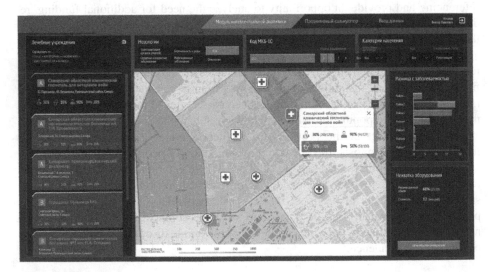

Fig. 6. Demand and supply spatial clustering on an interactive map.

For example, in one of the regions there is a center equipped with high-tech equipment for the diagnosis of cardiovascular diseases, while the demand for the use of this equipment is low. Consequently, it is required to redistribute the equipment to a medical facility located in an area with an increased level of cardiovascular diseases.

8 Conclusion

The proposed approach can be used to solve the problems of the location of new emerging institutions, shopping and entertainment centers, social services. The approach supports the formation of development strategies on the mechanisms of machine learning with the use of Big Data analysis to take into account the dynamically changing environment.

The semantic-statistical analysis allows building dependencies between objects generating demand, the automated search helps finding a balance between supply and demand, and the visualization is used to present the solution options. Using the introduced spatial clustering model we have developed an original concept of data organization based on multiple layer including digital map, semantic web (knowledge base), and overlay network.

Implementation of the developed software system based on the advanced approach allows for adaptation of the existing urban infrastructure objects accompanying the livelihoods of the population from the areas of health care, education, recreation and leisure, catering.

New approaches to organization of user interfaces allow increasing the effectiveness of situational monitoring centers through the implementation of intelligent interaction management technologies, taking into account the characteristics of the perception of the situation by decision makers.

Comparing the range of demand and supply actions on an interactive map, it becomes possible to accurately assess the efficiency of location, operating time, and characteristics of urban infrastructure, thereby improving the quality of customer service and improving business processes.

References

Surnin, O.L., Sitnikov, P.V., Ivaschenko, A.V., Ilyasova, N.Yu., Popov, S.B.: Big Data incorporation based on open services provider for distributed enterprises. In: CEUR Workshop Proceedings. Session Data Science (DS-ITNT 2017), Samara, Russia, 24–27 April 2017, vol. 190, pp. 42–47 (2017)

Mooi, E., Sarstedt, M., Mooi-Reci, I.: Cluster analysis. In: Market Research. STBE, pp. 313–366. Springer, Singapore (2018). https://doi.org/10.1007/978-981-10-5218-7_9

Ivaschenko, A., Khorina, A., Sitnikov, P.: Online creativity modeling and analysis based on Big Data of social networks. In: Arai, K., Kapoor, S., Bhatia, R. (eds.) SAI 2018. AISC, vol. 858, pp. 329–337. Springer, Cham (2019). https://doi.org/10.1007/978-3-030-01174-1_25

Stamp, M.: A survey of machine learning algorithms and their application in information security. In: Parkinson, S., Crampton, A., Hill, R. (eds.) Guide to Vulnerability Analysis for Computer Networks and Systems. CCN, pp. 33–55. Springer, Cham (2018). https://doi.org/10.1007/978-3-319-92624-7_2

Ester, M., et al.: A density-based algorithm for discovering clusters in large spatial databases with noise. In: KDD, vol. 96, no. 34, pp. 226–231 (1996)

Scitovski, R., Sabo, K.: DBSCAN-like clustering method for various data densities. Pattern Anal. Appl. 1–14 (2019). https://doi.org/10.1007/s10044-019-00809-z

Kassambara, A.: Practical Guide to Cluster Analysis in R: Unsupervised Machine Learning, vol. 1. STHDA (2017)

Monalisa, S., Kurnia, F.: Analysis of DBSCAN and K-means algorithm for evaluating outlier on RFM model of customer behaviour. TELKOMNIKA 17(1), 110–117 (2019)

Luchi, D., Rodrigues, A.L., Varejão, F.M.: Sampling approaches for applying DBSCAN to large datasets. Pattern Recogn. Lett. 117, 90–96 (2019)

Friggstad, Z., Rezapour, M., Salavatipour, M.R.: Local search yields a PTAS for k-means in doubling metrics. SIAM J. Comput. 48(2), 452–480 (2019)

Jeong, Y.J., et al.: K-means data clustering with memristor networks. Nano Lett. 18(7), 4447–4453 (2018)

Wang, S., Gittens, A., Mahoney, M.W.: Scalable kernel K-means clustering with Nyström approximation: relative-error bounds. J. Mach. Learn. Res. 20(1), 431–479 (2019)

Yang, Y., Zhu, Z.: A fast and efficient grid-based K-means++ clustering algorithm for large-scale datasets. In: Krömer, P., Zhang, H., Liang, Y., Pan, J.-S. (eds.) ECC 2018. AISC, vol. 891, pp. 508–515. Springer, Cham (2019). https://doi.org/10.1007/978-3-030-03766-6_57

Zhao, W.L., Deng, C.H., Ngo, C.W.: k-means: a revisit. Neurocomputing 291, 195–206 (2018)

Shaham, U., et al.: SpectralNet: spectral clustering using deep neural networks. arXiv preprint arXiv:1801.01587 (2018)

Shastri, A.A., et al.: Vector quantized spectral clustering applied to whole genome sequences of plants. Evol. Bioinform. 15 (2019). https://doi.org/10.1177/1176934319836997

Cai, M., Liang, Y.: An improved CURE algorithm. In: Shi, Z., Pennartz, C., Huang, T. (eds.) ICIS 2018. IAICT, vol. 539, pp. 102–111. Springer, Cham (2018). https://doi.org/10.1007/978-3-030-01313-4_11

Aparajita, A., Swagatika, S., Singh, D.: Comparative analysis of clustering techniques in cloud for effective load balancing. Int. J. Eng. Technol. (UAE) 7(3), 47–51 (2018)

Xia, T., Shen, J., Yu, X.: Predicting human mobility using Sina Weibo check-in data. In: 2018 International Conference on Audio, Language and Image Processing (ICALIP), pp. 380–384. IEEE (2018)

Perumal, M., Velumani, B.: Design and development of hybridized DBSCAN-NN approach for location prediction to place water treatment plant. In: Rajsingh, E.B., Veerasamy, J., Alavi, A.H., Peter, J.D. (eds.) Advances in Big Data and Cloud Computing. AISC, vol. 645, pp. 237–247. Springer, Singapore (2018). https://doi.org/10.1007/978-981-10-7200-0_21

Kuo, F.Y., Wen, T.H., Sabel, C.E.: Characterizing diffusion dynamics of disease clustering: a modified space-time DBSCAN (MST-DBSCAN) algorithm. Ann. Am. Assoc. Geogr. 108(4), 1168–1186 (2018)

Ramadani, V., et al.: Impact of geomarketing and location determinants on business development and decision making. Compet. Rev. Int. Bus. J. 28(1), 98–120 (2018)

Khalili Moghaddam, G., Lowe, C.R.: Mobile healthcare. In: Health and Wellness Measurement Approaches for Mobile Healthcare. SAST, pp. 1–11. Springer, Cham (2019). https://doi.org/10.1007/978-3-030-01557-2_1

Zaim, D., Benomar, A., Bellafkih, M.: Geomarketing solution: an ambient intelligence application in shopping (2018)

Kaar, C., Stary, C.: Intelligent business transformation through market specific value network analysis: structured interventions and process bootstrapping in geomarketing. Knowl. Process Manage. 26(2), 163–181 (2018)

Yarosh, O.: Digital geomarketing methods for analyzing the development of the economy of modern urban space. In: IOP Conference Series: Materials Science and Engineering, vol. 497, no. 1, pp. 012102. IOP Publishing (2019)

Rivera, R., Burnaev, E.: Forecasting of commercial sales with large scale Gaussian processes. In: ICDM Workshops 2017, pp. 625–634 (2017)

Ivaschenko, A., Lednev, A., Diyazitdinova, A., Sitnikov, P.: Agent-based outsourcing solution for agency service management. In: Bi, Y., Kapoor, S., Bhatia, R. (eds.) IntelliSys 2016. LNNS, vol. 16, pp. 204–215. Springer, Cham (2018). https://doi.org/10.1007/978-3-319-56991-8_16

Ivaschenko, A., Sitnikov, P., Andreev, M., Surnin, O.: Open services provider for supply chains. In: Proceedings of the 20th Conference of Open Innovations Association FRUCT, pp. 98–104 (2017)

Ontology-Based Approach to Organizing the Support for the Analysis of Argumentation in Popular Science Discourse

Yury Zagorulko[1(✉)], Natalia Garanina[1], Alexey Sery[1], and Oleg Domanov[2]

[1] A.P. Ershov Institute of Informatics Systems, Siberian Branch of the Russian Academy of Sciences, Acad. Lavrentjev avenue 6, 630090 Novosibirsk, Russia
zagor@iis.nsk.su
[2] Institute of Philosophy and Law, Siberian Branch of the Russian Academy of Sciences, Nikolaeva str., 8, 630090 Novosibirsk, Russia

Abstract. The paper presents an approach to modeling and analyzing the argumentation found in popular science literature. Argumentation is modeled using an argumentation ontology based on the AIF base ontology expanded by the means for modeling the target audience and allowing for a more detailed description of the arguments' content. In terms of this ontology, the authors give the descriptions of argumentation schemes, arguments' structure and elements, as well as of the network of arguments and their constituent parts extracted from the texts under study. To analyze argumentation, a software system is being developed. It provides tools for modeling and identifying the structure of argumentation on a corpus of texts relating to popular science discourse. In addition, the system can examine the extracted argumentation with the purpose of revealing and analyzing argumentative strategies and rhetorical methods used in scientific and popular science texts. The paper describes the specific features of the proposed argumentation ontology and presents the architecture and functionality of the software system designed for argumentation analysis.

Keywords: Argumentation · Argumentation scheme · Argumentation analysis tools · Ontology · Popular science discourse

1 Introduction

An important factor in the development of modern science is the trust of society and state. Science is becoming more complex, the problems that it solves are becoming more specific, and it is becoming increasingly difficult for outsiders to perceive and evaluate the results of scientific activity. The necessity to present scientific ideas and innovations to outside experts or consumers (in the form of grant applications, popular science or educational articles) dictates the need to switch from the specialized language of science to the common language understandable to the consumers of scientific knowledge. This creates the conditions for the penetration of argumentative discourse and specific rhetorical means of persuasion into the language of science. Today, popular science discourse is becoming an integral and essential element of scientific

S. O. Kuznetsov and A. I. Panov (Eds.): RCAI 2019, CCIS 1093, pp. 348–362, 2019.
https://doi.org/10.1007/978-3-030-30763-9_29

activity, as it acts as a mediator providing communication between scientists in special fields and an unprepared audience. Note that within the framework of this study, "discourse" is understood as the unity of two entities: the process of language communication and the resulting object, i.e., text. Thanks to this, discourse can be studied as a process unfolding in time and as a structural object.

Indeed, popular science discourse is less formal than the language of science, though stricter than a common natural language. As a rule, discourse contains arguments (convincing elements) "for" or "against" a particular concept/theory, argumentative strategies and rhetorical techniques implementing various persuasion methods.

In connection with the above, there is a need for a closer study of popular science discourse as a genre of human communication; the more so as it is much less studied than other genres, in particular, scientific articles and news reports. The problem of studying argumentation methods and rhetorical techniques used in popular science texts is especially acute because of the need to draw up recommendations for writing persuasive articles intended for general public.

The paper discusses an approach to modeling the argumentation found in popular science literature and analyzing the argumentation schemes, argumentative strategies and rhetorical techniques used. Argumentation modeling assumes an ontological description of the argumentation schemes (models), their implementation and examples of their use in the texts under study. For analyzing the argumentation we use a software system allowing researchers to find in the source texts and extract from them fragments making up the content of the argumentation and to analyze the strategies and techniques used in a particular text or in the whole corpus of texts.

The rest of the paper is structured as follows. Section 2 provides brief information concerning the argumentation theory. Section 3 presents an information model of argumentation used in the software system developed for the analysis of argumentation. Section 4 describes the features of the argumentation ontology, which is the core of the information model of the software system for argument analysis (SSAA) designed to analyze argumentation in popular science texts. Section 5 presents the architecture and describes the main functions of the SSAA. In conclusion, we summarize the interim results of the work on creating a tool for analyzing argumentation in popular science discourse and make plans for the future.

2   Some Information About the Argumentation Theory

The theory of argumentation is a complex discipline at the junction of a number of scientific areas engaged in the study of human communication and cognition. These areas include logic and philosophy, history and sociology, linguistics and psychology, computer science and artificial intelligence. The theory of argumentation studies the ways to influence people's beliefs. These methods are many: reference to experts' opinion, experience, more general principles, tradition, common sense, etc.

Actually, argumentation is presenting arguments (reasons) in order to change or create a certain conviction (position/view/opinion) of the other party (audience). It should be noted that "argumentation" is not only the procedure for presenting arguments in support or against a certain view, but also the totality of such arguments.

However, finding arguments and all their components in the text (discourse) is not always easy. This task is further complicated by the fact that not all elements of the argument are explicitly represented in the text. Therefore, the analysis of an argument often begins with the restoration of the sequence of statements (premises) leading to a conclusion (statement).

One of the most famous models of argumentation is the Toulmin model [1]. According to this model, an argument generally includes six elements (Fig. 1).

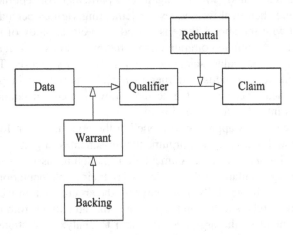

Fig. 1. Model of Toulmin's argumentation.

Claim is a thesis, i.e. approval or conclusion presented to the audience (which may not correspond to the initial beliefs of the audience);

Data are initial data (facts, statements, assumptions) related to the situation in question that make the basis for the acceptance of the thesis (Claim);

Warrant is a statement justifying the making of the thesis (Claim) from the data (Data);

Backing is information (statements) supporting the Warrant;

Rebuttal is a statement describing the limits of an argument applicability, i.e. a situation where the thesis cannot be accepted;

Qualifier is a statement expressing the degree of confidence in the thesis (modality).

Claim, Data and Warrant are considered the mandatory elements of an argument, whereas other elements may be missing.

In this model, counter-arguments are also arguments that can attack any of the first four elements (Claim, Data, Warrant or Backing).

In practice, we have to deal not with one argument, but with a set of them. In this case, any argument can be the starting point (premise) for another argument. Any thesis can be considered as a potential rationale for another thesis. Also, different arguments can have common premises as well as common theses. Thus, the arguments are connected and form a network. In practice, the network of arguments is usually visualized as a graph; therefore, in the future we will also use the terms of the "graph of arguments" or the "argument graph."

Various models of argumentation have been developed, but all of them, in one way or another, rely on the Toulmin model. Therefore, this model can be considered basic.

There are three categories of argumentation models [2]: rhetorical, dialogue and monologue. The first two models consider argumentation as a dynamic process: rhetorical models emphasize the audience and convincing intent; dialogue models describe the ways in which arguments are connected in dialogue structures. The monologue model, by contrast, emphasizes the structure of the argument itself, including the relationship between the various components of the argument.

Another well-known classification of models in computational argumentation distinguishes between abstract argumentation and structured argumentation [3]. Abstract argumentation considers each argument as an atomic entity without an internal structure while structured argumentation takes into account the internal structure of each argument.

Currently there are many models of structured argumentation. The most famous and popular is the Douglas Walton model [4], where a structured argument is defined as a set of statements consisting of three parts: a set of premises, a conclusion, and a conclusion from the premises of the conclusion.

To model the arguments, Walton, together with Reed [5], proposed the concept of an "argumentation scheme". Argumentation schemes are the forms of arguments describing the structure of an argumentative inference. This concept allows authors to identify and evaluate the common types of argumentation used by all people. Such schemes can be used to represent the knowledge necessary to provide arguments and explanations. They reflect common stereotypical thinking patterns that are generally not deductive or monotonous. Such schemes of arguments are called models of defeasible inference, in the sense that if the premises of an argument are true, then the conclusion is presumably true.

Each scheme has a name, conclusion, set of premises, and set of critical questions. Critical questions make it possible to identify the weaknesses of an argument based on this scheme. They can be used to simulate additional premises or to generate implicit premises (premises not explicitly presented in the text or omitted in the argument) that will support the argument.

Walton and his coauthors give a compendium [6], containing 60 basic argumentation schemes, many of which have variants (sub-schemes). However, as they point out, some schemes are not included in the compendium and are discussed separately.

Walton's schemes have been used in a number of argumentation tools (Araucaria [7], OVA [8], Carneades [9], ArgDF [10]). In this paper, we will also rely on them when modeling argumentation.

3 The Information Model of Argumentation

Like any software tools designed for text processing, the SSAA system uses some information model. For SSAA, the base of this model is the argumentation ontology. We describe argument structures, elements of arguments, argumentation schemes and argument networks found in texts in terms of this ontology.

Our ontology is based on the AIF (Argument Interchange Format) [11, 12]. De facto, this ontology format is accepted by the international community as a standard notation for describing arguments and argumentative structures. We have chosen the AIF format for two reasons. Firstly, it is a highly expressible formalism for describing the arguments and argumentation schemes used in several systems of argumentation processing. Secondly, the AIF is a convenient format for sharing the results received by the users of different systems using various presentation languages and formats in argumentation analysis.

3.1 The AIF

The AIF is a core ontology of concepts necessary to describe arguments. This ontology is naturally divided into two parts: the ontology of an upper level and the ontology of forms. The former defines the basic building blocks of AIF argument network, types of nodes and edges while the latter provides a conceptual description of elements of the AIF-network: inference schemes, premises, conclusions, exceptions, etc. Nodes defined in the upper level ontology are used to build a network of arguments at the instance level. The nodes of these networks fulfill (instantiate) the forms of the corresponding argument schemes from the ontology of forms.

Figure 2 shows the specification of the core AIF ontology. Here, the white nodes correspond to the classes of the upper-level ontology; the gray nodes correspond to the classes of the ontology of forms. Different types of arrows denote different types of relations between ontology classes. For example, the arrow of the first type indicates that the *Inference Scheme* class is a subclass of the *Schema* class. The arrow of the second type denotes that an instance of the *RA-node* class instantiates (*fulfils*) a subclass of the *Inference Scheme* class. The third type arrows connects the *Deductive Inference Scheme* class with the *Premise* class.

The core AIF ontology can generate a representation of arguments as nodes in a directed graph called a network of arguments. Every node can also have several (internal) attributes of its own, which correspond, for example, to the author of the argument, date of creation, degree of confidence, acceptability status of the argument, etc. Since these attributes depend on a particular application, they are not part of the main ontology.

The core AIF ontology includes two disjoint types of nodes: information nodes (or I-nodes) and scheme nodes (or S-nodes). The I-nodes depending on a subject domain represent statements containing information included in premises, conclusions and other elements of arguments. The S-nodes are used to represent the argument schemes that are subject-independent patterns (models) of reasoning. These schemes are similar to inference rules in deductive logic and can also support other types of inference.

The elements of argument schemes are premises, assumptions, exceptions, and a conclusion.

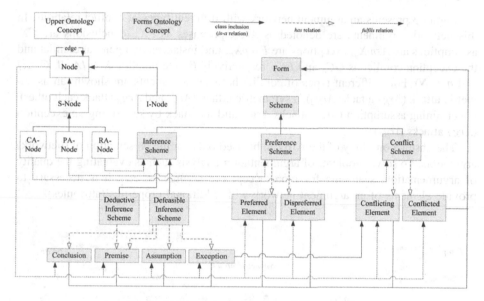

Fig. 2. Specification of the core AIF ontology.

There are three disjoint types of the S-nodes: application nodes for inference rules (*RA-node*), application nodes for preferences (*PA-node*), and application nodes for conflicts (*CA-node*). For these types in the AIF, the word "application" means that these nodes function as instances, not as classes. The *RA-nodes* represent both deductive and defeasible inference rules. The *CA-nodes* define a conflict relationship (for example, between a statement and its negation). The *PA-nodes* realize a preference relationship among evaluated nodes.

3.2 AIF Argument Network

The core AIF specification does not specify the types of edges. Their semantics can be understood from the types of nodes they connect. There are two types of edges: (1) *scheme edges* from the S-nodes support the conclusions of other S-nodes, which can be either I-nodes or S-nodes; and (2) *data edges* from the I-nodes to the S-nodes, which provide information for the implementation of argument schemes. That is, there are I-to-S edges (information edges), S-to-I edges (conclusion edges), and S-to-S edges (warrant edges). These restrictions do not allow output edges of the I-nodes to be input to another I-node. This ensures that a relation between the two information elements must be explicitly defined through an intermediate S-node. For a given network of arguments, node A supports another node B if and only if there is an edge from A to B. We define the network of arguments formally.

Definition 1 (*Argument Network*). The AIF argument network is a digraph $G = (N, E)$, where:

$N = I \cup RA \cup CA \cup PA$ is the set of nodes, where I is the set of I-nodes, RA is the set of RA-nodes, CA is the set of CA-nodes, and PA is the set of PA-nodes; and $E \subseteq (N \times N) \backslash (I \times I)$ is the set of edges.

Figure 3 presents an argument network with different types of conflict relations. In this network, arguments are denoted as Arg_n, premises as PX_n, conclusions are CX, assumptions are $AsmX_n$, exceptions are $ExcpX_n$, and instances of a general conflict and the exception conflict as GC_n and EC_1, respectively (in the notation $X \in \{A, B, C, ...\}$ and $n \in N$). Four different types of conflict between arguments are shown: an asymmetric attack (Arg_1 attacks Arg_2), a symmetric attack (Arg_2 and Arg_3 attack each other), undermining assumption (Arg_3 attacks Arg_4) and an attack by supporting an exception (Arg_4 attacks Arg_1).

The abstract ontology of the AIF can be used only for the presentation of (network) arguments. To solve problems of argumentation analysis such as evaluating the quality of argumentation, searching for more acceptable arguments, etc., it is necessary to provide elements of an argument network with additional properties (attributes).

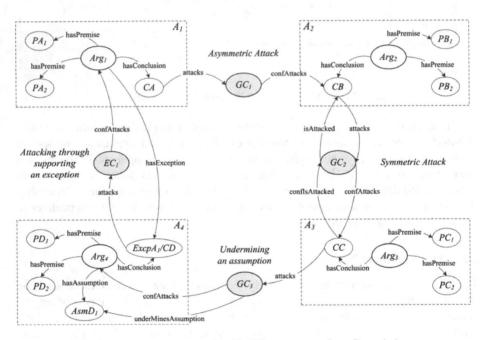

Fig. 3. An argument network with different types of conflict relations.

3.3   AIF Argument Network

The first version of the AIF ontology was implemented in the RDFS to describe arguments and argumentation schemes. A pilot web system, ArgDF, is based on this ontology [10]. This system allows creating argument structures in the RDF and searching in it.

The OWL version of the AIF ontology was implemented in 2012. Currently, this implementation is the only version available. The OWL version of the ontology is much more expressive than the RDFS version [13]. In particular, it contains a new definition of the AIF format specification and argument schemes as ontology classes (which are instances of classes in the RDFS version). Due to this format, the argument schemes can be explicitly classified. Another achievement is that the new ontology makes it possible to directly use DL solvers to classify arguments and schemas.

4 Enriched Argumentation Ontology

We take the AIF ontology as the basis of the information model for the SSAA, our software system of argumentation analysis. We have enriched this ontology with the means for modeling the target audience of argumentation and means for a more detailed description of the argument content (see Fig. 4).

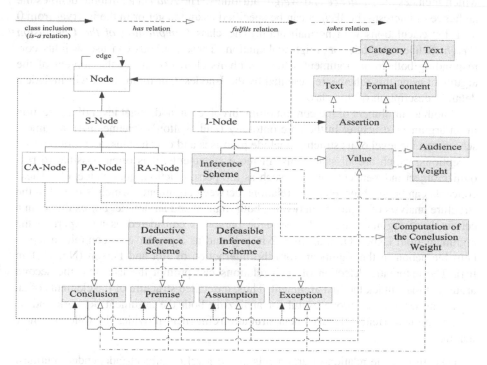

Fig. 4. A modification of the core AIF ontology.

In processing arguments, it is often necessary to take into account the way of thinking and the value system of various audiences. For example, arguments meaningful for teenagers may be less important for an older audience. At the same time, reference to the opinion of influential scientists will matter more for researchers than for schoolchildren.

To process the value of arguments and their elements, we have enriched our ontology with weights as attributes of classes of argument schemes, elements of argument schemes, and statements. In [14], the authors developed an abstract algebra, which in combination with the AIF ontology allows analyzing an argument network using the weights of their elements. This algebra also allows to represent attacks, supports, and aggregation of arguments. When calculating the weight of the argument conclusion, their model takes into account the weights of its premises and its relations with the other arguments of the network.

We have added to this model the ability to take into consideration the weight of an argument scheme. The reason for this addition is that for different audiences the same argument scheme may have different weights. For example, for the scientific community, the argument from Analogy (No. 7 in [6]) may weigh little, while for the lawyers adhering to the precedent-based legal system this argument may be strong. Our model can also take into account the weights of assumptions and exceptions of arguments. Depending on the audience, weights are specified using the *Value* class, which includes the *Audience* and *Weight* attributes. The *Audience* attribute denotes the audience of interest. The *Weight* can be specified as an integer or in the interval from 0 to 1 for calculations with normalization. The class *Computation of the Conclusion Weight* defines methods for weight calculation. These methods can use weights corresponding both to an argument scheme with its elements and to the content of the argument using this scheme, represented by the I-nodes. Our future work will include a detailed description of this class.

Another enrichment of the core ontology involves an additional level of abstraction in an argument structure. In the core ontology (and Walton's schemes [6]), argument schemes at the level of its structure include premises and conclusions, assumptions and exceptions, which are all statements. In these statements, it is often possible to recognize object-independent concepts such as the person, action, goal, value, etc. These concepts can be used for reference relations between arguments, which is useful in the structure analysis of argument networks, both manual and automatic. For example, in a certain large argument network, the same person is considered as an expert in the argument from Expert Opinion (No. 2 in [6]) and as a person who commits a reprehensible action in the argument from the Interaction of Act and Person (No. 18.1 in [6]). The automatic detection of such relations can prompt the user that the second argument may attack the first argument. Thus, a detailed structure of the elements of an argument scheme can prove useful for analyzing both the argument network and its underlying text. Hence, the argument structure refinement provides the following new features:

1. Detection of the relation of arguments at the level of subject-independent entities;
2. Automatic prediction of support and conflict relations;
3. Automatic prediction of arguments;
4. Automated extraction of arguments.

To refine a structure of statements, we have introduced the *Assertion* class. Its instances have two attributes: the *Text* attribute and *Formal content* attribute. The values of the former are the text contents of the corresponding elements of the argument scheme, while the latter specifies pairs (*Category, Text*) to describe the statement entities of interest. All I-nodes which instantiate elements of the argument schema belong to the *Assertion* class. Each argument scheme has its own set of *Categories* for describing the entities presented in the scheme (for example, *Person, Action, Value,* etc.). Also, the *Assertion* may have a value depending on the audience.

Figure 4 shows a modification of the core AIF ontology implementing the enrichments proposed above.

5 Developing a Software for Argument Modeling and Analysis

In this section, we are discussing the architecture of the software system allowing for argumentation modeling and detecting the text fragments containing argumentation. Being detected, the argumentation parts will allow the researcher to analyze which argumentative strategies and rhetorical methods have occurred in the text or, more generally, in the corpus.

5.1   Argumentation Analysis: Toolsets Review

Currently, there are a lot of software systems supporting argumentation modeling and analysis. Each of them is customized for a specific set of tasks and languages. Though almost all of them are based on the widely known Toulmin model, their functionality may vary greatly.

First of all, they may vary in the approach to representing the source material, i.e. text or corpus. Some software systems can only take text if it is split into Elementary Discourse Units (EDU) [15, 16], which are then combined to make Argumentation Discourse Units (ADU). Each ADU can be constructed only from EDUs. Other systems allow the user to upload an arbitrary text, and use any interval as a part of ADU [7, 8]. Some systems, however, do not allow users to work directly with the source text and build a graph of argument explicitly, providing them instead with special forms. In order to describe an argument of interest, the user should fill the form with the fragments of the source text [9].

Second, the software systems for argument analysis may differ in how they model the subject area, which is the Theory of Argumentation. Some systems allow building an argumentation graph of an arbitrary form, where nodes correspond to text fragments, and edges are customized by the users. Other systems expect all arguments to be based on the predefined schemes, which usually are a subset of Walton's schemes. Note that generally such systems allow defining new models.

As we can see, even though there is the generally accepted Toulmin model, approaches to its implementation and using this implementation for argument analysis are very diverse. Many systems were developed in the frames of scientific research projects, and hence their support was discontinued after the projects were closed.

Among the best known projects, it is worth to mention Araucaria [7], Online Visualization of Argument (OVA) [8], ArgDF [10], and Carneades [9]. The first two were developed at the University of Dundee of Great Britain together with other research teams as part of the European scientific project. These systems represent argumentation schemes based on the AIF model. Users build an argumentation graph explicitly by selecting an argumentation scheme, marking text fragments, making nodes from them, and then connecting these nodes through the scheme selected. Researchers can create new schemes, and share them along with the graphs they made using the AIF Database. An example of a graph of arguments in the form represented by the OVA system is shown on Fig. 5.

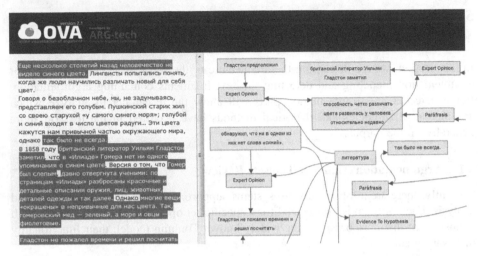

Fig. 5. Representation of an argumentation graph in the OVA system.

A System for Authoring and Navigating Arguments (ArgDF) [10] is a Semantic Web-based system. It also uses the AIF data model (AIF-RDF) and enables the users to create and manipulate semantically annotated arguments and also to re-use parts of existing arguments when creating a new one. Evidently, the ArgDF allows the users to create new argumentation schemes. According to its authors, the ArgDF is "an open platform not only for representing arguments, but also for building interlinked and dynamic argument networks."

The Carneades project was started in 2008. According to the latest news, its development team includes Douglas Walton, the developer of widely known argumentation schemes. The approach implemented in the Carneades software system differs from those used in Araucaria and OVA. The user has to fill in a form in order to create a new argument. The look of the form depends on the scheme the user has selected. As the system does not support the representation of the source text, the users have to complete the form fields manually, copying fragments from source text. In other words, the representation of argumentation is not a network or a graph, but rather an analytical textual form.

Currently, there is a need for software systems that would allow marking and then analyzing arguments not only within one text, but within an entire corpus of texts. One of the reasons for this is to increase interest in argumentation mining. There is a hope that corpus analysis will provide researchers with statistical data that will help them to identify argumentation patterns, and maybe prepare training sets for the ML-algorithms. At the same time, it is still important to have an opportunity to save and share research results, especially if they are presented in accordance with the generally accepted standard.

This means that in addition to the tools we need a data representation model. The AIF model is widely used, and there are other models, such as the Legal Knowledge Interchange Format (LKIF) [17], Collective Attack Framework (CAF) [18], etc. The AIF, however, is the only model that is more than a data interchange format. The AIF Database [19] provides researchers with access to argumentation schemes, text corpora, and graphs of arguments. Note that the AIFdb is primarily designed for the English speaking users.

It could be said that currently there are a lot of software tools developed for argument analysis. Yet none of them provides facilities to address all the tasks we set in our project. It is also important that none of them allows working fully in Russian. In this paper we suggest an architecture of a software system based on the suggested ontological model. This system is designed to support argument modeling and argument analysis in Russian popular science texts.

5.2 Software System for Argument Analysis

The software system for argument analysis (SSAA) is designed as a web application. We describe the system architecture as having three blocks, or tiers: Data tier, Server tier, and Client tier (Fig. 6).

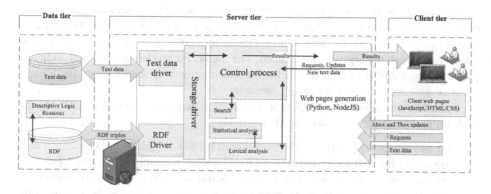

Fig. 6. Architecture of a software system for argument analysis.

The data tier includes two storages separated from each other, data storage and text storage. Argumentation data is represented as a set of RDF triples. The descriptive logic reasoning machine also works on the data tier.

The server tier implements data processing and representation of results. The application server includes data drivers, the RDF driver and text data driver. In addition, the application server implements and serves all backend operations: lexical analysis, corpus analysis, statistical analysis, search engines, etc. Together they form the basis of the system's functionality. The web server performs user authentication and generates web pages for the system's end user, like any web server does. It also gets requests and parameters from users, and sends them to the application server modules. There are widely used development tools, such as Python and NodeJS, to implement web server functionality.

The client tier contains an implementation of the interface of the end user. It takes requests from users and displays web pages in return. The main development tools of the client tier are JavaScript and HTML/CSS.

The design of the user interface (UI) of the SSAA is very important, because users judge the functionality and merits of the system by its interface. The interface helps the researcher, when he/she surfs a scientific popular text, looks for arguments, and links them together, building a graph of arguments. It was previously mentioned that some of the systems for argument analysis allow the users to build a graph in an explicit manner, selecting text fragments and making graph nodes from them. Other systems, like Carneades, offer a textual representation of arguments. We suggest implementing both types of argument representation in the SSAA so as to put together their advantages.

The user interface of the SSAA hides the actual complexity of the ontology. We focus on two types of users: linguists and specialists in argument analysis (e.g. philosophers). Linguists usually work with texts, terms, concepts, and objects; philosophers are used to work with statements, arguments, and argumentation schemes. Neither of them can work with the ontology directly, i.e., it can be used and edited only by knowledge engineers and system developers. The UI should be able to provide each type of users with sufficient tools based on the corresponding part of the ontology.

Advanced users can optionally use the new ontology additions for detailed description of an argument content and modeling the target audience of argumentation. The detailed argument content allows facilitating automatic detection of implicit relations between the arguments extracted. The means for modeling the target audience by assigning weights to argument schemes and argument elements allow for a more accurate assessment of the arguments strength.

Summing up, in order to support argumentation analysis on a corpus of texts, the SSAA should include the following functionality:

1. Text management operations. The user should be able to upload a text, create a new corpus, add the text to the existing corpus, create a hierarchy of corpora, etc.
2. Text annotation operations. The system should provide facilities to annotate a source text with arguments by marking fragments corresponding to the various parts of arguments: claims, premises, etc. It also includes creating a graph of arguments and navigating the graph.
3. Creating new argumentation schemes.
4. Support the analysis of argumentative strategies and linguistic means. This category includes almost everything the application server does: lexical analysis of texts, collecting and representing statistical data (e.g., information of how argumentation schemes are distributed across the collection of texts), searching for schemes and texts in database.

6 Conclusion

The paper presents an approach to modeling and analyzing argumentation found in popular science literature.

We model argumentation using the argumentation ontology based on the core AIF ontology. We have enriched the AIF ontology by taking into account the values and mentality of a target audience of a particular scientific text and by tools for giving a more detailed description of an argument content. The structure and elements of the arguments, argumentation schemes as well as the argument network and parts of the arguments found in texts under study are represented in terms of this ontology.

The software system SSAA for argument analysis is under development. In this paper, we describe its architecture and functionality. The SSAA provides tools for modeling and identifying the structure of argumentation on the corpus of texts related to popular science discourse. This system can also be used for studying the argumentative strategies and rhetorical techniques used in these texts.

Our software system provides text and corpus text management, creation of argumentation schemes, argumentative text markup and argumentation graph construction, as well as support for the analysis of argumentative strategies and their linguistic means. This system also includes support for lexical text analysis, collection and presentation of statistical data, search in the schemes and texts.

By now, we have developed an ontological model, the SSAA architecture and a set of modules for creating and visualizing argumentation networks.

Acknowledgment. This work was financially supported by the Russian Foundation for Basic Research (Grant No. № 18-00-01376 (18-00-00889)).

References

1. Toulmin, S.: The Uses of Argument. Cambridge University Press, Cambridge (2003)
2. Bentahar, J., Moulin, B., Bélanger, M.: A taxonomy of argumentation models used for knowledge representation. Artif. Intell. Rev. **33**(3), 211–259 (2010)
3. Besnard, P., et al.: Introduction to structured argumentation. Argument Comput. **5**(1), 1–4 (2014)
4. Walton, D.: Argumentation theory: a very short introduction. In: Simari, G., Rahwan, I. (eds.) Argumentation in Artificial Intelligence, pp. 1–22. Springer, Boston (2009). https://doi.org/10.1007/978-0-387-98197-0_1
5. Reed, C., Walton, D.: Argumentation schemes in argument-as-process and argument-as-product. In: Proceedings of Conference Celebrating Informal Logic. OSSA Conference Archive 75, University of Windsor, Windsor (2003)
6. Walton, D., Reed, C., Macagno, F.: Argumentation Schemes. Cambridge University Press, Cambridge (2008)
7. Reed, C., Rowe, G.: Araucaria: software for argument analysis, diagramming and representation. Int. J. Artif. Intell. Tools **13**(4), 961–979 (2004)
8. Janier, M., Lawrence, J., Reed, C.: OVA+: an argument analysis interface. In: Computational Models of Argument: Proceedings of COMMA 2014, vol. 266, pp. 463–464, IOS Press, Amsterdam (2014)

9. Gordon, T.F., Walton, D.: The Carneades argumentation framework – using presumptions and exceptions to model critical questions. In: Proceedings of the 2006 Conference on Computational Models of Argument: Proceedings of COMMA 2006, pp. 195–207. IOS Press, Amsterdam (2006)

10. Rahwan, I., Zablith, F., Reed, C.: Laying the foundations for a world wide argument web. Artif. Intell. **171**(10–15), 897–921 (2007)

11. Chesñevar, C.I., et al.: Towards an argument interchange format. Knowl. Eng. Rev. **21**(4), 293–316 (2006)

12. Rahwan, I., Reed, C.: The argument interchange format. In: Simari, G., Rahwan, I. (eds.) Argumentation in Artificial Intelligence, pp. 383–402. Springer, Boston (2009). https://doi.org/10.1007/978-0-387-98197-0_19

13. Rahwan, I., et al.: Representing and classifying arguments on the semantic web. Knowl. Eng. Rev. **26**(4), 487–511 (2011)

14. Budán, M.C.D., Lucero, M.J.G., Simari, G.R.: An AIF-based labeled argumentation framework. In: Beierle, C., Meghini, C. (eds.) FoIKS 2014. LNCS, vol. 8367, pp. 117–135. Springer, Cham (2014). https://doi.org/10.1007/978-3-319-04939-7_5

15. Kirschner, C., Eckle-Kohler, J., Gurevych, I.: Linking the thoughts: analysis of argumentation structures in scientific publications. In: Proceedings of the 2nd Workshop on Argumentation Mining, pp. 1–11. ACL, Denver (2015)

16. Sonntag, J., Stede, M.: GraPAT: a tool for graph annotations. In: Proceedings of LREC 2014, pp. 4147–4151. European Languages Resources Association, Reykjavik (2014)

17. Hoekstra, R., et al.: The LKIF core ontology of basic legal concepts. In: Proceedings of LOAIT 2007, vol. 321, pp. 43–64 (2007)

18. Murphy, J., Sassoon, I., Luck, M., Black, E.: An investigation of argumentation framework characteristics. In: Black, E., Modgil, S., Oren, N. (eds.) TAFA 2017. LNCS (LNAI), vol. 10757, pp. 1–16. Springer, Cham (2018). https://doi.org/10.1007/978-3-319-75553-3_1

19. AIF Database. http://www.aifdb.org. Accessed 05 May 2019

Ontological Approach to Providing Intelligent Support for Solving Compute-Intensive Problems on Supercomputers

Galina Zagorulko[1](✉), Yury Zagorulko[1], Boris Glinskiy[2], and Anna Sapetina[2]

[1] A.P. Ershov Institute of Informatics Systems, Siberian Branch of the Russian Academy of Sciences, Acad. Lavrentjev avenue 6, 630090 Novosibirsk, Russia
gal@iis.nsk.su
[2] Institute of Computational Mathematics and Mathematical Geophysics, Siberian Branch of the Russian Academy of Sciences, Acad. Lavrentjev avenue 6, 630090 Novosibirsk, Russia

Abstract. The paper describes an approach to providing intelligent support for solving compute-intensive problems on supercomputers, based on the ontologies and decision rules helping the users choose a computational method suited best to their task and supercomputer architecture. The authors focus on the concept and following components of intelligent support: the ontology of the problem area "Solving Compute-intensive Problems of Mathematical Physics on Supercomputers", an information-analytical Internet resource based on this ontology, providing the users access to information necessary for solving compute-intensive problems on supercomputers and an expert system helping users develop a parallel code based on ready-made software components. The paper describes in detail the conceptual scheme of intelligent support and the ontologies developed. To avoid possible errors in designing an ontology, in model means for knowledge representation absent in the ontology description language, to systematize and facilitate populating an ontology with concept instances, we have developed and applied a number of structural and content patterns.

Keywords: Supercomputers · Intelligent support · Ontology · Mathematical physics · Decision support system

1 Introduction

Currently, supercomputer technologies are widely used in the mathematical modeling of various physical phenomena and processes. However, the development of programs for supercomputers is becoming more complicated with an increase of parallelism and use of heterogeneous architectures. In this connection, creation of intelligent support means for solving compute-intensive problems on both modern and future supercomputers is an emerging priority.

The main idea of the intelligent support (IS) for solving computationally complex tasks of mathematical physics on supercomputers is using the knowledge of a problem

© Springer Nature Switzerland AG 2019
S. O. Kuznetsov and A. I. Panov (Eds.): RCAI 2019, CCIS 1093, pp. 363–375, 2019.
https://doi.org/10.1007/978-3-030-30763-9_30

area (PA). This includes the comprehensive knowledge of the methods and algorithms for solving such problems on supercomputers and their implementations, as well as the experience of solving such problems presented in the form of techniques and software components (fragments of parallel code).

As a conceptual basis of intelligent support, we propose to use a system of inter-related ontologies, including the ontology of computational methods and parallel algorithms, as well as the ontology of parallel architectures and technologies.

To ensure the success of solving tasks on the supercomputer, the users need information support: convenient access to the information on the available methods and algorithms, on the capabilities and limitations of each of them, and on the character-istics of their implementations. The means of such support is the information-analytical resource created on the basis of the above ontologies, supplied with an advanced user web-interface providing content-based access to this kind of information.

At the stage of developing a code to solve the user's problem, component support plays an important role. The opportunity to choose ready-made software components implementing the necessary algorithms can significantly simplify and speed up developing the code executed on a supercomputer. A means of supporting the solution of this problem is a library of previously developed software components equipped with unified specifications, which can serve as a basis for integrating the components into a parallel code.

Another means of intelligent support is an expert system, which should help the user to choose the implementation of a computational method and a supercomputer architecture optimal for his task.

The paper describes the ontological approach to providing intelligent support for solving compute-intensive problems on supercomputers. Section 2 provides an over-view of current information resources that support solving tasks on supercomputers. Section 3 details the concept of intelligent support. Section 4 describes the ontologies underlying the IS.

2 Overview of Information Resources Supporting the Solution of Tasks on Supercomputers

At present, there are several projects in Russia developing and supporting solving tasks on supercomputers. However, their support is limited to systematizing the knowledge on this topic and providing access to it.

The most significant Russian project is AlgoWiki [1], which provides an infor-mation resource positioned on the Internet as an open encyclopedia on algorithms' properties and peculiarities of their implementation on various software and hardware platforms, from mobile to exaflops supercomputer systems enabling collaboration with the entire world community.

The stated objective of the AlgoWiki resource is to give a comprehensive description of each algorithm, which will help to assess its potential in relation to a particular parallel computing platform. For this, AlgoWiki provides each algorithm with a detailed description, including a description of its parameters necessary for serial and parallel numerical implementation, indicating the most time-consuming parts. In addition, AlgoWiki provides references to ready-made packaged solutions.

The second most important Russian web resource is parallel.ru [2]. This resource is aimed at informing the users about all important events and updates in the supercomputer community (new technologies, software products and tools for developing parallel code, conferences, new supercomputers, latest news).

The above-mentioned resources systematize information about their subject areas without resorting to ontologies, which reduces their capabilities dramatically, both in terms of knowledge and data presentation and ease of access to them. Nevertheless, the presentation of information about the subject area, covering the problems of solving compute-intensive problems on supercomputers, in the form of ontologies can provide not only convenient access to it, but also support the user in choosing the optimal algorithms and parallel architectures in solving his applied problems due to the possibilities of logical inference on the ontology.

The need to create resources based on ontological descriptions, for various fields of science (physics [3], geology [4], biology [5], astrophysics [6, 7], etc.) has been also discussed abroad. Currently, there are three web resources on astrophysics [8], on genomics [9], on geology and geophysics [10]. However, similarly to the Russian resources, they do not provide to the user the comprehensive support, that will be provided by the resource proposed in this work.

The authors also explore how ontologies can be used to improve the efficiency of computational resources and support the users who solve their problems on them.

For example, in [11], it is suggested that ontologies can be used to describe Grid resources, which would simplify and structure the construction of Grid applications by composing and reusing existing software components and developing knowledge-based services and tools. For this purpose, an ontology of the Data Mining knowledge area has been developed. This ontology makes it easier to develop Grid applications focused on identifying knowledge from data. It offers experts in this area a basic (reference) model for various data analysis tasks as well as methodology and software developed to solve these tasks, and helps the user in choosing the optimal solution.

In [12], authors propose an approach that uses an ontology describing the metadata of a Grid resource and the reference mechanisms on it for more efficient management of Grid resources.

[13] discusses the use of ontologies and ontology reference mechanisms to assist users in solving compute-intensive problems on heterogeneous computing architectures, in particular on clusters equipped with NVIDIA GPGPUs and Xeon-Phi coprocessors in addition to the traditional Intel processor. Here, ontology inference mechanisms help to find the best possible solution by combining hardware, software, and planning strategies. The paper demonstrates the application of the approach to solving bioinformatics problems.

The described approaches to the use of ontologies are close to our approach, but they focus on other areas of knowledge and architectures.

3 The Concept of Intelligent Support

As mentioned above, intelligent support for solving compute-intensive problems of mathematical physics on supercomputers is based on using knowledge of this problem area presented in the form of ontologies and experience in solving such problems, embodied in the form of techniques and parallel code fragments.

Figure 1 shows a conceptual diagram of intelligent support for solving compute-intensive problems.

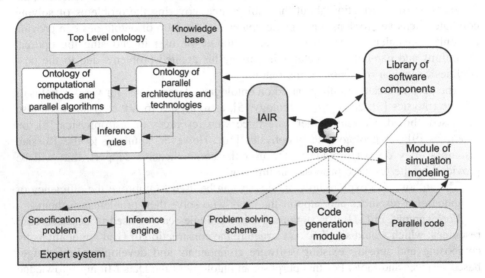

Fig. 1. Conceptual scheme of intelligent support for solving compute-intensive problems.

Intelligent support is provided by the following components: a knowledge base, an information-analytical Internet resource for supporting the solution of compute-intensive problems on supercomputers (IAIR SSCIP), an expert system (ES), a library of software components and a simulation module.

The core of IS is the knowledge base including interrelated ontologies: the top level ontology of the PA "Solving Compute-Intensive Problems of Mathematical Physics on Supercomputers", the ontology of computational methods and parallel algorithms, the ontology of parallel architectures and technologies, as well as inference rules that expand the logic of these ontologies.

The library of software components includes the code fragments implementing the necessary algorithms executed on a supercomputer. Software components are provided with unified specifications, which enable their integration into a parallel code. Also, this library provides the user with ready-made software packages that he/she can use when solving the task.

The knowledge base is used by an information-analytical Internet resource for supporting the solution of compute-intensive problems on supercomputers (IAIR SSCIP) and an expert system (ES) that helps the user in building a parallel code.

The ontology-based IAIR SSCIP is designed to provide the user with information support in solving compute-intensive problems. It provides complete information about the methods and algorithms available, capabilities and limitations of each of them, and characteristics of their implementations. This resource is equipped with an advanced user web-interface providing meaningful access to this kind of information. The user will be able to obtain detailed information necessary to solve his/her task: methods and algorithms currently available, their description and numerical implementation features, tools available for creating a parallel code, available supercomputer architectures and their features, as well as features of programming for these architectures. These capabilities of the IAIR SSCIP minimize the time required for an in-depth familiarization with the problem area, since all the necessary information is structured and collected in one place.

The expert system is designed to assist the user in building a parallel code that solves his/her problem on a supercomputer. The users submit to the ES the specification of their compute-intensive problems, and at the output they get a scheme for solving the problem, and then a parallel code.

In addition to the knowledge base, the ES includes an inference machine (solver) and an automated code generation module.

The inference machine uses the knowledge base and specification of a compute-intensive problem written by the user to build the optimal scheme for solving the problem.

The module of automated code generation supports the creation of the parallel code that solves the problem. This module inserts the corresponding code fragments from the software component library (SC) into the problem solving scheme. If there is no suitable component in the SC library, the user can substitute the necessary component by taking it from a standard library or writing a new one.

The module of simulation modeling [14], which evaluates the scalability of the resulting code, is also included in the intelligent support contour. The main purpose of this module is to select the optimal number of cores for implementing the code by studying its behavior with different numbers of cores in model time.

4   Ontologies

The backbone of the IS knowledge base is the ontology of the problem area "Solving Compute-intensive Problems of Mathematical Physics on Supercomputers". This multi-level ontology contains several interrelated ontologies; important among them are the ontology of computational methods and parallel algorithms and ontology of parallel architectures and technologies.

Consider the upper level of the ontology of the PA "Solving Compute-intensive Problems of Mathematical Physics on Supercomputers" (see Fig. 2).

The main Objects of research in this field are Physical Objects and Physical Phenomena, which are studied in certain divisions of science and are based on the Fundamental laws of nature derived, in turn, from Experiments and observations. The objects of research are considered in the form of an approximate Physical Model, described by the Mathematical Model, which formalizes the Fundamental laws of

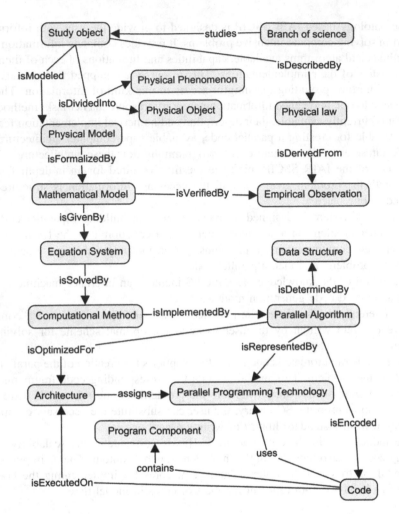

Fig. 2. The top level of ontology of the PA "Solving Compute-intensive Problems of Mathematical Physics on Supercomputers".

nature, is given by a system of equations and verified in the course of Experiments and observations. Consequently, we have a Mathematical model in the form of a System of equations satisfying the initial and boundary conditions containing all parameters (equation of state, values of coefficients, etc.). Since we are considering a limited field of mathematical physics, the system of equations will correspond to this area.

The system of equations is resolved by the Computational Method, which, in turn, is implemented by a Parallel algorithm, determined, among other things, by the Data Structure. The parallel algorithm implementing the Computational Method is optimized for the parallel architecture available to the user and is represented using certain Parallel Programming Technologies. The final representation of a parallel Algorithm is encoded by a program code consisting of a set of Software components and executed on a parallel Architecture.

The ontology described contains the basic concepts of the PA and their interrelationships. Since concepts such as the Computational Method, Parallel Algorithm, Parallel Architecture are very important for this PA and define the specifics of solving computationally complex problems, their descriptions are discussed in more detail and divided into two separate ontologies: the ontology of computational methods and parallel algorithms (Fig. 3) and ontology of parallel architectures and technologies (Fig. 6).

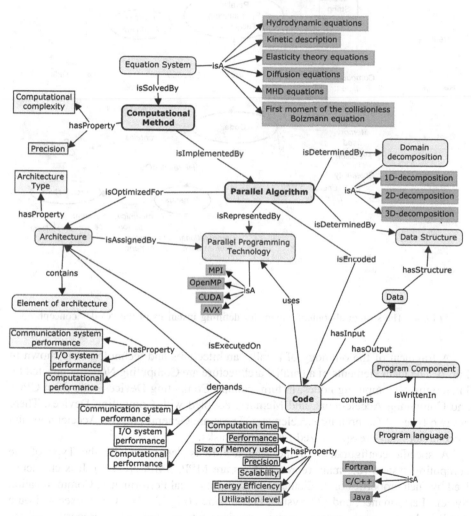

Fig. 3. Ontology of computational methods and parallel algorithms.

To systematize and facilitate populating these ontologies with the instances of their concepts, appropriate ontological design patterns have been developed [15, 16]. Figure 4 presents a structural-content pattern describing the class Code, which is one of the main classes of the ontology of computational methods and parallel algorithms. Class Code is characterized by such interrelated properties as Performance, Computation time, Size of memory used, Precision, Scalability, Energy Efficiency, Utilization level (of memory or processor). The structural-content pattern describing the class Parallel algorithm is shown in Fig. 5.

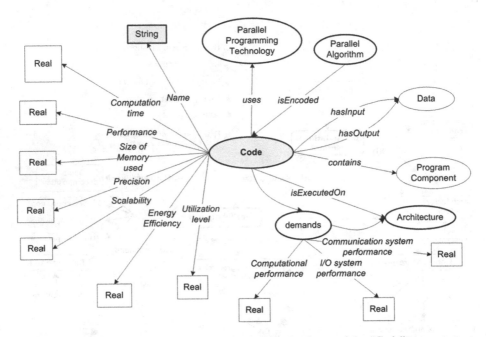

Fig. 4. The structural-content pattern for defining instances of the "Code" concept.

A fragment of the ontology of parallel architectures and technologies is shown in Fig. 6. The main elements of a parallel architecture are Computing Nodes connected by Interconnect. Computing nodes, in turn, contain Computing Devices—the main CPUs and Computing Accelerators, and Memory, coupled with Computing Devices. There are two types of Computing Accelerators. These are General-purpose Accelerators and Accelerators that are specialized for specific tasks.

A specific configuration of the Architecture is determined by the Type of the computing system (the main representatives are MPP, SMP, NUMA). It is characterized by such properties of its Elements as Computational Performance, Communication System Performance, and I/O System Performance (Fig. 7). The Code, executed on a parallel Architecture, imposes certain requirements on the listed properties of the Architecture Elements.

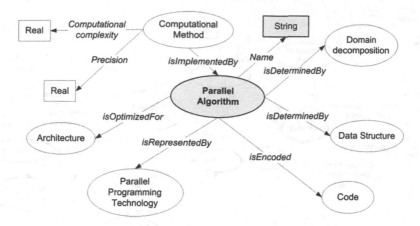

Fig. 5. The structural-content pattern for defining instances of the "Parallel algorithm" concept.

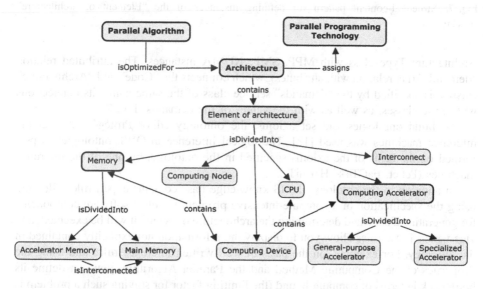

Fig. 6. Ontology of parallel architectures and technologies.

The above ontologies are described in the OWL language [17] and include descriptions of classes and their properties, as well as instances of classes that make up the knowledge base filled with specific methods, algorithms, software components and elements of parallel architectures.

As noted above, to systematize and simplify populating the ontologies with the instances of their concepts, a number of ontology design patterns have been developed (Figs. 4, 5 and 7). In addition, the patterns are used to model the techniques for representing some useful constructions not found in the OWL language. For example, the domain values of the type of a parallel Architecture are represented by the

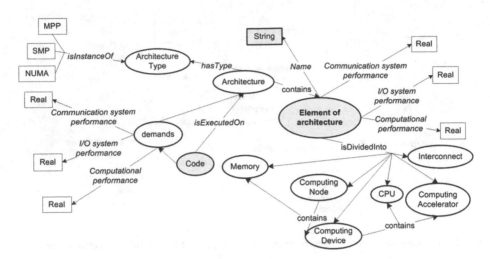

Fig. 7. Structural-content pattern for defining instances of the "Element of architecture" concept.

Architecture Type class with MPP, SMP, NUMA instances. The attributed relation "demands" (i.e. relation with attributes), which connects the "Code" and "Architecture" classes, is specified by the "demands" service class of the same name, its connections with these classes, as well as with the values of the demands (Fig. 7).

To build ontologies and set axioms, the ontology editor Protégé 5.2 with the inference machines was used [18]. The logical inference in OWL-ontologies is performed on the basis of the axioms specified in the ontology, by one of the inference machines (Pellet, FaCT++, HermiT).

In addition to the ontology, the IS knowledge base contains expert rules allowing using the specification of a compute-intensive problem to select software components for generating a code and determining the architecture on which it will be executed, and vice versa. These rules allow you to display the information not explicitly contained in the ontology. For example, on the basis of well-written inference rules and using the Properties of the Computing Method and the Parallel Algorithm, you can define its bottleneck in terms of compute-bound (the limiting factor for solving such a problem is the speed of the processor) and memory-bound problem (the limiting factor is the speed of access to memory).

Further, guided by the correct inference rules, one can give qualitative and quantitative estimates of the Properties of the Code executed on the Architecture, focusing on its Properties. Also, inference rules may allow setting the requirements that the Program Code imposes on the Properties of the Architecture (Fig. 4). For example, if the performance of the communication system of the Architecture is not high enough, efforts to improve the performance of the Code will be in vain. Thus, the inference rules define implicit links between the Computational Method, Parallel Algorithm, Target Architecture, and Code. Guided by them at different stages of problem solving, you can quickly find the optimal approach to the solution of your problem.

To represent the expert rules, the SWRL (Semantic Web Rule Language) [19] is used. (Note that the rules written in the SWRL are, in fact, Horn clauses, which greatly simplifies their construction and understanding.)

Let us give examples of the SWRL rules involved in the choice of the architecture on which the code can be executed.

The first rule checks whether the Computing Device has enough power to execute the code.

Code(?c), Architecture (?a), ComputingDevice (?cd), contains(?a, ?cd),
demands(?d), makesDemandsCode (?d, ?c),
makesDemandsArchitecture(?d, ?a),
demandsComputationalPerformance(?c, ?cpc),
ComputationalPerformance (?cd, ?cpa),
swrlb: greaterThanOrEqual (?cpa, ?cpc)
→ comparableToComputationalPerformance(?c, ?cd).

The second rule checks whether all the code demands for the architecture are satisfied and decides whether the code can be executed on the given architecture.

Code (?c), Architecture(?a), ComputingDevice(?cd), contains (?a, ?cd),
IOSystem (?ios) contains (?a, ?ios),
Interconnect (?i), contains (?a, ?i),
comparableToComputationalPerformance(?c, ?cd),
comparableToPerformanceInputOutputSystem (?c, ?ios),
comparableToPerformanceCommunicationSystem(?c, ?i),
→ isExecutedOn(?c, ?a).

5   Conclusion

The paper presents an ontological approach to providing intelligent support for solving compute-intensive problems of mathematical physics on supercomputers. Primarily, this support is necessary for regular users, who, as a rule, have little understanding of multiprocessor system architectures and software capability for creating parallel programs. Another group of users who will benefit from the IS are specialists in computational technologies, well versed in supercomputer architectures and parallel languages, but less familiar with computational methods.

Intelligent support is provided by the following components: the ontology of the PA "Solving Compute-intensive Problems of Mathematical Physics on Supercomputers", an information-analytical Internet resource to support solving compute-intensive problems on supercomputers, and an expert system helping users develop a parallel code based on ready-made software components.

It is vital to note that in order to help supercomputer users to create effective programs, it is most important to have detailed ontologies, a fairly complete library of software components implementing parallel algorithms and fragments of parallel code, and a well-chosen set of decision rules formalized as inference rules, which will generate the program code taking into account the specific features of the problems being solved and the available multiprocessor system architectures.

At the moment, the efforts of developers focus on the implementation and improvement of these intelligent support components.

Acknowledgment. This work is financially supported by the Russian Foundation for Basic Research (Grants no. 19-07-00085 and no. 19-07-00762).

References

1. AlgoWiki: Open Encyclopedia of Algorithm Properties. https://algowiki-project.org/ru/. Accessed 05 May 2019
2. parallel.ru. https://parallel.ru. Accessed 05 May 2019
3. Cvjetkovic, V.: Web physics ontology: online interactive symbolic computation in physics. In: Proceedings of 2017 4th Experiment@International Conference (exp.at 2017), Faro, Portugal, pp. 52–57. IEEE (2017)
4. Xiaogang, M.: Ontology spectrum for geological data interoperability. ITC, Netherlands (2011)
5. Cook, D.L., Neal, M.L., Bookstein, F.L., Gennari, J.H.: Ontology of physics for biology: representing physical dependencies as a basis for biological processes. J. Biomed. Semant. **4** (1), 41 (2013)
6. Sarro, L.M., Martínez, R.: First steps towards an ontology for astrophysics. In: Palade, V., Howlett, R.J., Jain, L. (eds.) KES 2003. LNCS (LNAI), vol. 2774, pp. 1389–1395. Springer, Heidelberg (2003). https://doi.org/10.1007/978-3-540-45226-3_188
7. Louge, T., Karray, M.H., Archimède, B., Knödlseder, J.: Semantic interoperability in astrophysics for workflows extraction from heterogeneous services. In: van Sinderen, M., Chapurlat, V. (eds.) IWEI 2015. LNBIP, vol. 213, pp. 3–15. Springer, Heidelberg (2015). https://doi.org/10.1007/978-3-662-47157-9_1
8. ESPAS. https://www.espas-fp7.eu/portal/browse.html#ontology. Accessed 05 May 2019
9. SemGen. http://sbp.bhi.washington.edu/projects/semgen. Accessed 05 May 2019
10. Awesome geoscience semantics. http://www.geoscience-semantics.org. Accessed 05 May 2019
11. Cannataro, M., Comito, C.: A data mining ontology for grid programming. In: Proceedings of 1st International Workshop on Semantics in Peer-To-Peer and Grid Computing (In Conjunction with WWW 2003), Budapest, Hungry, pp. 113–134 (2003)
12. Amarnath, B.R., Somasundaram, T.S., Ellappan, V.M., Buyya, R.: Ontology-based grid resource management. Softw. Pract. Exp. **39**(17), 1419–1438 (2009)
13. Faheem, H.M., König-Ries, B., Aslam, M.A., Aljohani, N.R., Katib, I.: Ontology design for solving computationally-intensive problems on heterogeneous architectures. Sustainability **10**(2), 441 (2018)
14. Podkorytov, D., Rodionov, A., Choo, H.: Agent-based simulation system AGNES for networks modeling: review and researching. In: Proceedings of the 6th International Conference on Ubiquitous Information Management and Communication (ACM ICUIMC 2012), Paper 115. ACM (2012)
15. Gangemi, A., Presutti, V.: Ontology design patterns. In: Staab, S., Studer, R. (eds.) Handbook on Ontologies. IHIS, pp. 221–243. Springer, Heidelberg (2009). https://doi.org/10.1007/978-3-540-92673-3_10

16. Zagorulko, Y., Borovikova, O., Zagorulko, G.: Development of ontologies of scientific subject domains using ontology design patterns. In: Kalinichenko, L., Manolopoulos, Y., Malkov, O., Skvortsov, N., Stupnikov, S., Sukhomlin, V. (eds.) DAMDID/RCDL 2017. CCIS, vol. 822, pp. 141–156. Springer, Cham (2018). https://doi.org/10.1007/978-3-319-96553-6_11
17. Antoniou, G., van Harmelen, F.: Web ontology language: OWL. In: Staab, S., Studer, R. (eds.) Handbook on Ontologies. INFOSYS, pp. 67–92. Springer, Heidelberg (2004). https://doi.org/10.1007/978-3-540-24750-0_4
18. Protégé. https://protege.stanford.edu. Accessed 05 May 2019
19. SWRL: A semantic web rule language combining OWL and RuleML. http://www.w3.org/Submission/SWRL/. Accessed 05 May 2019

Author Index

Printed in the United States
By Bookmasters